God's Inspiration of the Scriptures

William Kelly

w.K.

Scripture Truth Publications

GOD'S INSPIRATION OF THE SCRIPTURES

First published 1903 by T Weston, London
Second edition published 1907 by T Weston, London
Photographic reprint 1966 of 1903 edition by C. A. Hammond Trust Bible Depot, London (& Bible Truth Publishers, Addison, Ill.)
Re-typeset and transferred to Digital Printing 2007
First paperback edition March 2007

ISBN: 978-0-901860-51-4 (paperback)
ISBN: 978-0-901860-56-9 (hardback)
© Copyright 2007 Scripture Truth

A publication of Scripture Truth

All rights reserved. No part of this publication may be reproduced, stored in a retrieval system, or transmitted, in any form or by any means, electronic, mechanical, photocopying, recording or otherwise without prior permission of Scripture Truth Publications.

Most of the scriptures quoted are William Kelly's own translations from the original Hebrew or Greek text.

References to The Authorised Version are to The Authorised (King James) Version. Rights in the Authorised Version are vested in the Crown. Reproduced by permission of the Crown's patentee, Cambridge University Press.

References to the Revised Version are to "The New Testament of our Lord and Saviour Jesus Christ, Translated out of the Greek: Being the Version Set Forth A.D. 1611, Compared with the Most Ancient Authorities and Revised, A.D. 1881". Oxford: Oxford University Press, 1881

or "The Holy Bible containing the Old and New Testaments translated out of the original tongues : being the version set forth A.D. 1611 compared with the most ancient authorities and revised". Oxford: University Press, 1885.

Cover photograph ©iStockphoto.com/stevenallan (Steven Allan)

Published by Scripture Truth Publications
Coopies Way, Coopies Lane,
Morpeth, Northumberland, NE61 6JN

Scripture Truth is an imprint of Central Bible Hammond Trust, a charitable trust

Typesetting by John Rice
Printed by Lightning Source

Preface to 2007 Edition

This edition comprises the re-typeset text of the 1966 photographic reprint of the 1903 edition.

To assist the twenty-first century reader, minor changes in presentation (but *not* content) have been made. The use of quotation (speech) marks has been updated. Abbreviations have been expanded and Roman numerals have been replaced by Arabic, to facilitate ease of reference. In chapter 5 of the original the section numbering moves from 32 (Acts) to 34 (Romans). The opportunity has been taken to renumber the sections in the present edition and the valuable case studies in chapter 4 have been given headings and listed in the Contents.

The greater part of this volume (chapter 5) is devoted to a book-by-book synopsis of the entire Bible, focussing on the particular evidence of inspiration which each book provides.

William Kelly clearly sets out what divine inspiration is, and is not; provides a robust defence against common attacks on inspiration; and demonstrates how each and every part of the Scriptures displays evidence of its one animating and directing Author.

His desire was that this work should be of help to the spiritual understanding of all who value the Bible from beginning to end. May it be so!

John Rice

GOD'S INSPIRATION OF THE SCRIPTURES

Introduction to the 1966 Edition

Many volumes have been written defending one or other of the various theories of the Inspiration of the Scriptures, whether verbal or mechanical, fallible or infallible. Mr Kelly's thesis is rather to demonstrate from the scriptures themselves that they are what they claim to be, God-breathed writings (2 Timothy 3:16) coming forth from His very Self, a revelation of His mind given through men to us all. "Holy men of God spake as they were borne along by the Holy Spirit" (2 Peter 1:21) and their matter no less than their words were preserved by Him from all imperfections in being transmitted through frail human channels.

Much of this volume is devoted to showing the divine design in the structure and message of each book separately and of the whole. Though recorded over many centuries with a rich variety in style and form, all display the wisdom and purpose of the gracious and holy God who in them makes His mind known to man and claims his submission for eternal blessing.

The original manuscripts may have long since passed from our ken, but patient copying and later translation have brought to us in our own tongue the substance of what was first communicated. The few uncertainties introduced by these subsequent human instruments do not obscure the source or impeach the authority of the Scriptures, at least to those who study them in subjection to the Holy Spirit, their divine Author.

May God grant that His servant's labours now made available to a new generation, may be fruitful in helping humble souls to an unshakeable confidence in the unerring scriptures of truth.

H Harle

Preface

There is no question agitated in Christendom of greater moment than the true character and claim of the Scriptures. Nor has their divine authority been more widely denied all over the world than in our own day; and this, not merely by avowed sceptics, but by professing Christians of practically every denomination, and by many of their most distinguished representatives. But when the adversary comes in like a flood, the Spirit of the Lord does not fail to lift up a standard against him.

In this volume my heart's desire is to furnish a help to souls that seek the light of God which inspiration furnishes to those who tremble at His word. I have presented the positive proofs that God speaks in it to every conscience and heart, more particularly of Israel in the Old Testament, and of the Christian in the New though all scripture is his food. Men may refuse to hear, or hear to despise; but this they do at their peril; for God is not mocked. Such unbelief has a deeper brand of evil, after men have professed the Lord's name, than when the written word was first committed to human responsibility. It is the spirit of apostasy diffused by the great enemy of God and man, before the apostasy itself is established as a public fact, which is at hand.

In the face of a preparation so dark and ominous, which scripture announces as certain (2 Thessalonians 2:3), there are children of God all over the earth, who acknowledge with grateful thanksgiving His faithfulness in turning the attacks of Satan and his dupes to their confirmation in the faith, and the more profound enjoyment both of scripture and of Christ therein revealed by the Holy Spirit. May the reader by grace be helped to share a privilege which bespeaks itself divine, the best antidote to that unbelief which enfeebles where it does not quite destroy the divine energy of every revealed truth. To human tradition I give no real weight, less if possible to the speculations of men on grounds which they deem probable. As the traditional school is one form of rationalism, so is neo-criticism another, the one adding to God's word, the other taking from it, to His dishonour. Legitimate criticism is the servant of faith in seeking to eliminate errors of transcription; but it receives without question every word that was originally written. What is called "scientific inquiry" rises up in its empty pride against the divine authority of Christ, who has ruled what it dares to deny.

LONDON, *April, 1903*.

Contents

Introduction to the 1996 edition 5

Preface 7

Introduction 13

1 Divine Authority 21
2 Apostolic Doctrine 31
3 Its Uniformity 47
4 The Human Element 53
    4.1   The Genealogy in Matthew chapter 1 ... 61
    4.2   The Synoptic Gospels 65
    4.3   The Preface to Luke's Gospel 68
    4.4   1 Corinthians chapter 7 72
    4.5   Personal Communications 76
    4.6   The Second Epistle of Peter and the Epistle of Jude 81
    4.7   The Second and Third Epistles of John .. 85
5 Divine Design 93
    Introduction 93
    5.1   Genesis 103
    5.2   Exodus 112
    5.3   Leviticus 120
    5.4   Numbers 127
    5.5   Deuteronomy 135
    5.6   Joshua 145
    5.7   Judges 149

5.8	Ruth	152
5.9	1 Samuel	153
5.10	2 Samuel	156
5.11	1 Kings	158
5.12	2 Kings	160
5.13	1 Chronicles	163
5.14	2 Chronicles	166
5.15	Ezra	168
5.16	Nehemiah	171
5.17	Esther	173
5.18	Job	174
5.19	The Psalms	179
5.20	Proverbs	191
5.21	Ecclesiastes	194
5.22	Solomon's Song	196
5.23	Isaiah	198
5.24a	Jeremiah	203
5.24b	The Lamentations of Jeremiah	207
5.25	Ezekiel	209
5.26	Daniel	214
5.27	Minor Prophets	232
	5.27.1 Hosea	233
	5.27.2 Joel	234
	5.27.3 Amos	235

CONTENTS

5.27.4	Obadiah	236
5.27.5	Jonah	236
5.27.6	Micah	238
5.27.7	Nahum	240
5.27.8	Habakkuk	241
5.27.9	Zephaniah	242
5.27.10	Haggai	244
5.27.11	Zechariah	246
5.27.12	Malachi	248

New Testament 250

5.28	Matthew 250
5.29	Mark 259
5.30	Luke 272
5.31	John 286
5.32	The Acts of the Apostles 293
5.33	The Epistle of Paul to the Romans 308
5.34	1 Corinthians 322
5.35	2 Corinthians 342
5.36	Galatians 351
5.37	Ephesians 359
5.38	Philippians 371
5.39	Colossians 379
5.40	1 Thessalonians 389
5.41	2 Thessalonians 393

5.42	1 Timothy	397
5.43	2 Timothy	404
5.44	Titus	410
5.45	Philemon	417
5.46	Hebrews	420
5.47	James	425
5.48	1 Peter	432
5.49	2 Peter	440
5.50	1 John	446
5.51	2 John	454
5.52	3 John	457
5.53	Jude	460
5.54	The Revelation	466

6 Conclusion 479

Introduction

No considerate Christian will question the momentous weight of Inspiration, both in itself and as it bears on every question arising in things divine. It is no disparagement to scripture that we need also a new nature, a purged conscience, and a heart purified by faith. Let us add the Holy Spirit given, as He is now, to know the only True God and Jesus Christ Whom He sent. For this is life eternal, inseparable from the object of our faith, of the Father's delight, and of the Holy Spirit's testimony. "He that believeth hath life eternal"; he has life in Christ the Son, as truly as the apostle John, who wrote expressly to the family of God for all, babes no less than fathers in Christ, that they might *know* that, believing on the name of His Son, they have life eternal (1 John 5:13).

When thus assured of a portion precious beyond reckoning, we are in a condition to appreciate the scriptures as becomes children of God. What a contrast between the rich grace that shines in Christ, the personal Word, for every believer to enjoy, and the hesitating spirit among the baptised to appropriate these divine communications! Blessed be the God and Father of our Lord

Jesus Christ! didst Thou not bless every child of Thine with every spiritual blessing in the heavenlies in Christ? Are they not to-day for the most part questioning whether they are Thine or not? Are they not in doubt whether their sins be really all forgiven for His name's sake? And is not this painful uncertainty as plain in the third or fourth century after Christ, as in the eighteenth or nineteenth? And why is it, but that souls then as now were in general as feeble in believing God's written warrant as in receiving God's salvation by Christ and His work? How sad that a saint should even seem to be always learning and never able to come to the knowledge of the truth!

Undoubtedly in God's mercy there are all over the world simple-hearted believers, in the aggregate a great multitude, who rest with cloudless confidence in the grace and truth that came by Jesus Christ; who accept for themselves, and attest for all others that believe, the absolute reliableness of God's love and Christ's redemption; who know the Holy Spirit's presence with and in us for ever. Hidden ones too far beyond our thoughts there may have been, in all ages since our Lord died and rose, to profit by faith; whereas the recognised leaders prove by their remains how quickly and far the christian profession departed from their proper privileges and divine joys. For it would be intolerable to doubt that those who express what prevailed were as real in Catholic times of old, as in Anglican or Puritan times nearer us. Far be the thought! The fall from grace was deep and wide-spread; the truth was clouded with dark traditions of men, ancient and modern. Scripture itself is plain how soon such changes came in even among the best-taught confessors of Christ. And the inspired men, Paul and Peter, John and Jude, prepare us for profound departure without one promise of restoration, still less of progress, for Christendom. These facts accentuate the all-importance of the written word, which then as now is the standard of truth and the sole means of recovery, applied by God's Spirit to remove obstructions, that Christ might give them light once more, yea that He should be formed in them.

Thus it is sadly, humblingly, true that God has been dishonoured throughout christian times by unbelief of their best blessings in those who have borne the Lord's name; as, not least of all, we were warned of false teachers among them as of false prophets in Israel. In teachers and taught our own day beholds the bold and growing development of what is nothing less than sheer and systematic infidelity. This assumes the euphemistic name of "higher criticism", and puts forward the plea of fuller inquiries into the literary history of the scriptures. If we listen to themselves, it is in conflict neither with Christianity as a whole nor with any articles of the faith. But it is really a system as imaginative for the process they call the building up of (at least the earlier books of) the Bible, as is the Darwinian hypothesis for excluding God from creating species in the natural world, and for assigning this process to Time, the late Mr. Darwin's great god, and to Natural Selection, his goddess. When souls are thus seduced to abandon the divine authority of scripture and to deny its inspiration in any real sense, it is no consolation to feel that deceivers are themselves deceived. Nor indeed is there a fact more notorious, than that the men beguiled to disbelieve God's word readily show themselves the most credulous of mankind.

Take an instance clear and sufficient. In hardly any thing are the "higher critics" more unanimous or jubilant than as to Astruc's theory of Elohistic and Jehovistic documents, and the audacious consequences deduced from that assumption. But if it have any apparent sense as applied to the Pentateuch, how does it bear on Job? How on the Psalms? on Proverbs? on Ecclesiastes? or on the prophets, say Jonah for example? Did then Ezra and Nehemiah (or the inspired writers of these books) compile the annals of their own days from Elohistic and Jehovistic documents? If the theory hung together, to this absurdity it would fairly lead. The truth of God, conveyed by the admirable propriety with which inspiration employs these and other divine names, is wholly lost by such superficial guess-work. But this short introduction is not a suitable occasion to go into the minute and full proofs, on the one hand of the rationalist blunder, and on the other of the divine wisdom and beauty displayed in the inspired choice of the divine designations, in all scripture from Genesis to the Revelation, as well as in the books of Moses.

These considerations make it an urgent duty to survey the subject afresh, and with such a measure of precision and comprehensiveness as grace may supply for guarding souls in this increasingly evil day. The Christian wants divine certainty in his relations with God. Probability is all that man, as man, seeks or can have because he knows not God. But believers have ever craved and ever taken the wholly different ground of divine certainty by God's word. They had it and were blessed in it by faith long before there was a single scripture. Abel knew it, and Enoch, and Noah before the deluge, not to speak of other elders conspicuous in Hebrews 11 for the various characteristics of their faith. So it is with all that are taught of God. All rest on His word, whatever the special result in each by grace. It wrought long before there was a people of God like Israel. It remained vigorous when, on the temporary ruin of the Jews, God formed the church the body of Christ, calling out of Gentiles as well as a remnant of Israel. Thus every believer as of old, only now with immensely superior privileges, stands on ground of divine certainty, and not on probability however reinforced or strong.

It is here that the Tractarian party proved the unsoundness of their position. So Dr. J. H. Newman lets us know in his "Apologia". Mr. J. Keble, with all his melodious strains, was no better in principle. They were alike and all along on a plane which inclined to Romanism, the former being more consistent than the latter in going to Rome at last. Hence Newman's attempt to supplement probability, "the guide of life" (61, 62), with faith and love within, to give it more force (69). Of natural life it may be so with conscience as the monitor. The question is of our new life in Christ, of which philosophy takes no account. But no assemblage of concurring and converging helps of whatever kind can raise probability to absolute certainty. God's testimony received by faith does, and alone can, give divine certainty.

The Cardinal though professedly at the opposite pole of thought, was really in the same quagmire as his sceptical brother, Professor F. W. Newman. It is the case with all rationalists, be they superstitious or profane. Their ground is human, not divine. There are found the "higher critics" with any others who renounce God for man. Reasoning may predominate here, imagination and religious sentiment there; as others betake themselves to erudite speculation. But in no case is it the faith of God's elect, even if ensnared believers yield to it. What the word, and now the written word, was given to produce by the living operation of the Holy Spirit in the believer's heart, is divine certainty. But it is exactly what the "higher criticism" tends to destroy, even more directly than do the rank weeds of superstition which choke the good seed.

Such are the two schools which are today struggling for the mastery. They unite, as we have seen, in untiring effort to withdraw men if they can, from simple thorough subjection to God's word in faith. Of this they are alike jealous, and alike they cast scorn on it, though such faith alone becomes man, alone honours God. For it finds the God-given centre in Christ, full cleansing by His work, life's exercise in His service, and its joy in His love and the Father's, by the power of the Holy Spirit. Nor is this all. For by one Spirit were we all baptised into one body, and therein have our place and fellowship as worshippers, no less than as saints, one with another. Those on the ground of probability can never breathe this pure atmosphere freely; they have never emerged from the fog of nature. They betray their dark state by their inability, whether natural or religious rationalists, even to understand what is meant by such a scripture as "the worshippers, having been once cleansed, would have no more conscience of sins." Yet it is simply the common christian position in this respect (but to both those classes unintelligible), because it is the fruit of Christ's perfecting work, made known to the Christian only, above man's intellect and beyond his conscience, though faith enjoys its divine certainty. Confidence (one may not say faith) in the church can no more impart it, than reliance upon criticism higher or lower. It is the will of God now established, the work of Christ now finished and accepted, and the witness of the Holy Spirit now received in full assurance of faith according to

INTRODUCTION

scripture. Hence all joy and peace in believing is as unknown to the gloomy man of superstition, as to the airy higher critic.

GOD'S INSPIRATION OF THE SCRIPTURES

Chapter 1
Divine Authority

We open the Bible. Its first words are necessarily either a revelation or an imposture, either God's word or man's guess claiming His authority. A middle ground here is impossible.

The first and in extent the greatest of all miracles is revealed. "In the beginning God created the heavens and the earth." There is no specific date given. It is expressly indefinite. Many have confounded verse 3 with verse 1, with feelings some hostile, others friendly, to revelation. Both were inexcusably wrong, because both carelessly overlooked the scripture before their eyes. For these words of God, even were there no others confirmatory, affirm in verse 1 the original creation of the universe, then in verse 2 its chaotic condition. The earth was not created empty and waste when first called into being (Isaiah 45:18). It may have become so often, if able geologists are to be heeded. It certainly was so immediately before the days of man's world began, which commenced, not with creating light, but with its activity renewed after ruin and darkness. "And God said, Light be, and light was."

Thus verse 2 does not describe God's creation like verse 1, but a state of utter contrast with it, when total disorder ensued for the earth. Neither the one fact nor the other called for more than passing notice, as being physical and in no direct way the sphere of God's moral dealings with man. Yet was it of moment to have facts of deep interest briefly disclosed, which were entirely beyond the ken of man, lost in contending dreams of eternal matter in the West, and of emanations in the East, illusion and falsehood both of them into which evolution, the fashion of our day, no less surely entices unwary souls. Whatever of detail Genesis 1 may furnish is solely about the formation of the world as it was prepared for the human race; eventually for Christ the Man of God's counsels. It was no speculation of some "Hebrew Descartes" or Newton, but God's account of His own work by His servant and prophet Moses. It is worthy of God, deigning in love to communicate what man could not discover and yet ought to know.

Science is powerless to speak of the beginning of things. So the inductive philosophers own, ashamed as they may well be of all the cosmogonists, Egyptian, Phœnician, Greek, Oriental, or any others. There stands God's revelation, simple, majestic, and complete for His purpose, without even a rival throughout all ages, against which the pride of man can allege nothing but his own errors of haste and misapprehension. How could such a chapter have been written but by divine revelation? Search, ye men of science, ransack all your stores; scrutinise the reports and transactions of the most renowned societies. Did not your wisest own himself but as a child picking up a pebble here and there on the ocean shore? Did not he own reverently this inspired record of creation?

But is there not what some foolishly call a "second account" in Genesis 2? The first chapter reveals simply that which Elohim "created to make", closing with the sabbath He blessed and hallowed (chapter 2:1-3). Then follows from verse 4 Jehovah Elohim presenting man, formed specially and in moral relationship to Himself, and so not merely (as in chapter 1) the head of creation. Hence it is that here only, not before, we have the garden with every tree pleasant and good for food, and the trees of solemn import to humanity, life and responsibility— the last, a moral test applied to a condition of innocence; man exercising his lordship over all the lower creation, yet with no like helpmate; and then woman's peculiar formation out of man. These things and more pertain to God as moral governor (Jehovah Elohim), and therefore demand as they have a new section of scripture with a new and suited name of God.

How quickly the fall brought in death and ruin on man, an outcast from paradise! But grace revealed the Second man, the woman's Seed, to crush the old serpent, the tempter. Clearly then, far from being another and inconsistent narrative, Genesis 2:4 as a new subject begins the moral trial of Adam, and in it his wife too playing so grave a part, in that scene of paradise formed, no less than themselves, to give it the best effect in His wisdom Who put man to the proof.

Hence chapter 3 under the same divine title reveals the result, so glorifying to God, so humbling to the creature, yet a needed key to all that followed here below, with assured hope of the conqueror of Satan in a bruised Saviour to be born of woman. It continues what began in chapter 2.

In all the Bible there is not, save in Christ's person and work, a fact so momentous as the fall, nor a revelation more essential than Genesis 2, 3. God alone could have given us the truth as there made known. It is monstrous to conceive the guilty pair adequate witnesses of all said and done there. Who then else but God?

There it is, the unadorned truth, still more profound morally than chapter 1, in Christ revealing the grace of God to the utmost, God's glory in His person with man's ultimate deliverance, and thus of the highest moment to the salvation, well-being, and happiness of the believer. All comes out in plain facts, such as a child could take in, yet involving principles truer and deeper than any ideas evolved by the most philosophic of mankind. Herein lies an essential difference between revealed truth and all its rivals. Take Vedaism, Brahmanism, Buddhism, Lamaism, or aught else in India and the adjacent lands; take Confucianism, Taoism, Foism, in China; take Sabaism, Jovism, Fetishism ancient and modern: can any one of these systems allege a single fact as its basis? The religion of the Bible, Old or New Testament, Judaism or Christianity, rests on distinct realities, not on mere ideas of man's mind.

Whether a partial dealing of a moral nature by law within a particular people, or the full world-wide revelation of grace and truth in the Lord Jesus Christ, God's word was the divine communication of immensely momentous facts. The related divinely inspired writings are precisely those which rationalists, claiming to be Christians, devote their efforts to discredit, dislocate, and destroy, like Pagan philosophers of old. Like fallen Adam, I am born and have lived an outcast from God. Revelation, God's revelation, His word, is the only possible way of making God known to me. Now rationalism has not, more than Paganism or its philosophy, any just sense of the fall, or of sin, or of God's remedy for it in Christ. Here in the earliest revelation we have the fact unmistakeably brought out in its relation to present government on the earth, with light sufficient for faith to higher and everlasting things, as we see in Abel, Enoch, &c.

Nor is it otherwise with the law any more than the promises. As the latter was no mere aspiration proceeding from the heart of the fathers by the Spirit, but an objective revelation made to Abram, Isaac, and Jacob; so still more manifestly was the giving of the law by Moses for the sons of Israel. Not the least detail was left to the genius of that great man: everything was presented and regulated by the commandment of Jehovah.

So it is in Christianity, wherein is the revelation to us by the Holy Spirit of what is wholly beyond man's eye, ear, and heart; in the written word is the unswerving standard as well as the richest means of communicating all. All is established on sure and infinite facts; for the Incarnation, the Ministry, the Atoning death, the Resurrection, and the Ascension, of the Lord Jesus are grand realities. No doubt, now that the believer's conscience is purged, they may well exercise heart and mind, even to the uttermost by the word and Spirit of God. Still they are facts, attested by divine testimony to God's glory through man and for man, to be made good also in man by faith and love, by experience and obedience, by life-service and worship. There can scarce be a stronger contrast than between law and gospel, the earthly calling and the heavenly. But this at least is common to them both, that their groundwork is one of facts, not mere thoughts of the mind; and these facts are communicated to us with the known certainty of God's mind and word, such as the Holy Spirit alone could give.

Hence we may observe there is no formal claim in the opening of the Bible. The great of this world may enter with a flourish of trumpets, naturally if not necessarily. Not so the divine record. Who could speak of creation but God? or tell it adequately in its relational light but Himself taking His relative name to His people? Who but He in both ways could fully let us know the cause, history, and consequences of the deluge? Who else, what led to the rise of nations, languages, &c.? or to the call of Abram and the fathers who followed of His chosen and separate people? Yet even here throughout we have "Elohim said" and wrought; and so with His name as "Jehovah", wherever suited and requisite. He is an enemy who denies its absolute truth and divine authority.

Then comes Exodus, where the redemption of His people appears first, with the bitter bondage and oppression that preceded and brought judgment on their enemies, and His dwelling in their midst that followed, with the law but not without the shadow of the good things to come. Here accordingly we have His name of relationship specially bestowed (6:3). Here yet more abundantly "Jehovah said" and acted. But, whether historically, or when His nature is introduced, it is "God" as such, *i.e.* Elohim. No man or varying document has the least to do with this, but His own wisdom in the inspired word. The book must be a romance or imposture like the Koran, if it be not God through Moses. The peculiarities of it (such as reserving to chapter 30, where it even looks out of order, the altar of incense, the atonement-money, the holy anointing oil, and the holy compound for

Jehovah) flow from the deep design of God, instead of the blunder of legends, or the incapacity of an editor, to which the imbecility of "higher criticism" rashly and ignorantly ascribes them. The repetitions, as of the sabbath, &c., which they regard as self-evidence of several scribes, are due to a like divine design; and those only learn and profit who bow to divine authority.

Leviticus is even more manifestly "Jehovah" speaking from first to last, with the least of history in it, but quite as manifestly by divine authority. It deals with access to Him, and hence begins with sacrifices and offerings, and priesthood. Thence it treats of unclean things and state; of the central truth of the Day of Atonement, and of blood reserved to God; then of evil relationships and holy ones; of the feasts, &c.

Numbers is a book too varied for so brief a notice as the present; but it treats of the people's journeyings, and its characteristic moral facts are selected by the inspiring Spirit for God's permanent record, above all the wisdom of the writer or of any man at any time. The apostle in 1 Corinthians 10 declares the typical character of the events recorded, for which God alone was competent, to say nothing of copious and special injunctions to Moses, to Aaron, and to both, or of the wondrous predictions Jehovah spoke through Balaam compelled to bless Israel.

Deuteronomy has not only its task of rehearsal in a way beyond human thought, but is anticipative of their possession of the land, and solemnly insists on obedience to

Jehovah's word, and on a covenant distinct from that of Horeb. But we need not say more than express the horror which a believer unsophisticated by the spirit of the age must and ought to feel at the blasphemous denial of the New Testament testimony to Moses as the writer, and of its divine authority.

It would be too much to glance at every book, as we have at those which compose the Pentateuch. But all else in the Old Testament as in the New has the same authority of God. Hence the Old Testament scriptures are called as a whole by the apostle Paul (Romans 3:2) "the oracles of God"; as Moses is said by Stephen (Acts 7:38) to have received "living oracles" (not dead legends) to give unto God's people. And the Lord Jesus when risen said to the disciples, "These are the words which I spoke unto you, while I was yet with you, that all things must be fulfilled which were written in the law of Moses and prophets and psalms concerning me" (Luke 24:44). This covers the entire Hebrew Old Testament as the Jews present it to us. And herein the Latin church has proved a faithless guardian by adding apocryphal Greek writings to that Canon, which even Jerome in his Prologus Galeatus to the Vulgate admits to be not properly included. So similar unfaithfulness was essayed in early days by reading publicly uninspired writings, and joining them, as an Appendix, to the copies of the Greek New Testament. But even Rome did not commit itself to so gross an imposture as this last.

The great apostle in his First Epistle to Timothy (5:18) quotes Deuteronomy 25:4 and Luke 10:7 as "the scripture". He might have quoted Matthew 10:10 from one an apostle like himself; he was led of God to quote from one who was a prophet, not an apostle. For we are built upon the foundation of the apostles and prophets (Ephesians 2:20). This stamps Luke as no mere amanuensis expressing Paul's mind, according to the tradition of Eusebius, but as an inspired writer whom the apostle cites when writing in the Spirit. So 2 Peter 3:15, 16 shows us the apostle of the circumcision referring in this inspired document to Paul's Epistles as part of the scriptures. Thus we learn the unerring and far-seeing provision of allusion, which might to some seem casual, but is the fruit of infinite wisdom, and weightier to faith than a world of human reasonings. Indeed the intrinsic character of the New Testament is so unequivocally self-evidencing, that only the pride of unbelief in Jew or Gentile can account for one who accepts the Old as divine hesitating about the New as no less.

GOD'S INSPIRATION OF THE SCRIPTURES

Chapter 2
Apostolic Doctrine

We are not left to facts however momentous, nor to incidental statements though abundant, plain, and reliable. The New Testament pronounces the most distinct and conclusive doctrine on so all-important a subject. For it concerns not man only but God's honour, and the character of His word in both Testaments so called. "For thou hast magnified thy word [saying] above all thy name" (Psalm 138). Let us weigh a few of these testimonies.

The Lord Himself in John 14-16 prepared the way not for fresh promises, but for the fullest revelation of the truth by the Pentecostal gift of the Spirit. It was indeed to comprehend the power of enjoying every privilege and of supplying every need for the new creation, for the children of God, once scattered, now to be gathered together into one. "I have yet many things to say unto you, but ye cannot bear them now. Howbeit when he, the Spirit of truth, is come, he shall guide you into all the truth; for he shall not speak from himself, but whatsoever things he shall hear shall he speak; and he shall declare to you the things that are to come. He shall glorify me; for he shall take of mine and shall declare it to you." He had already announced that the Paraclete or Advocate, the Holy Spirit, Whom the Father would send in His name, should teach them all things, and bring to their remembrance all that He said to them. At Pentecost He came and made all this good.

1 Corinthians 2 is remarkably full as well as precise. The Old Testament left "secret things" belonging to God, which were then unrevealed: so intimated the law (Deuteronomy 29:29); and the greatest of the prophets acknowledged that it was not theirs to lift the veil (Isaiah 64:4). The apostle refers to this last, and contrasts the silence of old with what the Holy Spirit was now disclosing. "But to us God revealed [them] through the Spirit; for the Spirit searcheth all things, even the depths of God. For who of men knoweth the things of the man, except the spirit of the man that is in him? Thus also the things of God knoweth no one except the Spirit of God. But we received not the spirit of the world but the Spirit that is from God, that we might know the things that were freely given to us by God; which [things] also we speak, not in words taught by human wisdom but in [those] Spirit-taught, communicating spirituals by spirituals. But a natural man receiveth not the things of the Spirit of God, for they are folly to him; and he cannot know [them] because they are spiritually examined. But the spiritual examineth all things, while *he* is examined by no one. For who knew Jehovah's mind that he shall teach Him? But *we* have Christ's mind" (verses 10-16).

Here in fact is the whole case. God by His Spirit revealed what had been hidden, even His depths, which He only knows. We, says the apostle, received His Spirit that the things freely given to us by Him we may know as they are. The first is revelation of the truth, of His counsels.

Next comes the making known to others what God thus revealed: "Which things also we speak not in words taught of man's wisdom but in Spirit-taught, expounding spiritual [things] by spiritual [words]." Thirdly, follows the necessary spiritual condition to apprehend them. For a natural man neither receives nor can know what is scanned spiritually. It is the Spirit of God Who works in the Christian, the last stage, as He wrought in the first and the second. Thus we have God's gracious power by His Spirit, first in revealing divine things, next in communicating them verbally, and lastly in real reception or communion. Thereby have *we* Christ's mind, beyond even prophets of old.

The chief question lies in the word (verse 13) translated "comparing". As it undoubtedly has this meaning in 2 Corinthians 10:12, it was a natural temptation to understand it similarly here. But notoriously words are modified by their context; and as we have no other occurrence in the New Testament, we must search into the usage of the LXX or the like. For the sense of "comparing" is wholly unsuitable to the intermediate process, of which the apostle treats, though it might well form part of that which pertains to the reception or understanding of what was already written. Now in the Septuagint the most prevailing application of the word in its cognate forms is to the expounding or explanation of what God was pleased to reveal (Genesis 40:8, 12, 16, 18, 22; 41:12, 15), as in vision or dream (Daniel 2:2, 5, 6, 7, 9, 16, 24, 25, 26, 30, 36, 45; 4:3, 4, 6, 14, 15, 16, 17, 21; 5:7, 8, 13, 16, 18, 20, 28; 7:16).* As however in our text it is no question of a dream or vision to be interpreted, the sense naturally admits of a larger modification, and

---

* It is also used in Numbers 15:34 with the sense of "determined", or "decided".

hence in this instance requires "communicating" or some such equivalent.

This accordingly and perfectly falls in with the bearing of the clause and the demands of the context. For the clause is occupied, not with the spiritual man's apprehension of what is propounded, but with the conveying it to him in words taught by the Spirit. They were as to this expressly not left to man's wisdom or ability. Not only divine ideas were seen in the Spirit, but moreover the wording was no less taught by the Spirit. Herein "comparing" has no propriety and is therefore inadmissible. And though "interpreting", "expounding", or "determining" might convey the sense in substance, none of them seems to give it at this stage so unambiguously as "communicating". The connected words also acquire a definite force, free from the liability to different meanings which add nothing of moment. For "comparing" opens the door to vague and uncertain adjuncts; whereas with "communicating" the sense is fixed to "spiritual [things] by spiritual [words]". He had already spoken of the things of God, here designated "spiritual things", and he had also treated of words Spirit-taught; now brought together briefly in communicating "spiritual [things] by spiritual [words]". "To spiritual men" would be premature in verse 13; for he takes up this question only in the verses that follow.

His latest Epistle (2 Timothy 3) gave the apostle the fitting occasion to lay down the distinct and full dogmatic decision of the Holy Spirit on the scriptures. He had himself been raised up, not only as "minister of the gospel" but as "minister of the church", to fill up the word of God, as he tells us in Colossians 1:23-25. To Timothy he writes in view of difficult times to prevail in the last days, men who presented its evil traits being already there to turn away from. For if they had a form of piety, they denied its power. They had their prototypes in those who withstood Moses, and their folly should be quite manifest to all, as theirs too became. But Timothy had followed up Paul's teaching, conduct, purpose, faith, long-suffering, love, endurance, persecutions, sufferings; what things befell him at Antioch, at Iconium, at Lystra; what persecutions he endured, and the Lord delivered him out of all. But wicked men and impostors shall advance to worse, leading and led astray. "But abide thou in the things thou didst learn and wast assured of, knowing of whom thou didst learn, and that from a babe thou knowest sacred writ that is able to make thee wise unto salvation through faith that is in Christ Jesus."

Here we learn the safeguard to be in no way the church's witness; for therein it is that we see the awful spectacle of a veneered Christian form, yet a moral heathenism, with hypocrisy added, the grossest ways only concealed or withdrawn (compare Romans 1). The man of God rests on no Unnamed one, great or small. He was well aware of whom he learnt the truth, even the apostles; as he thoroughly knew what sort of life was his with whom he had the closest intimacy. For what is teaching without practice akin? Here it was maintained in face of persecutions and sufferings, with the marked deliverances of the Lord throughout; as indeed all should expect persecution who desire to live piously in Christ Jesus. Thus was manifested a marked difference in the later revelation as compared with the earlier. For its witnesses and instruments were contemporaries, bringing out the truth finally and together by the Spirit after Christ's advent and redemption; as the earlier writers had done their piece-meal work, spread over more than a thousand years, yet with a unity most marked.

But was it not the Old Testament that Timothy knew from a babe? Unquestionably. Would any one with wicked heart of unbelief thence seek to question or lower the New Testament? Let him learn that the apostle, while upholding God's ancient oracles as "sacred writ" (ἱερὰ γράμματα), is careful to affirm in the most comprehensive terms the divine authority of all, or rather "every", scripture, not old merely but new. For he reserves the due appropriated word, γραφή, which he declares in its every part to be inspired of God, or God-breathed, as is no other writing. It runs through the four Gospels, the Acts, and the apostolic Epistles in this sense alone, singular and plural.

The more general sense was expressed by γράμμα, a writing, which might mean a "bill" (Luke 16:6, 7), or "letter" in the abstract (Romans 2:27, 29; 7:6; 2 Corinthians 3:6), "alphabetic characters" (Luke 23:38; 1 Corinthians 3:7; Galatians 6:4), "epistles" (Acts 28:28), "letters" or learning (John 7:15; Acts 26:24), or "writings" (John 5:47), which needed the epithet ἱερὰ, sacred, &c. to stamp them as scriptures. But γραφή in Greek New Testament usage means nothing else, even without the article here or elsewhere, as our idiom also bears.

"Every scripture [is] God-breathed, and profitable for teaching, for conviction, for correction, for instruction in righteousness, that the man of God may be complete, equipped completely for every good work" (verses 16, 17). The Revisers, like some others, take "inspired of God", not as the predicate but as qualifying the subject; and the clause would then run, "Every scripture inspired of God [is] also profitable". But who will say that this is the natural meaning? who can deny that it involves a twofold awkwardness, but both by withholding the understood copula where one cannot but look for it, and by supposing it where it jars with the flow of the sentence? None of the constructions within or without the New Testament cited by Dean Alford approaches the one before us. One near in some respects is 1 Timothy 4:4, where it would be intolerable to make καλὸν (good) part of the subject. Still nearer perhaps is Hebrews 4:13, where nobody doubts that "naked and laid open" is the true predicate; if so, "God-breathed and profitable" ought to be thus taken here.

The truth appears to be that the conjunction καὶ though indubitably genuine was overlooked by early versions, as the Memphitic, Peschito-Syriac, and many of the Latin copies, besides the Clementine Vulgate: so too some fathers Greek and Latin. This error necessitated, one may say, the view that "God-breathed" belonged to the subject. Other Latin copies, with the Gothic, Harklean-Syriac, Armenian and Aethiopic, interpreted καὶ in the sense of "also" as introducing the predicate. Taken thus, καὶ is here feeble, and so superfluous that it was easily forgotten; whereas, wherever it is correctly so taken, it has an emphatic or supplementary force, as in Luke 1:36, Romans 8:29, 34, Galatians 4:7. It would certainly become those who contend for their construction to produce a sentence where a like severance occurs, or indeed can be, between two adjectives ostensibly connected by a conjunction.

But, if possibly allowed as grammatical, can this rendering be counted tenable on internal grounds? For if θεόπνευστος be treated as part of the subject, it must be taken either as an assumption, or as a condition. If it be assumed that scripture is God-inspired, nothing is gained by those who favour so harsh a construction. The sense is substantially alike, whether you assume or assert the inspiration of every scripture. But if the aim be to understand a condition (*i.e.* "if divinely inspired", rather than "*being* divinely inspired)", you are confronted with the acknowledged fact that γραφή in the New Testament is appropriated to scripture and spoken of no other writing. Hence the conditional construction, in order to apply, contradicts the known usage, and would require the wholly unauthorised sense of mere "writing": "every writing, if inspired of God, is also profitable", &c. If we understand γραφή as we must, in the sense of "scripture", and take the epithet with the subject, we gain nothing but a strangely incoherent phrase, yet in substance agreeing with its natural sense: "every scripture, being inspired of God, is also profitable", &c., as in fact Origen long ago took it, but not Athanasius, nor Gregory of Nyssa, nor Chrysostom, who held as the Authorised Version.

The Revised Version, whether intentionally or not, is ambiguous: "every scripture inspired of God [is] also profitable", &c. If it was *not* meant to raise a doubt, why was it so left? If it *was*, is it possible to conceive an object more opposed to the context? For the Spirit of God is furnishing the invaluable and needed safeguard against the difficult times of the last days; and after dwelling among the rest on the fact of Timothy's privilege in knowing from a babe the sacred writ of the Old Testament, he crowns all with the universal principle (which applies to the New Testament no less than to the Old, and to what might yet be written as well as to what was), "every scripture [is] God-inspired, and profitable for teaching", &c.

APOSTOLIC DOCTRINE

The apostle gives first, as was most reverent and worthy, its relation to God, the Author of this incomparable boon as of all others; next, its profitable uses for the blessing of the man of God. For as no creature but man in virtue of his spirit can know the things of man, no more can one know the things of God save by the Spirit of God, Who both revealed and communicated them, and enables the believer to discern them, as we have already seen. Scripture teaches us in our ignorance, convicts us of obstinacy or errors, corrects us when shirking or straying, and disciplines us in righteousness inward and outward, that in our stand for God we might be complete on every side, and with equal fulness furnished for every good work.

A learned dignitary (in loco) speaks of "God-inspired" not excluding verbal errors or possibly historical inaccuracies, and those of human transmission and transcription. But is not this doubly a mistake of grave import? It would first make the written word a divine guarantee of untruth, both originally as well as in its dissemination. Next, how he could mix up the two points is hard to say; for clerical blunders have nothing to do with the question of God's inspiration, solely with man's responsible use of its fruit. The former is a virtual denial of "God-inspired", unless the God of truth can lie: if He sanction errata in trifling matters, why not in greater things? But "scripture cannot be broken", said the Lord. Compromise is unworthy of faith. "It is written" was His answer to Satan's temptations, and is the guide and standard of all saints since grace gave scripture. It is not a question of *man's* spirit, but of God's, Who is beyond doubt able to secure the truth absolutely, as the Lord and the apostles and the prophets everywhere assume and assert. To imply such weakness in man as is beyond the power of God is a feeble, not the full, inspiration, taught in the Bible. But when philosophy is sought as the ally of divine truth, the issue cannot but be vacillating, inconsistent, and misleading. "Ye do err, not knowing the scriptures nor the power of God." It is a singularly loose comment on "*every* scripture is also inspired of God", &c. One can scarce doubt that a rendering so halting and strange tempts to a hesitating interpretation, even though not a whisper be given that they hold any scripture to be *un*inspired. Yet it is a plain and peremptory utterance of the apostle, calling for a version and a comment of no uncertain sound.

In ordinary thoughts and discussion on inspiration it is not always remembered that the apostle claims it authoritatively for "every scripture". This goes far beyond what men uttered from God, moved or borne along by the Holy Spirit (2 Peter 1:21). For we are taught, not only what the Holy Spirit gave by His living instruments, but that what is written by Him abides now of at least equal divine authority. It is painful to see the readiness of any Christian to allow the compatibility of this divine power with historical or any other inaccuracies, natural enough to man's spirit. But the apostle Paul in the text before us leaves no room for evasion or uncertainty. "Every scripture" is either assumed, as some argue, or asserted as others believe, to be God-inspired. Does *He* fail to exclude verbal errors? Is *He* capable of historical or any other inaccuracies?

The imputation really leaves God out, as every measure of scepticism does. It dwells on human infirmity and ignorance, which no believer ought for a moment to forget. But God's inspiration of "every scripture" gives to faith the certainty that no such inaccuracies attach to the written word as it came from Him; and this is all that plenary inspiration means. It in no way excludes mistakes in transcription, translation, or interpretation. But it is an abuse of language, calculated to deceive the simple and gratify the enemy, if one allow divine plenary inspiration in word and then annul it in deed. For as God cannot lie, so He does not pledge His inspiration so as to sanction errors ever so small. He used men of God as the vehicle for carrying out His purpose in giving His word; He employed their mind and heart as well as their language and style; but He communicated His own wisdom in fulfilment of His design beyond the measure of the instrument, and in absolute exclusion of mistake.

For any then to contend that plenary inspiration admits of "leaving" inspired men to themselves in any respect is really to leave out God, and to blow hot and cold in the same breath. It is openly and absolutely to contradict the apostolic canon here laid down. Not only were the writers moved by the Holy Spirit, but "every scripture is God-inspired". Scripture is no mere accident, nor simply a providential arrangement, where blemishes may naturally be. If it was God's purpose to give us His word, the Holy Spirit wrought to effectuate it in a wisdom, power, order, and end which bespoke Himself. One can understand unbelief blind even to the grace and the truth which came through Jesus Christ, and seeing only discrepancies and blunders in the Gospels, where spiritual intelligence finds the deepest demonstration of the divine mind, and a perfect result produced to Christ's glory before the eyes of faith. How strange and distressing that any who hear that word and believe Him Who sent the Lord fail to perceive that, of all theories, none is less satisfactory, tenable, or reverent! For it means that the Holy Spirit Who inspired the evangelists recalled facts and words imperfectly to their remembrance, and stamped misleading memoirs with the authority of God's word. What more inexplicable than that there should be no less than a divine Person for such compilations, supposed to be mutually inconsistent as well as defective in small points?

Here is not the place to show, not only how baseless is this unbelief, but the divinely admirable truth which the Holy Spirit set out in these inspired accounts of our Lord as everywhere else in the Bible. It would demand volumes and can be found by those who seriously enquire. But such speculations ought never to have been entertained for a moment. Their source is evil, though good men be ensnared by them. "Every scripture is God-inspired." We are entitled as believers to set one's seal to it that He is true; so is His word. We are bound in simple faith to deny errors or discrepancies in scripture as He wrote it. We may not be able to answer every objection, or to clear up every difficulty which ingenious ill-will or even weakness may muster; for this depends on our intelligence, which may be small. But if we believe the apostle's deliverance on the Bible to be "the commandment of the Lord" (as he claims generally and for smaller things in 1 Corinthians 14), we are warranted to rest in the peaceful certainty that "every scripture is inspired of God".

So our Lord acted with friend or foe. So He taught His own, as He had confronted the great enemy. "It is written" was the conclusive answer to temptation and to question; and if scripture were perverted, "It is written again" is the short and best refutation. What an example for us, so ready to trust in our dialectic skill of defence or in dissecting an adversary's ignorance and error! The simplest believer can reckon on the word and Spirit of

God. This honours Him and His word, and is for us the humblest, holiest, and safest ground.

In vain then do men argue that there are many things in the scriptures which the writers might have known, and probably did know, by ordinary means; that for some things they must have been supernaturally endowed; and that other things again required nothing less than direct revelation. The aim of this is unconsciously to lower scripture, and bring as much as possible within man's capacity. Now no believer need question God's use of means, if He pleases, or rising above them if for His glory. But "every scripture is inspired of God" settles all questions. We have there wicked men's hypocritical words, and their rebellious ones; we have even Satan's temptations and his accusations in scripture; but "every scripture is God-breathed". To present the least fact, to record the simplest word in scripture, was as truly of God's inspiration, as to reveal "the mystery" or to disclose the future glory of heaven and earth. Documents or none, the insertion in scripture was God-inspired: else the apostolic rule were infringed. But as our Lord said (John 10:35), "the scripture cannot be broken".

As Jehovah magnified His saying above all His name, so did our Lord take His stand on the written word, the scriptures, as the most authoritative of all testimonies. All scripture, every part of it even, is God-inspired for permanence, and the true end of controversy for those that believe; while such as believe not must learn their sin and folly in the judgment. The question is in no way, whether the writers knew or did not know what they wrote (for both are found abundantly in scripture), but whether they were inspired of God to write it. And "every scripture" is so inspired. This alone makes it God's word, not its known truth or usefulness, but His inspiring it; and this we have in every scripture. Some writers may be sublime and others simple; some may be pathetic and others severe; but all are God-inspired; and the plain proof is that they are part of the scriptures. In the New Testament we have differences as wide as sever the Epistle of James from those of Paul, and the Gospel of Mark from that of John. But inspired they are equally, as their writings are part of the scriptures. Inspiration of God is a fact, and does not admit of varying degrees.

It is quite within the power of the Holy Spirit in giving God's word to adopt the style of each individual writer. But no effort on a writer's part could make his words to be God's. Even before any adversary the Lord told the twelve to have no anxiety how or what to speak, for in the hour of need it should be given. "For it is not ye that speak, but the Spirit of your Father that speaketh in you" (Matthew 10:20). How much more was that divine energy wanted and given, when not their vindication was in question, but the communication of God's mind and will for His own and for ever! Indeed it is no more than the certain fact; for every scripture is God-inspired.

Speculation into the "how" of inspiration is a prying into what is not revealed, and therefore unwise and unbecoming. We are not told how God inspired the writers of the scriptures. It is probable that none could know save those who were so energised. Theories "mechanical" or "dynamical", so called, are out of place and explain nothing. As 1 Corinthians 2 maintains the principle, the necessity, and the fact of Spirit-taught words, so 2 Timothy 3:16 speaks, not of the revelation before the mind only, but of "scripture"; and decides for it as inspired of God. This is the all-important truth conveyed. It is God Himself in scripture removing all doubt about scripture, and even about every part of it. One can conceive no other communication more distinct or conclusive. The language is as plain as its aim is spiritually momentous; and its intimation is of the utmost practical interest and value.

Chapter 3
Its Uniformity

We have dwelt the longer on the claim demanded by the great apostle for "every scripture", because it really settles for the believer all the questions which the busy mind of man can raise. For we are not now debating with the Atheist or even the Deist, who openly disbelieves a revelation from God, but meeting the difficulties raised among professing Christians, though it may be too often originated by real sceptics. Doubts are more guilty now than in the days of our Lord Who reproached the Sadducees with not knowing the scriptures nor the power of God. For not only was He come as the True Light to shed light on every man, and to give an understanding that we might know Him that is true, but the entire book of the final revelation from God has been added since by the Holy Spirit sent forth from heaven. And it is in one of these latest communications of divine truth that we have God attesting His own inspiration of "every scripture".

This was as it should be in view of man's need, and especially for the safeguard of believers, soon to be left without the living presence of apostles. But from the beginning of revelation God took care that they who read or heard His word should be assured that it was His truth in His power and by His authority, that His people might believe and obey Him. Thus in that last book of the Pentateuch, which it is a modern fashion to imagine of late date, in Deuteronomy 4:2 we read, "Ye shall not add unto the word which I command you, neither shall ye diminish aught from it, that ye may keep the commandments of Jehovah thy God which I command you." As with the Law, so it was with the Prophets: "Jehovah hath spoken", though by Isaiah (1:2); "The words of Jeremiah ... to whom the word of Jehovah came" (Jeremiah 1:1, 2); and so with the others. It did not differ with the Psalms, as their chief writer says, "The Spirit of Jehovah spoke by me, and his word was in my tongue" (2 Samuel 23:2).

The Lord Jesus when here set the scripture in the clearest light, in the simplest way, and on the firmest ground. He repels Satan's temptation with "It is written"; and when Satan uses the word, He answers by its right use, "It is written again." It is remarkable and instructive, that all these replies are taken from Deuteronomy: the book that reveals the obedience of faith when the people should be ruined through failure under the law. He appealed to the earliest history (Genesis 2) as God's word. He also prepared His disciples for those new communications of grace and truth which the Holy Spirit would come to make on His own departure (John 14, 15, 16): these we have now in what is called the New Testament. So the apostles themselves declare (Romans 16:25, 26; 1 Corinthians 2; 14:36; 2 Corinthians 13:2, 3; Colossians 4:16; 1 Thessalonians 2:13; 5:27; Hebrews 1:1, 2; 2:1-4; 12:25; 2 Peter 3:2, 15, 16; 1 John 4:6). 2 Timothy 3:16 has been already before us. Apparently "occasional and fragmentary", the writings of the New Testament have a real completeness unmistakably divine.

It is because this divine character of all scripture is not held in simple faith that men, and even pious men, have yielded to human thoughts which dishonour God's word and have opened the door to sceptical evil more and more ungodly. As the Old Testament consists of the Law, the Psalms, and the Prophets, so does the New Testament of the Gospels and Acts, the Epistles, and the Apocalypse. Its basis is grace and truth come through Jesus Christ, Who on His own departure sent the Holy Spirit as the other Paraclete to be with and in us for ever. Again, the Epistles form quite as characteristic a part of the New Testament as the Gospels, following up those memoirs with the truth dogmatically (which saints could not bear before redemption); as in the Acts we have historically the Holy Ghost's action when personally descended and present.

Hence the contrast is greatest with the Psalms or poetic portion of the Old Testament; and it is the Epistles, which to us stand over against them: of all compositions the most familiar and intimate. Therein it is no longer outpourings which anticipate Messiah's coming, sufferings, and reign in Zion, with groans and cries meanwhile; but heart communicating to heart in the Spirit the grace and the glory of the Son of God already come and gone, but about to come again to have us with Himself in the Father's house as well as to appear and reign, as we shall with Him, in that day. No wonder that a new walk (Ephesians 2:10), and a higher, nearer worship, go along with the new relationship most fully brought out in the Epistles. The closest analogue to the Old Testament is in the Apocalypse, which alone answers to the Prophets but rises above while it confirms them, completing the whole to the glory of God and the Lamb.

The development of all, whether in the Old Testament or in the New, gives occasion to the most delightful variety in God's communications through His chosen instruments. But this only the more strikingly manifests the unity of the Divine Author. "Every scripture is God-inspired." No notion can be more false or superficial than to infer from their variety of matter and manner a difference in the degree of inspiration. Neither the revealed facts nor the revealed doctrine allow an idea so baseless, unreasonable, and dangerous. Scripture pronounces that "every scripture is inspired of God". One can understand cavils or disbelief about its parts, or even the whole where scepticism is extreme; but, for any one who admits scripture to be from God, a varying inspiration is negatived by divine authority.

This suffices to prove without further ado the egregious error of the late D. Wilson, Bishop of Calcutta, in his Evidences of Christianity (i. 508). "By the inspiration of *suggestion* is meant such communications of the Holy Spirit, as suggested and detailed minutely every part of the truths delivered. The inspiration of *direction* is meant of such assistance as left the writers to describe revealed truth in their own way, directing only the mind in the exercise of its power. The inspiration of *elevation* added a greater strength and vigour to the efforts of the mind than the writer could otherwise have attained. The inspiration of *superintendency* was that watchful care which preserved generally from anything being put down derogatory to the revelation with which it was connected." There are no such kinds of inspiration taught in the Bible, which speaks of God's inspiration pure and simple, and predicates it of "every scripture" alike. Dr. Wilson's first kind is the only real inspiration, though even it is not fully stated. The other three are not the inspiration of any scripture, but such direction, elevation, and superintendency as His servants look for, and not in vain, day by day. But none of these is true inspiration, which conveys God's mind or will as perfectly as it excludes every error of man.

Doctors Dick (Essay on Inspiration), Pye Smith (Scripture Testimony to the Messiah i.), Henderson (Lect. on Inspir. 36 sec.), and others have put forth a similar hypothesis of different degrees in inspiration, influenced partly by the free thinking of modern Germans, partly by a name so respectable as that of Dr. Doddridge (Works v.) of older date. There is modification; for Henderson makes five degrees, while Doddridge states no more than three. But all agree in the hypothesis of differences which oppose the authoritative declaration of the apostle, without the semblance of warrant from any other scripture.

To what source then are we to attribute these unbelieving speculations? It would seem mainly to Moses Maimonides (AD 1131-1204), from whom Benedict de Spinoza borrowed much, followed in that at least by Le Clerc, as Grotius derived it directly from Jewish channels. In his "Moreh Nebochim" Maimonides conceives eleven "degrees of Prophecy". These the Portuguese Jew, Abarbanel (AD 1437-1508), melted into three degrees of inspiration for the Old Testament, answering to the three divisions of the sanctuary and its court: the Thorah, the Nebiim, and the Ketubhim, the Law, the Prophets, and the rest of the Old Testament or Hagiographa. That Moses personally enjoyed the divine Presence, as no ordinary prophet did, is certain:

Numbers 12 and Deuteronomy 34 are as to this explicit. John the Baptist (and we have our Lord's authority for it) was a prophet, and greater than a prophet. None of woman-born was greater than he; yet he neither wrote a line nor wrought a miracle. But whosoever wrote, inspiration is a fact, and admits of no varying measures. "Every scripture is God-inspired"; and God is equally true at all times and by all persons He employed to write or even speak His word. It was certainly a monstrous position of the Jewish scheme that the lowest in the scale of the inspired should be assigned to the Holy Spirit; for He, as we know, is the divine agent in man of all divine inspiration, and He does not differ from Himself.

Such then is the murky ditch whence the Jews have derived their chief theory on the books of the Old Testament. Such men abide still in the unbelief for which the branches were broken off from the olive-tree of promise. No other origin perhaps can be assigned to the low and debasing influences, otherwise enlarged, which are in our day working to greater ungodliness among professing Christians. Can any thing be more humbling to one who loves Christ and the church? How all-important to cleave to God and the word of His grace! This, and nothing else at bottom, is able to build us up (instead of leaving us a sport to every wind of doctrine), able also to give us an inheritance among all those that are sanctified. It is the truth, the Father's word, that sanctifies His children. Error, all error, defiles. What error more poisonous, next to heterodoxy on Christ's Person and work, than the dishonour of God's word, the great means of making divine truth known to us? How imminent and far-reaching the peril of tampering with humanitarianism as to scripture!

Chapter 4
The Human Element

Nobody doubts that scripture without exception has a human element. In it God speaks and writes permanently to man, and therefore in human language. It were unintelligible otherwise. As the general rule Hebrew was employed in the so-called Old Testament, Greek in the New. We can readily perceive His wisdom in thus writing by man to man (Deuteronomy 5:22; 9:10; 10:4), save in the most solemnly exceptional case: the law with all its variety of meaning in the language of His ancient people; the gospel with all the fulness of grace and truth in the chief tongue of the Gentiles.

But God was pleased to do much more—even to work to this end on man and in man, so that the reproach of "mechanical" is unfounded, no less than the setting up of "dynamical" is cold and insufficient. The inspired are through His goodness far beyond being His pen or even His penmen, as it has been said. Their minds and affections He uses as well as their language. There was indeed dictation in certain parts of scripture, as in His promises and His threats, His predictions, His ordinances, statutes, and judgments. Such is the latter half of

Exodus, and almost the whole of Leviticus, a great part of Numbers, and not a little even of Deuteronomy, special as its character is. So there was to the Prophets, where they had to search, like their readers, what or what manner of time the Spirit of Christ which was in them did point out, when it testified beforehand the sufferings that belonged to Christ and the glories after these; "to whom it was revealed that not to themselves but to you they ministered those things which were now reported to you through those that evangelised you by the Holy Spirit sent from heaven" (1 Peter 1:11, 12).

In New Testament days, as we learn from 1 Corinthians 14, men were not to speak in a tongue without the gift of interpretation. If there were no interpreter, such an one, gifted as he was, must be silent in the assembly, because all things there must be done to edifying, whereas even the man's own spirit was unfruitful. The great thing was to speak with the spirit and with the understanding also. Hence the apostle thanked God that he spoke with tongues more than any of them; but in the assembly he preferred to speak five words with his understanding that he might instruct others also, than ten thousand words in a tongue. What a rebuke to the childishness which doats on the display of power! What strengthening of holy love that all might learn and be encouraged!

This of course was not inspiration, but it furnishes a principle for estimating intelligently the various forms which the Holy Spirit adopted in that work also. Nor can any right mind overlook on the one hand that, where it was God's power conspicuously and unmistakeably working in a tongue, it holds far from the highest place for the assembly; it was (without the presence of an interpretation) excluded, as having no more title in itself to be there than the performance of a miracle, a sign for unbelievers, not for the faithful. And so they and the like are classed together, the lowest in the scale of these divine gifts (1 Corinthians 12, 14). Prophesying on the other hand has the highest value; for he that exercises this gift speaks to men's edification and encouragement and consolation; he edifies the church, which the speaker in a tongue cannot do, unless there be also interpretation with it. Thus God gave the better place where His Spirit brought in the distinct element of profit for others. Power, though plainly God's, is subordinate to spiritual blessing, order, and love.

So it is with the fruits of inspiration. All have alike divine authority. All are of the Spirit, and in their place and for their end give God's mind. Scripture says little of the mode in which He wrought in each case; but the little that is said shows that all were not favoured with the same degree of intimacy in the manner, while the utmost precision was taken to affirm that "every scripture is inspired of God". Some may exhibit simplicity, others majesty; some are models of terseness, others are rich and flowing; some are familiar with human life, its difficulties, dangers, disappointments, and snares; others are occupied with the trials of conscience and the affections God-ward. Then again some are historical (as Genesis), but with the momentous aim of giving us God's mind and principles of moral government as found nowhere else. This indeed is but a small part of its scope, which takes in the germs of almost all that God will do till time melts into eternity, as developed elsewhere by the Prophets. Others, like the Kings, are historical in presenting the conduct of His anointed rulers and of His people under law, where are episodes (rare indeed in men of faith) of kings, priests, prophets;

where man's ways are stated just as they were, and God's ways thereon as no earthly historian ever gave or could. In all this the human element has a very large place; but inspiration yields God's word throughout, and thus the Bible is unique.

Take a quite different instance and a book outside Israel directly, yet devoted to solving the problem individually which applies to that people. The book of Job brings before us a godly man set on by the unseen adversary, and suddenly cast down from honour and affluence into such loss, bereavement, and personal suffering as never was allowed to fall on another, yet through causes that looked ordinary. Was God indifferent? On the contrary (and expressly to prove not only to Job but to all others who might be tried here below, that He can overrule even now the enemy for the good of His own), it was He that initiated the entire transaction by His gracious notice of the saint before Satan's envious and malicious ears. Job needed to judge himself before God as he had never yet learnt, and to bow to God confidingly. The bearing of his friends does what Satan's cruel wiles wholly failed in; and Job breaks down in impatience, as his friends in misjudgment. Elihu intervenes, when they were reduced to the silence of vexation (but Job still unbroken), and proves that, if the present world be as far as possible from being a reliable manifestation of divine government, God nevertheless carries on His government of souls in a most efficient and unfailing manner. And Jehovah Himself in His majesty ends the controversy by an answer to Job which humbles him in the dust, yet shows Himself very pitiful and of tender mercy; as He also puts to shame and censure the self-righteous friends (who deemed the sufferer a hypocrite), now dependent on Job's intercession who was blessed doubly more at the end than in his beginning. Here the human element abounds in the most instructive way. It was not that God approved all that Job said, still less what his friends uttered in their pride and self-complacency, to say nothing of Satan or of Job's wife. But inspiration gives the entire, perfectly to let us know where they all were, and to give us God's mind and aim from the first and to the last. Only He could have furnished the scene, where sacrificial offering had its due place, and righteous government ruled in the face of all appearances to the contrary.

The style of the history too is notable. How touchingly Jehovah is heard in Genesis adapting Himself to the childhood of mankind! "It is not good that man should be alone: I will make a help-mate for him, his counterpart." "And they heard the voice of Jehovah God walking in the garden in the cool of the day." Hear too His expostulation when they sinned, and His mercy toward man glorying against judgment in His curse of the Serpent. Hear it with Cain when nursing the wrath which was soon to slay his holy and righteous brother, yea after that impious murder. What grief at His heart appears over the race in Genesis 6:5-7! What ready recognition of Noah's holocaust after the deluge, as He said in His heart, "I will not henceforth curse the ground any more on account of man." How vigilant for the life of man, whoever might shed his blood! "And the bow shall be in the cloud; and I will look upon it", not man merely from below! Compare also Genesis 11:6, 7; 18:20, 21. So too as to His people it is in Exodus 2:23-29; 3:7-9 before their deliverance from Egypt.

It is not that divine majesty is lacking. The opening words of the Bible, simple, sublime, and absolutely true, proclaim the mind that inspired, no less than the words of the first day's work which drew out the admiration of the heathen Longinus. But "the philanthropy" of God, as the apostle calls it, could not be hidden from the first before the day of its full display; and this not only in His works and ways but in His word. Only the dullest of readers could fail to observe the varieties of style which pervade both Testaments. From Moses to Malachi each writer preserves his peculiarities intact; and it is precisely the same from the Gospel of Matthew to the Revelation of John. This is a fact patent, in presence of the still more wondrous fact of a mighty purpose flowing from One self-evidently divine wrought out in and by so many different agents with the most marked diversity of position and character, of time and place. It is just the human element maintained and governed by the divine; and so far is there aught inscrutable in this, when we see its admirable result in the scriptures, the believer feels that it is altogether worthy of God and gracious toward man. The difficulty indeed, now that we know it as a subsisting reality, would be to conceive any other mode emanating from Him that could so satisfy His mind and love. Thus is man morally elevated and best enlightened; thus alone is God's glory secured, while His grace has the fullest scope and exercise. *We* have nothing to reconcile: *God* has done it perfectly in scripture. It is for us to believe and be blessed, even to true and living communion with the Blesser; a blessing impossible for man save in Christ through the word and Spirit of God.

The wonder is deepened immensely when we recall the marked and radical difference of the two volumes, as we may call them, Hebrew and Greek: the one characterised by the law and the land; the other by the gospel and heaven. Yet it is the same living and true God, only now revealing Himself in the Son incarnate, and by the Holy Spirit sent forth from heaven. And therefore it is that the New Testament acquires a human character yet more pronounced and more profound than the Old Testament. For not only did the Son become man, as He will never cease to be, but through His redemption the Holy Spirit deigns to dwell in the believer as He never did or could before, and acts as a Spirit of communion, not merely as One of prophecy (Revelation 19). The assembly too or church is God's temple, His habitation in virtue of the Spirit Who dwells there. Yea, as baptised by Him it is Christ's body. Hence the human element shines as never of old, of the deepest interest and with the richest intimacy of grace, and only second in moment to the divine, because in their perfection we know and have both in the Lord Jesus Christ. He is the True God and Eternal life; and this we have in Him. But we are also "members of His body"; for "He is the head of the church".

Now the Old Testament discloses a state of things under the kingdom of God wholly distinct from that of the gospel and the church, wherein Jew and Gentile cannot be, nor bond nor free, nor male and female, all being one in Christ Jesus. Whereas in the age to come Israel is to be restored and exalted, Zion to have the first dominion, and all the nations to be blessed, and the whole world set under His reign in manifest power and glory, Who is alike Messiah, Son of man, and Jehovah. And the New Testament confirms the same blessed prospect for the earth and all its families in that day; while it alone reveals the heavenly portion of the glorified, and the church's marriage with the heavenly Bridegroom, sharing the inheritance with Him Who is the Heir of all things.

This therefore imparts unequalled ground and occasion for the human element in God's counsels and ways, as it is no less reflected in the inspired communications of the New Testament. The Epistles are accordingly the fitting form of God's mind thereon; as the Christian himself is Christ's epistle as well as the apostle's, known and read of all men, written not with ink but with the Spirit of the living God, not in stone tables but in fleshy tables of the heart.

Yet the Old Testament proclaimed the coming of the New, and that ruin of the chosen people through the rejection of the Messiah which made their own fall necessary, and thus opened the way for Christ's exaltation on high, the call of the Gentiles by the gospel, and the formation of the church in union with the Head by the Spirit come from heaven. Hence too the new volume of inspiration authenticates the new work going on till the Lord comes, but seals the truth of the Old Testament which it replaces for the Christian and the church. Yet it assures that the Law and the Prophets are verily to be fulfilled in the day that is rapidly nearing, when Christ shall be hidden no more but appear to gather together in one all things in Him, the things in the heavens and the things on the earth.

It is evident that a human element is in one form or another characteristic of inspiration, that it is even more "prophetic" in the New Testament than in the Old, and that it is only second in interest and importance to the divine which is there. But it is a phrase employed to insinuate liability to human error in some respect if not in all; just as men avail themselves of the Incarnation to overthrow or undermine the personal glory of Christ. Such unbelief is in both altogether unfounded and unworthy. Scripture is most explicit in guarding souls from thus dishonouring God's Son or His word; and all the more because appearances afford a handle to such as seek this occasion. For scripture, like the Lord Jesus, is a grand moral test; and those who desire not God's will can readily find reasons against both out of that will which is declared to be "enmity against God". To impute human defect to scripture is to deny its inspiration of God.

4.1   The Genealogy in Matthew chapter 1

As an important instance to test the unbelieving cavil, take the genealogy in the first chapter of Matthew's Gospel. This, pseudo-criticism will have to be a compilation of ignorance and mistake. It is often assumed that Matthew simply adopted the existing Jewish register. Gaps in such pedigrees were quite understood and made no difficulty where the line was sure, and give no real ground for the charge of discrepancy with other lists. Compare Ezra 7:1-5 with 1 Chronicles 6:1-15 for the stem of Aaron. This was open to the inspiring Spirit here as elsewhere, if such were God's will. But the genealogy here has marks of design which we find only in scripture. It opens with marking out the Lord as "son of David, son of Abraham", the beginnings of the kingdom as settled of God for ever, and of the promises. Then it presents from Abraham to David fourteen generations, from David to the Babylonish migration as many, and the same from that migration to the birth of Christ.

It is universally known that three generations are omitted from the intermediate series. Nobody can with candour conceive that Matthew, whose Gospel displays pre-eminent and profound acquaintance with the Law, the Psalms, and the Prophets, did not perfectly well know that Ahaziah, Joash, and Amaziah were here left out between Joram and Uzziah. Even an unenlightened Israelite could not be ignorant of a fact so patent. It was therefore due to purpose, in no reasonable way to oversight or confusion. It was intended to arrange the line with but twice seven in each of its three sections: the beginning of the stock of promise down to the king of God's choice; the course of the kingdom till its utter evil and humiliation in Babylon; and the faithfulness of God notwithstanding in preserving the royal line to the virgin's Son according to prophecy. As therefore some links must be dropt to effect this aim, who could be so fittingly omitted as these three descendants of the foreign and murderous Athaliah? The Jews themselves may well have done this in some register of theirs, assuredly not ignorant of what they did, but with moral design. Whether this was so or not, we cannot say, as the registers were lost at the destruction of Jerusalem. But the omission is plain at this point and to the extent of leaving the intended links of fourteen generations. Whatever may have been the motive of the writer, the fact is before all; and the character of the Gospel altogether refutes the imputation that it was lack of care, intelligence, or honesty. If he was inspired to give the genealogy, it is impossible that God could either lie or err.

But the proof of divine design appears in other features also. Think of any one on human grounds selecting such women as are here named in the earlier chain! Think of a Jew on his own motion inserting these only in his pedigree of the Messiah! Not a word about Sarah or Rebecca, of Leah or Rachel; but "Judah begot Pharez and Zarah of *Thamar!*" Certainly it was no accident to drag out a history so scandalous into the light of the

New Testament, risking the dishonour of the Messiah. And is it "after the manner of men" to blazon the fact that "Salmon begot Boaz of Rahab?" or even that "Boaz begot Obed of Ruth?" And when we come down to "David the king", what can one say of recalling the chief shame that stained his life? "David begot Solomon of her [that had been wife] of Uriah?" An incestuous woman! a harlot! a Moabitess! an adulteress! Never was there such a choice, and in the face of so many admirable and saintly wives passed by!

No; it is incredible that any priest or scribe or lawyer ever drew up as a legal document such a genealogical roll. Further, it is not conceivable that Matthew himself would ever have thought or dared to do it without the power of the inspiring Spirit working in him to this end. It is at first sight as opposed as can be to every natural instinct. Nothing can account for it but the direct and deep purpose of God, Who was pleased to disclose to us the depths of sin abounding in Messiah's ancestry, calmly but expressly singled out, that we may see in His redemption, where sin abounded, grace surpassing yet more through Christ to God's glory. And if the Holy Spirit be the true author, and the result God's word, who and what are they who venture on their petty and unhallowed criticisms?

Again, the same spirit of unbelief objects to the genealogy that it is Joseph's line; whereas what they want is Mary's! Here extreme ignorance is betrayed; for the genealogy needed to satisfy an enquiring Jew was and must be descent from Solomon. This was solely through Joseph. If our Lord had not inherited legally his title, He could not have been David's Son in the direct royal line. And this was given to Matthew, who proves Him to be beyond doubt the Heir through Solomon whose succession Jehovah confirmed with an oath: the true and expected David's Son Who was David's Lord, yet born of the virgin and so marked off from all others, Emmanuel, yet Jehovah, Who should save His people from their sins.

On the other hand, Luke's genealogy (which is quite mistakenly counted Joseph's, but can be shewn demonstrably to be Mary's*) was essential for the due proof that our Lord was her Son, not legally merely but really, Son of God and Son of man in one Person, and thus "Light for revelation of Gentiles, as well as glory of God's people Israel": so all this Gospel illustrates. He was truly man: how else had He reached all mankind, or even Israel, as the Saviour? He was as truly God: else He had never revealed Him adequately in His life, nor availed efficaciously in His atoning blood and death, as all the Gospels testify and above all John's. Christ was thus according to the law Joseph's heir, both naturally and supernaturally Mary's Son; above all He was the Only-begotten Son of God through eternity. This last is given by John, who furnishes no earthly genealogy any more than Mark, though for a wholly different reason: John, because He is presented as being God, and therefore far above it; Mark, as becoming Servant of God for

---

* The true way of taking Luke 3:23 is: "And Jesus himself, when he began, was about thirty years old (being, as was supposed, son of Joseph); of Eli, of Matthat, of Levi, &c." Mary was, as even the Talmud admits, daughter of Eli in descent from Nathan. "Being, as was supposed, Joseph's son" is the correct parenthesis. It is natural that Satan should seek to set in opposition two genealogies, Joseph's and Mary's, which are in fact distinct, yet are both necessary for the truth. The mistake of most has been through viewing the allusion to Joseph, not as parenthetical which it evidently is, but as the starting point of the line which really begins with Eli, Mary's father.

every need of man, wherein nobody looks for a genealogy.

4.2 THE SYNOPTIC GOSPELS

The next case we may here review is the inextricable difficulty some critics have found in comparing the Synoptic Gospels, and in particular on the supposition that the writers which succeeded each other had before them the Gospel or Gospels that preceded. The conclusion is that they had a common oral tradition or teaching, while each was left to tell his own story with all the modification incident to human weakness where there was also veracity. Let me cite the late Dean Alford on the example in question, which seemed to him not only typical but peculiarly plain and sure from his frequent allusion to it. "The *real* discrepancies between our Evangelistic histories are very few, and those nearly all of one kind. They are simply the results of the entire independence of the accounts. They consist, mainly in different chronological arrangements expressed or implied. Such for instance is the transposition, before noticed, of the history of the passage into the country of the Gadarenes, which in Matthew 8:28 ff. precedes a whole course of events which in Mark 5:1 ff. and Luke 8:26 ff. it follows. Such again is the difference in position between the pair of incidents related in Matthew 8:19-22, and the same pair of incidents found in Luke 9:57-60" (Greek Testament, Prolegomena [chapter] 1, [page] 12, fifth edition). He gives these up as "real discrepancies", complaining on the one side of enemies who would thereby overthrow the truth, and on the other of the orthodox who would harmonize at the expense of common fairness and candour.

Now why is it that one who sincerely loved the Lord and His word felt driven to so helpless a dilemma? Because he failed to hold unflinchingly that "every scripture is inspired of God", and allowed under that standard that the writers were "*left*, in common with others, to the guidance of their natural faculties!" But this is *not* divine inspiration. It does not rise above the gracious guidance of the Spirit every Christian looks or ought to look for day by day. If the Dean would confine it to "much variety", *i.e.* discrepancy in points of minor consequence, he could not resist the demands of others who apply it to any or every statement, be it of the highest moment. He thus surrenders the unwavering standard which faith finds in God's inspiring "every scripture".

Is there then any insuperable obstacle in the way of believing that the differing arrangements, being equally inspired, are to be received implicitly as God's word and absolutely true? Why impute the difference to man's weakness? Why not to God's wisdom? One can heartily sympathise with a believer who says, Here is a difficulty beyond my solution; and so I wait and search with prayer to Him Who gave it by His Spirit for my comfort and instruction. Therefore, as I am sure it is all and equally true, I hope yet (if it please Him) to see the apparent discrepancy cleared, perhaps in my own reading, or yet more probably through another believer. For we are members one of another; and thus the Spirit loves to help. Far be it from me to lay on God's word the blame which belongs to my own spiritual dullness.—In the present case, without in the least claiming power of the Spirit to meet every hard question or to answer all possible objections, let me say that the special design of each Gospel (ascertainable by grace from its own contents) is the main key.

THE HUMAN ELEMENT

Matthew was led of God frequently to depart from the mere order of the facts with the deeper end of the Spirit in setting out the dispensational change from Jehovah-Messiah's presence, and His rejection by the Jews. Luke was led to act similarly in presenting the moral principles which shone in Christ's words and ways as the Holy Thing born of woman, the Son of God, Man on earth among men. Chronology was on these occasions subordinate and vanished before the weightier aim of the Holy Spirit. In ordinary cases it was preserved; and so we may observe it to be all but invariably in the Gospels of Mark and John, the divine design in them not interfering with the simple order of occurrence.

Matthew 8 opens first with the Jewish leper cured; then follows the Gentile centurion's servant healed. Yet the fact of the leper occurred before the Lord went up the mountain in chapters 5, 6, 7, as is certain from comparing Mark 1. The centurion's servant was not healed till He came down. Again, Peter's mother-in-law was restored to strength from fever, and of course the crowd of sick and possessed after sunset of the same sabbath, before even the leper, as the same chapter of Mark proves beyond cavil. For in his Gospel we have the day specified and the order of events kept; whereas it is not so in the part of Matthew we are examining, where we have only "and", "and", "and", leaving the time open, save in the connecting verses 16, 17 with verses 14, 15. Further, it is quite clear from Mark 4:35—5 that the passage across the lake and the storm which obeyed the Lord's rebuke were on the evening of the day when the Lord gave utterance to the great parables of Matthew 13; and that the two demoniacs were delivered on the other side after that, Mark and Luke being inspired to dwell on the more desperate case of Legion. There is not even the semblance of discrepancy; because Matthew states the facts without any note of time, and states them in the order suited to give a display of the Lord's power in detailed testimony on earth showing the dispensational change that was imminent. Mark gives them as they happened in His ministry; which enables us to see how hasty are those who set one account against another. The design explains each and all.

It may be added that Luke 9 appears to indicate that "the pair of incidents" which illustrate Christ's position in Mark 8 occurred historically after the transfiguration given in Matthew 17. Hence we have there no note of time in the First Gospel. This cuts off all ground for the charge of "real discrepancy". It is unworthy of a believer that anything of the kind should issue in a wanton insult to scripture, due to one's own haste and ignorance.

4.3 THE PREFACE TO LUKE'S GOSPEL

There is a passage which is constantly adduced by those who contend that scripture itself denies its own divine character and claims no more than diligence in using human means to arrive at authentic history. It is the well-known preface to Luke's Gospel. Does it warrant such an inference? Does it in the least contradict 2 Timothy 3:16? Is not a Gospel as fully inspired as an Epistle? Are they not alike God's word? And is not the word of God such in reality as in name?

"Forasmuch as many took in hand to set forth a narrative concerning the matters that are fully established (or, believed) among us, according as they who from the beginning were eye-witnesses and ministers of the word delivered to us, it seemed good to me also, having accurately followed up all things from the outset, to write with order to thee, most excellent Theophilus, that thou mightest fully know the certainty about things (or, words) in which thou wast instructed" (Luke 1:1-4).

Can there be a more striking witness of divine design and special character? This Gospel more than any other developes the ways and words of the "man Christ Jesus who gave himself a ransom for all" (1 Timothy 2:6): not the Messiah rejected by the Jews, not the Servant of man's need and specially of the gospel, nor yet as the Divine Word become flesh, the Only-begotten Son. Here pre-eminently He is the Son of man among men, and so traced up to Adam, though carefully shewn to be the Son of God as no one else. Here have we the beautiful sketch, not only of the Babe just born, but of His youth; here the sabbath in the synagogue at Nazareth, where He read the beginning of Isaiah 61, closing the book (or, roll) exactly where it was fulfilled that day. On their expression of unbelief, He reminded them of Israel's long famine when God's mercy flowed to the Gentile widow of Zarephath, and of the Syrian cleansed when there were many lepers in Israel.

Here we learn more than elsewhere of His praying; here only we find the widow of Nain whose only son He gave, raised from the bier of death, to his mother. Here is given the affecting story of the penitent woman in Simon the Pharisee's house, forgiven, saved, and in peace. Here we read of the many women blessed in various ways whom He allowed to minister to Him of their substance. Here we are told of James and John rebuked for their lack of grace toward certain Samaritans. Here is found the mission of the seventy, and the Lord's call to a joy in heavenly privilege rather than in power over the enemy. Here the Lord teaches Who is my neighbour? by the good Samaritan. Here Mary's good part is declared to anxious and bustling Martha. Here the rich fool is laid bare to rebuke such too as would make Christ a divider of inheritance. Here waiting is shewn to be beyond working for the Lord, though His own are called to both.

Here men who prate of judgments are warned to repent lest they all perish alike. Here the great supper comes before us, and man's contempt for God's inviting goodness. Here are presented the combined parables of the lost sheep, coin, and son, here too the Father's love and joy in saving. Here meet us the prudent that sacrifice the present in view of the future; here the light of the unseen shows us Lazarus exchanging extremest misery on earth for Abraham's bosom, and the rich man his sumptuous ease for torment unspeakable. Here the repentant tax-gatherer is justified rather than the self-trusting Pharisee. Here the Son of man brings salvation to the rich Zacchaeus. And here at the end the rejoicing disciples praise God for "peace in heaven and glory in the highest", as the heavenly host at the beginning ascribed "Glory to God in the highest, and on earth peace, good pleasure in men." So here only we have the touching assurance to denying Simon Peter of his restoration through the Lord's intercession, and of his subsequent confirming his brethren. Here only do we read of an angel strengthening Christ and of His bloody sweat; here of Jerusalem's daughters warned; here of the converted robber to be that day with Him in Paradise. Here lastly have we the walk of the risen Jesus to Emmaus; here the preaching, unto all the nations, of repentance and remission of sins in His name, beginning with Jerusalem; here His ascending from Bethany to heaven, while He blessed His own on earth.

Thus we have distinct facts and words indicating a marked design, and doubtless a design far deeper than

THE HUMAN ELEMENT

Luke's mind, though God wrought in his affections and his understanding powerfully, as He did in each of the inspired men. But it was given to him in particular to trace Christ morally and in His grace to man universally. So his preface savours of that design; and he speaks of the motives that animated his writing to another fellow-disciple, instead of plunging into his task without a word about himself or Theophilus. The human element is therefore at its height here as throughout. This is exactly the special character with which God was pleased to invest the beloved physician whom He employed, (himself distinguished with others from those of circumcision in Colossians 4,) to write to a young Christian who was a Gentile. Hence this Gospel, though commencing with "the Jew first", like the great apostle, breaks quickly forth out of Jewish trammels, and reveals in the Saviour what God is to man in grace.

Just so is it with the preface and introduction and dedication to Theophilus with his Gentile title. Luke contrasts rather than compares his account of our Lord with the composition of others. If the "many" who undertook the work had done it with the certainty requisite, there had been no need for him. The others had drawn up their reports, in accordance with the tradition of those that from the beginning were eye-witnesses and ministers of the word. Nor does he censure them or their accounts. But it seemed good to him also, having accurately followed up all from the first, to write in an orderly way that Theophilus might know the certainty respecting what he was instructed in.

How he had had his full and accurate acquaintance with all this history of infinite interest and importance, he does not tell us, as none of the inspired do more than he.

But he does open out his mind and heart in a way peculiar to himself, yet in perfect accord with the Gospel throughout, so as to bear the stamp of the Holy Spirit working in him unerringly to that end. "Every scripture is inspired of God"; and Luke's Gospel no less than any other portion. But if the gracious and godly motives of the writer appear in the preface in a way quite unusual; so the absurdity and superficial narrowness of the critics are evident in perverting that fact, beautifully characteristic, to lower the divine authority of this book of scripture he was employed to write. It is on the contrary an additional and powerful evidence, in passing, of God's inspiring him to do the work in a way beyond the power of man, who fails even to see it when done.

It is unfounded too, as may be remarked here, that Luke says he derived his knowledge from what was delivered by other people, as they did who undertook the accounts alluded to, which were evidently not the Gospels we have. He, like the other evangelists, wrote his Gospel with full knowledge of its exactitude. But it was not the usual way of inspired men to speak of that divine power which gave them, each and all, to communicate the truth in words which the Holy Spirit teaches. The truth shines in its own light, and needs no taper of man that it may be seen. It is light from God, though the blind may not see: only His gracious power can open their eyes.

4.4   1 CORINTHIANS CHAPTER 7

1 Corinthians 7 has been appealed to confidently as going even farther, and disclaiming inspiration! This would be strange indeed if true, seeing the Epistle is not only one of the most important of the communications in the New Testament but is opened expressly with the

writer's claim of apostolic authority. It is therefore one of those Epistles which the apostle Peter classes among the "scriptures" (2 Peter 3:15, 16). Still as it is alleged to prove that the apostles "sometimes candidly admit that they are not speaking by inspiration", we are bound to refute the perversion.

Any such inference drawn from verse 6 is wholly baseless: "But I speak this by allowance, not by commandment." The apostle means that he speaks here not as commanding but as conceding. No compulsion was laid on the saints as to the advice given in verse 5; but he recommends this to them. He was inspired thus to speak. The mistake lies in the sense of the Lord's permission of him to write; whereas he means that it was not compulsory on them, but for their discretion before the Lord. Compare 2 Corinthians 8:8.

But verse 10 is also adduced, and quite as much misapprehended: "But to the married I enjoin, not I but the Lord, that wife be not severed from husband." This the rationalist would make a distinction between inspired and non-inspired. Whereas the apostle is drawing attention to the fact that the Lord had Himself settled this question personally; and therefore it was not now left to His servant: see Matthew 19:6, and Mark 10:12. This is made remarkably clear in verse 12, "But to the rest speak I, not the Lord." For the case now in question had not been ruled by the Lord, as shewn in the Gospels. Therefore the apostle in the Holy Spirit determines it here by authority given to himself. But it must have been and was from the Lord, though not the Lord deciding in person. For the question is of the mixed marriages that arose as the gospel spread. Then according to the Old Testament the Jew was bound to abandon the Gentile. On the contrary, the apostle shows that grace now intervenes. Hence if a brother has an unbelieving wife, and she consents to dwell with him, he is *not* to leave her; and a woman that has an unbelieving husband who consents to dwell with her is *not* to leave the husband. Here then if anywhere divine authority was required in an absolute way. Is it possible then, that this decision could be no more than the "human element"?

The very fact that the Lord when on earth had not spoken as to this case made all the more conspicuous the authority of the apostle, who under the gospel supersedes what the law demanded of a Jewish man or woman in analogous circumstances of old. God owns no longer the feebleness or the partial dealing of the law. Grace now reigns; the truth is spoken according to God fully revealed; and the apostle, not the Lord in person, was here the spokesman, as the Epistle is the inspired communication, that we might have it livingly here, as we had the other for permanent guidance in the Gospels. Clearly then it is hardly possible there could be a more cogent disproof of the rationalistic aim than the true force of verses 10 and 12 before us. Not only is there not the most distant thought of lowering the character and weight of what the apostle writes, in comparison with the Lord, but the passage brings out in a singularly striking manner the authority conferred on the apostle in consonance with gospel liberty to remove the shackles imposed by the law on the ancient people of God when marriage had been contracted with Gentiles. Not the Lord when on earth, but Paul now by His authority from heaven abrogates the Jewish restrictions, which, without this apostolic word, would have surely clogged the question and hindered the will of the Lord in the church. "And thus I ordain in all the assemblies" (verse 17). What can be stronger evidence?

But there is another case, not as to the mutual conduct of believers in the married state, nor yet about the mixed condition of those so related (a believer and unbeliever), but the virgin or unmarried in the latter half of the chapter. Here the apostle declares that he has no commandment of the Lord but he gives his judgment, as having received mercy of Him to be faithful (verse 25), which he winds up with the words at the close (verse 40), "And I think that I too have God's Spirit."

Here is equally certain the absurdity of supposing that the apostle conveys one word derogatory to his own apostolic authority. But this last case is an interesting illustration of what many have failed to see in the ways of God as to His word. Everything written therein is inspired, the latter part of the chapter just as truly as the former. But as the apostle had shewn in the former that the Lord had decided the general rule of marriage, and himself the special case of mixed marriage, so here he was inspired to give for the unmarried not any commandment from the Lord, but his own judgment who was entitled assuredly to form and express one, if ever man could. Yet the intention of God in thus inspiring the apostle was to distinguish this particular case from the Lord's commandment, which in all other unrestricted matters he declares what he wrote to be (chapter 14:37).

Thus we have in scripture as the rule the "Lord's commandment". But we have here what inspiration carefully distinguishes as a distinct spiritual judgment, given as such from the faithful apostle to the faithful for profit and guidance. By divine design it was not inflexibly bound on the conscience, but set before the saints with the exceeding value of one who laboured more in the gospel than any who ever lived, of one who revealed the church's nature, character, and hopes as no other, even apostle, did. What this exceptional passage is, rationalist unbelief would like to make all scripture; not the Lord's commandment, but the holy view taken of an important question for Christian practice by a most eminent servant of the Lord, and conveyed to us. Only they fail to see that inspiration admits of a godly judgment commended to our consideration, no less than of the words of worldly and wicked men, or even of Satan, where no reasonable man could imagine them to be the Lord's commandment. But they are all alike inspired of God, because they are scripture, and every scripture is so inspired. Now the nature of the case decides that the record of evil counsel, or the counsel of evil beings, cannot be the Lord's commandment. So the apostle distinctly excepts from the category what he gives of his own spiritual judgment. In this instance, it must be perverse not to receive it as such. Still worse would it be to deny to be the Lord's commandment what he wrote without any such restriction. It is the exception that proves the rule. He discriminates his judgment in this particular case to be what it really is, and what God meant it to be. All else is the Lord's commandment. But even a judgment thus characterised as his is scripture; and every scripture is inspired of God.

4.5 Personal Communications

1 Timothy 5:23 and 2 Timothy 4:13 are a fair sample of texts which unbelief regards as unworthy of divine inspiration. It may be of interest and profit to consider in our measure as believers, why God was pleased to give each of them a place in His word. To the neo-critics such vulgar details, wholly lacking in the theological

THE HUMAN ELEMENT

element, seem beneath the operation of the Holy Spirit for permanent use.

It will be observed that they both are found in the Pastoral Epistles, and in the two addressed by the apostle to the fellow-servant who had his most intimate affection. The Epistle to Titus contains no such tender or familiar communications. This was just as it should be. To Philemon there is again a shade of difference, which is of exquisite moral beauty in its place. All are of the utmost value for that instruction or training in righteousness which God purposed to give by these scriptures. In various forms they each illustrate the power of the Holy Spirit dwelling and working in man, and even in his body now made a member of Christ (1 Corinthians 6:15) and a temple of the Holy Spirit that is in him which he has from God. For he is not his own, but bought with a price, and so is to glorify God in his body. This by the way, seeming strange and low in natural or philosophic eyes, led to early tampering with the text by the addition, "and in your spirit, which are God's." But there is no doubt of the genuine text amply attested by the best manuscripts and most of the ancient versions, &c. As little should we doubt the general doctrine of the believer's body, as now claimed for God (Romans 6:12, 13, 19; 12:1; 2 Corinthians 4:7, 10, 11; Philippians 1:20). It was no peculiarity of the heathen or Gnostics to pretend holiness in spirit, while giving licence to the body. Scripture leaves no loophole for such antinomianism. The body is for the Lord, and therein dwells the Holy Spirit. God is wise. Man cannot improve scripture, but injures it by his supplements or corrections.

Now it is the gift, the Pentecostal gift, of the Spirit which gives its distinctive character to New Testament inspiration. This is displayed in the Epistles, following up the infinite fact of the Son of God revealing the Father, and accomplishing redemption, sending out the gospel, and building the church as the Gospels tell. It would indeed have been extraordinary if the human element had not been given a new and far richer place than ever, just when God was making Himself fully known and had effected that work in which He is perfectly glorified. Christ is the key to both and the perfect manifestation of both; which indeed could not be, had He not been as verily God as man, and so manifested.

Take the Epistle to the Romans. There the apostle elaborately develops God's righteousness in the face of man's proved unrighteousness; and the holy practice to which the Christian is called. Yet from this immense scope of divine truth and grace the last chapter turns to the most touching salutations of love with an individuality of cordial interest in each beyond parallel; and the more striking because the Epistle is written to all the saints in the metropolis of the world, which he had not as yet visited. Yet there his heart went out into characteristic details of their service, many of them lowly men and women, honoured and loved for Christ's name by him who was alike His greatest servant and greatest sufferer. Was not this truly divine? Yet where was the human element more conspicuous? It is equally God's word, in which one has well said, Nothing is too great for man, nothing too small for God. As He can afford, so He effectually works in Christ and by His Spirit.

It is not otherwise in the confidential letters the apostle sent to his true and beloved child in the faith. The weightiest injunction is in the First Epistle laid on Timothy; not only as to godly order but also fundamental truth, but along with directions for befitting decision in his public position, tender solicitude for his bodily health and frequent illnesses. So in the still more solemn dangers which the Second contemplates, with the apostle's speedy departure. Timothy's affectionate care in what the apostle wanted at that time is fully counted on, as love ever does. Such episodes would be doubtless entirely out of place in a Bishop's Charge or a Pope's Encyclical; but they admirably bring out the wholly different atmosphere of scripture, and in particular of the New Testament. There the Holy Spirit working in man delights in blending zeal for the eternal principles of God's nature and glory in the gospel, and in the church as the witness of His truth, with consideration for an earnest man of God, lest he should yield overmuch to abstemious scruple and forego that liberty in the use of the creature which his bodily well-being required. There, even when the imminent and hopeless ruin of the Christian profession was intimated along with the holy and unfailing safeguards for the most difficult times, the same Spirit does not fail to show that His entering into the least details of life are perfectly compatible with the solemn last words of the great apostle. Do we not find the same principle in the dying charge of the Saviour Himself (John 19:27)?

Here are the passages. "No longer be a water-drinker, but use a little wine on account of thy stomach and thy frequent infirmities" (1 Timothy 5:23). "The cloak, which I left behind in Troas with Carpus, bring when thou comest, and the books, especially the parchments" (2 Timothy 4:13).

In the first case divine wisdom overrules the morbid tendency of a truly devoted servant. The body is for the Lord, as the Lord is for the body. Hence as impurity is evil, so is asceticism alien, though flesh may glory in the latter, as it might indulge in the former. Christ alone maintains both holiness and liberty; and the apostle was here inspired so to exhort Timothy. A Rabbi, a theologian, might regard such a reference beneath the dignity of a divine mandate for all time. But thus they only betray the empty arrogance of the earthen vessel. Here we have the treasure in it. Here we own the condescension of God's love, as we do the majesty of His truth and the purity of His ways, in the same context, pressed by the awe-enforcing words, "I charge in the sight of God and of Christ Jesus and of the elect angels, that thou keep these things without prejudice, doing nothing according to prepossession" (verse 21).

In the second case, what a lesson for us to read, at such a crisis of the apostle's life, and in delivering his final message in the Spirit to the same cherished fellow-labourer in tones of the deepest gravity, and on truth meant to be the stay of the godly when seducers wax worse and worse, deceiving and being deceived! He was again a prisoner, already being poured out, and the time of his release come, looking for the crown of righteousness, which the Lord would render to him, and not to him only but also to all who love His appearing. He bids Timothy use diligence to come to him quickly, but withal to bring with him the cloak left with Carpus in Troas, and again to come before winter (verse 21). Is not this a pathetic glimpse why he wished "the cloak"? God was not unmindful of his need nor of ours. Whether he had no means to procure a new one, or he judged it of God rather to request the old one, have we nothing to learn? Nor are "the books" without guidance to us. I do not believe he meant either "the sacred letters" of the Old Testament (chapter 3:15), nor "scripture" generally (verse 16), but his "books" of an ordinary kind. The apostle was no fanatic, but as far as possible from it, as this testifies, particularly at such a moment. "The parchments" he wished especially. They were wanted for more permanent use, and seem to have been not yet written on. Did he desire them for copying his Epistles, now that he had his departure in immediate view? Oh! the grace of the Lord in giving what is here conveyed, not as a private note but in an Epistle of his, which is among those which the apostle Peter pronounces to be "scriptures". It is the human element of God's word.

4.6 THE SECOND EPISTLE OF PETER AND THE EPISTLE OF JUDE

We may now compare the Second Epistle of Peter with that of Jude. For erudite ignorance loves to set one against the other, lowering one if not both, and denying God's inspiration of the two in any adequate sense. In comparatively early days unbelief worked in the active minds of Origen, Eusebius of Cæsarea, Theodore of Mopsuestia, and many more. Nor was this surprising; as they were no less daring in their speculations on Christ's person, and as to revelation generally. It is easy to feel difficulties and suggest doubts. It needs distrust in self and faith in God to await His solving the one and dispelling the other, as far as it may seem good. In every case the positive weight of revealed truth is so great in all the disputed Epistles of the New Testament, as against not only the early spurious writings but the best remains of the post-apostolic writers, that to discredit the former is as inexcusable as to accept the latter. Circumstances might be adverse, and influence carry away souls for a season in this place or that. But as those writings which compose the New Testament were in the earliest days received as divinely inspired without any known question, so even in face of a deeply fallen and degenerating state the objections and reasonings of incredulity passed away into their own nothingness. Individuals now and then revived these, until the rage of free-thinking in modern days emboldened men far and wide to flatter themselves that faith in revelation is well nigh perished from the earth. How little they are aware that such are the precursors of that dark and destructive hour which awaits Christendom when the apostasy shall come and the man of sin be revealed! Yet this the apostle Paul was given to reveal in one of his earliest Epistles. He furnished the light of God: they spread the darkness of the pit, before that day.

The fact is that both these Epistles carry the indelible marks of divine inspiration. We cannot doubt that their writers were familiar one with another, and both with the Old Testament as well as the Christian revelation. The facts and the truths of which these Epistles are full were habitually before their souls till the Holy Spirit saw fit to prompt their communication in this permanent form. No considerate believer can wonder that there is not a little common ground of solemn warning and urgent importance. But it is of the deepest interest to trace that difference of spiritual design which God alone ever did or could effectuate. This rationalism quite fails to discern. Yet the proofs of it are intrinsic and even plain, irresistible too in the measure of our faith. So it ought to be in a moral book like the Bible, where mathematical demonstration would be not only absurd and impossible but destructive of its character and aim. No doubt the two Epistles confirm each other, both being perfectly true and occasionally touching the same facts and truth. But they were given of God for the more momentous task of bringing out His mind in distinct ways of the utmost gravity, which one only, perfect for its own purpose, could not have done.

Both Epistles treat of the growing ruin of Christendom, Peter's as a question of unrighteousness to God, Jude's of departure from His grace.

We may readily see that Peter's two Epistles are characterised by the place given to God's moral government: the first chiefly with the believer, redeemed and begotten again to a living hope by the resurrection of Jesus Christ from the dead, and passing through the wilderness world as a stranger and sojourner, suffering for righteousness' sake and Christ's name; the second, rather on the difficulties created by the rebellious wickedness not only of the world, but of those who bore the Lord's name falsely and in unrighteousness, with God's judgment impending, sure, and everlasting.

Jude treats of the narrower scene but profounder evil of ungodly men who crept in privily, turning the grace of our God, and denying the only Master and our Lord Jesus Christ. It is more special apostasy, not general unrighteousness as with Peter, but evidently and particularly found in the Christian profession.

Hence in his Second Epistle Peter does not say more of the false teachers than their denying the Master that bought them. They reject the universal title which the Sovereign Master has by purchase. Accordingly, as the saints received like precious faith with the apostles through the righteousness of our God and Saviour Jesus Christ, and were exhorted to add the becoming moral qualities, the false teachers are warned of God's righteous and unslumbering judgment. And the examples chosen are viewed in this light. God spared not angels when they "sinned", nor the old world when the deluge came on the "ungodly", though He preserved with seven others Noah a preacher of "righteousness". And so afterwards He reduced Sodom and Gomorrah to ashes, rescuing Lot "a righteous" man; as subsequently Balaam is dwelt largely on who loved "unrighteousness' wages". In chapter 3, where Peter predicts the mockers at the end of the days, he vividly sets out the day of the Lord and the total dissolution of all nature on the solidity of which such men build, and God's bringing in new heavens and a new earth wherein dwelleth "righteousness".

Jude on the other hand draws attention to the fact that the Lord, having saved a people out of Egypt's land, in the second place destroyed those that believed not. Of this Peter did not speak but Jude, who treats of departure from grace, not of simple opposition to righteousness. Thence when he speaks of angels, it is of those that kept not their own first state. They were apostates. And when we hear next of Sodom and Gomorrah, it is as, in like manner with them, going away after other flesh. Michael the archangel is specified by Jude as in contrast with railing. So a far fuller picture of Christian apostasy is given in verse 14, Cain and Korah as well as Balaam. In Korah's gainsaying, where apostasy is clear, they are to perish. Again, we have Enoch's prophecy here only on the terrible end; for that holy man in the vision saw the Lord coming judicially. And Jude shows us Him that is able to set the saints exulting and blameless before His glory: the special hope, and not the general blessedness of which Peter spoke so appropriately.

It would be no difficult thing to draw up a detailed comparison of the minute verbal proofs of the different designs which pervade the two Epistles. But this would afford evidence interesting chiefly to the student, and would be quite in place in an exegetic comment of that kind. The aim here is simply to furnish proof, overlooked by those who boast much of erudition, but quite accessible to every believer, that there is not the smallest ground for the cavil of Peter borrowing from Jude, or Jude from Peter. On the contrary there is incontestable certainty from their own words, that the Holy Spirit gave each of them his own distinctive line, both Epistles contributing their very solemn and united testimony, and each in its differences of purpose and aspect of the highest value, to give us the complete truth of God. The more salient features are ample for what is now in hand; the details, if honestly and intelligently followed up, will furnish accumulative confirmation.

4.7 The Second and Third Epistles of John

We may conclude this chapter with a brief examination of the Second and Third Epistles of John. Many years ago I remember Cardinal Wiseman (then Rector of the English College in Rome), in his zeal for Romanism, challenging the Christian as to these two Epistles. How demonstrate from internal facts their inspiration? Why could they not have been written by a very holy and pious man, without any aid whatsoever from that special work of the Holy Spirit?*

---

* Lectures on the Doctrines and Practices of the Roman Catholic Church (London, Hodson, 1836), Lecture ii. 28. But finding that this was not "authorized", and that an edition was afterwards sanctioned by the author, I quote from it also (Volume i. 38. London. Joseph Booker, 61 New Bond Street, 1836). "I would ask what internal mark of inspiration can we discover in the third Epistle of St. John, to show that the inspiration *sometimes* accorded must have been granted here? Is there anything in that Epistle, which a good and virtuous pastor of the primitive ages might not have written? Anything superior in sentiment or doctrine, to what an Ignatius or a Polycarp might have indited?"

Thus it is that the Romanist takes ground similar in principle to the infidel. In his anxiety to exalt the claims of his own sect, which he assumes to be God's church, he denies the intrinsic self-evidencing power of the scripture. The infidel indeed rejects it absolutely, and denies more than man in the case; the Romanist regards the church as the voucher for the written word, so that scripture is thus subordinated to ecclesiastical authority.

For the essence of faith is that one believes God's testimony, because it is *He* that speaks or writes. If one requires somebody else as his warrant in order to believe His word, this is in effect to believe that other warrant, rather than to believe God. Yea, it is to frustrate the very aim and the desired end of faith; for this is to put the soul by believing His word into immediate relationship with God. It is true that He reveals Himself in Christ; but does this hinder? On the contrary He above all promotes and effects perfectly that immediateness of association with God, being God and man in one person. He Whom God sent speaketh the words of God. *Through Him*, says 1 Peter 1:21, we believe in God that raised Him up from the dead and gave Him glory, so that our faith and hope are Godward. If Christ were not God, there would be interposed a barrier to keep the soul away from God; but as the image of the invisible God, and the Only-begotten Son, He shows us not only God in His nature but the Father in the richest gift of His love and in the deepest nearness of His relationship, that we through Him dead and risen may know His Father our Father, and His God our God.

"Never man spake like this man", said those whom His enemies sent to apprehend Him (John 7:46). Yet what can be more striking than His own testimony to the scriptures for which men claim the validating or sealing authority of the church? "How can ye believe, receiving as ye do glory one of another, and seek not the glory that is from the only God? Think not that I will accuse you to the Father: there is one that accuseth you, Moses, on whom ye have set your hope. For if ye believed Moses, ye would believe me; for about me he wrote. But if ye believe not his writings, how shall ye believe my words" (John 5:44-47)? Thus, where the Lord is enumerating the witnesses to the Jews why they should believe on Him, He gives pointedly the highest place, over spoken words, to the written word as having a permanence from God peculiar to itself. Not to believe scripture is virtually that God did not and could not make it bind the conscience to receive it as His without the church's authority to stamp it. The church is bound to be a witness and keeper of God's word, and all the more because blessed beyond measure through it; but to set up to be its necessary and authoritative warrant is shameless arrogance and unbelieving profanity.

How then do these two short Epistles carry in their own contents the evidence of God, as they do of "the beloved disciple"? They are a pair, like those to the Ephesians and the Colossians. Yet have they the genuine mark of originality, in form and wisdom from above, in object and execution. They both insist solemnly on the truth, on love, on obedience; and this because Christ is all, alike to writer, readers, and the saints. The glory of the Father and the Son, the confession of Jesus Christ coming in flesh, is even more peremptorily urged in the Second Epistle than in the Third. Yet the Second is addressed to an elect lady and to her children, the Third to Gaius the beloved. For in the former case the foundation was at stake; in the latter no such peril existed but a turbulent self-seeking man, who opposed the free service of Christ in the truth, whereas Gaius is exhorted to go on as he had begun in its gracious support.

It is well known what doubt exists among the learned,* and from early days till the present to whom the Second was written. And no wonder. God no more meant us to know the name of the lady here than of the sinful woman in Luke 7 on which so much foolish conjecture has been spent. It is as plain Greek as could be written for "an elect lady", whom with her children the apostle loved in truth. But she was not meant to be named; while the solemn duty laid on any was meant to be perpetuated whenever the like danger arose. Thus, while the injured glory of Christ claimed this service from the apostle, under the touching and lowly title of "the elder", while a lady and her children were the object of the Holy Spirit's inspired injunction (to cut off all plea that *they* were surely to be spared this painful token of loyalty to Christ), the written word expressly omitted to register the name in such a distressing case and paramount obligation. It is not "the" but "an elect lady".

His experience, however, must be small, if not familiar with the artifices of heterodoxy in taking advantage of a woman and of young persons. Let us not forget that

---

* Thus, Capellus, Grotius, de Lyra, Bishop Middleton, Wetstein, Wolff, &c. took Eclecta for the proper name, as Bengel, Benson, Carpzov, de Wette, Fritzsche, Heumann, Jachmann, Lange, Lücke, Rosenmüller with the Peschito Syriac, took Kyria (lady), while Beza, Aretas, Baum-Crusius, Corn-a-lap, Doddridge, Lardner, Mill, like the Authorised & Revised Versions, Heidegger, Luther, Piscator, Wells, &c. preferred "to the elect lady", some suggesting Drusia, Martha, or the Lord's mother Mary. Greek and Latin fathers inclined to the church in general; as moderns to a particular one here or there. Even Dean Alford in his third edition gives "lady" in his notes, but in his Prolegomena gives his suffrage for Kyria. J. D. Michaelis suggested the wild idea of elect church assembling on a Lord's day!

even those branded as antichrists once seemed as fair and zealous as others. One of the most hideous in our own age began his career as a clergyman with earnest evangelicalism and conversion work in numerous souls. If he called on a Christian household which used to honour him and his work, after that the deadly error betrayed itself, how natural for *him* to enter on the old terms, and for them to welcome one of whom personally *they* knew only good! "I am but a woman, not a brother, still less an elder: who am I to sit in judgment on a dear servant of God? And my children so young in the faith, are they to refuse his kindly visit? Surely we do no wrong in showing love, as the poor brother has had to bear such fearful censure from the brethren." No! the elder was inspired of God to cut off any such excuses of weakness, reminding the lady and her children of the infinite worth of Christ, and causing them to wax valiant in fight, as truth and love pointed, and in no way yielding to the enemy. "If any one cometh unto you and bringeth not this doctrine [the truth of Christ's person], receive him not into the house, and greet him not; for he that greeteth him partaketh in his wicked works."

Wholly different in circumstances, the Third Epistle rests on the same basis of Christ. It is, as in the Second, life eternal shown in the walk of truth, love, and obedience. Gaius was prospering in his soul; so that "the elder" wishes him to prosper, not surely "above" but "about all things", and be in health too, for in such a case it would not be misused. In the work and among the workmen of the Lord disappointments occur. Gaius persevered in loving aid, notwithstanding difficulties and trials. "The elder" rejoiced exceedingly in the testimony borne, not only to his walking truthfully in the truth he knew, but to his faithful identification in love with the labouring brethren, even when strangers, setting them forward on their way worthily of God; and all the more, because for the Name they went forth, taking nothing from the Gentile sort. Nay, the apostle went so far as to say emphatically, "*We* therefore ought to receive [or, welcome] such, that we might be fellow-helpers to the truth." What grace on the apostle's part!

Now the nice propriety here is as manifest as in the preceding Epistle. On the one hand, a woman, indeed we might say "a lady" in particular, needs to watch against what her affections might prompt, and what (she thought) might be expected of her. Looking to Christ would guard and guide her, where she had adequate testimony that there wrought the deceiver and the antichrist. In and for His name to shut the door would make the house a fort impregnable for her and her children. Did they not owe supreme allegiance to Him? On the other hand a man is not so lively in his affections and therefore less exposed to yielding thereby; he is apt to confide in his judgment, and liable to shut up his bowels of compassion if he fears being imposed on. But Gaius, being a good man, persevered in love as he walked in truth; and thus to go on is far more than to begin warmly. Nor must he be cowed by the imperious party-spirited surliness of one in the assembly, like Diotrephes, who loved the first place, prated with wicked words against such as the apostle, and set himself violently against the brethren that went about, carrying Christ's name every where. This was heartbreaking enough; but let him think of one that did good like Demetrius, testified to by all and by the truth itself; even as John did, whom Gaius knew to give a true witness.

THE HUMAN ELEMENT

In these two Epistles then we have an admirable provision of inspired wisdom for individual guidance in "the last time"; as in the First Epistle God gave us the fullest unfolding of Christ in His person especially, but also in His work, when antichrists abound. Where such an evil dares to enter, even a lady and her children are called to act in the most decided manner, lest they might be entrapped into misprision of treason. They are therefore warned not to receive even into a house him that brought not the doctrine of Christ, no matter how fair appearances might be. Christ admits of no compromise; a lady and her children must not shirk their responsibility. But the beloved Gaius *is* by name exhorted to receive those who did good in Christ's name. Here no delicacy need preserve silence as to his person. As he was doing faithfully and in love, let him not grow weary, but be all the more zealous in gracious consideration of Christ's messengers. He was to imitate not what is evil, glaring as it might be in Diotrephes, but what was good; and this, as he knew it to be of God, he might find in Demetrius. It is well then not to be in despair but to be in our watch-tower, when we prove how many deceivers are (not entered, but) "gone out into the world". But let us rejoice that in the darkest time we are cheered by the love and fidelity of a Gaius and a Demetrius; and as they have apostolic sanction, so also then especially are "the friends" to greet and be greeted. In short we have instruction for a time of exceeding and increasing danger, whom to receive, and whom to refuse. It is invaluable and imperative to him.

To the Cardinal all this might seem wild and uncanonical. He ask if this (and much more of which we need not speak) might not be within the scope of a pious and holy man. Divine authority is *nil* to him without the church's.

Alas! ritualism blinds almost equally with rationalism, as both stand opposed to the truth that is according to godliness. But these Epistles strikingly attest, not the absence of the human element, but the power of divine inspiration adapting the truth, with apostolic sanction and a prophetic insight wholly beyond the creature, to the exigencies of each case, one of them fundamental, both of great moment.

Chapter 5
Divine Design

INTRODUCTION

Among the marks of God's word, none is more impressive or important than the design which the Holy Spirit was pleased to stamp indelibly on the various books individually and on the entire collection as a whole; and this not only on the Old Testament and the New Testament separately, but on both as forming what we, Christians at least, call the Bible. There are faults of transcription in the Hebrew as in the Greek. There are shortcomings and errors of translation in ancient as in modern versions. There are yet more abundantly mistakes in the commentaries from the earliest extant down to our own day. But all these flaws together, though some may conceal the witness of a detail, cannot deface to the instructed eye of the believer (save in a very small degree) the exquisite beauty of the Scriptures, "For ever singing as they shine, The hand that made us is divine." And this is as much above the orbs of the sky, of which one of our own poets used the words, as what is material sinks below the expression of God's word, mind, gracious affections, and glorious purposes, for His children and His people, and all the nations too, which find their centre, their aim, and their accomplishment in Christ the Son of His love and the Lord of all.

That unbelief fails to hear God in His word goes without saying. So Scripture itself testifies; and such is its experience since it was written and diffused in every age, land, and tongue. Nor could it be otherwise with man fallen into alienation from God as a race. "The mind of the flesh is enmity against God", says the apostle to the Romans (8:7). "The world by wisdom knew not God", writes he to the Corinthians (1 1:21). Who can wonder when he reads the overwhelming words to the Ephesians (2:1-3)? "And you, being dead in your offences and sins, in which ye (Gentiles) walked according to the age of this world, according to the ruler of the power of the air, the spirit that now worketh in the sons of disobedience; among whom we (Jews) all too had once our conversation in the lusts of our flesh, fulfilling the things willed by the flesh and the thoughts, and were by nature children of wrath even as the rest." "And you, being once alienated and enemies in mind by your wicked works", writes he to the Colossians (1:21). There is therefore innate repugnance to God and His word in every child of Adam. Hence the absolute necessity of being born anew, as our Lord assured Nicodemus (John 3:3-5): "Except one be born anew, he cannot see the kingdom of God." And if they believed not when He told them the earthly things, how would they believe if He were to tell them the heavenly things? For God's kingdom embraces both, Christ being the Heir of all things, already set on high, as He will soon be manifested Head over them all.

But all this, and, yet more, the ground of it in His personal glory and in the efficacious work of reconciliation through His death, are unknown to and scorned by the haughty unbelief of man. This sees in the scripture (say of the Pentateuch, the very foundation of the Old Testament and no less maintained as divine in the New Testament) only a patch-work of antique human legends which do not even agree, if not an imposture, at least a romance put together as a whole in Samuel's or even Josiah's day if not later still. But so abominable a fraud is the baseless imputation of old English Deists, burnished up to date by the mischievous ingenuity and the ponderous learning of their modern successors, chiefly in Germany and Holland, to say nothing of their English-speaking disciples.

"The fool hath said in his heart, There is no God. Corrupt are they and have done abominable iniquity; there is none that doeth good. God looked down from the heavens upon the sons of man to see if there were any that did understand, that did seek God. Every one of them is gone back; they are together become corrupt; there is none that doeth good, not even one" (Psalm 53:1-3). So it is that those self-styled "higher" but really sceptical critics treat His word. They exclude God from the authorship of the Scriptures. Not one of them honestly accepts the Lord's ruling by the apostle Paul (2 Timothy 3:16): "every scripture is God-inspired, and profitable for teaching, for conviction, for correction, for instruction that is in righteousness". It is a sentence expressly affirming divine inspiration, not for the writers only but of every whit, even to be written, as Scripture. So he had already spoken of the Old Testament in verse 15, distinguished by a different term so as to lend the greater emphasis; thus he takes in every part of what grace was supplying as God's latest communication. Of course the word that Timothy knew applies to what was written of old; for the Scriptures, like other boons from God, are committed to the care of His own, ever liable to fail in keeping intact, and duly understanding, and conveying to others, the holy deposit. To remove such human intrusions is the legitimate function of the critic; so that the reader may have the truth, the whole truth, and nothing but the truth. In no other book but the Bible is this found; no, nor in all others put together.

Now the neo-critics start with the preliminary lie that the Scriptures are in no real sense the word of God. They hence deprive themselves and their followers of all confidence in what is written, where no question arises of its primitive text. As they do not truly believe in God's inspiring any Scripture, so still less if possible do they look for His revelation of Himself in it, either in its wondrous unity, or in each part consistently and perfectly contributing to that grand end; and this throughout the varied dealings of God with man, before sin came in, and afterwards, when there was neither the law of God, nor the government of man ordained by Him; when the promises to the fathers were made, and when the law was given by Moses to their sons; when the Levitical system was introduced, and the shadows of the coming good things accompanied it; when the judges followed till Samuel, and kings were set up; when the prophets became more distinct and pronounced, developing on God's part what Moses predicted more generally, from the first judgment of Israel, then of Judah's idolatrous departure and every other from Jehovah, "till there was no remedy"; and times of the Gentiles began by His people becoming Lo-ammi (not-My-people), and the world-power given meanwhile to the Four Empires. Under the Fourth or Roman was sent the Messiah, pre-

DIVINE DESIGN: INTRODUCTION

sented too with every evidence of grace, truth, and power of God in humiliation, but for this very reason rejected by all, even and worst of all by the Jewish remnant which had returned under the Second empire from captivity in Babylon. Thus was fulfilled the word of the prophets, both in God found by Gentiles that sought Him not, and in the Jews losing their place for the time as a rebellious people to whom He had spread out His hands all the day. Compare Isaiah 65:1, 2, with Romans 10:20, 21.

Hence the Lord Jesus, the Messiah, the Only-begotten Son of God, brought out not only the lost and evil state of man, but that of the Jews more guilty still. For in the cross, which was the deepest proof of their combined iniquity, was accomplished fully by Christ the will of God, in virtue of which we have been and are sanctified through the offering of the body of Jesus Christ once for all (Hebrews 10:10). The gospel of God's grace to all mankind, and the church (the body of Christ in the baptism of the Holy Spirit sent from heaven), are the blessed consequences which required that new revelation of God commonly called the New Testament. This fully confirms the Old Testament in every respect as divine, fulfilling it notably in prophecies of Messiah's person, God and man; His unique walk, mission, and service; His death too, not only through man's hatred but in God's atoning grace; His resurrection and ascension; and His return to raise the dead, to restore the kingdom to Israel, to bless the earth and all the nations, having put down the higher or spiritual powers of evil.

But the New Testament, besides sealing the truth of the Old Testament, reveals for the Christian and the church the mysteries of the kingdom, showing a state of things quite different from the old, and yet more the mysteries with regard to the church, wholly incompatible with Israel's position either in the past or in the future. This therefore only comes into actuality and view when that people as a whole had for a while forfeited its privileges by adding the cross of Christ to its idolatry. Indeed man's responsibility as under law, and still more widely God's government, run through the Old Testament, though there is also prophetic testimony to His purpose in Christ.

But the New Testament gives us the Son of God come, a man yet the True God and Eternal Life. This brings in the greatest change. It is no longer as in the Old Testament God hidden and dwelling in the thick darkness, but God manifested in Him, Who is Son as none else is or can be, the Word become flesh. His death, as sacrifice for sin, goes farther still: not simply God in man tabernacling among men, full of grace and truth, but the veil rent, sin judged in the cross, and the man, at least believing man, brought to God, all the offences forgiven, himself once and completely purged so as to have no more conscience of sins, and God's Spirit thereon abiding in him for ever. Such is the Christian; nor is it all the privilege which might be said. This gives a nearer, a more intimate, character to the New Testament generally; but divine authority belongs equally to both Old and New. Its authority is because God speaks in both through His instruments. If we do not hear *Him*, we have no living faith. A tract or a sermon, a parent or a preacher, may be the means of presenting the truth to my soul; but if I have not believed God, my faith is human and worthless. We are thus born of God, receiving Christ, the object and spirit of the word, as the apostle says in 2 Corinthians 3:17: "Now the Lord is the

DIVINE DESIGN: INTRODUCTION

spirit" (referring to verse 6, not the letter but the spirit of the Old Testament).

When men rest on the redemption that is in Christ Jesus, they receive the Holy Spirit Who guides into all the truth. Doubtless we only know in part; yet even spiritual babes (1 John 2) are assured that they know all things. Ere long it is learnt that each book (remembering that such as the two of Samuel, and their continuation in the Kings, &c. go together), has its proper design permeating it, whether in Old Testament or in New. Of this its own contents must be the evidence, as will by grace be presented severally ere long. To draw it out fully would demand many large volumes doubtless, even if one had spiritual ability for so serious and difficult a task. Here but a small space can be devoted to the purpose. This means that no more can be attempted at present than a cursory view of the various writings which compose the Bible. Such a sketch however involves the advantage that the proofs which scripture furnishes in each case will stand forth free from those clouds of commentary which so often overload and disguise the text.

There is thus no more striking characteristic of Scripture than the design God has imprinted on its various books. Old or New Testament makes no difference. The poetic portion attests it no less than the prose, the prophetic as clearly as the historical. It is not at all unlikely that the various writers may have been unconscious of any intention on their part to effect such a result. All the more instructive and sure is it that one animating and directing Author presided over each several part, imparting a special character to it, and at the same time causing all to contribute to the common purpose of revealing His counsels of glory and His ways of grace, while fully making known the weakness or the wickedness of the creature in resisting His will and doing its own. For that such is the fact, not obviously on the surface but indelibly and deeply underlying the entire body of the Scriptures, is the inevitable conviction produced on the Christian by the careful examination of the Bible as a whole and by the intelligent comparison of its component parts.

Evidence to appear consecutively and in due time will be set before the reader, unstrained, clear, and abundant, that the Scriptures are ruled from first to last by a moral purpose which discloses the wisdom and goodness of God rising above the failure of the creature, and especially man's sin giving occasion to the resources and the triumph of His grace in Christ for heaven and earth, time and eternity, for man, Israel, the saints of old, the church, and the nations. Who but God could have intimated so vast and far-reaching an intention from the first writing that ushers in all the books which follow through many generations, not only those composed in Hebrew (with Aramaic in a small degree), but such as after a marked interval appeared in Greek, revealing in that one generation of the New Testament the Son of God come, the gospel, and the church, the latest book being the suited answer to the earliest, manifestly also closing the complete compass of inspiration?

That in the Pentateuch or Five Books of Moses we have the firm and ample foundation of the Old Testament can be disputed by no reader subject to the truth. They are called the Torah or Law, as this is the institution of God given so fully in Exodus and Leviticus, with supplements drawn out by the journeys of Numbers, and the moral rehearsal of Deuteronomy in view of the entrance into the land of Canaan across the Jordan.

DIVINE DESIGN: INTRODUCTION

The Prophets, early and later, as the Jews distinguished the books that succeed as well as the openly predictive books to which we give that name, attest the growing departure from the law, and hold out the bright vision of Messiah's Kingdom, not only for the restored people of Israel but for all the nations of the earth. Then the hosts of the high ones shall be punished on high, and the kings of the earth upon the earth. Then Jehovah shall be exalted, and the inhabitants of the world learn righteousness. Then the wilderness and the solitary place shall be glad, and the desert shall rejoice and blossom as the rose.

The Psalms constitute the third division, the leading portion (as in the other sections) giving its title to various books of an emotional and ethic character. Here too we find a class of writings which bear witness quite as strongly as the others to the grand design of God in His word: the ruin of the first man; the blessedness of the Second, even for all those of the ruined race that put their trust in Him (Psalm 2:12). In the Prophets we have formal witness indeed to a new covenant with the house of Israel and with the house of Judah, which shall supersede that of the law; when the promises to the fathers shall be made good in the true Seed.

It would be idle to impute to the New Testament in the least degree any imitation of the Old Testament. The fresh revelation has the distinctive power of a divine testimony to the Son of God, the Man Christ Jesus, manifested here below and ascended to heaven after accomplishing His great sacrificial work for man to God's glory. Yet one cannot fail, when attention is drawn to the new collection as compared with the old, to find the unmistakable proofs of a common plan, not named by a single writer, but evident when we have all before us. For there is a similar basis of fact historically presented: not the first but the Last Adam with the new creation dependent on Him, and associated with its Head; and instead of the Law (given alike on a day of Pentecost), the Holy Ghost sent forth from heaven to abide for ever. Here only is the "perfection", which was not possible by the law, though this made its need felt and was its shadow or even its foreshadow.

Then, after the Gospels and the Acts, we have the Epistles, which answer and more than answer to the Ketubhim or "writings" of the Old Testament, and unfold the grace and truth in Christ and His work and offices, with the blessed hope, all bearing on the heart and walk and worship of the saints.

Finally there is the one wondrous book of the Apocalypse preceded by not a little in the Gospels and Epistles as in the analogy of the Old Testament. Therein all the predictive revelations of Scripture are co-ordinated and completed, not only till the establishment of the displayed kingdom of the Lord Jesus filling the heavens and the earth to God's glory, but right on to the endless issues of all in eternity, when evil is finally and for ever judged, and the new heavens and earth are come, wherein righteousness, instead of ruling by power, can and does dwell unbroken and absolutely perfect, God being all in all.

Thus is there, where much else differs, a very distinct correspondency in the two volumes, the Old and the New, without the least effort after it by any writer in either volume. What could more indicate without a cloud one Divine mind of infinite purity and goodness, Light and Love, communicating in the Scriptures, as He will accomplish in fact, those purposes worthy of

Himself and of His Son, full of blessing for all who believe, but of everlasting judgment to those that love Him not and despise His word?

Let us now test the reality of distinct purpose on God's part attributed to His word, beginning with the earliest book of Scripture.

5.1 GENESIS

The Bible opens with the creation, distinguishing the beginning when man was not nor our environment of nature, and intimating a state of convulsion for the earth at least, which followed the original act and preceded its formation for the human race (1:1, 2). The week is then detailed which ushers in Adam, God (Elohim)'s work and rest (1:3—2:3).

The true commencement of chapter 2 is in verse 4, where the name of Jehovah Elohim, or the LORD God, necessarily appears as in chapter 3 also. For the design was to identify Elohim, the Creator, with Jehovah, the moral Governor, Who established man, not as a living soul merely, but by His inbreathing into him only in immediate relationship with Himself, and set in a paradise planted for him, yet with moral responsibility put to the proof and provision for life if obedient, but if disobedient with death the penalty. Nor this only, but man's relation to his wife, builded out of himself to be his intimate counterpart and so named by himself, is here; as he also gave names to the subject creation of the earth, bird, and beast.

Chapter 3 shows how man fell through the woman by the wiles of a mysterious foe who availed himself of the serpent as medium, and so acquired to the end the title of "the old serpent, who is the Devil and Satan"

(Revelation 20:2). The design here required the same divine designation as in the chapter before, the form of which is all the more apparent from the omission of Jehovah by the serpent and by the woman parleying with the tempter (1-5). But the solemn sentence of death was not passed on the head of the race, now knowing good and evil, without a previous curse on the serpent, wherein was intimated the blessed assurance of the woman's Seed, bruised in heel, to bruise the enemy's head. Coats of skins were given to the guilty pair, who knew themselves not the less naked for their fig-leaf aprons. The divine covering for sinners had its source in death; it was grace, but in righteousness.

Thereon follows the essential difference between Adam's sons in chapter 4. Abel by faith brought a sacrifice. Cain, hard and unbelieving, brought an offering of the fruit of the ground, and, incensed at Jehovah's acceptance of Abel and his offering, slew his righteous brother. What a picture of man's worship! so the close of the chapter is of his world with art and science and pleasures of life to hide that he is an outcast, a vain substitute for paradise. Here accordingly Jehovah's name appears with strict propriety; the exceptional case in verse 25 only confirms it, as Eve's natural expression, disappointed in her spiritual thought of verse 1. Yet is Seth the appointed seed that succeeds the slain Abel, and men call on Jehovah's name: so it will be, as it was.

In chapter 5 is a review of the race down to Noah and his offering. Adam and his sons, long as they might live, died at length. For if Elohim created and made, death entered through sin; but Enoch walked with God, and was not, for God took him. It was not simple government, but Elohim known and acting according to His nature. On the other hand Jehovah as properly is used in verse 29 where His moral dealing is in view. Of all those, two men are divine witnesses, respectively of heavenly grace, and of earthly judgment yet with mercy glorying against it.

Then chapter 6:1-8 proceeds with righteous judgment under Jehovah's name, which is no way inconsistent with "the sons of God" in 2 and 4, as in Job a regular designation; whereas Elohim along is found in 9-22. The expression is as accurate as the design is evident. Relationship was violated; and nature was corrupted; but if judgment must ensue, the Creator duly perpetuates the creature.

So in chapter 7 Jehovah has respect for Noah and his house too, enjoining clean beasts and birds by sevens, not two as in His name of Elohim; and Noah obeyed in both (5, 9). Oh, the blindness of pseudo-critics, who fancy inconsistency, when the divine wisdom was as plain in His acts as His design is in His word! What ignorance and folly to account for all this by the imaginary patchwork of tradition! See also the absurdity of an Elohist and a Jehovist in the same verse 16, where the two motives of divine action meet in Noah subject and kept safe. Truly "all have not faith": woe to those who believe not! particularly if they profess the Lord's name.

Chapter 8 conversely has Elohim only in 1-9, but in 20-22 Jehovah no less instructively. This instruction pseudo-criticism denies and destroys, as far as it can, by the childish fancy of different legendists. Truly they labour for the fire and weary themselves for vanity.

So chapter 9 designedly gives Elohim throughout, save that the special blessing in Shem's case brings in Jehovah his God in 26, whereas in 27 of Japheth is said Elohim only. Conceive the imbecility as well as the unspirituality of supposing here two authors, where so much of the force depends on the One, Who first uttered all by one mouth, then writing all by a single pen in due time! As the end of chapter 8 shows the world that was resting for its order on sacrifice, so 9 begins with the principle of government committed to man's hand, to which was added the sign of no deluge more.

In chapter 10 we have the rise of nations divided in their lands, every one after his tongue, from Noah's three sons; and even in those days Nimrod's assumption of despotic power, where alone Jehovah occurs, as right relationship was violated. But in the earlier verses (1-9) of chapter 11 we have Jehovah judging the moral cause for the scattering of men, bent on making themselves a name in one vast republic. From verse 10 the generations of Shem are traced to bring in "the fathers", and afterward "the sons", of Israel.

Chapter 12 presents Jehovah's call of Abram. He had left Ur of the Chaldees for Haran at the end of chapter 11. Only when he "went as Jehovah had spoken to him" does he arrive in Canaan. He first has the promises, father of the faithful, as Adam of all mankind. Abram is a pilgrim, with "this land" promised to his seed, and has not a tent only but altars he built to Jehovah. His was the walk and worship of faith. Under the pressure of famine he goes down into Egypt, and denies his true relationship to Sarai; so that she was taken into Pharaoh's house, and he became very rich with the king's gifts. Thus it was total failure; but Jehovah plagued Pharaoh, delivered Sarai, and dismissed Abram, who had no altar in Egypt and returns to the place where his tent had been at the beginning, unto the place of his altar there.

Chapter 13. Thereon strife among their herdmen leads to the separation of Lot from Abram, who has Jehovah's promise more fully renewed, and consequently builds another altar.

But chapter 14 shows Lot swept away in the world's wars, as he had already betrayed his worldly-mindedness. But Abram defeats the conquerors who led Lot captive. Then Melchizedek king of Salem blessed Abram on the part of God Most High, possessor of heaven and earth, and blessed God Most High Who delivered Abram's enemies into his hand. It is a picture which closes the first part of Abram's history, the type of the day of blessing, of "bread and wine", not of sacrifices nor of intercession above and unseen, which sustains now, based on sacrifice. Here the distinctive name is Jehovah, but qualified by God Most High (Elyon), the victory of faith when enemies are put down and rival gods vanish; heaven and earth unite in the blessing of God and His own under the priest Melchizedek reigning. How plain yet profound is this typical climax! Who could have designed it all but God?

From chapter 15 we have a fresh and subsequent order of things personal, rather that public, closing with chapter 21, where the question of the heir is solved fully and in various points of view. First we have Jehovah's word coming in a vision, and the seed after the flesh in prophetic detail, and a sacrificial covenant by which the limits of the land are guaranteed. In chapter 16 we see failure in the faith so bright in the chapter before, and the carnal impatience which sought it illegitimately, to her sorrow especially who had first suggested it. Not Hagar but Sarai must be the heir's mother. Compare Galatians 4. In chapter 17 Jehovah (for such is the name here also) appears to Abram revealing His title, specific for the patriarchs, of El Shaddai, God Almighty, and enlarging his name to Abraham, as his wife's was to be Sarah. Yet it is said to be Elohim so talking and saying: so baseless is the fancy of different documents or authors; and so perfect is the design in putting these elements together. Nations and kings were to come of Abraham and Sarah by an everlasting covenant established with Isaac, but with circumcision (expressing death to the flesh) which extended even to the connected stranger. Chapter 18 gives Jehovah's next appearing in intimate condescension; and the time of the heir's birth is announced, but after this too the judgment just about to fall on the guilty cities which draws out Abraham's intercession. This stopped short of what his heart yearned after; but Jehovah delivered Lot and his daughters, while punishing his wife's disobedience, as in chapter 19 with its sad sequel. In chapter 20 Abraham again denies his relationship to the mother of the coming heir; but Elohim warns Abimelech who also restores Sarah intact. God's grace alone shines throughout; but Jehovah had judged the deed (verse 18) in His righteous government. The series concludes with chapter 21, when the heir was born, and (soon after) the bondmaid's son was cast out, though preserved in respect for faithful Abraham. But more now; for Abimelech, instead of reproving, stands reproved; and Beersheba attests the inheritance of the world, Abraham planting a tamarisk or grove and calling on the name of Jehovah, the everlasting God (El Olam). The inheritance, wide as it is, may not compare with His grace Who gives all; but it is glorious. Who but One could have indited these communications? Did He leave them like Sibylline leaves to be blown about, and gathered by Elohists, Jehovists, or such like imaginary ghosts? His word is truth.

Chapter 22 lays the foundation in the Son's death and resurrection figuratively for new and heavenly things; chapter 23 is the passing away of the mother, Israel; chapter 24 the call of the bride for the risen bridegroom;* and chapter 25:1-10 indicates other descendants of Abraham endowed with favour, but not to the disparagement of the heir of all; after which the father dies in a good old age. Here the futility of different hands, Elohist or Jehovist, is as manifest as before. Elohim tempted or tried Abraham's faith; yet the angel of Jehovah interposed after the proof that he feared Elohim; and so to the end of chapter 22. Neither occurs in 23; but Jehovah the God of the heavens and the God of the earth &c. is in 24. In chapter 25:11 Elohim blessed Isaac, yet after the generations of Ishmael (12-18), Jehovah appears in those of Isaac: what more simple, intelligible, or accurate from one and the same hand? So it is Jehovah yet the God of Abraham in chapter 26 even on Gentile lips; and again in chapter 27. There we read "Jehovah hath blessed; and Elohim give thee" (verses 27, 28): plain and sure evidence against the variorum hypothesis; and so is chapter 28:3, 4, 13, 16, 17, 20-22.

Now we enter on Jacob's varied experience, hearing no more of Isaac but his death in chapter 35:28, 29, after a life spent exclusively in Canaan as contrasted with Abraham and Jacob. Divine design is evident in the scripture as well as in the fact. Isaac typified the Son who after death and resurrection is the church's Head and Bridegroom in the heavenlies. Compare chapter

---

* In Joseph's case we have the type of the bride repeated, but this to mark the fact that it w as when he who became the bridegroom was sold by and separated from his brethren, exalted to a glory by them unknown. The truth needs both figures; and each tale is true and has its own characteristics, as Moses' case has in Exodus 2.

24:3-9, 37-41. Just as strikingly he who was even called Israel knows the greatest vicissitudes, as we see in the remaining chapters of the book. Was this casual? Did it not flow from God's design? It is Jehovah in chapter 29 and Elohim in chapter 30:2-23, yet in the next verse (24) Rachel says not Elohim, but Jehovah; and thus it is in 27 and 30. The notion of different writers is mere fancy, explains nothing, and hinders all due enquiry into the divine motive for the change of name. See also chapter 26:3, 5, 7, 9, 11, 13, 16, 24, 29, 42, 49, 50, 53; chapter 32:9, 28, 30; and chapter 33:5, 10, 11, 20.

One cannot wonder that neither name is in chapter 34 or in 36, 37; but it is Elohim, God in His nature, God sovereign in His action, which appears in 35:1, 3, 7, 9, 10; only the revealed El Shaddai, dropped with Isaac save in reference to Jacob (28:3), here reappears (11). Then Elohim is in 13, 15. But Jehovah is the name in chapter 38:7, 10, where His rights were violated flagrantly in Judah's family; as His marked blessing was on Joseph in 39:2, 3, 5, 21, 23. What could be more correct? On the other hand Elohim alone suits 40:8, 16, 25, 32, 38, 39, 51, 52. It is the historic as well as abstract expression; and hence in 42:18, 28; 43:23, 29; 44:16; 45:5, 7, 8, 9; 46:1, 3; 48:9, 11, 15, 20, 21; 49:25; 50:17, 19, 20, 24, 25; whilst in 43:14 and 48:3 it is El Shaddai, and in 49 Jehovah as specially due. God, or Elohim, is in contrast with man; Jehovah is His name of relationship; El Shaddai is the proper patriarchal title, as El Elyon is that of the kingdom in figure.

But how manifestly we have divine purpose in progressive warning through Esau as before through Ishmael! For Esau was worse, a profane man despising his birthright, which Jacob, however faulty, was far from; but God is faithful in wanderings caused by his unbelief and given with much detail. It is the picture of Israel's sad history, the pledge of their future and blessed restoration to the promised land; as indeed God announced in chapter 46:4, and predicts in Jacob's last words (chapter 49). To this also point the burials there of his body and Joseph's.

Nor can one fairly overlook the tale of Joseph, the general hatred on the part of his brethren, the special guilt and special recovery of Judah, the sale of Joseph to the Gentiles and their subsequent evil, Joseph's interpretation of God's mind in his humiliation, his elevation to administer the kingdom over the Gentiles with a wife then given him, and finally his reception of his brethren now penitent before his glory. A plainer type cannot be of God's dealings, much accomplished though some not even yet, all settled and sure if we believe the scriptures in general which teach these truths explicitly elsewhere as to Christ.

Is not then divine design throughout the book of Genesis established of God beyond just question? How vast the scope from the absolutely first act of creative energy! How wise the details only when man was to be created! How important to distinguish the fact of the Adamic earth from the relative position of all concerned, and to show how soon and complete was the ruin through sin! Yet do we see immense long-suffering, till the violation of all order, added to man's growing corruption and overspread violence, draws down divine judgment, yet Noah and his house prepared by grace to begin the world, set under sacrifice on the one hand, and the principle of human government brought in on the other. Instead of filling the earth at God's command, the wilful effort to combine and make themselves a name was met by the confusion of tongues, which scattered mankind.

Thus began the nations divided in their lands, everyone after his tongue and his family. Then, when men began to serve other gods, as Joshua 24 tells us, Abraham was called out of country, kindred, and father's house, separated to the true God as His witness. To him was promised the land of Canaan, and yet more all the families of the earth to be blessed in him. Isaac typifies the risen Son in the heavenly places, with a bride called out from the world to join Him there. Jacob represents the earthly people, to be blessed at length in the kind after bitter experiences in and out of it, the effect of their own faults. In the midst of this history Joseph foreshadows Christ separated from his envious and hating brethren, but manifesting God's wisdom in his low estate, and exalted to the administration of a kingdom of the world. He is thus made known to the Jews, now humbled and owing their preservation to him as all others do; yet was his heart set on the people and land notwithstanding; where the great prophecy of chapter 49 shows they are to be at the end of days. Is all this a concourse of atoms? or the certain work of divine purpose?

5.2 Exodus

Very different from the first is the second book of the Pentateuch. Here, instead of the vast variety which meets us in Genesis, we have in the main one great truth developed, with the antecedents which made its necessity felt, and with the most characteristic consequence which ensued in God's wisdom and goodness. For here in a way peculiar to itself we have redemption accomplished for Israel, the foreshadow of an eternal one in Christ, in its foundation, its display, and its effects. The basis one must be blind not to see typified in the Paschal sacrifice; and the displayed power in the passage of the Red Sea: the death and the resurrection of the Lord Jesus. The effect is seen in God's tabernacling in their midst. What lends it the greater force is that, multifarious as are the counsels and the ways of God which Genesis presents to us in germ, redemption is wholly absent from its contents. The very word occurs only once toward the close in its general or figurative application to Jacob's life; and thus is quite distinct from that precise sense which the type in Exodus vividly supplies. Can any proof of specific design on God's part be asked more powerful than this, supposing the facts to be made out clearly and without violence? Let us then examine the evidence.

Chapter 1 opens with the sons of Israel after Joseph's death waxing many and mighty but, under a king that knew not Joseph, bitterly oppressed. The then king of Egypt sought even to destroy the males. This was counteracted at first; but in chapter 2 the murderous aim was pressed so far that Moses could not be longer hid. Him when exposed Pharaoh's daughter found and brought up as her son; who, when not only grown up but going out to see his afflicted brethren, slew an Egyptian evildoer, but finding no right feeling in the objects of his care, had to flee the king's resentment. The time was not yet come; and Moses in Midian protects the daughters of its priest-king, one of whom he marries; and his son "Gershom" witnesses that he was no settler there but a sojourner, who remembered his brethren: so God did His covenant with their fathers as He heard their groans.

In chapter 3 when "Jehovah" saw that he turned to see the bush that burnt, unconsumed with fire, "Elohim" called to him (verse 4). How irrational as well as unspiritual to imagine more than one writer! Jehovah is relative name, Elohim is God in nature. Compare verses 7 and 14, where He adds "I AM THAT I AM" as the name to assure His despairing people, and sends Moses and their elders with the petition to let them go. Then in chapter 4 Jehovah gives two signs and even a third for his mission, and makes Aaron to be his spokesman when hesitating, as once too precipitate. So Moses bids his father-in-law farewell, and with wife and sons returns to Egypt, but not without a solemn reminder of a neglected duty for both husband and wife. Aaron meets him at Jehovah's command on the mountain of God, and the people bow and worship when they heard. Next in chapter 5 they lay Jehovah's message before Pharaoh, who scornfully flouts it, and cruelly aggravates the burden of the Israelites under penalty; so that they suffer more than ever, and Moses pours out His plaint.

But Jehovah (chapter 6) assures him that He would act so that Pharaoh should drive them out of his land. And here He formally inaugurates "Jehovah" for Israel, in contra-distinction from the patriarchal revelation of "El-shaddai" (God Almighty), as the pledge of also bringing them into the promised land. But the people hearkened not for anguish, as Moses told Jehovah, when He bade him speak to Pharaoh. Both Moses and Aaron He charged with the same errand. Thereon follows a remarkable genealogy, as in Genesis; but as each there has its own character, so has this, which, starting with Reuben and Simeon, stops at Levi and his sons, giving prominence to "Aaron and Moses" (20-26) in natural order first, but lastly (verse 27) in spiritual power "Moses and Aaron". Is this then man's folly, or God's wisdom and design? For men have not been wanting to blow on it in their ignorant presumption. Let them learn His mind and give thanks.

After the preliminary sign in chapter 7 the plagues follow God's demand refused:—1, The river which they gloried in and adored was turned to blood for seven days at the time when even a red appearance never occurs; 2, Frogs swarmed so as to torment then in their houses, beds, ovens, everywhere; 3, The dust became lice or some equally noisome insect on man and beast; 4, So did flies swarm yet more grievously, but none in Goshen; 5, A deadly murrain overspread Egypt, but not Israel's quarter; 6, A boil broke out on all in Egypt man and beast; 7, Hail followed, and fire mingled, and thunder, without example in that land; 8, Locusts beyond parallel; 9, Darkness for three days that might be felt; 10, The first-born slain of man and cattle from the king to the slave, but Israel untouched (8—11).

Then came redemption by the blood of the lamb, chapter 12. Without this, as Israel's ground before Jehovah, He could not go with a people sinful and degraded. But where He saw the blood, He would pass over (verse 13). On His own estimate of that blood, which pointed to the one efficacious sacrifice, He acted; as they at His word had sprinkled it on the door-posts of each house. Pilgrims now, they fed on the lamb's flesh with bitter herbs (repentance) and without leaven (the emblem of corruption rejected). There is no type of redemption so clear and comprehensive. Who but God could have given it? or would have put it here, the most suited time and place in all the Bible? Israel, not the priest yet, was separated to Jehovah by it; and this marked by their first-born of man and beast, as well as by the feast of unleavened bread (chapter 13) continually, in remembrance of the slain first-born of Egypt and judgment executed against all their gods. Chapter 14 completes the picture: redemption by power, which brought Israel dry-shod through the waters of death when they engulphed the flower and forces of Egypt. The song in chapter 15 celebrates their salvation and their enemies overwhelmed, but Jehovah's holiness glorious. But they pass through a desert world, where the bitter waters need the tree cast in to sweeten them; but where they come to springs and palms in all fulness for refreshment by the way. The sabbath, figure of rest, is marked by the manna that typified Christ; as the living water, *i.e.* the Spirit, was given from the smitten rock (chapters 16, 17), followed by conflict with the enemy, where victory depends on the continued intercession of the Mediator. This series of grace closes (chapter 18) with the type of the orderly government of the kingdom; where the Gentile worships and eats bread with Israel, confessing Jehovah greater than all gods.

From this reign of grace to glory we turn in chapter 19 to law accepted as the condition of blessing and finding themselves under curse, instead of owning their sinfulness and pleading the promises. All is changed to menace of death, to thunder, lightning, and thick cloud; to trumpet's sound exceeding loud, and a voice of words more awful still, so that Moses quaked. Then the Ten Words were spoken; and national judgments were given afterwards (chapters 20-23). Blood sealed this covenant on the ground of the people doing all the words Jehovah had spoken: death was the solemn sanction of all; and Israel's elders eat and drink in God's presence. But Moses ascends higher to receive the tables of stone, and abides on high forty days and nights.

In chapter 25 Moses is directed that the Israelites should bring Him a heave-offering, as their heart prompted, of all the requisites in precious metals and stones, in dyes, skins, wood, oil, fine cotton or byss, incense and aromatics, for the priesthood and the sanctuary, with all the parts and vessels of which He would show the patterns. They represented heavenly things, as we learn in Hebrews. Of these the ark is first with the mercy-seat and the cherubim in the holiest; then in the holy place the table, and the lamp-stand. Thus did Jehovah provide for manifesting Himself in His dwelling in the midst of His people. For to this grand effect of redemption are we now come. The ark was His seat in relationship with Israel, but in truth as the Judge of all; there divine righteousness was attested. For on the day of atonement the blood was sprinkled upon it once, before it seven times. Christ Who alone glorified the Father in living obedience glorified God about sin on the cross. But there was also in the supporters the witness of judicial authority that would make Him respected. The table with its loaves set forth divine nourishment in man, as the lamp-stand divine light in the Spirit; of both which Christ is the fulness and perfect witness.

Chapter 26 presents the tabernacle itself with its curtains, boards, bars, and veil which severed the holy place from the most holy. Christ too was the true tabernacle or temple, though it had a wider application too. Next in chapter 27 we have the copper-laid altar of Burnt-offering, and the court of the tabernacle with the requirement of oil for the light. This altar represents God's righteousness in Christ, as far at least as man's sin thoroughly judged, but in grace to the sinner, where he is and can come before Him freely.

To rationalistic eyes it seems unaccountable disorder that the command for the consecration of the priesthood should be given in chapters 28, 29. It is really divine wisdom; for thus is separated that part of these patterns of the heavenly which relates to God's manifestation of Himself to man, from what brings out the presenting of man to God in the sanctuary, though some may partake in a measure of both. But there is a true distinction; and the priesthood is the transition, as they were the medium which represented Israel therein. Aaron and his sons represented those of the heavenly calling in the grace of Christ minutely displayed and throughout those two chapters, as is plain enough to every instructed believer. Then in chapter 30, the due place for it, comes first the altar of incense, as the type of Christ in intercession for the saints, a continual sweet savour, on the horns of which too the atoning blood was put. Next came the atonement-money, the same half-shekel for every one rich or poor; then the laver of copper for purifying Aaron and his sons; the holy anointing oil also for them; and the perfume of aromatics holy to Jehovah. All these are types of what Christ is for us; not the manifestation of God to us, but the means needful for our being presented to Him. But who could have initiated this but Jehovah? Then in chapter 31 comes the qualifying of the workmen by Jehovah for the construction of all; the sabbath too here again appears as the sign that God's rest is His people's hope; and Jehovah gave Moses the tables of testimony.

Below, how sad the contrast! The people of Israel corrupted themselves away from Jehovah; and Aaron helped them in it. Hence Jehovah bids Moses go down to *his* people, corrupt as they were, and offers to make of him a great nation. But Moses pleads, and not in vain. Yet when he saw the golden calf and heard their songs, he shattered the tables in his indignation and summoned those that stood for Jehovah. When the sons of

Levi responded, he called on them to consecrate themselves in His name, and they slew about 3,000 men. The same Moses turns to Jehovah in intercession the next day, and offers to be blotted out for them. But God, accepting his mediation, modifies the terms by His long-suffering goodness while still leaving them under His law, and bids Moses lead them on with His angel going before. It is thus no longer law, pure and simple as at the first, but now a mixture of grace with law, to which 2 Corinthians 3 refers as a ministry of death and condemnation, even though Moses' face shone as only on the second time (33, 34). It is at this time too that Moses left the camp and pitched the tent outside, calling it the tent of meeting, whither went every one that sought Jehovah, anticipating the tabernacle that was to be established. There God revealed His merciful name on that separation from corruption.

In chapter 35 Moses again speaks of the sabbath, and enjoins the heave-offering on all the willing; to which they answered promptly. He told them once more that Jehovah called Bezaleel and Aholiab in chief to the work. In chapters 36, 37 it proceeds with abundant zeal, set out in detail, not only there but in chapters 38, 39, "as Jehovah commanded Moses". Is this true? If any one bearing the Lord's name dare to say it is false, it is well that Christians should know with what they have to do. Chapter 40 tells of the tabernacle set up and of the priesthood consecrated according to the command of Jehovah, all anointed. The cloud then covered the tent and the glory of Jehovah filled the tabernacle. How true is the book to the divine design of showing redemption, and the worthy end of God dwelling in the midst of His own then realised in type, as the effect of redemption!

5.3 Leviticus

As scarce a book in the Old Testament consists so much of the express words of Jehovah, so none gives fuller evidence of divine design from first to last. One great theme governs as in Exodus; but it is approach to God in the sanctuary, not redemption as there. The title we employ like most is vaguely if at all appropriate; for from its nature the priesthood are essential and prominent, not the Levites who figure here but little. The Jews do not attempt distinctive titles, but name the books from the opening word in each.

It is Jehovah speaking, not the Ten words from the darkness on the top of Sinai, but out of the tent of meeting in the midst of His people, to lay down the conditions of their relationship with Him. Hence His relative name to Israel is used throughout, and only in the later chapters from 18 have we occasionally "your" or "thy" God added to it, or connected with it. Hence not a shadow yields room for the dream of an Elohist, senior, junior, or in any wise. It is Elohim in relation with His people, and therefore "Jehovah" calls, speaks, and commands throughout. Even the historical episode of 8—10 is all and only Jehovistic, and so is the briefer one in 24:10 to the end of the chapter. But it is the more untrue and illogical to make this fact depend on a special writer; for the writer, though giving uniform predominance to "Jehovah", identifies Him as surely with "thy" or "your" Elohim.

Access to Jehovah then is the design of this book, as redemption is of Exodus; access to Him in the sanctuary, as individuals or as His people, according to the law. Not only are the means defined, which required sacrifice and offering, with the priests duly inaugurated, but the duties and state of the people, as well as their privileges, with those of the priestly family. Then follows the ruin which disobedience and apostasy must entail; yet would He in judgment remember mercy, and the covenant with their fathers, anterior to the law and dependent on promise. Also the vow of devoting persons, beasts, or land should result, on Israel's failure, in Jehovah's rights, when Christ as both Priest and King will order all to His glory. Not Moses, nor any other mere man, left to himself, was capable of a design so profound, and of evidently prophetic character; but if Moses was inspired to give what Jehovah spoke throughout, all is plain and holy and true. Rationalism may impute departure from original integrity and other faults suggested by the pettiness of man's mind; those who do so must take the consequence before Him Who is its Author. Let us look into the details as they stand.

The book opens with the basis of all access to Jehovah, sacrifice and offering. As not the first man but the Second is His object, He begins with the Burnt-offering (1), the Meal-offering (2), and the Peace-offering (3), and only then enters on the Sin-offering and Trespass- (or, Guilt-)offering (4—6:7), with the laws of each (6:8—7). Such is the divine institution: when application comes, as with the priests (8:14, &c.), the Sin-offering precedes, or with a leper, the Trespass-offering (14:12, &c.). Who but God could so order? The first three oblations are alike Fire-offerings of sweet savour to Jehovah. They represent the positive excellency of Christ as offered upon the altar, in death as in life man holy, and for communion; together they form the first communication from Jehovah. Offerings for sin follow in chapter 4, with a transition of mingled character in 5:1-13, after which to 6:7 we have the

Trespass-offering fully; and the regulations, which deal mainly with the question of eating or not, are given to the end of chapter 7. From the Trespass-offering in chapter 5:14 are no less than seven distinct but connected communications from Jehovah.

In chapters 8, 9 is given the institution of Aaron and his sons to the priesthood. Here we find another, and if possible brighter, witness to the unique excellency of Christ. For the high priest alone, as typifying Christ and duly attired, was anointed without blood (8:10-12), and at the same time the tabernacle with all therein. He to Whom Aaron pointed was entitled to the energy of the Spirit in person and inheritance; and He is Heir of all things. No mortal would ever have so thought or spoken of himself; only Jehovah Who inspired Moses. His sons also, duly attired, required the Sin-offering; and as Aaron personally was a sinner like them, all laid their hands on the victim's head (verse 14), and Moses put of its blood on the altar, and thereon burnt the fat and the rest of the body without the camp. Then the ram for a Burnt-offering was duly offered; but that for consecration had its blood put by Moses, first on Aaron's right ear, thumb, and toe, then on his sons similarly. After the rest of that rite was completed, Moses took of the anointing oil and of the blood, and sprinkled it on Aaron and his garments, and on his sons and their garments with his. On the eighth day the glory of Jehovah appeared, the plain prefiguration of what will be for Israel when He shall sit and rule upon His throne, not for heaven only but manifested for the earth. Chapter 10 is the affecting history of the failure of the priesthood at once, even Eleazar and Ithamar only spared by intercession. Next are the chapters that refer to discernment of food clean and unclean (11), and priestly dealing with defilements natural (12), also typifying sin and its cleansing (13, 14), and others occasional (15).

Then comes the momentous Atonement-day (16), the fast of the sacred year, on which all hung for priests and people, the high priest acting for both in access to God. How any believer can fail to own that Jehovah alone could have designed it, not only for the time then present, but as prophetic of the first coming of Christ and His work, and even of the still unaccomplished second coming when it is applied to Israel's pardon and spiritual restoration, is strange indeed. The New Testament interpretation is unmistakable in Hebrews 9 more particularly. The Christian blessing is identified with Aaron and his house, in virtue of the one offering for them in the sanctuary. When the high priest comes out will be the application of the scapegoat, but on the ground of Jehovah's lot, to the repentant people. To regard Azazel, the living goat sent away associated with the slain one, as a demon or evil genius, is a monstrous perversion whether of ritualists or of rationalists, blind to the full efficacy of Christ's atoning work and to the hopes of the Jews. The two goats figure one Christ offered to Jehovah for propitiation and substitution. But who beforehand could have anticipated the truth?

This is followed by communications to guard priests and people from the dishonour of Jehovah, in the matter of blood, and especially against eating it (17); in natural relationships against impurity (18); in the maintenance of holy ways and comely practice, far from profanity (19); and especially in abhorrence of heathen and unnatural abominations (20): all, as became a people in holy nearness to Jehovah, and separated from the peoples to be His. Chapter 21 insists on a still higher sanctity on the part of Aaron's sons, and especially of the high priest, in view of their access to the sanctuary; and chapter 22 adds other disqualifications even if but transient. Then the people are joined with the priests in the caution against a blemished offering, and due heed claimed for Jehovah's injunction as to times, &c.

Chapter 23 presents the Feasts in which, especially in the greater ones, Jehovah gathered all the males around Himself as their centre. Here the prophetic character is yet more marked than in the great Day of Atonement; as in it there is plain historical sequence, so that it is easy enough to distinguish the fulfilled from what remains to be so, when the Lord returns in power and glory. Now who is, who could be, competent for these things? Only Jehovah, Who spoke to Moses concerning these "set times" of drawing near to Himself.

The Sabbath has this speciality of being revealed before the Feasts proper, as it will be accomplished at their close, when the true sabbatism will no longer "remain" but be realised for the people of God (3). It alone recurred week by week.

The Passover is the foundation of all blessing as it prefigures Christ sacrificed (1 Corinthians 5:7), the head or beginning of months (5).

In immediate sequence is Unleavened bread for seven days, the feast we now celebrate, not with old leaven nor with leaven of malice and wickedness, but with unleavened [bread] of sincerity and truth (6-8).

Then comes the Wave-sheaf on the next day after the sabbath, the clear type of Christ risen from the dead; for Whom therefore was no Sin or Trespass-offering, but Burnt and Meal-offerings with the Drink-offering thereof (9-14).

And the Feast of Weeks follows, seven weeks complete from the day of the Wave-sheaf, or fifty days till the morning after the seventh sabbath. It is Pentecost with its two Wave-loaves of fine flour, but with leaven: not Christ now, but they that are His, and therefore the leaven. Here then not only have we a Burnt-offering, with oblation and Drink-offering, but a Sin-offering. For it is short sight to deny the old man in believers; it is their joy that by Christ's death the evil is annulled to faith. This new oblation to Jehovah has His injunction appended, not to reap or glean so as to clear the field's corners, but to leave for the poor and the stranger. It is a provision for those who are to follow the souls who now believe, during the age's completion (15-22).

Next is announced a new speaking of Jehovah to Moses. It is a fresh testimony, a memorial of blowing of Trumpets. This new Feast, like those that succeed, are all in the seventh month; and this on its first day. It is Jehovah summoning His ancient people from their sleep—from their "graves" as Ezekiel calls it figuratively. Compare Isaiah 26:19, Daniel 12:2. The Christian call is past; the Jewish appeal will then begin and go on. Grace is preparing a people for Jehovah on earth, as now under the gospel for heaven.

On the tenth day is the day of the Atonement, when Israel no longer unbelieving but repentant shall afflict their souls, and mix up no works of theirs with His work, long despised, now understood and honoured. It is the application of the cross of Christ to their souls, deeply feeling their sins and His grace.

The fifteenth day opens the Feast of Booths or Tabernacles seven days to Jehovah: a complete cycle for *them* when "glory shall dwell in their land", as *we* have in keeping the feast of Unleavened bread. Only an eighth day follows, which points to the glory in resurrection connected then, the heavenly things of the kingdom with the earthly. Compare John 3:12, Ephesians 1:10, Colossians 1:20.

Now who was capable of such a living, comprehensive, all-important scheme of divine dealings from the beginning? Look at it from the purpose of rest couched in the pledge of the sabbath, till that day which shall display the Heir of all things centring in Himself all creation, heavenly and earthly, not only reconciled to God by His blood, then applied in power, and ourselves reigning with Him, being already reconciled by faith, as Israel will be "in that day" with all nations joined and no more at enmity. Christ is the One on Whom all turns: if received, life, peace, holiness, blessing, with access to God and to His glory; if rejected, wrath and indignation, tribulation and distress, when the vanity of present things and the carnal show of man can no longer hide the truth. What could imaginary Elohists or Jehovists avail to put together such a wondrous plan? All is simple, and only so, if Jehovah spoke to Moses, and Moses wrote of Christ. And who or what are they who blasphemously deny it? For He has testified to it.

Chapter 24 furnishes the solemn contrast of Israel according to purpose and as they are through their unbelief. In the one aspect shines the light of the Spirit through the High Priest during the dark night of their slumber; and the twelve loaves, with the pure frankincense, are on the table as a memorial for Aaron and his sons to eat (1-9). In the other we see the actual state under the "son of an Israelitish woman whose father was an Egyptian", blaspheming the Name and cursing. "His blood be on us and on our children" was their cry; as

Blood-field (Aceldama) is their land to this day. So do they bear their sin (10-23).

In chapter 25 we have the sabbath of the land every seventh year, and the hallowed year of Jubilee, the fiftieth year proclaimed on Atonement day. What affecting regulations in view of the trumpet which will usher the people of Jehovah, long outcasts for their sins, into the land which He will make theirs! for it is His, as He will prove against the mightiest foes. Let Gentiles beware who intrude. As this is prophetic, so is chapter 26. Israel made and worshipped idols; Israel rebelled, despising their nearness to Jehovah; Israel braved His chastenings; Israel brought waste on their cities, and desolation on their land. But away in exile shall they confess their iniquity and accept its punishment from Jehovah Who will remember His covenant with their fathers and remember their land. Mercy shall glory over judgment; and Jehovah's end is that He is full of tender compassion and pitiful.

The last chapter (27) brings in the priest again, but Moses' estimation. There may be vows of persons or beasts (not of the first-born, already Jehovah's), of house or land; but if all fail or be lost through man, God's rights abide. All was gone before God, when Christ was worth no more in Jewish eyes than the price of a slave. Yet will He retrieve all for them, having glorified Jehovah in all. Is this a human book?

5.4 Numbers

The Fourth Book of the Pentateuch is inadequately described by the title given in the versions generally. Nor is the usual Jewish expedient of the first words better rendered, "And spoke"; others say what is given later in the verse, "In the wilderness", which fairly presents its scope. For, as we have seen in its predecessors, this book has no less impressed on its contents a worthy divine design, which we as Christians are enabled by the Holy Spirit to apprehend and enjoy, in a way impossible to the Israelites or even to Moses its writer. "Now all these things happened to them as types; and they were written for our admonition on whom the ends of the ages are come" (1 Corinthians 10:11). This to the believer is decisive authority, far from excluding the book of Exodus, but fully extending to Numbers. The history, as far as it goes, is thoroughly reliable; but the typical instruction, as we are taught, was the aim and motive of the Holy Spirit. And this it is which accounts for repetitions and a seeming disorder in parts, which is the best order for the truth intended by the divine Author. If the Neo-critics had only reverent faith to learn, they would be kept from a wholly ungrounded pretension to judge what is above their powers, and might apprehend the goodness and wisdom of God's revealed mind to their blessing for evermore.

The book contemplates, as does none other, the desert journeyings of Jehovah's people, the walk in the wilderness. Hence here only are the people numbered (1), and arranged (2), at the beginning; and for an equally important reason they are numbered again toward the end. As service attaches to this condition, here we have (not in Leviticus) necessary prominence given to the Levites who are separately numbered, and their tabernacle duties (3, 4); whereas in the preceding book, which treats of access to Jehovah, the priesthood has that prominent place. Hence too the preservation of the camp as a whole, and of each individual, from defilement is here fully provided (5); as is the converse case of special devotedness in its various forms (6, 7). The High

Priest lighting the lamps next appears in chapter 8 morally connected; and the consecration of the Levites. Gracious consideration follows for any unintentionally unclean, that they too might not be debarred from observing the fundamental feast for all the people, the Passover (9). Hence here is the great and common call to guide the journey and the encampment according to the commandment of Jehovah. Nor was there "the cloud" only, but the silver trumpets for special occasions (10). Yet when their first march was ordered, grace interposed beyond prescription, and if Moses leaned on Hobab, the ark of the covenant of Jehovah went before them three days' journey, to seek out a resting-place for them. What a God of all consolation for the earthly pilgrimage! And Moses could now in the Spirit suitably speak when the ark set forward, and when it halted.

Such is a brief review of the first division of this book. Could any mere man that ever lived have conceived and adjusted such an introduction? Were this the fitting occasion to enter into the details, for instance for carrying the tabernacle and the vessels of the sanctuary in chapter 4, the typical force would add incalculably to the impiety as well as absurdity of fancying such ill-omened sprites as Elohists, Jehovists, and Redactors, where every thing points to the One Divine Spirit Who employed Moses to write, not for Israel only, but for all that fear God at all times. The literary mania of Jew or Gentile (one is ashamed to say of professing Christians) is a suicidal and destructive snare of Satan when it sits in rationalistic judgment on God's word. It is blind to that manifestation of God in Christ here portrayed in the holy vessels, &c., and their respective coverings, only here found, only here suited, whether for the day that now is, or for that which is to come for His people on the earth. Further, "holiness becometh thy house, O Jehovah, for evermore." The desert journey is just the responsible scene for maintaining it; and therefore is chapter 5 in its precisely right place, whatever be the objection of shallow and reckless speculation. So is the counterpart in chapter 6 of Nazarite separation to Jehovah: special defilements, and special devotedness, closing with the blessing of Jehovah on Israel pronounced by the entire priesthood.

Then, as we have said, follows the free-will offering from the twelve chiefs of the tribes, given to the Levites according to their service (chapter 7), the dedication-gift of the altar. And the Voice from above the mercy-seat speaks, in chapter 8, first of the candlestick, a striking figure designedly here, whatever rationalist presumption may say; then the Levites purified and set apart for Jehovah's work. That the sons of Israel laid their hands on them is a wholesome hint for ritualists to ponder. Jehovah gave them to Aaron and his sons for ministry. The Passover fitly comes at this point as uniting all Israel in the feast of redemption, with a gracious provision here only for such as were hindered by uncleanness from a dead body (chapter 9). The direction by the cloud is next given. The sounding of the silver trumpets opens chapter 10; then the first move with its deeply interesting accompaniments already noticed. Various subdivisions may be observed within this first division; but we must first forbear.

The second general portion opens with the moral history of the people in their journeyings. They murmur, and Jehovah judges but hears the prayer of Moses. They lust after flesh, weary of the manna; all fail, even Moses and Joshua in a measure; and Jehovah smote the people severely (chapter 11). Envy shows itself in Miriam and

Aaron; but Aaron confesses, and Miriam stricken with leprosy is healed at Moses' cry (chapter 12). As unbelief let in these evils on the way, so in chapters 13, 14 we see as to the hope. The pleasant land is despised through fear of the sons of Anak. In the same unbelief, instead of allowing self-judgment, after a carnal mourning, they went up without a word from Jehovah and were cut to pieces, as far as Hormah by the Amalekite and the Canaanite hill-men. How marvellous and opportune the grace, which there and then drops these evil ways of Israel and their inevitable chastenings, to instruct them (chapter 15) what to do when come into the land of their habitations which Jehovah gives them! To offer Fire-offerings to Him with the Drink-offering of joy! To offer Him the first of their dough as a Heave-offering throughout their generations! Let us admire also the provision for sin unwittingly (only the gospel could meet worse evil): the presumptuous sin dealt with by a death which all joined to inflict; and the fringe of blue to promote remembrance and obedience. What man of his own notion would have ventured such an episode? No wonder that unbelievers cavil, because they know not God. Chapter 16 is the culmination of the sad story here in the gainsaying of Korah, with other chiefs. The worst part of the rebellion lay in the ministry arrogating the priesthood; which, as Jude declares, has its answer in the apostasy of Christendom. Jehovah decided by consuming fire; and, when the assembly murmured, by the plague that destroyed more than 14,000.

We may consider chapter 17 as introducing a fresh division, where the power of priestly intercession is shewn in the fruitful rod of Aaron, living after death, alone able to lead the failing people through the wilderness. In chapter 18 the relative place of priests and Levites is explained. Aaron and his sons bear the iniquity of the sanctuary. How far is this from human, earthly, ambition! Theirs were the hallowed things to eat. The tithe was for the Levites, not for the priests save a tithe of the tithe given by the Levites to Aaron.

As these chapters are by divine design in their exactly right places, so in chapter 19 the Red Heifer is here alone given; for it alone suits this book as the special provision for the defilements of the wilderness in general and in this place of grace particularly. The standard for every Israelite is the holiness of the sanctuary. The blood was put in its completeness of efficacy, as the basis needing no renewal; the ashes mixed with living water were applied to the unclean. It is the remembrance of Christ's suffering by the word in the Spirit. In chapter 20 Miriam dies; and the people, wanting water, contend with Moses. Jehovah being appealed to directs Moses to take the rod, and speak to the rock which should give its water. Here Moses and Aaron quite fail to represent Jehovah's grace. For instead of speaking with Aaron's rod of priestly grace, Moses smote the rock with his own rod of power. The waters flowed; but Moses and Aaron were doomed to die outside the land, as they did. Edom, we are told, opposed the direct way; and Israel turned from them as akin however hostile. Aaron dies on mount Hor, and Eleazar succeeds.

Chapter 21 appears to begin a new series. King Arad's coming out against the Israelites is said by Dr. Perowne (Smith's Dictionary of the Bible ii. 581) to be "clearly out of place". But the comparison of chapter 33:40 confirms the assurance that it certainly is in its true place. Only the supplied "*when*" of the Authorised Version is a mistake; this is not written. But now the Canaanite made head, till Israel vowed to Jehovah to deal with the accursed race as He adjudged. Yet after fresh impatience and murmuring against the bread from above, they are smitten by the enemy's deadly sting, and find the only remedy in what figures Christ made sin for us. Then comes joyful refreshment in the well dug by the staves of their chiefs; and Sihon and Og assail them to their destruction, leaving their possessions to Israel. On the plains of Moab, with only Jordan severing them from Canaan, Satan makes a new and final effort to thwart Jehovah by cursing His people. But the false prophet was compelled to bless in repeated strains of unequalled beauty, before which the odes of Pindar and Horace are as inferior as their heroes and the occasions of their laudation. They are not only prophetic but Messianic throughout, indirectly and directly. Elohim, Jehovah, El Elyon, and El Shaddai are used with perfect propriety, but so as to expel from the field of spiritual intelligence the flimsy rag of Astruc wherewith rationalism seeks to cover its nakedness. Poor as His people are in themselves, here God gives His mind and purpose about them: separateness, justification, beauty, and glory (chapters 22-24). Never did such thoughts grow out of the heart of man; and God will verify them all in His time. The day is at hand.

In chapter 25 we see Balaam's will in corrupting the people, but Phinehas avenging it and staying the plague. Then in chapter 26 is renewed the enumeration of the people; and chapter 27 has daughters secured in the coming inheritance; while Jehovah bids Moses, in view of his decease, lay his hand on Joshua to lead the people in. Chapters 28, 29 follow the analogy of kindred insertions, and treat of what Jehovah calls His bread, His offerings at the set times, not as Leviticus 23 did in picturing the course of dispensations, but viewed intrinsically and as displaying the worship rendered by His people on earth. Then in chapter 30 we have the secret of man's or Israel's failure, and the way grace takes to surmount it and deliver the weak. Next is the holy war to execute Jehovah's vengeance on Midian, with (not Joshua the soldier, but) Phinehas the priest for leader and the alarm-trumpets in his hand. The victory is complete, and the seducers destroyed. But chapter 32 indicates the fact, so sadly natural, that whole tribes prefer their inheritance outside the Jordan: still they fight as Jehovah's people against the enemy. Then comes the interesting list of the journeys as far as God was pleased to relate them in chapter 33; and in chapter 34 the borders of the land on the other side of the Jordan, to fall by lot to the nine and a half tribes of Israel. This leads to the cities of the Levites (chapter 35), who had no inheritance in the land, and to the provision for him who might have slain unwittingly: a striking figure of what grace will yet reckon to the repentant remnant of Israel. The last chapter guards the security for heiresses from disordering the inheritance by passing out of the proper tribe.

If it be objected that not a little of this book refers to the land of promise, not yet possessed by the people, as adverse to the character of pilgrimage, the answer is that the looking onward in assured hope is precisely what is needed to cheer those who pass through the difficulties and dangers of the wilderness. The thing objected to is therefore in perfect keeping with its divine design. So we saw in the riband of blue only given in Numbers 15, like the water for separation in chapter 19, however differing in character; for the one recalls the light of heaven to those walking on earth, who also specially need the means of purifying from the defilements of the way.

How superficial are the critical censures of unbelief! how deep and precious are the helps of the divine word to faith!

5.5 DEUTERONOMY

The last book of the Pentateuch is as definitely marked as each of its predecessors. It alone was written in view of Israel's crossing the Jordan and entering on the land of their inheritance. It is therefore wholly different from Genesis which has a primary character, and is all but universal in its range, the word of Him Who knows the end from the beginning. Neither does it converge on redemption from Egypt, like Exodus; nor on access to Jehovah, like Leviticus; nor yet on pilgrimage through the wilderness, like Numbers. The title in the Authorised Version follows the Latin Vulgate, as it the Septuagint, but is at least nearer the mark than in the other cases; for the book largely consists of a special recapitulation of the law. Only we must allow for the divine affluence of scripture; which, when interpreting a vision, or a parable, or even a particular symbol, not merely repeats but adds very strikingly.

If we believe the book (and he is God's enemy who does not), Moses spoke and wrote on the eve of his approaching death. This could not but impart a peculiarly earnest and solemn tone. Ethic, affectionate, and expostulatory elements predominate beyond what we find in any other of the five books. As Moses says, in closing the brief preface of chapter 1:3-5, he began to declare or expound this law. Obedience is urged continually, and the spirit of it in the heart. It is the people as a whole therefore, who are in general addressed directly throughout, on their responsible tenure of the land. Typical teaching is comparatively rare, moral abounds, not without prophecy at the close especially. "The priests, the Levites" only appear for specific reasons, and Levites also as such. But the people are regarded as under the moral government of Jehovah their God in the land; and this accounts for its characteristics. Those born in the wilderness had been uncircumcised, and so disqualified for the privileges of Israel. This was no longer to be tolerated. Israel must henceforth take their normal place of obedience in Jehovah's land. So the book urges anticipatively.

From chapter 1:6 to the end of chapter 4 is an introduction, in which Moses first sketches in the rest of chapter 1 the journeying from Horeb to Kadesh, with the previous choice of rulers to judge, and the subsequent one of the spies, their rebellious unbelief, and its punishment. Then in chapters 2, 3 we have their final advance, after long abidings and marches in the wilderness. They were not to meddle with Edom, Moab, or Ammon. When Sihon and Og opposed, they slew them and their people, taking all they had as spoil on that side of Jordan, and giving their lands and cities to Reuben, Gad, and half of Manasseh, who were as eager to possess at once even outside Canaan, as Moses pleads in vain to go over and see the good land. Chapter 4 turns shameful Baalpeor into an appeal to obey Jehovah's word, neither adding nor diminishing; as they alone have Him so nigh with His statutes and judgments, heard His voice, yet saw no similitude. Therefore were they called to abhor every image and created object, lest Jehovah should expel and scatter them among the idolatrous nations. But even there are they encouraged to turn and obey Him. The chapter closes with three cities chosen for the manslayer in the country beyond Jordan taken from the Amorite kings, Sihon and Og. Such a refuge was due to

Jehovah, Who would not tolerate the shedding of man's blood on the one hand, nor on the other allow mischance to be dealt with as murder. Where His people dwelt, even though outside their proper barrier, His rights must be respected. We may observe how distinct is the setting of these refuge cities in Numbers, where they are given within the portion of the Levites, and in view of the decease of the anointed priest: a typical connexion of which Deuteronomy here shows no trace, but has its own appropriate reason. What a testimony to the divine inspiration of both! What we have had hitherto suits no book but the one that has it.

From chapter 5 to the end of 11 are given the general moral principles on which Israel were set before Jehovah. Chapters 12-26 are rather the special terms in statutes and judgments made with the people.

In chapter 5 Moses repeats the law according to the Horeb covenant, made not with their fathers but with them; as was said just before in the face of Beth-peor to impress their danger, but in the land they had won to cheer them. Similarly to the fourth commandment is annexed, not the recall to creation as in Exodus 20, but the remembrance of His deliverance from Egypt Who now commanded its observance. Chapter 6 is a homiletic application of the first commandment, as 7 is of the second. Chapter 8 impresses the whole from their wilderness experience of God and of their own heart with Canaan in view. Chapter 9 reminds them of their weakness, though assured of victory by Jehovah's grace, and of their grievous sins and rebellion, of Moses' own indignant smashing the tables though inscribed by God's own hand, yet of his deprecating divine wrath; so that he came down after other 40 days and nights with freshly written tables for the ark, as he states in a parenthesis of chapter 10 from verse 1 to 9, the more singular for containing another parenthesis in 6-9. For if Aaron died at a later day, Levi "at that time" gained a good degree by devotedness, and Jehovah gave the tribe an honoured place of service. Obedience therefore is insisted on most touchingly; and in chapter 11 love too in presence of His wondrous ways of mercy as well as judgment, and this to their enjoying the good land. He repeats therefore in conclusion the all-importance of keeping Jehovah's words, they and their children, as in chapter 6, that they might be blessed and their foes put down, instead of reaping a curse on their disobedience.

Now there is no place in the Pentateuch, nor in all the Bible, where such appeals are so suitable as in the last words of the prophet and legislator. The very repetitions are not vain but deeply pathetic, and only despicable in the eyes of men as stiff-necked as those who kicked against them of old. It was the adaptation of the law to the new need of the generation about to enter and possess Canaan; but no language is clearer than its claim to be of Moses. If this be untrue, the book is an imposture; if true from Jehovah, what are they who undermine and defame it?

This design accordingly governs the enactments. They regard Israel as if in Canaan. This determines which reappear, and which do not. It has nothing to do with later times or various authors; nor is there real discrepancy with the previous books. For Jehovah's land is required for His people obedient and true to His relationship, eschewing false gods and images, with one centre to His name for their sacrifices, and their offerings, or either; yet with leave to kill and eat flesh (not the blood) within all their gates (12). For the same reason, prophet or dreamer that enticed to other gods must be put to death; so must be the nearest relative that enticed, however secretly; and if a whole city were thus drawn away, it must be devoted to destruction, as a traitor to Jehovah (13). As sons of Jehovah they must adopt no foreign custom, nor eat unclean food, but were to truly tithe corn, wine, oil, and first-fruits, bringing them or their value to Jehovah's central place. Even another tithe at the end of three years is claimed for their homes, and for the Levite and the sojourner, the orphan and the widow, besides that carried to the holy centre (14). For the people would thus be shewn in immediate relationship with Jehovah, while His sanctuary had its place also. What a witness of the book's divine design is this added tithe, here only in the Pentateuch, where alone it could be! It is the people's joy in fellowship with Him Who not only redeemed and kept them, but gave them the land, the Levites &c. (who had none) being graciously prominent. Chapter 15 follows this up by release of a debtor by a neighbour at the end of seven years, and by a call to constant liberality, as a people blessed of Jehovah. For which reason also the hallowing of male firstlings from herd and flock is here pressed for Jehovah's centre; but if a defect existed, to be eaten within their gates as hart or gazelle.

Chapter 16 is so weighty a proof of the same design, that it claims a little farther notice. It enjoins the three feasts of the year which gathered all the males to Jehovah's chosen place in the land, and not empty but according to His blessing given them. It is not the full typical circle of God's ways as in Leviticus 23, nor the witness of God's worship yet to be rendered on the earth as in Numbers 28, 29. In our chapter we have, first redemption, then the liberty of grace, and lastly, after the harvest and the vintage, the "whole joyfulness" of glory.

Yet even so only the seven days are here, because it looks not beyond the blessing of Israel in the land, the scope of Deuteronomy. The close from verse 18 takes up the means of sustaining the people in righteous order and in abhorrence of idolatry before Jehovah. Chapter 17 first commands integrity of conscience in sacrifice, then joint clearance of disloyalty to Him; and if any had recourse to the priests, and to the judge in those days, with meekness to bow to that decision. This leads to the question of a king, who from them was to be chosen of Jehovah, to avoid fleshly and worldly ways, and to write a copy of the law for his personal guidance. Then we have the priests, indeed the whole tribe of Levi (18) with their dues. Next are denounced for Israel, the heathen abominations for which the Canaanites were dispossessed; and the promise of the great Prophet from their midst is given. Acts 3 is conclusive authority that Christ is meant; and so is Acts 7: both Peter and Stephen attesting that Moses so said to Israel.

The same principle applies to chapter 19. They when possessing the land were to separate three more cities of refuge for the unwitting slayer: the murderer must surely die. Landmarks were not to be removed, and testimony guarded. In chapter 20 we see how the fear of Jehovah controlled war, both within and without. It was not a rival to be got rid of, but the abominable races who in fact held the land, to be destroyed by and for Israel to whom the land was divinely given. But chapter 21 presents moral truths of interest in the man found slain, the captive woman, the child of the hated wife, and the rebellious son: if these refer to Israel in the land which Jehovah will have hallowed, and to inconsistency judged, the close (we know) points to Him Who became a curse in infinite grace to deliver the people and bless the land: the contrast of all who defile it.

On the other hand chapter 22 fosters gracious and even delicate feeling, forbids mixture of principle, punishes impurity, and protects the weak innocents against brutality. Again, in chapter 23 relation to the congregation of Jehovah is guarded, making a difference, and the seemliness even of the camp maintained; the runaway slave shielded from oppression; prostitution and its gain scouted, and interest too from a brother; vows established; kindness enjoined as to vineyard or field, but selfishness forbidden. In chapter 24 divorce was allowed under law; but the Lord brought in better things under grace. Many and various ordinances follow keeping flesh in check to the end of chapter 25.

This is closed by the unique worship in chapter 26 where the Israelite in possession of his inheritance puts the first of his fruits in a basket, goes to the chosen place, and says to the priest that shall be in that day (for Deuteronomy is the anticipation of faith), "'I profess this day to Jehovah thy God, that I am come unto the land that Jehovah swore to our fathers to give them." Then the priest takes the basket and sets it down before Jehovah's altar. And the offerer says, "A perishing Syrian was my father, and he went down to Egypt" &c. "And now, behold, I have brought the first of the fruit of the ground, which thou, Jehovah, hast given me." This set before Him, the Israelite worshipped: else he was free and called to rejoice in all the good which Jehovah had given him and his house, "thou, and the Levite, and the stranger that is in thy midst."

Can any thing be conceived more Deuteronomic? Or more distinct from the preceding books? To call these specialities inconsistent with foregoing observances is absurd and wrong. Are critical eyes evil because Jehovah's eye is good? Hope and its accomplishment call out gratitude and generosity, as in the tithes of the third year, a characteristic institution beyond the ordinary Levitical tithes and its tithe to the priests. It was the festive and overflowing joy of the people before Jehovah when put in possession of His land. Amos (4:4) alludes to it ironically, because the people were steeped in transgression which tainted all; Tobit (1:7, 8), though of no divine authority, relates the fact, as does Josephus (Antiquities of the Jews, Book 4, chapter 8, §22). It is worship, not intermediary in the sanctuary but direct, personal or household. But the priest in the sanctuary remains none the less; to set the one against the other is only rationalistic shallowness and ill-will. The joy of communion with Jehovah's manifested goodness is provided for in the new order of things assured.

The chapters which follow are in the exactly right place. Chapters 27 and 28 are supplemental, and each where it should be. They express the sanction of the law. First, on passing Jordan into the land, great stones were to be set up and plastered, with "all the words of this law" written on them; an altar of kindred nature also for Burnt-offerings and Peace-offerings. But a most solemn sign followed: six tribes told off to bless on Gerizim; six to curse on Ebal. Yet, whatever might be the fact, the chapter gives the Levites loudly proclaiming to all Israel *nothing but the curses*. Such is the basis of the apostolic word to the Galatians (Galatians 3:10), "As many (persons) as are of works of law are under curse"; not merely those who transgressed, but all on that principle, like the Galatians bewitched. Spiritually, it was no use to tell us of the blessings on Gerizim. Chapter 28 speaks, not of the personal curse, but of governmental blessings or curses and therefore temporary; whilst chapter 29 applies all to the conscience: only the last verse refers to the secret or hidden things belonging to Jehovah. This is of the deepest interest. The things revealed were as to the law; but there were secrets in divine purpose, only alluded to prophetically till the rejection of Christ, when they too were revealed. Chapter 30 illustrates this, if we compare with it the apostle's words in Romans 10:4-9.

Moses then in chapter 31 announces Joshua, not himself, as their leader over Jordan under Jehovah; and exhorts them to be courageous and strong in His going with them. "This law", it is definitely said, Moses wrote, and delivered it to the priests, the sons of Levi, and to all the elders of Israel, with the command (at the release of every seven years, when all Israel met before Jehovah at His chosen place) to read it in their ears, men, women, children, and even the stranger within their gates. Then Joshua receives his charge at the tent of meeting and, as Jehovah directed, Moses wrote that day a prophetic song, His witness against the sons of Israel. Indeed "this book of the law" too was to be put by the side of the ark for the same purpose. For Moses well knew their rebelliousness, and the evil to befall them at the end of days; but he rejoiced that Jehovah's purpose is unfailing and irrevocable.

Chapter 32 begins with the song, before which Horace's lyrics are flat and Pindar's froth. Its holy grandeur has no equal. Its prophetic insight justifies the present grace to Gentiles (21) during the hiding of Jehovah's face from His ancient people, and His future vindication of Israel when humbled and believing (35-42); and then will be the fulfilment, not inchoate but complete, when the nations shout for joy [with] His people, or speak aloud their praises, as some Jewish versions say, and in substance the Vulgate but not the Septuagint. Yet all point to the glorious future. It is utterly groundless that the stand-point is other than Moses then took whether on Jehovah's side or on the people's, though anticipating, as indeed is the aim of all Deuteronomy, their entrance on their predestined inheritance. Alas! they disobeyed and became idolaters; but Jehovah abides, and will avenge the blood of His servants, and will render vengeance to His adversaries, and will make expiation for His land, for His people. After a few words more from Moses to the people, Jehovah bids him go up Nebo, and when he had seen the land, to die.

But this was not before blessing the sons of Israel in chapter 33. His blessing is in view of Jehovah's government of His people in relationship with Himself in the land, the key-note of the book. In this way it differs from Jacob's in Genesis, which is historic and prophetically complete. Yet there is no inconsistency, but each true to its own divine design. What triumphant fervour in both the exordium and the conclusion! and what critical shortsightedness in thinking that it was not suitable to the prophet Moses in Deuteronomy to say, "He thrust out", "and said, Destroy", and "Israel dwelleth" or any other form in 27, 28!

There is no need whatever to take chapter 34 as written by Moses before his death. Others followed inspired like him. But, as to the contents, Jehovah buried the dead law-giver; and Jude tells us what none had revealed till then. Satan would have turned a willing people to idolize him dead, whom living they strove against. No man knows his sepulchre unto this day. The testimony to the blessed man of God, as in Numbers 12:3, better suits the successor to whom it was given of God.

5.6 Joshua

The book of Joshua is closely akin to the last book of the Pentateuch, which it immediately follows; but it has its own proper design impressed by God. It is no longer the mediator, no longer the apostle and high priest, but typically the power of Christ in Spirit leading His own in conflict with spiritual powers of wickedness in the heavenlies. The book does not prefigure the personal presence of our Lord appearing from heaven, when He takes the inheritance of the universe in power and establishes the undisputed reign of His glory at the end of the age. Joshua represents the intermediate action of Him Who, dead, risen, and ascended, works by His Spirit in His saints to realise their heavenly title and inheritance in the face of their not yet extirpated enemies. What can be clearer than that Ephesians 6:12 warrants, as well as suggests, this as the just application?

It is not heaven now entered individually after death, nor the enjoyment of God's rest when we are all conformed to the image of His Son and are with Him in the Father's house; but our death and resurrection with Christ, and sitting in the heavenlies in Him, with our consequent responsibility to wrestle against the world-rulers of this darkness on high, who strive to hinder our laying hold of our heavenly blessedness in Christ. If the popular Puritan allegory expresses evangelical shortcoming (to say the least), the Romanist and even the Catholic view is still darker. Both ideas betray the loss in this respect of the due and characteristic privilege of the Christian and of the church, developed specially in the Epistle to the Ephesians.

How inimitably chapter 1 prepares the way necessary to God's design! On Moses' death, Joshua is called to "arise and go over this Jordan, thou and all this people, unto the land which I do give them." For the people redeemed from Egypt the wilderness was not Jehovah's purpose, only His way. Compare Exodus 3:8, 17; 6:4-8; 13:3-5; 15:13-17. The Jordan sets forth our death and resurrection *with* Christ, as the Red Sea does Christ's death and resurrection *for* us. Energy and courage were imperative and unswerving adherence to the word. So it is for the Christian; he is set free, yet bound, to obey God.

In chapter 2 how bright the accompanying grace to a hitherto worthless and despised Gentile! Salvation to her, and even to her house, was attested by the scarlet line. She believed Jehovah, and this likewise in the midst of His people, before a blow was struck in Canaan. Then in chapter 3 came the wonder wrought in Jordan when it overflowed all its banks: the ark of the covenant was borne in by the priests, and the waters fled before it, till all Israel passed over on dry ground. It points to the new position with and in Christ for the heavenly places, as the Red Sea prefigured our justification by His death and resurrection, needful even for our pilgrimage through the wilderness. The latter was out of Egypt, as the former into Canaan under Joshua. We died with Christ and were raised together with Him; and therefore should we mortify our members that are on the earth (Colossians 2, 3). So we see the full witness of life out of and over death in the memorial of the twelve stones of chapter 4 and the circumcision of Israel in chapter 5 at Gilgal, when, and not before, the reproach of Egypt was rolled off. Thus "the old things passed away; behold, new things are come; but the whole, of the God that reconciled us to himself through Christ" (2 Corinthians 5:17, 18). The passover was kept as the Lamb's death.

Next, the resurrection food, the old corn of the land, took the place of manna. In fact and in spiritual force this could only be now. Compare 2 Corinthians 5:16. As in the wilderness, we eat the manna, and we celebrate His death; but as heavenly (for "all things are ours"), we feed on Him risen and on high.

Thus, after the vision not of the unconsumed bush for the desert, but of the Captain with drawn sword for Canaan and holiness in His presence, we have in chapter 6 the first and greatest lesson of Jehovah in Jericho's fall: absolute subjection on man's part; the means seemingly unmeaning or absurd; but Jehovah the real accomplisher, as Joshua learnt of Him and told the people before the siege began. But man as he is was faithless; soon the wickedness of Achan brought defeat on Israel who failed to enquire of Jehovah before assailing Ai. That sin must first be sifted out and judged. Even then self-confidence is rebuked in chapter 8: for all must march even against so small a place, and a special ambush be laid, and a signal appointed by Him be obeyed, when victory comes.

But the land was owned as Jehovah's according to Deuteronomy 21:22, 23, and by the altar of Ebal which proclaimed Israel's responsibility to obey. Gibeon in chapter 9 disclosed that the chiefs failed in vigilant faith; for Israel was then deceived into an oath to spare a race whom Jehovah had devoted to destruction. But chapter 10 shows a mighty discomfiture of the hosts that gathered against Gibeon, when sun and moon, or rather Jehovah, hearkened to Joshua's voice, who passed on, smiting the whole country, the mountain and the Negeb, and the lowland, and the slopes, and all their kings. He let none remain; but he utterly destroyed all that breathed, as Jehovah the God of Israel commanded.

There was no more doubt of their wicked abominations than of his divine warrant to execute judgment. Thence is the return to Gilgal, whence he went up: there, was the memorial of death and resurrection; there, the mortification of the flesh. When weak, then are we strong. A new combination by the king of Hazor (chapter 11) only brought the word of Jehovah for a complete victory to Joshua till the land had rest from war. Chapter 11 rehearses the conquest and the land acquired.

Yet the second half of the book tells us how imperfectly man's part was done. The failure was assuredly not in Jehovah, but in His people: so it ever is. Caleb received his portion, but not even Judah made good his lot by dispossessing the enemies of Jehovah. Ephraim and half Manasseh did no better. On these details, so full of interest to those who will re-enter and never more leave the land, one need not dwell now. Who but God could have given us such a book, on the surface so simple, but with depths beyond man's plummet? So Caleb was not forgotten, neither were Zelophehad's daughters; nor did Joshua show favour to the sons of Joseph, but faithfulness. At length also he rebuked the slack tribes, in order to taking possession by lot, as we learn in chapter 18, 19.

The cities of refuge were appointed (chapter 20) on this as on that side of Jordan; and the Levites received their forty-eight cities with their suburbs (chapter 21), and the two tribes and half were sent away (chapter 22). But they built an altar before crossing Jordan, which roused the alarm of Israel, who sent Phinehas and other representatives to remonstrate. On disclaiming any thought save of a witness between them and their God, that they too had portion in Jehovah, peace prevailed.

In chapters 23, 24 are two charges of Joshua, the first more general, the second more detailed and emphatic, in which the departing leader set blessing and warning before them, but not a word about his own achievements in either. In the latter he reminds them how Abraham was chosen out of an idolatrous house; how Egypt was plagued, and Israel brought out; how the Amorites opposed and were effaced; how Balaam was forced to bless; how the nations in Canaan were delivered into their hand. Then he puts their danger from all false gods, avowing fidelity to Jehovah from him and his. On the people declaring their loyalty, Joshua owns his just fears, whilst they repeat their allegiance; and a covenant was thereon made in Shechem. The book closes with the death and burial of Joshua in the hill-country of Ephraim: so Joseph's bones had been laid there too, and Eleazar's also, each in its own quarter.

Not only was the book of Joshua of the highest interest and importance to Israel as the evidence of Jehovah's accomplishing in power what His mouth had promised; but it sets out to the Christian the present privilege of realising our spiritual blessing in the heavenlies as in no other part of the Old Testament. If the types in the first half reveal the mighty work of God in Christ risen and ascended, the second speaks most practically to our souls also. It was written by one who "passed over" Jordan that day (Joshua 5:1); but it was and must be by God's unerring hand and mind and love, let unbelief rail as it may.

5. 7 JUDGES

Is this book less marked by the finger of God? Here it is not slackness but growing failure, and grievous forsaking of Jehovah; and Bochim succeeds to Gilgal, so that

He sold them into heathen hands. Yet it attests His ear open to their cry, and deliverers raised up in answer. It is the book beyond all others of revivals on God's part, when to His mercy His people appealed out of their misery from their shameful sins. Historically and morally the book could only be where it is; the divine design is exactly suited to the facts.

To chapter 3:7 is an introduction, as chapter 17 to the end is a dark yet needed appendix. Joshua's death did not hinder Jehovah's blessing when He was looked to by Judah, and for Simeon too. Othniel's early story is repeated. Yet did they all like Benjamin fail in energy: so too did Manasseh, Ephraim, Zebulun, Asher, Naphtali, and Dan. Nor was it felt, till Jehovah's angel (chapter 2) came up from Gilgal to Bochim with the dread word that He would not drive out the accursed race whom they had spared. Thus they sunk lower and lower, as each deliverer died. Tears cannot do the work of faith. The evil was within and against Jehovah. Humiliation came from heathen without, instead of self-judgment by the word.

Their first oppressor was Cushan-rishathaim, king of Mesopotamia, till the Spirit of Jehovah wrought in Othniel, and the land had rest for forty years. Then came the dominion of the Moabite Eglon, till Ehud was raised up, and the land rested eighty years. Shamgar followed for deliverance from the Philistines (chapter 4). Again Jabin of Hazor mightily oppressed Israel twenty years, when Deborah was used by God to subdue the Canaanite through Barak; and they sing Jehovah's praise in the noble ode of chapter 5.

On fresh evil Jehovah delivers Israel into the hand of Midian; but when they cried to Him, Gideon was raised up to be a saviour. But what lessons of faith to make the weak strong in chapters 6, 7, 8! Yet never were the people lower morally. And so it came out openly when Gideon died; and retribution fell on Abimelech and the men of Shechem (chapter 9).

Afterwards as we read in chapter 10 came Tola, and Jair with his thirty sons; but when Israel sank into the worship not only of other strange gods but of those of the Philistine and the Ammonite, Jehovah sold them into the hands of those neighbouring peoples; and their cry arose, and His soul was grieved for their misery. Jephthah (chapter 11) the despised became their leader, on whom was the Spirit of Jehovah; and Ammon was subdued. But the haughty men of Ephraim, graciously answered by Gideon, met a severer judge in the Gileadite; after whom came Ibzan, Elon, and Abdon (chapter 12).

A worse relapse brought a stern and nearer chastening from the Philistines. Here therefore the deliverer was a Nazarite: separation to Jehovah was the condition of suited mercy. Yet Samson was weak enough morally, and his work more individual, and rather prowess physically, than in any previous case. His strength lay in maintaining the secret of Jehovah; and when he gave it up basely, he became as another man for a while, but his vision gone, till God visited the vain-glory of the Philistines with a disaster at his hands greater in his death than the victories of his life (chapters 13-16).

The tale of Micah in chapters 17, 18 is not in chronological order, but here given after the history, to lay bare the lawlessness in religious matters which prevailed in the days of the judges; as that in chapters 19-21 lets us see the frightful demoralisation in those days, and the calamities it brought on Israel, when Benjamin was all but extinguished as a tribe. How marvellous the grace which turned their shame to profit, both in self-judgment from God, and in recovery of fraternal affection! Who but Himself could or would thus have lifted the veil off His people for good?

5.8 RUTH

It is not our task to search into the motives which led the later Jews to take the book of Ruth from its place, as indicated in our Bibles as well as in the Septuagint (the Greek Version rendered long before our Lord came), and class it with the Lamentations, Canticles, Esther, and Ecclesiastes, as the five Megilloth, part of the Khetubim or Hagio-grapha. Following Judges and preceding the books of Samuel, it is just where it should be. It falls within the days of the judges, and most fittingly points on to the Beloved whom Jehovah chose to be His anointed, coming to the throne when Saul fell.

But what a contrast with those old anomalous days, especially with the horrors of the appendix! The Holy Spirit here brings before us from within that period a tale of surpassing beauty, in particular of her whose name is the title.

The death of Elimelech ("whose God is King") left Naomi a widow, the type of Israel. Her two sons also died, and she returns from among strangers to the land of promise, hearing that Jehovah had visited His people in giving them bread. Only did Ruth cleave to her. So it will be after the people's sins and desolations: a remnant will return, after Lo-ammi had been long written. This is vividly typified by the Moabitess daughter-in-law; but meanwhile Naomi owns herself as yet Mara, not "my pleasantness" but "bitterness". But come back to

Bethlehem, they meet with Boaz ("in him is strength"); and Naomi, encouraged by his kindness and character, instructs Ruth to claim her Levirate title. Another, who represented the nearer claim of the law in flesh, refuses to take the inheritance with Ruth; while Boaz represents the risen Heir, and as the kinsman-redeemer accepts the widow to raise up the name of the dead upon his inheritance. And out of their union sprang Obed, father of Jesse, father of David. So it will be in the last days, when the godly remnant will be owned in grace by the Redeemer, before the kingdom is established in power and glory. Types of the Kingdom will soon appear in the books that follow this: personally in David the warrior king and in the son of David, the man of peace, both needed to give an adequate view of the Messiah in relation to Israel.

That these anticipations of Holy Writ are true can readily be proved to men of faith. All men however have not faith; but if the words are of God from first to last, if they will be surely fulfilled in the grand events of the latter day, what can one think of the spirit, aim, and state of those who, bearing the Lord's name, strain every nerve to darken and destroy these living oracles, reducing them to legends haphazard and of varying merit, but really denying that God wrote them by His inspired servants, that they might be worthy of all acceptance?

5.9   1 Samuel

The wisdom of God is no less apparent in these four books, which are parts of the same design. They open with the failure of the priesthood, as distinctly as the people had failed both in the wilderness and in the land. "By strength shall no man prevail." Since sin entered, and death through it, grace alone avails, as in Hannah

(1, 2), and expressed in her prayer-song, and by the man of God prophetically to Eli in the marked change of even the faithful priest walking before Jehovah's Anointed for ever. Thus was the King foreshadowed in sovereign grace, before the evil heart of unbelief wearied of Jehovah, and would have "a king like all the nations". Hitherto the high priest was "the anointed". Soon was there to be the anointed King before whom the priest would walk, which finds its complete realisation only in the Lord Jesus.

The word of Jehovah meanwhile calls Samuel, to whom He revealed Himself for all Israel (3); and the ark abused by selfishness passes to the Philistines (4). But if this was Ichabod for people and priests, the enemy and their idol were forced to bow before the vindicating judgments of Jehovah, only too glad to send the ark away with their guilt-offering (5, 6). If the men of Beth-shemesh indulged in profane curiosity, a yet more severe blow befell those who ought to have known better. To Kirjath-jearim is the ark brought, and abides there twenty years. It never returns to the old order, and only enters its due place when David's son set up in peace the picture of glory, which still awaits the people under Messiah and the new covenant. When Israel lamented, Samuel calls them to repentance and gathers them to Mizpah where his prayer rises because of a counter gathering of the Philistines, who were driven out into their border (7). But if Samuel judged in faith, he could not make his sons judges beyond the name, when Israel, revolting from them, revolted also from Jehovah (8); and He putting aside Samuel's indignation, gave them a king in His anger and took him away in His wrath, as says Hosea. This episode occupies to the end of the book; but within it is the tale of him who was made the type of the true Beloved, His king, to sit on His holy hill of Zion. Saul was the chosen, higher than any of the people, according to the heart of Israel (9), saluted as king, by all save some base fellows (10), and achieving a crushing victory over the Ammonites (11). Samuel, acknowledged to have been faithful, warns them of their responsibility, but assures them of his continued intercession (12); whereas Saul after two years is heard summoning "the Hebrews", as a heathen might say who believed not that they were Jehovah's people (13), and offered the burnt-offering in his disobedience. Jonathan wrought with God, his father Saul only spoiling the victory and only kept by the people from making Jonathan the victim of his superstition (14). Samuel let him know, on his fresh disobedience as to Amalek, that Jehovah rejected him from the throne of Israel (15).

Jehovah in chapter 16 takes the initiative, and has Jesse's youngest son anointed by the prophet. Meanwhile he is sought to soothe with the harp the king troubled by an evil spirit. Then follows his victory over Goliath in chapter 17, with Jonathan's love, and Saul's jealous hatred, Merab given to another, Michal to him as a snare, but only proving Jehovah to be with David who escaped the king's murderous hand (18, 19). In 20 Jonathan, slow to believe his father's ill-will, renews his covenant with David, who becomes now an exile, and receives the shew-bread from the priest with Goliath's sword. This brings death on the sons of Aaron at Doeg's hand (21, 22) and gives occasion to many a psalm of plaint and praise, as David hides in Keilah, Ziph, and Engedi (23, 24). Nabal's folly is as plain as Abigail's faith in chapter 25. But if David's generosity puts Saul to shame at Hachilah (26), his faith breaks down in 27, and an interval in no way to his praise follows in Ziklag. Saul seeks the witch of Endor, when Samuel's soul appeared, not her familiar spirit, and tells him the approaching doom (28). David is refused as an ally by the Philistine lords, and returns to find Ziklag burnt, and the families of him and his men captive (29, 30), but defeats the Amalekite spoilers, as the Philistines smite Israel, Saul, and his sons on Gilboa (31).

5.10 2 Samuel

The second book (1) opens with David's resentment at the stranger who falsely taxed himself with the slaying of Saul to please him, and with a genuine lament over the fallen house. In chapter 2 at the word of Jehovah he goes to Hebron, and reigns over Judah seven years and a half. For two years reigns Saul's son Ishbosheth over Benjamin and Israel generally, through Abner's influence, with whom Joab contends. David only had title from God who let the hindrances pass, without the least sympathy on his own part with the guilty instruments (3, 4). In chapter 5 all the tribes come to him in Hebron, and anoint David king, who reigns in Jerusalem over all Israel thirty-three years more. The stronghold of Zion falls; and Tyre sends gifts. In vain the Philistines gather against David, who enquires of Jehovah, instead of going at once in the confidence of prowess and old victories. Again they come; but David only acts as Jehovah commands. Still the ark remained in Abinadab's house; and David desired its presence (6). But he did not enquire, nor did he search the scriptures, how it should be done. So it ended in death, as it began in error. And the ark was carried into the house of Obed-edom for three months of blessing to all the house. Tidings of this awakened the king to the homage of faith; and the ark was duly carried into the city of David with joy. It was not yet the temple, but the provisional tabernacle beyond which David could not go. The rest of glory was reserved for Solomon, type of Christ in peace, as David was of His wars. All this appears clearly in the prophets who came afterward; here its analogue comes historically; but who could have done either but the Holy Spirit? David is not viewed as a priest on his throne, but acts by grace as a servant, and so thoroughly as to rouse the fleshly anger of Michal, who pays the penalty of her contempt.

How proper did it seem as we read in chapter 7 to build Jehovah a palace as the king had done for himself! But Nathan the prophet is corrected by Jehovah the same night: David's son, who shall be Jehovah's son, is to build that house; and his house shall be established for ever. So it shall be in the most glorious way. If this be the truth, who but God could have so revealed? and how perfectly in keeping with the divine design in this book! David could no more build the temple than Moses could enter the land. Hence we may note his subduing the Philistines, Moabites, Syrians, &c., in chapter 8. He typifies the warrior still. The man of peace shall build. Christ will answer to both in the fullest perfection. David's grace to Jonathan's son shines in chapter 9. But chapter 10 shows how the type fails; chapter 11, how far he fell shamefully; and chapter 12, how the sword should never depart from his house in Jehovah's moral government. What a rebuke was Amnon's lust in chapter 13! What another was Absalom's blood-guiltiness! Nor was this all. For if through Joab Absalom returns (14), his rebellion breaks out, as chapter 15 shows, and David's flight in chapter 16. Ahithophel comes to nothing in chapter 17; and Absalom perishes by Joab's hand in 18. Touching is the king's sorrow; but he returns in chapter 19. Sheba's rebellion ends with the traitor's death, but not without Joab's guile and cruelty in chapter 20; as chapter 21 gives the striking proof that Jehovah punishes in king Saul's house perfidy toward even the accursed Hivites of Gibeon.

Then how remarkably comes in here David's song of deliverance from all his enemies and Saul too (22)! followed by his "last words" in chapter 23 when he long reigned, but also had the grief that "his house is not so with God"; and though he could say the covenant was all his salvation and desire, yet "He maketh it not to grow." Judgment must intervene; which Christ alone could execute perfectly. Who but God could have so written? even as He will accomplish all in its day. Then follows the roll of David's worthies on the one hand, and the plague that devoured the thousands (chapter 24), about whose numbering he sinned in the pride of his heart, in painful contrast with Him Whom he foreshadowed so much. But even there mercy glories against judgment at Jerusalem, and the threshing-floor of Araunah becomes the site of the altar to Jehovah, the meeting-place of reconciliation for His people for ever.

Directly and indirectly we thus see that the books of Samuel are God giving man's choice of a king superseded by the figure of the true Beloved, reducing His enemies to subjection; as the Lord will when He comes in power and glory at the end of the age, before He reigns in peace.

5.11 1 Kings

The first book of Kings pursues the history of the kingdom, not only to the division under Rehoboam, but to the death of Jehoshaphat and the reign of Ahaziah. A design similar to 1 and 2 Samuel pervades it and its successor. So in the Septuagint and in the Vulgate they are together entitled the Four books of Kings. But they essentially differ from all other annals, in that prophets in this case were the historians: a character which rationalism does its utmost to doubt, darken, and destroy, but in vain. Only Christ stands, and will, in every relation in which the first man failed; and as king it will be displayed power and glory on earth as in the heavens. Who but an unbeliever cannot discern a greater than David in Him Who, delivered from the strivings of the people, is made Head of the nations?

Here we have the type set in responsibility, blessed and a blessing in the measure of fidelity, and bringing in ruin through unfaithfulness till there was no remedy. But Jehovah cannot fail nor His Anointed, as the consummation of the age will prove to a wondering world. These books testify what the kingdom was in its decline and fall with the assured promise of the "morning without clouds", when judgment clears the way for His reign Whose right it is. Such is the divine design of all four: in the first two, David's history in this point of view; and now Solomon's, who is seen established on the throne, the more for Adonijah's rebellion, in which fell crafty Joab, and later, Shimei, with Abiathar the priest (chapters 1, 2) in God's righteous government. Though affinity with the Gentile has its expression in chapter 3, and Solomon was blessed with wisdom and much more, a feebler faith appears in his cleaving to the brazen altar and the great high place in Gibeon, as compared with David's appreciation of the ark. But the splendour of the kingdom was great, the peace maintained, Israel prosperous and glad, the Gentiles filled with his fame, and subservient to his glory (4, 5). Then follows (6, 7) his building in seven years the temple of Jehovah, himself but a shadow of Him Who is to sit and rule, a priest on

His throne, according to Zechariah 6; his house in thirteen years, and that of the forest of Lebanon, with the porch of judgment, and a house for Pharaoh's daughter. In chapter 8 at the feast of Tabernacles he dedicates Jehovah's house in prayers, to which Jehovah answers (chapter 9) in language only to be fulfilled in Christ's reign when His world-kingdom is come (Revelation 11:15). And the queen of Sheba (10) prefigures the Gentile powers coming to the brightness of His rising Who is far greater than Solomon. But darkness falls on the king in chapter 11, and prophecy tells of approaching judgment. So it is with the first man.

Under his son Rehoboam it comes in part and soon; for Jeroboam rebels with the tribes of Israel, leaving Judah. Rehoboam must bow to the word of God (chapter 12). Prophets rise into marked prominency, and especially in Israel now apostate and idolatrous; as Jeroboam was made to feel (13, 14), though he adheres to his sin. Abijam follows Rehoboam in evil; Asa shows piety, but trusts in a Syrian alliance to his sorrow (15). The godly Jehoshaphat succeeded, though he too failed in allying with Ahab and Ahaziah. At this time was the ministry of Elijah the prophet and of Micaiah (17-22). But we need not dwell on the details, of wondrous interest and instruction though they be.

5.12 2 Kings

Ahaziah fights against Jehovah and perishes (chapter 1). Jehoram is no better. Where the king, as in Israel then, was not a link of relationship with God, but rather a witness against Him as being idolatrous, the prophet was so in extraordinary grace. But now Elijah was to be caught up, yet not before Elisha is called, as it were from that ascension, and hence has a character of grace as marked as his in righteousness who retired to Horeb, confessing that all was over as to Israel. Jericho is relieved from the curse, though the mockers are punished (chapter 2). Moab fights in vain (3). Miracles of mercy abound, even to deliverance from death and to the outside Gentile (4, 5); so that the baffled foe comes no more. The famine yields to unexpected plenty (chapters 6, 7). Israel will yet be restored (8), whatever humiliation may be even for Judah, whatever changes in Israel (9, 10). Judah seemed menaced with the destruction of the royal house: but a branch is hid, the pledge of sure blessing (11) at the end, and of judgment preceding. The Syrians meanwhile oppress both Judah (12) and Israel (13), though dying Elisha helps the king who failed in faith to consume the foe. The pride of Judah's king received its humiliation (14); and Jehovah relieved the bitter afflictions of Israel.

Then the Assyrian is bought off by Menahem, during the long reign of Azariah (or Uzziah) over Judah (15). But Pul is followed by Tiglath-Pileser who sweeps into captivity the north of the land. In Jotham's time the kings of Syria and Israel begin to act against Judah; but in the days of Ahaz, wicked as he was (16), Jehovah pronounces the failure of their confederacy. Yet later, in the reign of Hezekiah is Samaria taken, and Israel as a whole carried away (chapter 17), according to Jehovah's judgment of their apostasy; whereas the Assyrian Sennacherib has his blasphemy punished by an unexampled blow from Jehovah in one night, as he was slain afterwards by his own sons in the house of Nisroch his god (chapters 18, 19). The trustful son of David typified the final fall of that power, when Messiah shall reign, great even unto the ends of the earth (Micah 5:1-6). But *his* rising as it were from death is followed by vainglory before the ambassadors from Babylon; when the prophet announces Judah's captivity to this power, not to the Assyrian (chapter 20).

The revival in that day no doubt gave rise to fond hopes; but it is succeeded by the enormous wickedness of Manasseh (21), and his imitating son, Amon. The pious fear of Josiah (22, 23) was but a brief stay of the impending ruin, which was hastened by the iniquity of those summed up in Matthew 1:11 as "Jechoniah and his brethren". Pharaoh and Nebuchadnezzar might contend for a little while; but the divine design had long been uttered. Out of Egypt Israel was called; into Babylon Judah must go (24, 25), and now, utterly corrupt and apostate, became the slave of the patroness of corruption; till all her graven images were broken to the ground, and the avenger said of Jerusalem, She shall be built, and to the temple, Thy foundation shall be laid. This however was but providential.

Grace only can really meet the need to the divine glory, crushing all the power of Satan; though for the earth God will be glorified in Israel. This Christ takes up in Isaiah 49 where He substitutes Himself for the utterly ruined people; while His rejection and atoning death become the pivot for deliverance and righteousness, power and glory. What design so worthy of God, so blessed for man and Israel? And this it is which runs through the four books just surveyed. All the wit of man would have failed to conceive or express the ways of divine government here traced. God alone was capable of forming such a moral already accomplished in the realities of that land under the sway of kings (for the most part failing and judged), but with ample foreshadow of overturning, until He come Who alone is worthy, to Whom the kingdom will be given.

5.13 1 Chronicles

That there is a purpose in the book of Chronicles, now divided into two, distinct from that which runs through the preceding books of Kings, is unquestionable. No "And" connects their beginning, as before. But the Septuagintal title of Παραλειπόμενα, "Things deficient or omitted", fails to describe it adequately. A great deal is repeated though not without characteristic differences, while very much is fresh with notable omissions of a markedly homogeneous kind. The introductory genealogy from man's existence on the earth ought to have shut out the notion of a mere supplement, and prepared for a special design of God; Who here points out, in the midst of general ruin, His sovereign mercy and blessing bound up with the house of David and the tribe of Judah, whatever His chastenings because of their sins. They were a spiritual retrospect, like Deuteronomy, which also is not in continuity with its predecessors, though to the believer undoubtedly of Moses, as the Chronicles in all probability of Ezra, both admitting of a little inspired addition to complete them. But there is no such ground to insist on Ezra here, as on Moses there, who claims the book with unusual precision; so that one must accept this, *or* treat it as a fraudulent romance and risk the consequence both now and before the judgment-seat of Christ.

The so-called first book parts into two sections, chapters 1-9:34, and 10-29.

In the nine chapters constituting the preliminary section we have the principle long after formulated by the apostle Paul, not first the spiritual but the natural, then the spiritual. Even the general genealogy of chapter 1 is governed by this divine purpose. That of the sons of

Israel from chapter 2 follows the same rule. In chapter 3 are named David's sons, born in Hebron and in Jerusalem, Judah thus occupying the space from 2:3 to 4:23, the sons of Simeon following who were allotted there and were specially associated as in Judges 1. How Reuben, the firstborn, lost the primacy which sovereign grace gave to Judah, though the birthright passed to Joseph, we read in chapter 5; and Reuben's war with the Hagarites, which leads to a brief notice of the Gadites and Manassites, his neighbours. Then comes the incomparably fuller view of the Levites and Aaron's sons in the long chapter 6; as those of Issachar, Benjamin, Naphtali, the other half of Manasseh, Ephraim, Asher, curtly follow in chapter 7. But Benjamin reappears particularly in chapter 8 to bring in Saul, his forefathers and descendants. Dan and Zebulun are not even noticed. Chapter 9 sketches the circumstances on the return from Babylon, when some of Israel, but especially the saved and the royal tribes came back, in and near Jerusalem.

We may regard the history opening with Saul and his house in chapter 9:35, but hastening to his sad end on mount Gilboa, with the Holy Spirit's moral comment on it in chapter 10. Thereon, for here too the spiritual was after the natural, follows the true king of Jehovah's choice, not in Hebron only but Jerusalem; Zion taken; and his worthies named in chapters 11, 12. Then we have the ark with the failures that first hindered in 13, while David was blessed when he was dependent on God (chapter 14); but at length he honoured God in due order and reverence for the ark to the joy of all but Michal (15). Yet was its place only provisional, whatever the blessing and praise on that day (16). David's son was to build Jehovah's house (17), and his thanks rise higher still in the assured and everlasting blessing of his own house.

David's conquests and prosperous reign through Jehovah's favour appear in chapter 18, and the Ammonite king insults him to the ruin of himself and his allies (chapters 19, 20). David's terrible fall in the matter of Uriah and Bathsheba is left out, as well as his tribulations before he reached the throne; not so in the pride that counted Israel, which drew from Jehovah pestilence, arrested at Ornan's threshing-floor, Mount Moriah, thereon bought by David as the site for Jehovah's house (chapters 21, 22). The sanctuary then becomes actively his concern, and his charge to Solomon to build it, and to the princes of Israel to help.

Then in chapter 23 David divides the Levites for their services, and in 24 the sons of Aaron into their twenty-four courses, as in 25 the singers and musicians into a like number. The doorkeepers and other officials are seen arranged in chapter 26. Then in 27 we have the civil officers for every month, and heads of tribes, and the royal controllers in their several places.

In 28, 29 the king repeats his charge before all the chiefs as to Solomon and the house to Jehovah's name, with its inspired pattern and his ample store of material, stirring up pious generosity in the men of means, and blessing Jehovah before all with sacrifice abundant. Solomon is again made king, with Zadok priest. And David's close is touchingly recounted, with Solomon reigning in his stead: the twofold type of Christ, as we have seen in Moses and Joshua. The episode of Adonijah, &c., is only in the Book of Kings.

5.14 2 Chronicles

The continuation begins with Solomon in the same aspect as David. It is the figure of the kingdom. How blessed when the Great King reigns, with Whom is no failure, but blessing to the full! Solomon's faults, like David's, it was not the point to name, save where otherwise it was required. "Jehovah his God was with him and magnified him exceedingly." But the brazen altar was before him as before the people, rather than the ark, David's delight. He asked wisdom of God, and received also riches and honour beyond all (chapter 1). But the house of Jehovah engaged him rightly, and the king of Tyre helped him, and all the strangers in the land served (chapter 2). This is described in 3, 4 and the assembly on its completion, with their hallelujahs when the glory of Jehovah filled God's house (chapter 5), for indeed He only is Elohim: so little have diverse documents to do with the terms. And Solomon's prayer goes up with blessing in chapter 6, and the fire came down from the heavens as answer in chapter 7. It was the feast of Tabernacles, as well as of the altar's dedication, kept with joy and gladness; and Jehovah appeared to Solomon, but not without solemn warning. The Gentile gives gifts (chapter 8), and Pharaoh's daughter has her separate house; and his fame spreads far and wide, so that Sheba's queen comes with her precious things and proving his wisdom (chapter 9), as indeed all the kings of the earth owned it.

Next Rehoboam fools away all but Judah and Benjamin, and Israel rebelled against David's house (chapter 10); but here the contrast with the preceding books is striking, for we have no account save of what adhered loyally and in faith. Even Rehoboam bowed to the man of God sent to prohibit his avenging Israel's defection (chapter

11); yet afterwards (12) forsaking the law he was chastened by the hand of Shishak. Abijah, who succeeded and had more faith, inflicted a severe blow on Jeroboam and Israel. So with Asa in chapter 14, before whom Ethiopia's myriads fell, and who was blessed in hearing Oded the prophet, chapter 15. But relying on Syria against Israel (chapter 16), he was smitten of God by a lingering death. The bright reign of faithful Jehoshaphat follows in 17-20, yet with the blot of joining himself with the idolatrous kings of Israel for state purposes to his shame more than once.

Of Jehoram and Ahaziah there is only evil to say in 21, 22; and the wicked Athaliah seemed to have extinguished the lamp of David's house; but not so: Jehoiada, the priest, conceals the heir in the house of God six years. In chapter 23 we read how the young king got his own again, and the murderous usurper came to her death. But Joash too forgot his debt to Jehoiada when his son Zechariah was slain by the people at the king's command; and he too (24) publicly and personally came to grief. Amaziah had a mixed career according to his behaviour and ended ill, chapter 25; and Uzziah reigned well and long, but he also transgressing in pride became a leper judicially till his death, chapter 26.

Jotham did better, as we read in 27, but Ahaz ("that is that King Ahaz") walked in the ways of Israel's kings, and spite of calls of grace (28), sank lower and lower. His son Hezekiah was simple and strong in faith, as we see in chapters 29-32, and honoured in the overthrow of the Assyrian. Yet he got lifted up at last; though here again the Spirit omits the details of his sickness, and his vain display before the ambassadors from Babylon, both only touched on in the Chronicles. The horrors of Manasseh's reign are shortly given, and also his repentance and restoration after captivity; Amon's evil follows in the same chapter 33, but punished by his own servants who were themselves punished.

In the midst of Judah more and more corrupt, how marked is the tender conscience of Josiah (34), with boldness for Jehovah's honour and hatred of idolatry and heed to the word of God! so that the passover was kept as not before since Samuel's days (35). But fighting without divine direction he fell before the then king of Egypt. The evil under Jehoahaz, Jehoiakim, Jehoiachin, and the profane Zedekiah brought on the destruction of the kingdom, of Jerusalem and the temple, with the captivity of the remnant in Babylon (36). "There was no remedy." After seventy years Cyrus the Persian according to the word of Jehovah proclaimed the return and the rebuilding of His house at Jerusalem.

5.15 Ezra

This book has its own design from God, manifestly distinct from that of Kings as well as Chronicles, even if the style of the latter did not point to the same writer, "a ready scribe in the law of Moses which Jehovah, the God of Israel, had given." In fact however the book before us was joined, not with the Chronicles, but with Nehemiah, though this was by the governor's hand, long designated together "the Book of Ezra", and it would seem, only late in the fourth century after Christ separated as we now have them. Ezra was not the witness of the facts in chapters 1-6, as he was of those in the remaining four; but there is no sufficient ground to doubt that he was inspired to give us all.

The overthrow of Babylon was an event of signal moment, not only in itself and its immediate consequences, but yet more as prefiguring the judgment of the Gentile dominion from the God of heaven on the actual apostasy and ruin for the time of Jehovah's people. This is made plain in Isaiah 13, 14 where, as none ought to doubt that it predicts the catastrophe that befell the beauty of the Chaldeans' pride by the Medes, &c., so none should overlook that "the Burden" does not stop short of the final downfall of the power which "the golden city" began. Then will Jehovah have compassion on, not on a mere remnant of Judah chiefly, but "on Jacob, and will yet choose Israel, and set them in their own land", and "they shall take them captive whose captives they were; and they shall rule over their oppressors."

This book of Ezra was of the utmost importance to show the divine account of the intervening provisional state in which they waited for the Messiah, and the fulfilment to the utmost when they are completely restored to the land, under the new covenant, and have the true David and David's Son reigning over them in power and glory. They are meanwhile Lo-ammi (not-My-people); they *are* (not "were") bondmen of the Gentile power. Compare Ezra 9:9, and Nehemiah 9:36 which makes the correction certain. Yet Cyrus had proclaimed more than liberty to return and even a charge to build Jehovah His house in Jerusalem according to prophecy. Withal he returned the captured vessels, gold and silver, by Sheshbazzar, prince of Judah (1); and the children of the captivity went up (2), every one to his city, upwards of 42,000 genealogically reckoned, besides their servants male and female. Most appropriately they set up, not first a wall, but the altar, and offered Burnt-offerings, and kept the feast of Tabernacles (for it was the seventh month), with other dues to Jehovah according to His word, before the foundation of the house was laid.

When it was laid before their eyes, greatly wept the old, loudly shouted the young (3). But the adversaries were on the alert, first pretending a friendly alliance, next accusing the returned remnant to Cambyses (≈Ahasuerus), and as he evidently would not oppose his father's decree, then to Smerdis (≈Artaxerxes), who lent them his ear; and the work ceased (4). But the prophets, looking to God, re-awakened their zeal by their prophesying (5); and the work went on, notwithstanding the opposition of influential antagonists, before the fresh letter to Darius Hystaspis brought out his decided confirmation of Cyrus' original proclamation. The house was finished in his sixth year, and its dedication kept with joy; and remnant though they were, shorn of their chief ornaments, they embraced all Israel in faith and subjection to the word; as in due time they kept the passover duly purified and joyfully, though owning the Gentile king in the bondage to which God had reduced them because of their departure from Himself (6).

After these things, in the seventh year of Artaxerxes Longimanus, Ezra the priest went up from Babylon, and with him other Israelites of all grades by the king's favour, and with free-will offerings, and authority for all Ezra wanted for the house of his God, and instruction and judging of the Jews: a witness alike of divine mercy through the Gentile, and of the abnormal position of Israel (7). The genealogy follows in chapter 8 of Ezra's companions, their fears, yet faith, and safe arrival. But this faithful servant of God, when he learnt the affinity of those already in the land with the Gentiles, sat down grieved and overwhelmed until the evening oblation; then he poured out with tears his humiliation to Jehovah (chapter 9). There Shechaniah confessed for the rest (10); and they agreed to put away the evil at a solemn assembly of all by proclamation. So too it was done, though not without resistance; for the sin was widespread, even among the priests.

5.16 Nehemiah

Not less distinct is God's design in the book of Nehemiah. But it is their civil policy, not their religious position. Both must be according to God, but in the lowly estate that became captives returned from Babylon. Pretension in either would have dishonoured God; but obedience is ever imperative: no ruin absolves from its obligation. In this book we have his own touching account of the grief that filled him even at the Persian court in Artaxerxes Longimanus's twentieth year, when he heard of the great affliction and reproach under which the remnant lay, the wall even still broken down, and the gates burnt with fire. So he gave himself to mourning and prayer to the God of heaven. Still He was God and would hear supplication (1). The great king perceived his sadness, though a forbidden thing there; and his cup-bearer, not without fresh prayer, made his request to build the city of his fathers' sepulchres, which was granted, to the vexation of new adversaries. But Nehemiah saw all with his own eyes, though by night; and only then laid his purpose to build the wall before the chief men, who were cheered and strengthened accordingly, whatever the scorn and despite of their neighbours (2).

Great things were far from Nehemiah, but jealousy for God and persevering love for Israel in their utter weakness and shame. Chapter 3 is the deeply interesting account of their labours in detail from the high priest down to the least. If nobles failed here, even a ruler's daughter repaired elsewhere. Great was the anger and indignation of Sanballat; bitter the contempt of Tobiah; but Nehemiah prayed and set a watch, and they built with swords girt on, and the trumpeter by the governor (4). What mortification and anger, when he heard of Jews exacting usury of their brethren, and even enslaving them as the issue! So he put them to shame and redressed the wrong; as his own unselfishness rebuked them (5). Then we see him in chapter 6 escaping the snare, as before the violence, of the foe; and the wall is finished, in spite of treachery in priests, prophets, and nobles. The genealogy of the returned captives under Zerubbabel here appears in chapter 7 in connection with his repeopling Jerusalem and building houses in it.

Next in chapter 8 we are told, as the seventh month was come, all the people gathered, and Ezra read the book of the law; and when the people wept, they were exhorted to good cheer; for a day that is holy to Jehovah does not call for gloom. But obedience is of all moment always; and so they judged all previous departure, as they had not done since Joshua's time. Chapter 9 shows them fasting shortly after, as becomes them, with a true repentance: so in Ezra's case before. Chapter 10 gives the list of those who sealed the covenant of separation from strangers and of confession of sins from the Tirshatha downwards; as in chapter 11 we have those who devoted themselves to reside in Jerusalem and its suburbs. Again, chapter 12 furnishes the names of the priests and the Levites that had first returned, and those descended till subsequent days. The dedication of the wall follows.

The closing chapter brings us down to the time when Nehemiah came again from the Persian court in the two and thirtieth year of the king (13:6). Then a fresh effort was made to separate Israel from the strange multitude, the house of God was purged from impurity, the sabbath vindicated, and mixed marriages put an end to. For even the high priest's son was guilty and repulsed by Nehemiah.

5.17 Esther

More striking still is the special divine design here, of which the omission of God's name is an essential part. It was intended to mark that, when the people, already Lo-ammi, were in such circumstances among the Gentiles that His name could not be named, His secret providence on their behalf comes out unfailingly. This is so sure and manifest, that no detailed proof is required. Yet deep religious feeling is latent throughout, as in the Jewish horror of the Agagite, the fasting of Esther, and the feast of Purim. It was indeed what people call an "invisible church" to the utmost.

The Septuagintal addition, we may add, brings in God's name to the destruction of that silence which so embarrasses Canon Rawlinson and most persons. When the people were in such a state that God could not own them, He unseen, unnamed, cares for them. How could He acknowledge a daughter of Israel married to the great king? The book looks at the dispersion, as Ezra and Nehemiah did at the returned remnant. It is thus unique as well as invaluable throughout its ten chapters.

As a type, it shows us the Gentile bride set aside who failed to display her beauty, and the Jewish one established in her stead. The enemy may rage in a last effort of destructive malice; but all ends in his own ruin and that of his instruments, but to the joy of Israel and of the nations under righteous rule throughout the vast dominion. How will not Christ administer the kingdom to the glory of God the Father!

5.18 Job

Having thus surveyed the historical parts of the Old Testament with a view to the question of divine design, it remains for us to apply the same research into the poetical books, at the head of which in the English and many other Bibles stands that of Job. No sufficient ground appears for doubting that it rightly opens this fresh division of Old Testament scripture. Even those free handlers of the Bible (who admit the impossibility of fixing the date of this book precisely, but would like to bring it down to Jeremiah's age) allow the weight of Ezekiel 14:14-20 for the true personality of the patriarch, his known righteousness, and the proved value of his intercession. The internal evidence of the book points to patriarchal times and manners; the religious observances, and even the idolatry which was spreading, though (like adultery) an iniquity for the judge, all confirm the bearing of his age. On the other hand the prologue and the epilogue naturally imply that the writer of the book was not earlier than Moses, though recounting the great debate which supposes God not so known. Indeed not a few of weight have been impressed by the similarity of its narrative to the book of Genesis.

This, however interesting in a literary way and otherwise, is quite subordinate to its inspiration. Nor do the neo-critics, though self-sufficient and scornful because of their inability to appreciate Elihu's speeches, fail to see the transcendent superiority of what Jehovah says here, as compared even with the grandest strain of Isaiah on a kindred theme. What then is the design of the book which proves God to be its author? What place does it hold in the Bible peculiar to itself, worthy of Him, and needed by man?

Here in the midst of the sacred writings of Israel stands a book, which no Jew of his own motion would ever have written or could even have conceived. For it authoritatively reveals the deepest interest of the true God in a man outside the fathers or the sons of the chosen race, a son of the east in the land of Uz, "perfect and upright, one that feared God and abstained from evil." Who can wonder at the outbreak of the early rationalism clearly as in Maimonides? Jewish pride would like to see in Job no more than a fictitious personage. Yet if even an inspired romance were really possible, the difficulty would remain. For the case presented is as overwhelming to Jewish narrowness, as it must cheer any soul on earth that knew it. The curtain is drawn (chapter 1) for the occasion from the unseen world, that the believing reader may know that God initiates the unparalleled trial about to open for the good of Job, and challenges the ever active Adversary. "Hast thou considered my servant Job? for there is none like him in the earth" &c. Satan imputes a selfish motive for Job's piety; and all belonging to him is left for the evil one to blast. This he at once willingly executes by natural means: a lesson of great value, nowhere else in the Old Testament taught so clearly. Satan fails. In the midst of family joy and his own piety messenger follows messenger, of Sabean and Chaldean raids, of lightning and tempest, which swept from Job all his oxen, sheep, camels, and children; but Job blessed His name as to all, and sinned not.

The Adversary reappears with the sons of God on high (chapter 2) and, challenged yet more, he obtains leave to touch Job's bone and flesh, apart from his life: not that this would have really made a disadvantage to Job; but it would have hindered the end of the Lord. Even when a mass and a spectacle of suffering, with his wife tempting him, Job cleaves to God, and Satan vanishes. But God carries on the trial; for the hindrance was not yet reached, and Job's self-complacency might and must have been enhanced by his patience in sad adversity, had all stopped there. So his three friends come, each from his own place; and their sympathetic grief brings out Job's passionate cursing of his day (chapter 3), and desire for death to close his trouble. He is being laid bare and humbled in his own eyes before God, as he never had been before.

His friends, though pious men, knew still less of God and of themselves than the afflicted and now complaining saint. They each and all come out in their own thoughts, farther from the truth God was teaching than Job; for they assume the adequacy of present results as the criterion of God's estimate of man. Now there is a providential government, which overrules evil, and which does good according to God's nature; but His word reveals only at the close righteousness governing, and later still righteousness dwelling when all things are made new. Meanwhile God makes all things work together for good to those that love Him, humbling them, pious though they be, with what they are, and giving delight in God and submission to Him. We thus learn ourselves as well as God.

In this sketch it is not called for that we analyse the discussion that ensues. Suffice it to say that there are three series of speeches: from Eliphaz more grave and courteous; from Bildad more formal and severe; and from Zophar more suspicious; to each of whom Job replies respectively. The third time, Zophar, the least weighty and the most violent, is silenced. But Job took up his parable again, as if for him also, unless indeed we may not better regard chapters 27, 28 as more general, and chapters 29-31 as a closing summary which contrasts his bright past with his dark present, whereon he then confidently appeals to God. It is anything but a religious drama, or epos, or philosophy, as it has been called. It is a divinely given disclosure in a living saint's case for the instruction of man at any time (independently of special position as of Israel in particular), though for his correction too as peculiarly needing it. There we have a saint in the relationship with God which faith forms, exposed to the conflict of good and evil. Thus, as we discern Satan's enmity here below behind second causes and his accusation on high, we may also know God's gracious interest all through as before heaven. Not only is thus proved the failure of any righteousness on our part as a standing before God, but the necessity for such a daysman (or mediator) as the Lord Jesus, perfect God and perfect man.

But the intervention of Elihu is of the greatest moment, however people may disparage it who do not enter into the truth or feel their personal need of it. For he speaks as the requisite interpreter, "one of a thousand", and while exposing the rashness of Job and the inability of his friends to solve the difficulty, he furnishes the key:— God uses trial and suffering for the blessing of souls. This he shows in chapter 33 as to man generally, to deliver him from going down to the pit; while in chapter 36 it is to open to instruction the ears of the righteous, who might be sadly wrong and fall.

This was much for the good of souls. But more was vouchsafed; for Jehovah answered Job out of the whirlwind (chapters 38, 39), not by argument nor even by instruction, but displaying the witness of His majesty and power, so that Job was constrained to say, "Behold,

I am of small account: what shall I answer thee? I lay my hand upon my mouth: once have I spoken, and I will not answer; yea twice, but I will proceed no farther" (40:3-5). Jehovah answers again out of the whirlwind, by presenting two creatures, behemoth and leviathan, to enforce Job's sense of powerlessness, and the folly of his presumptuous words, so that he again confesses (42:2-6), "I know that Thou canst do all things, and that no purpose of Thine can be hindered. Who is this that hideth counsel without knowledge? Therefore I uttered what I understood not, things too wonderful for me that I knew not. Hear, I beseech Thee, and I will speak. I will demand of Thee, and inform Thou me. I had heard of Thee by the hearing of the ear; but now mine eye seeth Thee: wherefore I abhor [myself] and repent in dust and ashes."

It is an unintelligent objection that when Eliphaz, Bildad, and Zophar are censured, and owe their pardon to Job whom they had wholly misjudged, Elihu does not appear. He had done his good work: Jehovah alone must be exalted. And the captivity of Job was turned when he prayed for his friends; and Job got twice as much as before. Typically it applies to Israel when the time comes for His mercy to the erring people, then blessed more than at the first. But meanwhile for souls from the day it was written what an unfolding of the divine ways with those that fear God! They, because they are His, must learn the folly of their own heart, and confide submissively in what He is, not only in Himself and His work, but this in His ways toward them.

That still higher and deeper things appeared in Christ on earth, and by the Holy Spirit when He went up on high, is true; but such divine and heavenly communications in no way set aside the immense worth of the book before us, the design of which is unique in the Bible. And who but God Himself could have given it?

5.19 THE PSALMS

The special character of the Psalms is undeniable. In no part of scripture is the design of God more evident. This is the more notable, because of the variety of writers concerned, and the profound arrangement of their contributions, not superficially according to source or time, but by a distinct and divine purpose which governs the due place of no less than 150 several pieces, some alone, others in groups, all falling under five large sections, each with its own scope and its marked conclusion.

Of these the first comprises Psalms 1 to 41; the second has 42 to 72; the third contains 73 to 89; in the fourth are 90 to 106; and the last gives us 107 to 150, where the end comes without any form of expressing it as before. The first section, as one may gather from its contents, presents prophetically the general principle of the godly discriminated from the wicked among the Jews. Yet they are still together for the city and the sanctuary; and the covenant name of Jehovah predominates accordingly. In the second, on the contrary, the godly are a remnant who are severed from the multitude with whom they used to pass along to the house of God, as its opening intimates. They are sorrow-stricken and ask Elohim to do them justice against an ungodly nation. Here accordingly, as deprived of public and common covenant privileges, they fall back on what God is in Himself, and the abstract name predominates. A striking proof of this appears from comparing Psalm 53 with 14. The third section, which has the divine names more mingled from Elohim to Jehovah, opens and goes through with the introduction of Israel as object of divine goodness, but such only "as are of a pure heart", with all the nations jealous and hostile coming under judgment. The fourth division, after an appropriate exordium, strikes the note of a psalm-song for the Sabbath, and is filled with Jehovah reigning when He again brings the First-begotten into the inhabited earth; and here with the covenant name we find also the Most High and the Almighty. The last part celebrates Jehovah in the redemption of His people from the oppressor's hand, and their ingathering out of all countries, east, west, north, and south. It furnishes a believing and moral review of all that had passed, the virtues of the law written thenceforward on Israel's heart, and an affecting series of songs of degrees, followed after due interval by an ever swelling chorus of Hallelujahs, universal and lasting while earth endures.

As the history of man and of Israel is but the history of sin and ruin, but on God's part from man's fall were given communications of grace in prophecy and promise, so we have in the Old Testament this beautiful and central book whose undercurrent is "the sufferings of Christ and the glories that should follow them." Here we have the Holy Spirit providing inspired effusions from the heart and for the heart in sorrow and in joy, that the expression might have a divine savour through mercy and in truth, for His people passing through vicissitudes beyond all others, more favoured yet more guilty, in respect not only of the law, but of the Messiah, but at length brought out of all guilt as well as distress unequalled, repentant and meek, into the over-abounding joy of grace and the everlasting glory of the kingdom, when everything that has breath shall praise.

The Psalms therefore obviously and assuredly have the prophetic bearing which is stamped more or less plainly on all scripture. But they have the peculiarity of expressing the heart's feelings to God, produced by the Holy Spirit in poetic form, when holy men passed through grievous trials, as for instance David particularly, far the most fertile writer of Psalms. But we have the Lord's authority and that of the inspiring Spirit that an infinitely greater was the object of God, in some of them personally, in all of them His Spirit. This accordingly gave rise in the saints thus tried to the richest exercise of heart and conscience; which the Holy Spirit produced and clothed in appropriate language for others in similar or even deeper trials, especially those in which the Jew will be involved at the consummation of the age. Deepest of all are those which none but the Lord Jesus could adequately feel and express, such as Psalms 8, 16, 22, 40 &c. Many are the Psalms on the other hand which anticipate the glory which is to appear, and the triumph not in heaven only but here below for Him Who was rejected and put to shame and by none so bitterly as by His brethren after the flesh.

In the Psalms therefore, beyond every other part of the written word, we have the divinely inspired expression of the hopes and fears, of the dangers and falls, of the confessions and recoveries, of the self-judgment and the thanksgivings, of the praises and the blessings, of God's people. We have the outpouring even of the Lord Himself, alone in atoning for sin, associated with others in governmental affliction, and leading the praise where and when this could be. Who but God could have supplied all this with a vast deal more, and beforehand? Who could have combined the experience of man's trembling and agitated heart, with the consolations of divine grace suited to his state, in a form worthy of God and a bearing for all time, even for that when the groans of creation shall be changed into the joy of the earth in unison with the heavens, and the field shall exult, and all the trees of the forest sing for joy, when the floods shall clap hands and the mountains chant together? For Jehovah will judge the world with righteousness, and the peoples with equity.

The order of the Psalms was a final act of divine inspiration as certainly as the substance of every several psalm. There is an exact propriety in the succession, which in no case could be disturbed without loss, and thus forcibly attests the finger of God. The titles, where given, are significant of a deeper mind than man's, though naturally unintelligible to such as look only for what lies on the surface. The absence of a title has its meaning, though it may not always be the same.

Thus Psalms 1 and 2 have no title, not only to link them together, but this at the start as the preface to the first section and indeed also to the entire collection: one laying down the character of the godly man before Jehovah, whose hope is in Messiah; the other, the titles of Christ, as Jehovah's Son and King anointed for His holy hill of Zion, as surely as He will crush the nations and their kings in His day.

From 3 to 7 it is not the godly alone, nor Christ alone, but the Spirit of Christ in the godly. It is not Christ personally, but in His Spirit setting forth great moral principles. Thus in 3 it is faith in Jehovah, howsoever many be hostile; in 4 Jehovah sets apart the godly to Himself and hears him; in 5 it is confidence of blessing through Jehovah's righteousness for the righteous; in 6 he bows in distress before Jehovah in the sense of His just displeasure and pleads for mercy; in 7 he looks for His judgment falling on the wicked. Psalm 8 closes the group by passing from God's purpose about Christ to

His suffering in fact as Son of man, and even now highly exalted in a wider glory, as in result Jehovah's name excellent in all the earth.

Again, Psalms 9 and 10 plunge us into the latter-day crisis as the time to which in general the psalms apply, not the period of the gospel and the church. Hence the issue is judgment executed on the quick (hostile heathen and wicked Jews), not the rapture of the saints glorified to heaven. They are a pair, and regard the enemies without and within. And they are followed up by a connected series up to 18 which express in 11-13 the experience and feelings of the godly in those days. Psalm 14 contrasts the character of the wicked and the righteous in view of that day; and 15 replies to the challenge, Who shall dwell with Him then? Then in Psalms 16 and 17 Christ is seen as taking in grace His place therein, and in righteousness; whereas Psalm 18 identifies strikingly Messiah with His people from the deliverance out of Egypt at the outset till the Abiding One, when He becomes head, not of the church as now, but of the nations at the end of the age.

Next, one can scarce fail to see, come the divine testimonies of creation and the law in 19, then in 20 of Messiah answered in the day of trouble, and glorified in 21; whilst Psalm 22 is Messiah made sin and so forsaken to God's glory, resulting in grace flowing out more and more widely, if not then so deeply, till all the ends of the earth turn to Jehovah, and His righteousness is declared to a people that shall be born, on the ground of Messiah's doing. For after all, as we read in 23, 24, He as Jehovah guards His sheep when evil reigns, and will Himself be owned as Jehovah King of glory in the kingdom and house of Jehovah.

Then commencing with 25, 26 we have confession of sins and integrity of ways united in those that are His, emboldened by His sacrifice to own the truth and pursue holiness: a fresh start for the psalms to come. Whom should such a one fear? says Psalm 27, and (whatever the distress) Jehovah is his shield, Who will judge the wicked according to their deeds, as in 28. Hence the challenge in 29 to the sons of the mighty to own Jehovah, as every one in the temple says, Glory! Psalm 30 celebrates deliverance: if weeping comes for the night, there is joy at morn. Yet for this Messiah died, 31. Thus only could transgression be forgiven, sin be covered, and true blessedness come, 32; and thus alone could the righteous exult in Jehovah as in 33, its companion psalm, while Psalm 34 rises to a strain yet higher and sustained "at all times".

The next four psalms, again, contemplate the way and power of evil judicially, also the path of the righteous, as well as a just sense of their sins confessed; whilst Psalm 39 owns that it is to their chastening, though man walks in a vain show. The section worthily concludes with Christ, after death and resurrection, praising in a new song, faithful in obedience, as also in bearing sins, in word and deed and suffering to the uttermost (40); and blessed is he that understands the Poor One, if His own familiar friend lifted up heel against Him (41).

The second section regards the godly remnant as forced to flee and be outside Jerusalem (42). Compare Matthew 24:15, &c. For those within are in league with idolatrous Gentiles, being alike ungodly and apostate (43). "Arise", pleads 44. Christ too is no longer viewed in general as graciously in their midst on earth, but gloriously on high; as we see in 45. Elohim appropriately is their refuge in 46, but Jehovah Most High is anticipatively celebrated in faith, and this for all the peoples, a great King for all the earth (47). Whatever present things may say, the utter rout of earth's kings is seen by faith, and Zion is the hill of His holiness (48). Psalm 49 is a homily thereon: that day proclaims the folly of unbelief. Man in honour and understanding not is like the beasts that perish. Their wealth, lands, sayings, glory, come to nought. Only the redeemed abide. The chosen people in Psalm 50 were no better than the world, yea more guilty; but the godly made a covenant with God over sacrifice. In 51 like David they own corruption and blood-guiltiness; they recognise man's might under judgment, 52, and the folly of "the many" 53. But all the resource of faith is in God, 54, though the wilderness was better than the city traitorous to Christ, 55. Psalms 56, 57 are an evident pair, expressing confidence, and growingly, in that day of danger and distress. So are 58, 59 when God's judgment is owned as the only means to convince man of fruit for the righteous, and that God rules in Jacob.

In 60 the Jew accepts God's chastening, but looks for victory. In 61 he cries "from the end of the earth" (and it is mainly for his soul and the king's life); in 62 with enlarging expectation. In 63 the praise and blessing and soul-satisfaction rise, though he be still an outcast from the sanctuary. Psalm 64 spreads before God the deadly craft and evil of that day, but is sure of God's intervention; and also in 65 the outburst then of praise, silent long in Zion. Yea, all the earth shall shout aloud to God; and the godly one who had fled will then go into His house and pay the vows made in trouble, 66. Next 67 closes this group by the blessing of the Jew as the means for all nations to know God's salvation, never before nor otherwise.

The triumph of God, as Psalm 68 exultingly sings, is in and by Christ ascended on high. So shall His enemies be scattered when He arises; so shall the isolated be made to dwell in a home, and the kings of armies flee, and Jehovah dwell in Zion for ever, and the kingdoms of the earth sing to God: blessed be God! But what was not Christ's humiliation in order that it all should be righteously? This, 69 declares of Him, Who here speaks of being smitten and wounded of Jehovah. Indeed Christ bore reproach for His sake, for which judgment must follow on His enemies. Psalm 70 pleads for His deliverance, but withal to the shame of His wicked adversaries, and to their joy that sought Jehovah, Himself afflicted in order to it. Psalm 71 turns this principle to Jewish deliverance, "old" as they might be, but yet to renew their youth in praise; and so this portion closes with Psalm 72 "for Solomon". It is not the aged David, the man of war, but the Prince of Peace, Who introduces the rest of God, when the prayers of Jesse's son are ended. Who can doubt the divine design thus far?

The third division bears out its larger character as bringing in Israel and their Gentile foes so plainly that fewer words are here needed. Psalm 73 speaks expressly of the people thus; as 74 of their and His enemies. In 75 Messiah intervenes, judging with equity; when earth and all its inhabitants are dissolved, He bears up its pillars. Can any one doubt Who He is? or when? Psalm 76 speaks of the catastrophe for the kings of the earth when He dwells in Zion; not when His presence shines from heaven to the destruction of the Beast and the False prophet. But there is inward deliverance also as in Psalm 77. And the history of the people is turned more than ever to "instruction" in that day as in 78. But even when Israel is back in the land, Gentile hatred once more breaks out as we see in Psalm 79, and the people are not yet established in the new covenant. In 80 they pray that the Shepherd of Israel may shine forth, and His hand be on the Man of His right hand, the Son of man.

Psalm 81 bids the trumpet be blown at the new moon. It is the awakening and gathering of Israel, as 82 warns the judges of His arising to judge the earth. Nor will the confederacy of Gentiles, small or great (83), avail against God's hidden ones; their greed after His holy places will only bring out that He alone Whose name is Jehovah is the Most High over all the earth. Psalm 84 then points out the blessing, first, of dwelling where Jehovah dwells, in His house; next, of going up thither. Psalm 85 celebrates His favour, though the result was far from complete; for glory is to dwell in the land. Compare Isaiah 4 for Jerusalem. A suited prayer of David follows in Psalm 86; and Psalm 87 contrasts Zion with the passing splendour of the earth's great ones. But none the less do the godly feel and express in 88 the terrors of a broken law; and they cry to the God of their salvation accordingly. They had utterly failed in their relationship; but the Spirit of Christ in no way held aloof from this righteous affliction, Himself holy and spotless. Psalm 89 is the song of Jehovah's loving-kindness or mercies, the centre of which is the Merciful or Holy One in verse 19. They had lost all but His mercies in Christ, which abide and will yet be theirs "for ever".

The fit opening of the fourth section is Moses' prayer, Psalm 90. The sovereign Lord alone can say to crumbling man, Return, children of men. But this turns on the Messiah, Psalm 91, Whose work brings in the true sabbath song, 92. Jehovah then reigns, higher than the highest of creatures; and holiness becomes His house ever more, 93. Yet vengeance belongs to Him, dishonoured from the first, and most of all at the last, 94. But when the workers of iniquity are cut off, then goes forth Israel's joyous call to sing to Jehovah, 95, as in 96 all the earth is invited to sing a new song. Is not 97 the answer to that, as 99 to 98 where Israel is in question? In Psalm 100 they are all summoned to shout aloud and serve Jehovah with joy. There is no narrowness of heart more. If "we" are His people, enter "ye" into His gates with thanksgiving and His courts with praise. Psalm 101 is Messiah setting out the terms of His reign, mercy and judgment. Psalm 102 gives the ground of all blessing in His humiliation, Who was not the cast down Messiah only but Jehovah, as truly as He who lifted Him up; for He is the Creator of all. Then, Psalm 103, what praise in Israel flows out! What praise in creation, Psalm 104! What thanks given in Psalm 105 where Jehovah's ways of grace are retraced from the fathers down till the sons entered on the lands of the nations! What thanks, in Psalm 106 not less deeply but here adding, "for His loving kindness (or mercy) is for ever." Grace opens their lips to confess how they had sinned with their fathers, and done wickedly throughout the self-same history, and later still when carried captive. Now they say, "Save us, Jehovah our God, and gather us from among the nations to give thanks to thy holy name, to triumph in thy praise."

The fifth division begins with Psalm 107, in substance like the concluding one of the fourth, but adding the weighty facts in verses 2, 3, and recounting their varied providential past, wise now to understand Jehovah's mercy. Compare Romans 11:30-32. Psalm 108 is the joy of the Spirit of Christ when Israel is put in possession of their long forfeited inheritance. Here it is His mercy, truth, and glory. Now in 109 we have Christ rejected but exalted to help the needy, with judgment on the son of perdition first and last. Psalm 110 is David's Son and Lord exalted. Though Priest for ever after Melchisedek's order, He is about to smite through kings in the day of His anger, especially the "head over a mighty land": the just reply to 109.

In 111 to 118 we have a group celebrating Jehovah successively in His works and wonders: 111, in His commandments and righteousness; 112, in His character and dealings; 113, in praise, all being Hallelujahs; then in 114 is the effect on the earth of the presence of Jacob's God, as 115 is the humbling effect on Israel to His glory, blessed and blessing; and in 116 their love in Christ's Spirit as delivered from death like Jairus' daughter. Again, 117 calls all the nations to praise Jehovah, as 118 closes the set with "His mercy for ever" sung by Israel, Aaron's house, and those that fear Him. Through sore trial Israel had passed, but destroyed their foes; but it was in His name Who set the rejected Stone at the head of the corner; and in His name Messiah coming they bless.

Next in Psalm 119 we have Israel's state shown, the law written on their hearts, and its virtues analysed fully and distinctively. Then follows the series of fifteen "Songs of degrees", or steps in Israel's restoration, not yet fulfilled. In 120 the deceitful foe is discerned; in 121 Jehovah is looked to for help; and in 122 Christ's Spirit kindles their joy in worship. Then in 123 their eyes are devotedly lifted up to Jehovah; and in 124 the snare is broken, and they bless Him. In Psalm 125 they confide in Jehovah, peace on Israel; in 126 joy is reaped after sowing in tears, by Christ above all. Psalm 127 is for Solomon, contrasting the house and the city of the rest of God with the Babel-building that preceded, and looking for a blessed posterity. The blessing of Jehovah-fearers duly ensues in 128 and their many afflictions can now, in 129, be calmly remembered with the assurance of shame to all that hate Zion. Then 130 tells how forgiveness with Jehovah taught them to fear Him, and wait for Him, and hope; as in 131 the moral effect goes forth in subjection of heart, deepening that hope. Psalm 132 asks Jehovah to remember for David all his affliction, the figure of infinitely greater; and to arise into His rest, with answers from verse 14 exceeding every request. Next 133 points us to the beauteous dwelling in unity that results from the power of the Spirit, honouring a greater than Aaron in the blessing— life for evermore; while 134 ends this series with blessing rising up: night brings no pause, and Jehovah blesses out of Zion, king and priest being here together in it.

Psalm 135 is more general praise, though it and the succeeding 136 may be regarded as replying to the psalms of degrees. They are rehearsals. The first begins and ends with Hallelujah; the second resounds with Israel's known chorus.

Special circumstances, of the people's sorrow, and of Jehovah's fidelity to His word, begin in Psalms 137 and 138, while 139 gives the individual heart-searching in goodness of the Eternal, which encourages to pray,

"Search me, O God, and know my heart", &c. As the last foe has not fallen before the kingdom is established in peace, we have in 140 a prayer for his fall; so in 141 for preservation and profit by the discipline meanwhile. It is even more urgent in 142 and in sense of loneliness. Psalm 143 takes the deep ground that in His sight no man living shall be justified. It is a question of divine righteousness. So in Psalm 144 "Jehovah, what is man?" Why should He delay judgment and blessing for him? for Jehovah only has and gives might.

Psalm 145 is the Spirit of Christ in the Jewish saints praising for the kingdom; and Hallelujah psalms swell in volume to the end. Psalm 146 is the contrast in the man of Jehovah delivering His people; Psalm 147 His mercy to Jerusalem and Israel's outcasts with His blessing of creation. In 148 it is His praise "from the heavens", and "from the earth", with all therein; as Psalm 149 is His praise in the congregation of the godly (for such are Israel henceforth). Psalm 150 is praise to El (the mighty One), everywhere and in all respects, with every instrument and by everything that has breath. How evident is the special design of God not only in each psalm but in their arrangement! Man without Him was incapable of either.

5.20 Proverbs

The collection of "the words of the wise" which next claims our heed is as different in character from the book of Psalms as one can conceive, though both may be in form poetical, the latter in the highest degree. But they are the inverse of one another: the Psalms mostly presenting to us Jehovah, or God in His nature rather than in covenant, the expression by the Holy Spirit of His people's and His own feelings in their varying experience, in hopes and fears, joy and distress, as well as in the acknowledgment of His ways; the Proverbs, His wisdom in view of the difficulties and trials, snares and joys, and all other circumstances in the earthly path. The fear of Jehovah is the key-note. The special design of the book is unmistakable. No other part of the Bible fulfils or even shares its place. It communicates Jehovah's wisdom in its authoritative instruction of His people. Hence "God" as such occurs very sparingly in the prologue, 2:5, 17; 3:4; not at all in the strict "proverbs of Solomon" (10-24); once in the supplement which Hezekiah's men transcribed (25:2); and twice in the appendix of Agur's words (30:5, 9). This however gives no countenance to the dream of Astruc, but one more plain proof that it is false, senseless, and misleading.

After the preface of 1:1-7, we have a very full and affectionate introduction in the first nine chapters. In contrast with the authority given to parents is the enticement in the world through independence and lust, which calls to violence in chapter 1 and corruption in chapter 2. But if that authority works early and within, wisdom on Jehovah's part cries without, warning of the judgment at the end on the wicked man and the strange woman, and assuring of the moral value and blessing at all times for those that hear and prize her voice. In chapter 3 not our own intelligence but Jehovah's fear and instruction can avail. Hence in chapter 4 wisdom's words are to be sought to get true intelligence, avoiding all other ways. In chapter 5 is shown that only remorse and ruin come from swerving to corruption, while Jehovah would have His own enjoy the relations He sanctions. Chapter 6 warns against suretyship and sloth, evil activity and adultery; as chapter 7 pursues the latter in detail to death and Sheol. In chapter 8 the wisdom of God, energetic and importunate in love, rises up to Him Who is Son; as Christ is said to be His wisdom in the New Testament (object of Jehovah's delight), and His delights not merely in Israel but "with the sons of men". In chapter 9 wisdom has built her house with her seven pillars, answering to the house of God, as it were, and not His call only, but contrasted with "the foolish woman" who leads her victims to destruction. Wisdom has an organisation of good, as the strange and "clamorous" woman has of evil.

The intermediate chapters to 24, with the supplement in 25-29, present us the detailed wisdom of Jehovah for His people on the earth. The special walk of the Christian is not contemplated; still less is the church of God before us; any more than Christ suffering as God's witness, or for our sins, or His exaltation on high as Head, and in the heavenly sanctuary as Priest. But we have those divine apophthegms on the earthly path, which have drawn out the admiration of the wisest among men. After all they are but a selection from the "three thousand proverbs" which Solomon spoke (1 Kings 4:32). For God gave the king wisdom and understanding exceeding much, and largeness of heart, even as the sand that is on the sea-shore. And Solomon's wisdom excelled the wisdom of all the children of the east country, and all the wisdom of Egypt. For he was wiser than all men, than Ethan the Ezrahite, and Heman, and Chalcol, and Darda, the sons of Mahol; and his fame was in all nations round about. What we have is a selection made by the Holy Spirit: a principle just as true of the "signs" wrought by our Lord (John 20:30, 31; 21:24, 25). Every scripture is of God's special design.

Of the concluding chapters 30, 31 we would say here little more than that they are in keeping with the book and worthy of forming its close. They claim the character of "prophecy"; and every word bears the stamp of God. The picture of the matron in the last 22 verses (acrostics) of the book is beautiful, and shows what woman might be under the law, even before Christ came and gave her a yet higher dignity.

5.21 ECCLESIASTES

On the face of the book stands revealed this striking difference from the Proverbs that here Elohim, or God, is found from first to last, never once Jehovah. Hence it is not the people in special relationship, but man as he is. Indeed some found on this fact the absurd inference that, if Solomon for the most part wrote the former, he could not have written the latter. The books claim to have emanated from the son of David. This however is nothing to a rationalist, save perhaps one incentive more to deny it. Leaving such a question, the case confirms the truth which we have often asserted, that the use of these divine designations depends on the different objects in view, not on separate writers. In Ecclesiastes it is no question of covenant relationship and its prescribed order, but of God, of the Creator, and of man vainly seeking happiness in a ruined creation. Here therefore Jehovah would be wholly out of place. It is moral suitability under the Holy Spirit which regulates the choice quite independently of the writer, whether the same or a different person. It is therefore Elohim, and man having to do with Him and His judgment.

Thus here again God's special design is manifest; and so is the shortsightedness of learning, or rather of unbelief, in overlooking the intimations of the written word for an hypothesis of pure imagination. The truth on the contrary, if it be only in the designation, edifies and helps us so far to enter into the scope of the book. Here it is a book which has its own peculiar place; none other even resembles it. It is the experience of a man unequalled in his capacity, in his circumstances, and in his means (for what can the man do that comes after the king?) for quest of happiness, and finding only vanity and pursuit of the wind in all "done under the sun". How could it be otherwise, if man is an outcast from paradise, and looks not in faith to Him Who is above the sun? Experience, even the exceptional power, position, and activity of Solomon, experience of all that promises most on earth, ends in "vanity of vanities", as surely as experience of self does to the man born of God who is occupied with himself (Romans 7:7-24). All in man or the world is fallen and most wretched. Nor did wisdom itself avail to help, but rather intensified, the dissatisfaction and the sorrow. Death comes, and what does man as such know of that which is after it? To outward eye he dies as the brute. What then is for him but to fear God and keep His commandments? For this is the whole of man. For God shall bring every work into judgment, with every secret thing, whether it be good, or whether it be evil.

This has been counted pessimistic and sceptical; and so it would be if it were all. But the book itself urges the thankful use of the good God gives in a ruin so pervading. And if He gives them to weary themselves, it is to cast themselves on His fear and obedience, wherein is no vanity. But it was in no way the aim of the book to unfold sovereign grace, and its saving provisions.

"The words of the wise" are not positive here as in the Proverbs, but negative, acting as goads to turn from seeking good in the creature, seeing that the end of all is death. Of this, as it closes on man, is given a most poetical allegory at the close; as the book opens with the constant change stamped on all the creature around and within. What a contrast with the rest of God into which the work of Christ (here entirely out of sight) alone can introduce such as we are, which from the beginning pointed to the Messiah and redemption based on sacrifice! Even when God's house is named, it is for man to hear, and pay vows conscientiously, and fear God; but the forgiveness with Jehovah that produces fear is no more entered on here than propitiation is in Romans 2:1-16, where the apostle lays down God's immutable principles in dealing with men, be they who they may. Man needs God as a centre for his heart which the creature cannot satisfy.

5.22 Solomon's Song

Quite as unique is God's special design in Canticles, wherein neither Elohim nor Jehovah is once found, only Jah descriptively and not as an object (7:6). It is the Beloved and His love, the Bridegroom and the Bride as revealed to Israel; not the great secret as to Christ and as to the church, but a communication fully disclosed to the ancient people of God. (Compare also Psalm 45 and Isaiah 62.). The one who drew the bride's heart is the King, Messiah Himself; as this Song of songs is Solomon's. This need not hinder its application to the believer, or *mutatis mutandis* to the church; for there is a principle of relationship common to them all. It was an early error, especially from and even before the Constantinian epoch, to conceive Israel cast off for ever, and the church the heir of earthly honour and power.

Men forgot the warning in Romans 11 that this is but Gentile conceit, which loses the church's present suffering and future glory with Christ, and also denies the mercy which, when the Gentile calling corrupts itself and is cut off, will restore Israel and be to the world as life from the dead when the Lord comes to reign. Thus the key to Canticles got hidden; and the book was either lowered irreverently, and sometimes grossly enough as is natural to a rationalist, or elevated in error to a heavenly object, which finds its proper unfolding in Revelation 19-22, not here strictly or fully.

The church is the body of Christ glorified at God's right hand on high by virtue of the baptism of the Holy Spirit sent down as the fruit of Christ's known redemption. This explains the peace and calm enjoyment of our peculiar relationship even now, before the day comes for the marriage of the Lamb above, as we read in Revelation 19 which adds and keeps for us, in all its fulness, the power of hope in Christ's coming.

It is a different state we find here where the relationship has to be formed or re-established under the new covenant. Hence the varied antecedent experiences for the heart of which this book so largely consists, and which grace will turn to the blessing of the daughter of Zion. Nothing of the kind is found in the New Testament any more than a collection of Psalms; but they are both provided in the Old Testament about the ancient people, though all is surely for our use and blessing, although not about us. We are supposed to be in such peace, liberty, and joy by the presence of the Holy Spirit, as to make and sing our own psalms and hymns (1 Corinthians 14, Ephesians 5, Colossians 3). The misuse of these scriptures, as if the church were Zion, Judah, Israel, &c., has done much to judaize the

Christian. The blessing of their direct use will begin for the godly remnant before the day breaks; after which all Israel will sing them together—with what joy in that day! But who save God could have provided this wonderful anticipation?

5.23 Isaiah

The vision of Isaiah is here unrolled before us. What is the special design? One does not enquire whether the noblest and most comprehensive of the prophets wrote without a purpose. The question is then, judging by its contents throughout, what did God mean His ancient people, ourselves too who now believe, to consider His aim to be in the book? What does He teach in it as a whole?

Jerusalem and Judah have a marked prominence; but from first to last the holy seer was given to judge the moral ruin of Israel by the word of Jehovah and the future glory under the sway of the divine Messiah, when all the nations shall flow to the mountain of Jehovah's house. What could be more odious than sacrifices and offerings, new moons and set feasts, from rulers of Sodom and a people of Gomorrah? If we must reject the traditional delusion that Isaiah 2 opens with the progress of the gospel, how can rationalist unbelief face the plain intimation that only by the judgment He will execute are the people to be restored? and this, not nationally only but also in their souls, that only thus will all the nations be brought into glad and willing subjection? What for so good and grand an issue has present experience to do with either outlook? Surely not the hypocrisy of the Jews, or the idolatrous iniquities of all the nations.

Yet such were the actual facts. What sign, then or since, of Jerusalem thoroughly purged or of the Gentiles learning war no more? No, the Holy Spirit led the prophet to foresee the "end of the age", and the judgment of Jehovah's adversaries; neither the one nor the other as yet accomplished facts. He shall reign Whose right it is. In that day all pride shall fall, and every disorder be rectified; even each petty female vanity shall vanish (3). Yet it will not be by the gospel nor the church; but the Lord shall scour out corruption and violence by the spirit of judgment and of burning; and Jehovah will create over every dwelling-place the glory to be a canopy (4). Such is the introduction, each part ending with Israel's restoration, as does each larger section prove save the intermediary one.

Then follows in chapter 5 a song of lamentation touching His vineyard, the house of Israel, and Judah the plant of His delight, followed by manifold woes on His people, which introduces the refrain of His anger not turned away, and His hand stretched out still, closing here with darkness and distress on the land and light darkened in the heavens thereof. After a striking parenthesis in chapter 6 followed up in 7 to 9:7, the refrain is repeated from chapter 9:8, till the end comes in the Assyrian who had been the rod of His anger (chapter 10:5), now to be punished and destroyed when the Lord has performed His whole work on mount Zion. "For yet a very little while, and the indignation shall be accomplished, and mine anger, in their destruction." Deliverance comes by divine judgment. Who He is that makes good both is given in chapter 11 with Israel's song of joy in chapter 12. But the parenthesis which is occupied with Judah and David's house had already prepared for this. For His divine glory is seen according to

John 12 in chapter 6; then in 7 His incarnation; in 8 His claim too (as Immanuel) to the land; and in 9, after the eclipse of His rejection, when Jehovah hid His face from the house of Jacob, His victory over the oppressor as in the day of Midian, when His glories are proclaimed. Thus the general course of judgment, as well as the parenthetic revelation of Messiah rejected but at last intervening for judgment of the foe, coalesce. Such is the remainder of the first section, ending in Jehovah's praise, and the Holy One of Israel great in the midst of Zion.

The second division consists of "burdens" or "oracles" of judgment from 13 to 23, ending with not the land only but "the world" languishing and fading away, and Jehovah punishing the high ones on high and the kings of the earth on the earth, but a fortress to the poor remnant of godly Jews, when the veil is destroyed that veils all the peoples; yea death is swallowed up in victory. Who can fail to discern the end of the age? For in that day shall be sung in Judah's land a song of victory; and a vineyard of verjuice no more, but of pure wine; and Israel shall fill the face of the world with fruit, as we read with much more in chapters 25-27. The end is full triumph for restored Israel, as throughout it appears briefly in each part. And how plainly the future is in view by beginning with Babylon and next Assyria! For historically every one knows this is not the order: compare Micah 5:4-7.

The portion that succeeds begins with "woe" to Ephraim, and "woe" to Ariel or Jerusalem, in chapters 28, 29, with moral "woes" going on to chapter 30 and in chapter 31 on those that go down to Egypt for help: Jehovah alone avails. In chapter 32 is the contrasted reign of Christ, and the Spirit poured out for that day on the earth, as already on the Christian for heaven. Chapter 33 is "woe" on the last spoiler, as 34 is the final slaughter in the land of Edom, which makes way for the wilderness and the parched land to be glad, indeed for all creation. And no wonder; for they shall see the glory of Jehovah, the excellency of Israel's God. The church, and all the glorified, will have a still more lofty and a deeper portion on high.

Then we have four prose chapters (36-39) of the greatest interest, evidently of prophetic type, and meant to brace together the two halves of this sublime prophecy by recounting the facts of Hezekiah's history, which begin with the blasphemous pride and the divine overthrow of the Assyrian, and end with the predicted removal to Babylon, occupying as it does large space in the unbroken stream of prophecy that follows. But even this interlude of external change would not have been complete without the inner revelation of the sickness unto death of the king, from which Jehovah raised him up (chapter 38), and which has its glorious counterpart in the infinitely greater Son of David, Who really died and rose again: the everlasting ground, not merely for the sure mercies of David toward Israel, but for all the divine counsels of blessing for all saints, for heaven and earth, for time and eternity. But what is this to the higher criticism so called? Alas! it derides true prophecy and miracle, and has no revealed future of blessedness or judgment, confessing neither the Father nor the Son. Is it of God, or of the enemy?

The profound and majestic dignity of the latter half (vainly attributed to "the Great Unnamed") is exactly suited to its more inward character, each section, though more secretly intimated than in the first half, centring in the Messiah. There are three distinct aspects in continuous flow. Chapters 40 to 48 are the first where Jehovah redeemed His servant Jacob, adumbrated by Cyrus' overthrow of Babylon, and his proclamation of liberty and return to the captive Jew. "There is no peace, saith Jehovah, to the wicked"; which only a far greater than Cyrus will effectuate. The second consists of chapters 49 to 57 where it is no question of idols judged in Babylon, as a chastening for the Jew but final and fatal for the heathen; but we have the still more impious and unbelieving guilt of the Jew in rejecting Jehovah-Messiah, with "no peace, saith my God, to the wicked." For this evil lies deeper and strikes at God Himself, not merely at His relative and continuous title as the God of ages, and governor of Israel. Lastly, the crown of blessing is to the end of the book, where faith in the Righteous Servant and in His atonement changes unrighteous Israel; and the elect from them become His servants, not only delivered from every foe at the last extremity, but brought into unchanging joy and glory; no longer a curse, but at the end of the age an everlasting blessing to all families of the earth, as was promised at the beginning of their history to their first fathers.

Who but God could have inspired so far reaching a plan, worthy of Himself and of His Son the Anointed! He, by unreserved obedience and infinite suffering in atonement, will deliver His people at last out of their manifold evil, wandering, and ruin, to become the ready servants of His good and holy will, and the honoured instruments as well as objects of His mercy in the great day, when Israel shall be as stable before Jehovah as the new heavens and the new earth which He will create. How sad the unbelief which doubts that the zeal of Jehovah will do this, and much more! How blind those who fail to see the glowing and splendid testimony of all the vision of Isaiah to it all!

Take the Incarnation so clearly predicted in chapter 7, yet in chapter 8 a stone of stumbling and a rock of offence to both the houses of Israel, while Jehovah hides His face from the guilty people, but has "disciples" given to the rejected Christ for signs, and for wonders, before the day of final victory and abiding joy. Then shall the nation be multiplied as in chapter 9 and say triumphantly, Unto us a child is born, unto us a son is given, and the government shall be upon His shoulders. And His name shall be called Wonderful, Counsellor, The mighty God, The Father of the age to come (or eternity), The Prince of Peace. Of the increase of His government and peace there shall be no end, upon the throne of David and upon his kingdom, to order it and to establish it with judgment and with justice henceforth even for ever. Is the trumpet's voice uncertain?

Take again His atoning death in chapter 53 and the glories surely to follow, though we have to wait for the Jews to look on Him Whom they pierced before He is set on Zion, and reigns as Jehovah over all the earth. How honestly deny true, divinely given, foresight in broad and clear instances like these, early and later? Indubitable fairly as they are, they serve to attest all the others as to Babylon, Cyrus, &c.—any of which have furnished matter for critical cavil. But the orderly design also of the book, both as a whole and in each of its seven parts, points to its divine author through Isaiah.

5.24a Jeremiah

The special object of Jeremiah's prophecy is no less evident than Isaiah's; yet is each as different in character and style from the other, as both are from Ezekiel and

Daniel. It was Jeremiah's lot to live and testify in the midst of guilty Judah hastening to utter ruin, and in the land for the most part during the crisis of its last kings of David's house. Instead of being the honoured prophet of the king (save Josiah of course), and dear alike to monarch and people, he was a weeping Seer. It was not his to see his prediction accomplished in the sudden judgment which befell the most arrogant of Assyrian monarchs, who in his retreat of shame perished by the hand of his own sons before the vain idol of his worship. We have before us the greatest and most constant sufferer among the prophets; and this at the hand, now of kings, now of priests and false prophets, now of princes, and of the people, the chosen people; who, after their rebellious contempt during his life, regarded him subsequently to his death as the chief of prophets.

No such immense sweep is compassed by the tender priest of Anathoth as in Isaiah's sublime vision with its rich and varied expression. But no book in the Old Testament is so distinguished as this of Jeremiah, on the one hand by entire identification with Jehovah's indignant denunciation of Jewish iniquity and apostasy, on the other hand by self-sacrificing love to the end toward his countrymen who despised and hated him for his faithful rebukes and solemn warnings. Yet the wicked Jews were not so wicked even at last as the higher critics. "That generation" in the spurious 2 Maccabees 2 represents him as appearing to their hero Judas Maccabeus as "a man with grey hairs and exceeding glorious, and a wonderful and excellent majesty to gird him with a golden sword": an imposture singularly out of harmony with all that scripture tells us of this prophet of sorrows, troubles, and woes. Yet as he was given to proclaim, not only the destruction of Jerusalem and the temple by Nebuchadnezzar and the captivity in Babylon, but also at the close of seventy years the downfall of that great city and the first of the proper world-powers, even "that generation" was not so incredulous as the self-exalting and God-defying scribes of the last century and our own, who are audacious enough to deny all true prediction as they do all real miracle, just as they reject the grace and truth that came by Jesus Christ and the future glory to be revealed.

Unbelievers may speculate about the Pentateuch generally, and Deuteronomy in particular; for nothing is easier than for sharp wits, armed by self-will, to conjure difficulties and doubts against books so ancient as they profess to be. But the prophet lived till the Four great Empires or the "times of the Gentiles" began, and extant human history more or less credible followed, to say nothing of monuments (spite of their vain-glory and too frequent lying), which confirm him in remarkable and unexpected ways. And as the authenticity of his writings cannot be justly questioned, so the punctual accomplishment of so striking a prediction deeply moved the Jewish mind. Thereby the saintly captive was led to look onward, not merely to the proximate and provisional return of a remnant to the land, but to the final and full and everlasting redemption of Jerusalem in the latter days.

Then Jehovah will turn again the captivity of His people *Israel and Judah*, who will possess (as they have not yet done) the land given to their fathers, and Jehovah will be the God of *all the families of Israel*. Yet it cannot be without the last and unparalleled time of Jacob's trouble; but he shall be saved out of it. "Behold, days come, saith Jehovah [not merely to "sow the house of Israel and the house of Judah", not for destruction and affliction, but to build and plant them], that I will make a new covenant with the house of Israel and with the house of Judah." It will not rest, as he declares, on man's weakness, but on divine grace. For Jehovah will put His law in their inward parts, and will write it in their hearts, and as He will be their God, so they His people knowing Him from the least of them to the greatest, and their sins remembered by Him no more.

But while Jeremiah laboured and testified, he had the bitter lot of his worst enemies among those he loved and pitied and censured so profoundly. This incredulity of Jehovah's word was caused by their rebellion of will against Jehovah Himself, as it ever is, whatever men say or boast. Nebuchadnezzar and his servants shone in honouring Jeremiah, in the most marked contrast with priests and false prophets and even kings Jehoiachim and Zedekiah. Nevertheless, as a true lover of God's people in their lowest estate and their base ingratitude to him, instead of going to Babylon where ease and honour were assured, he preferred to suffer affliction with the most despised in the land, who behaved as ill as ever and against his inspired warnings carried him down into Egypt, rather than abide in subjection to the Chaldean.

Who can doubt, whose ear is opened to hear, the specific design and unique place of Jeremiah's writings in the Bible? But, as before, a sketch of its parts is given in proof that the general estimate is only confirmed by the detail. Moral appeal to conscience in Jerusalem and Judah occupies the early half, or nearly so, chapter 1 being the prophet's inauguration as a young man. Nor is any fact more striking than the way in which the apparent disorder of the chapters as in 21-24, even in the Hebrew (to say nothing of the Septuagint), subserves the aim of God's Spirit by the truth. To characterise it as confusion among his writings owing to a violent death is a mere and arbitrary guess, which overlooks the moral purpose and design of God. Chapter 25 is a transition, declaring the providential judgment of nations, ominously putting Jerusalem and Judah in their forefront. In chapters 30-33 the entire people of God, all Israel, are promised restoration to the land with salvation (in its vital and blessed sense) in days to come, under a new covenant and the Messiah clearly announced to reign (as King in chapter 23:5), a Branch of righteousness unto David, as Jerusalem shall be called by the new name of Jehovah our righteousness. From chapter 34 to 38 is the word of Jehovah as to various kings of Judah, but not in historical order, save that they preceded the fall of Jerusalem; while those from 39 to 44 bear on what followed, 45 closing the section with the prophetic word to Baruch his amanuensis. The last series consists of predictions on foreign nations separately, as we may see also in the writings of Isaiah and Ezekiel. The last chapter 52 is expressly an appendix to the words of Jeremiah by the inspired editor. It is a most appropriate close of the prophecy and introduction to the Lamentations.

5.24B THE LAMENTATIONS OF JEREMIAH

It is notable, but by no means an unprecedented thing, that the book, which more than any other breathes the distress of a pious and broken heart, is clothed in a markedly artificial form. God meant His people to share the prophet's lamentation; and its predominant shape occupied his heart who wrote, and theirs who pondered and remembered it all the more. Its five chapters are five elegies. Chapters 1, 2 have twenty-two stanzas or verses, answering to the letters of the Hebrew alphabet, and each stanza with three parts. In the third chapter the initial letter occurs for each of the three parts, when the prophet speaks personally of his own sufferings, as before and after chapter 3 he pours forth his groans over the city destroyed with all its glories. In chapter 4 each stanza consists of two parts, each verse beginning with the successive letters of the alphabet. Though chapter 5 has twenty-two stanzas or verses of two parts, the initial letters do not follow regularly. It is throughout a true-hearted confession of sins. "The crown is fallen from our head; woe unto us for we have sinned! For this our heart is faint; for these things our eyes have grown dim, because of the mountain of Zion, which is desolate: foxes walk over it. Thou, Jehovah, dwellest for ever; thy throne is from generation to generation. Wherefore dost thou forget us for ever—dost thou forsake us so long time? Turn thou us unto thee, Jehovah, and we shall be turned; renew our days as of old. Or is it that thou hast utterly rejected us—art wroth with us exceedingly?"

The book has then a place quite unique, from a heart which answered to the love of Jehovah for His people, when they were most justly in the depths because of their sins and His chastisement, even to blotting them out from His land, city, kingdom, and house. It is thorough self-judgment in the heart's solidarity with them and clinging in the face and experience of all to Him. Can we not discern what a gap for the Bible if we had not Lamentations? What will it not be to the godly in their last tribulation? Did the writer forget his own purchase (Jeremiah 32) in faith of the word? or his prophecy of Israel under Messiah and the new covenant? Assuredly not; yet none the less did he mourn the ruin of Israel, and that Jehovah should have grounds so valid for His severe chastening.

5.25 Ezekiel

We have traced the distinctive character of Jeremiah as compared with Isaiah, and the special design by each. Ezekiel (≈ strengthened of God), who was a priest like Jeremiah, has his characteristic differences. Here rationalism seems less irreverent. As Christ is not so openly predicted, they are more indifferent to question and deny the truth. If the orthodox were decided in confessing the millennial city and sanctuary in his concluding chapters, we should hear of their opposition and vapid theories to get rid of divine truths. For Christendom it is all ideal enough; and the neo-critics can leave the visions of their coming glory undisturbed. Real and pronounced faith in others would soon awaken their enmity. But alas! when the Son of man comes, shall He find faith on the earth?

Now as Jeremiah prophesied long after Isaiah in the closing throes of the expiring monarchy of Judah, his mournful mission and messages from Jehovah lay up to the last in the land, till he was carried away by the unbelieving leaders of the remnant into Egypt. But Ezekiel was carried into captivity with Jehoiachin by Nebuchadnezzar, and given his place with others at Tel-Abib on the river Chebar. It was in the "thirtieth year" (he does not say of what epoch, but it would seem of Nabopolassar's era), the fifth of the Jewish king's captivity, that he saw the vision of chapter 1. It was the throne of the Lord Jehovah in unsparing majesty seen in Chaldea and judging Jerusalem and His sanctuary there. What a solemn change, not reigning, but vengeance on His house and city!

Here there appeared four living creatures, as a stormy wind issuing from the north, with cloud and a fire infolding itself, out of which indeed they came each with four faces and four wings, running and returning like lightning. But their four wheels too he beheld on the earth, and wheel within a wheel, with rims full of eyes, and the spirit of the living creatures in the four wheels. Overhead was the likeness of an expanse "as the look of the terrible crystal", and above the expanse the likeness of a throne as of sapphire, and as it were a man above upon it. As the appearance of the living creatures was like burning coals of fire, as the appearance of torches, so the man's likeness was as the look of glowing brass, as the appearance of fire within round about, and from the loins and downward the appearance of fire. It was at this time the suited display of Jehovah's glory, but in punitive judgment of Israel.

How strikingly different from the holy scene of the Lord in the temple, where Isaiah saw His glory with winged seraphim in attendance, and one touched the Seer's lips with a coal from the altar, that he might tell the people (who seemed so prospering in religion and all else) of the judicial darkness about to befall them and the desolation, to follow, though a remnant should be spared for the unfailing purpose of Jehovah. How different from both the call of Jeremiah, with its lowly symbols, yet hallowed before his birth to be a prophet to the nations, to pluck up and to break down, and to destroy and to overthrow, to build and to plant. He too learnt that out of the north should evil break forth on all the inhabitants of the land. Feeble and sensitive as he was, Jeremiah was to speak all Jehovah should command him: he was in their midst and tasted sorrows out of a full cup. Ezekiel is away from the land, which the divine glory visits judicially by Nebuchadnezzar. He, and not Jeremiah or Isaiah, is regularly called "Son of man" as Daniel but once. Hence it is not a dealing with conscience as with Jeremiah to restore; Ezekiel was to be dumb, and only to pronounce Jehovah's sentence. Yet is it constantly to Israel, or "the house of Israel", or the like, he refers, when as a prophet His mouth is opened to vindicate Jehovah's casting them off. They were more hardened than the heathen who knew not God; and he had to speak whether they heard or forbore.

Chapters 1 to 7 comprise the first division, the judgment that was sent on Jehovah's people. The next comprehends from 8 to 19 though with a subdivision at the end of chapter 11. The prophet was carried to Jerusalem in the Spirit that he might behold the abominations of all the remnant there, and especially in His house, which His glory visits in judgment. The city is also entirely given up, as well as the sanctuary. The last prince should go captive to Babylon, but should not see it, yet there die (chapter 12). Think of any but a profane scoffer here denying true prediction! It was not only in great events, but in a minute point like this, which seemed an enigma till the event made it as impressive as plain. And who were guilty? Not the king only, but the prophets, and the people down to the women in their petty ways (13). So were the elders, though they came and sat before Ezekiel (14). Famine, &c. must come to cut off man and beast; in such a crisis not even Noah, Daniel, and Job could deliver any but their own souls. The vine (15), being fruitless, was good only for fuel; such the doom for the capital. Jerusalem's father was Amorite and mother Hittite; Jehovah's love to win her she rejected; worse was she than Sodom and Samaria; yet would He establish His covenant with her for ever (16). After a parable it is shewn in 17 how Jerusalem's king despised Jehovah's oath and broke the covenant to utter ruin; but grace in the end is to Jehovah's praise. And chapter 18 declares that they need not complain of the old ground of national judgment: they would be dealt with each according to his works. This portion closes with a lamentation over the total ruin of the last princes of Israel in chapter 19.

The third part goes hence to the end of chapter 23. Here Israel is again prominent, and sin from the beginning, and that, idolatry; but in the end He will purge out the rebels and work for His own name. It is Israel contrasted here with Judah's lot. A fresh threat comes from verse 45 to the end; and 21 declares Jehovah's sword unsheathed against Jerusalem and the land of Israel because of the profane and wicked prince (Zedekiah) till He come Whose right is the crown: an allusion, we may presume, invisible to unbelieving eyes. Ammon shares the judgment (21). The prophet is to judge the bloody and unclean Jerusalem (22); and the fresh parable of Oholah and Oholibah enforces it in 23.

Chapter 24 is the utter rejection of Jerusalem, which the prophet is not to mourn: another contrast with Jeremiah who was unmarried; and as a sign, Ezekiel loses suddenly his wife whom he was forbidden to lament. It was in the ninth year of the captivity, as chapters 1-7 pertained to the fifth year, 8-19 to the sixth, and 20-23 to the seventh. Chapter 24 leads to 25-32, which take up the nations around or within the land dealt with by the Lord Jehovah, but no longer in chronological order like the first half of the book: a fact instructive for other books, inasmuch as the neo-critics do not dispute our prophet's hand. The arrangement is due to no disturbing cause, but to God's design above man's thought (or want of thought) and care. Like Jerusalem, Ammon, Moab, Edom, and the Philistine shall know that He is Jehovah.

So (26) shall Tyre and her towns. This is pursued with wide and accurate minuteness as to its commerce in chapter 27, and in 28 for the prince and the king of Tyre, with veiled reference to Satan's fall, the great world-ruler. The chapter goes on to Sidon's judgment, and closes with the assured restoration of Israel. The three chapters following contain Egypt's judgment under Nebuchadnezzar who had put down the rest.

Chapter 33 opens a new series by proclaiming individual responsibility henceforth, instead of national solidarity with their ancestors' guilt as in chapter 18. Chapter 34 gives their chiefs judged; and 35 Edom once more. But 36 is the work of grace inward and self-judging in Israel; as 37 is the nation resuscitated and united under the true David; ending with 38, 39, the judgment of Gog, the prince of Rosh, Meshech, and Tubal (all the Russias), who attacks Israel when peaceful in the land, and perishes with all the nations which fight under that banner. This done, the Solomon type will be fulfilled.

Chapters 40-48, the concluding series, furnish the grand picture of that day. In the visions of God Ezekiel is set on a very high mountain, on or by which was a city. But the primary object is the temple with its many chambers, into which comes the glory of Jehovah, the God of Israel. Therein the sons of Zadok shall minister to Him with burnt, sin, and peace offerings, as we find later the guilt and the meal offerings. A prince too of David's house represents Messiah (44), with a portion for priests and prince. The first of the month and the last of the week are remembered; the Passover and the Tabernacles, but no Pentecost, no Atonement-day, no Red Heifer. Chapter 47 presents the beautiful sight of waters issuing from under the threshold of the house, which soon rise into a river that could not be waded through; a river of healing where death reigned, only with an exception to show that it is not yet the new heaven and new earth absolutely and eternally. It is the kingdom that precedes; and the division of the land for the twelve tribes is such as never has been more than any other part of this vision. And the name of the city from that day shall be Jehovah-Shammah (Jehovah [is] there). The originality of Ezekiel, in God's special design, starts from Israel given up and judged of old, passing clean over the four Gentile empires or world-powers, till Jehovah takes up Israel (when this age ends) for His grand and unfailing purpose of blessing on all the earth. It is in no way typical of the church of God destined to heavenly glory.

5.26 Daniel

Have we clear and conclusive proof from its own internal evidence that the book is marked by special aim on God's part? Who can deny, as he weighs its testimony as a whole, that Daniel is, as no other, the prophet of "the times of the Gentiles"? There is a valuable but curt confirmatory witness in the later book of Zechariah subsequent to the Babylonish captivity. But neither there nor in all could be gleaned from every other prophecy put together any real ground of comparison with the pious captive Jew; who was called in God's providence to the highest position of counselling rule, not only at the Babylonian court under its mightiest monarch, but in the Medo-Persian which succeeded, to the days when Cyrus reigned sole and supreme.

While Israel was thus manifestly "Lo-ammi (not-my-people)", as the book indicates throughout, the striking fact is also disclosed of a provisional state for the Jewish remnant in the land, spiritual intelligence in a few, unbelieving blindness in the mass. This is revealed in chapter 9:24, &c. as coming into collision with Messiah the Prince, and His being cut off, without having anything (*i.e.* of His Messianic rights), and its ruinous consequences described thereafter "even unto the consummation", which is not come. But it also recurs in chapters 11:36-12:7, where we read the details of that consummation, when the same unbelieving generation of the Jews, who rejected long ago the true Christ, will receive the Antichrist to his and their shame and everlasting contempt. So the great Prophet Himself warned those of His day in John 5:43, before either of those awful catastrophes immeasurably more momentous, whatever rationalists think or say, than all the "decisive battles" of the world.

The unity of the book is now admitted even by most advanced freethinkers, save a few eccentrics of no weight. In the first half, having the historical form, Daniel is spoken of, and the Gentile chiefs are prominent (especially the first and greatest), though only the prophet could interpret. In the second half the prophet only has the visions as well as interpretations, which refer to "the saints" and "the people of the saints" in a way which the first did not. The best answer to cavilling sceptics is to read and believe "Daniel the prophet", as the Lord of all designated him.

Chapter 1 is a preface, from Jerusalem losing the direct government of God (who set up meanwhile Babylon in a fresh imperial position), down to the first year of Cyrus. Chapter 12 has also a conclusory character in the judgment of the Gentiles up to the deliverance of Israel. From chapter 2 to 6 Gentiles are prominent in an exoteric way. From chapter 7 to the end, only the prophet receives and communicates the mind of God intimately on all, with the glory of the Son of man and His saints on high, but His people here below. We may therefore call this half esoteric. What could so immense, as well as intimate, a range of truth have in keeping with Maccabean times? It is true that the Syrian king's furious persecution of the Jews, and his profanation of worship, find a marked place in the course of the book; but where it does, plain indication is given of a greater power and a worse evil typified thereby before "the end of the indignation". What sad belittling of an inspired book to make that king, audacious as he was and cruel, a blind not only to the final actor in that sphere, but to others on an incomparably larger scale, who are all to come under divine dealings at "the time of the end"—a time which assuredly is not yet arrived!

Chapter 2 conveys the interesting and important fact that "the God of the heavens" acted by a dream on the first Gentile head of empire, to show the general course of dominion then begun till its extinction: an image gorgeous and terrible, but gradually deteriorating as it descends, and closing with great strength and marked weakness also. Then He sets up another kingdom—His own, after destroying not only the fourth empire in its last divided condition of the ten toes (which did not exist when Christ suffered or the Holy Spirit came down) but the remains of all from the first—the gold, the silver, the brass, as well as the iron and clay. Only when judgment has been executed does the "little stone" expand into a great mountain and fill the whole earth. It awaits His second advent.

Here, as is well known, the rationalist coalesces with the ritualist in teaching the self-complacent chimera of an "ideal Israel", the church or Christendom. Yet in the church is neither Jew nor Greek, but Christ is all. It is the body of the glorified Head; and its calling is to suffering grace on earth, awaiting glory with Christ at His return. Crushing to powder the image of Gentile empires is in no way or time the church's work. The once rejected but now exalted Stone will do it, as He declared in Matthew 21:44 and in other scriptures. But the literal Israel will be then and there delivered, and become His earthly centre in power and glory. Such is the uniform witness of the prophets. We need not begrudge this to the remnant of Jacob then repentant; for we are called to far brighter glory with Christ in heavenly places. But, whether believed now or not, the first dominion on earth shall surely come to the daughter of Zion in that day, for as long as the earth endures.

The intervening histories in chapters 3-6 are in the fullest accord with the predictions of Daniel, two of them general (3, 4) and two particular (5, 6, as we shall find the prophecies are also); but none of them in fact refers to the peculiar scourge in the days of Antiochus Epiphanes. In not one is there a trace of Hellenism imposed on the Jews. Not even in Belshazzar have we the least real likeness to punishing recalcitrants against the gods of Olympus.

The aim of chapter 3 is to show how the Gentile entrusted with imperial power by God used it, deeply impressed as he had been by the lost secret which none but the Hebrew captive could interpret. Alas! man being in honour abides not; he is like the beasts that perish. So it had been with Israel under law, with Judah, and with David's house. New-fangled idolatry on pain of the most cruel death was the first recorded command of the Gentile world-power: a religious bond to unite by that act the various peoples, nations, and tongues of the one empire, and thus to counteract the divisive influence of gods peculiar to each of these races. But such a universal test gave God, thus ignored, the occasion to prove the nullity of that idol and of every other, the total and manifest defeat of supreme power even by its own captives cast into the fiery furnace, be it ever so heated. How grave the public lesson read to the Gentile empires, were not man as forgetful of God as he is bent on his own will!

The next chapter (4) is no less general, and the more impressive as the deepest humiliation was inflicted by God, after His slighted warning, on the same haughty head of imperial power. Nebuchadnezzar had ascribed all his glory to himself, and got debased, as none else ever was, to the bestial state till "seven times" passed over him. After that he "lifted up his eyes to heaven", a repentant and restored man owning the Most High, no longer like the brute but morally intelligent. It is childish to lower or restrain to the Seleucid prince a lesson *he* never learnt. It is infidel to doubt the facts of this chapter or of the preceding one. It is blind not to recognise that chapter 3 looks on to the deliverance of faithful ones (not "the many") at the end; as the next does to the day when the Gentile shall have a beast's heart no more, but will bless the Most High God, possessor of heaven and earth: the character of the divine display when this present evil age terminates. What connexion had either with the loathsome foe of the Jews, Antiochus Epiphanes? Nothing could be more telling than both displays of God's power during the "head of gold" "till the times of the Gentiles are fulfilled". It is Satan's work to disbelieve them; and a nominal Christian is far more guilty now than a heathen of old if he help Satan against God and His word.

The special aims of chapters 5, 6 are of no less serious moment. Neither the one nor the other represents or resembles Antiochus Epiphanes. In chapter 5 we see dissolute profanity eliciting a most solemn token of divine displeasure on the spot, and judged by a providential infliction that very night. Monuments or not, the word of our God shall stand for ever. Nothing more dangerous than to trust any thing or one against scripture; and what can be more sinful? What avail the brave words of men enamoured of Babylonish bricks, cylinders, etc.? Let them beware of the snares of the great enemy; not even resurrection power broke Jewish unbelief. In chapter 6 man was by craft set up for a while as the sole object of prayer or worship, which brought on its devisers the sudden destruction they had plotted for the faithful. What bearing had this, any more than the chapter before, on the grievous scourge of Antiochus Epiphanes? They evidently prepare the way, for the judgment of the future Babylon in the one (5), and for that of the Beast in the other (6), as given in the Book of Revelation, where both are shown to perish frightfully though with difference.

Next follow the more complicated communications of God's mind about the four "Beasts", the last especially, much fuller and more intimate than in chapter 2. The movement of heaven is disclosed, and God's interest in His people, and particularly in the sufferers for His name specified "as saints", and even as "saints of the high places". The dream of Nebuchadnezzar, condescending as it was to him and awe-inspiring in itself, contained no such vision of glory on high, no such prospects for heaven or earth, no such display of divine purpose in the Son of man.

But as in chapter 2, so yet more in chapter 7, the last and most distant empire, the fourth, is much more fully described than the Babylonish then in being, or the Medo-Persian that next followed, or the Greek that succeeded in its due time. For we have a crowd of minute predictions of an unexampled nature, the many horns in the last empire at its close, the audacious presumption and restless ambition of its last chief; who from a small beginning governed the rest, and, not content with trampling down the saints, rose up in blasphemy against God and His rights. But this calls forth summary and final judgment on all, with the action of heaven in establishing the everlasting kingdom of power and glory here below.

Such a revelation fundamentally clashes with the canons of the Higher Criticism, and demonstrates, if believed, their utter futility. Hence we can understand the wild efforts to get rid of the unvarnished truth Daniel sets before us in this vision. The attempt to separate the Median and the Persian elements, so as to make them respectively the second and third empires, is desperate and unworthy. Chapter 5:28 was explicit beforehand as well as chapter 6:8, 12, 15; and afterwards chapter 8 demolishes such contradiction of scripture. The bear in chapter 7 answers to the ram in chapter 8, which had two horns, the kings of Media and Persia—not two Beasts, but one composite power expressly. The leopard, therefore, with its four heads answers to the goat of Greece, for whose great horn, when broken, four stood up in its stead. The fourth Beast, different from all the Beasts before, is none other than the Roman Empire; which has ten horns in its final shape, after which, when further change comes, divine judgment falls in a form without previous parallel (7:11, 12).*

---

* As far as I know, Ephraem Syrus stands alone among the early eccle-

If we let in, as we are bound, the further light of the Apocalypse, where we cannot but recognise the same "Beast" which Daniel saw in the fourth place, we gain the fullest certainty from [Revelation] chapter 17 that the seven heads were successive governing forms, of which the sixth or imperial head was in being when John saw the vision (verse 10); and that the ten horns were contemporary, for all receive authority as kings for "one hour with the beast". It is preparatory to the last crisis, when they make war with the Lamb, and the Lamb shall overcome them (verses 12-14). This is also decisively shown in verse 16, "And the ten horns which thou sawest, and [not 'on'] the beast, these shall hate the harlot", etc., as they also give their kingdom to the "Beast" until the words of God shall be fulfilled. This, accordingly and absolutely, disposes of the attempt to make the "ten horns" mean only ten successive kings; so as to apply the list to the Seleucidae, and make it appear that Antiochus was the little horn of Daniel 7, who got rid of the three last of his predecessors. Such a scheme is mere perversion of scripture, wholly dislocates the chapter, and deprives us of the only true interpretation. For this supposes a divine interposition at the end of the age in judgment of the Roman Empire, revived to fulfil its complete destiny and to be judged by the Lord Jesus at His appearing.

The first empire had a simplicity peculiar to itself. The second or Medo-Persian had dual elements; and so has

---

siastics in treating Antiochus Epiphanes as the little horn of Daniel 7. An earnest man, extremely attached to monasticism, and vehement against the heterodox, he died in AD 378; but one has yet to learn why his differing from all other fathers earlier and later should have weight. Grotius and others, notorious for excluding the future and Christ, and for limiting prophecy to past history, followed in modern times, though early fathers enough led in the same path of unbelief.

the symbol two horns, of which the higher came up last. The third or Macedonian after its brief rise had four heads, of which two are noticed particularly as having to do with the Jews in the details of Daniel 11. The fourth empire, beyond just doubt, is the Roman, diverse from all before it, and distinguished by the notable form of ten concurrent horns, ere its destructive judgment by a divine kingdom which supersedes all, alone truly both universal and everlasting. Then shall the saints of the high places have their grand portion, surely not to eclipse the Son of man (as these sorry critics would like), but to swell the train of His glory Who is Heir of all things.

None but the Roman Empire corresponds with the feet of iron and clay; none other furnishes an analogy to the ten toes in one case and ten horns in another, the only true force of which is ten kings (subject to the violent change indicated) reigning together. Nor can any power that ever bore sway be so truly compared to "iron breaking and subduing all things", or a most ravenous nondescript brute with great iron teeth, which "devoured and brake in pieces and stamped the residue with the feet of it". The entrance of the Teuton clay indicates the brittleness of independent will (in contrast with the old Roman cohesive centralism); which, as it broke up the empire in the past, will culminate in the tenfold division of the future, on that revival of the empire which is presupposed in Daniel 7 before judgment falls, and is distinctly revealed in Revelation 17. This is a trait wholly absent from all previous empires, as well as from the Syro-Greek kingdom, which never was an empire nor approached it.

As the revival of the Roman Empire is so momentous a fact of the future and for "the time of the end", it may be well here to point out its clear and conclusive evidence in scripture. On the showing of Daniel 2 and 7 the fourth or Roman Empire is in power when the kingdom of God comes, enforced by the Son of man. But the Revelation explains how this can and will be. In chapter 13:1-10 is seen the "Beast" emerging once more from the sea or revolutionary state of nations, having seven heads and ten horns. These last have been ever held to identify it with Daniel's fourth empire. Again, the seven heads, now appropriately added, can only confirm it; for (explained as it is in Revelation 17:9, 10) this description applies to no known empire so significantly as to the Roman. Only we have to observe an absolutely new fact in connexion with the healing of that one of his heads (the imperial, as it appears) which had been wounded to death: that the great dragon (who in chapter 12 is declared to be Satan) gave him his power and his throne and great authority.

Pagan Rome was evil exceedingly, and had its part in the crucifixion of the Lord of glory. The same Roman empire will reappear at the end of the age, energized by Satan in a way neither itself nor any other empire had ever known. This gives the key to its extreme blasphemy and defiance of the Most High, as well as to other enemies; because of which the judgment shall sit and the dominion be taken away by the wrath of God from heaven, when the Beast with its hosts dares to make war against the Lord descending in power and glory. The horns will then act as of one will with the "Beast" that is then present to give imperial unity. For still more clearing the intimations of chapter 13, chapter 17:8 is most explicit: "The beast that thou sawest was, and is not, and is about to come up out of the abyss and to go into perdition." Again, at the close of the verse, "Seeing the beast, how that he was, and is not, and shall be present." (See also verse 11.)

The "Beast" without the horns was under the Caesars and their successors. Horns in their varying numbers were without the "Beast" in the middle ages and onward: "The beast was, and *is not*." But the wonder of the future is that the Beast, before the closing scene, is to arise not only out of the sea but with the far more awful symbol, "out of the abyss", the prelude of perdition. Here, again, the consistency of the truth asserts itself. To none but the Roman Empire can these predictions apply. To Alexander's empire they are irrelevant; how much more to a mere offshoot of it! No, it is the empire that rose up against the Lord in humiliation, which, blinded and filled by Satan's power, will make war with the Lamb when He comes in glory to its appalling ruin.

Chapter 8 is manifestly of a character and scope more circumscribed than the general prophecies of chapters 2 and 7. Yet it is none the less important for its design, because it takes up only a special part; but all alike conduct us to the catastrophe at the end. As this we have seen to be evidently true of the great general visions of the book, so is it equally of the particulars; which circumstance exposes the fallacy of identifying the objects. All come into collision with divine judgment; but they are distinct in character as in fact.

Here, then, we have the second empire of Medo-Persia assailed overwhelmingly by the third or Greek kingdom of Alexander the Great. How any upright mind can fail to apprehend this from the simple reading of the text is hard to account for. The great horn was broken when it became strong, and in its stead came up four notable horns. Out of one of these four kingdoms rose a little horn which became exceeding great, and also meddled peculiarly with the Jews and the sanctuary. It is a deplorable lack of intelligence to confound this oppressor with the little horn of chapter 7. The one was as manifestly the ruler over a part of the Greek empire in the East, as the other from a small beginning arrives to be the chief of the Western empire. Both are to be excessively impious and wicked, both surely punished by God beyond example. But to confound them is to lose the difference of the actors at the close, even wholly opposed as they are to each other, though both inflict the worst evils on the chosen people. Now there is the less need of many words here, as it is agreed that the vision in its later part from verse 9 does set forth the Seleucid enemy of the Jews and of their religion. And it would appear that verses 13, 14 apply to his defilement of the sanctuary and suppression of the daily offering.

As usual in Daniel and elsewhere in scripture, the interpretation not only explains but adds considerably, and in particular dwells, not on the typical Antiochus Epiphanes, but on the final antitypical enemy in the same quarter at the latter day. It is weak to pretend that the awful end predicted for the infamous personage of the future in this chapter and at the end of Daniel 11 could be fulfilled in the death of Antiochus Epiphanes, terrible as it was in the estimate of Greeks as well as Jews. Thus the real prediction of his history in the preceding verses of the same chapter 11 up to 32 does not dwell on it as comparable with that of him who is found "at the time of the end".

For the prophecy goes on to the consummation, when God interferes in unmistakeable power. Hence the angelic interpreter would make Daniel know "what shall be at the end of the indignation". Who can say with the smallest show of truth that this was in the days of the impious Syrian or of the Maccabean resistance? "The end of the indignation" will only be, when Israel are truly repentant and God has no more controversy with His people. Nor should this surprise any one who reads the scriptures in faith, for all the prophets look on to that happy time. The real person before the mind of the Holy Spirit at the close is one who will "stand up against the Prince of princes", but shall be "broken without hand" in a way far beyond its type in past history. A gap, therefore, necessarily occurs in every one of the prophecies. In no instance is continuity unbroken. Enough is said to make the general bearing plain; but in every case the Holy Spirit dwells on the final scene which connects itself with the subject matter before us; because then only will the judgment of God decide all absolutely and publicly, and introduce the kingdom of power and glory that shall never pass away.

Daniel 9 has its own peculiarities. Those who contrast this book with other prophecies, as lacking the predominantly moral element, only prove their own blindness. In no prophecy is it more conspicuous; and the same chapter which so profoundly tells out to God a heart that identified itself with the sins and iniquities ("*we* have sinned", &c.) of the men of Judah, and of the inhabitants of Jerusalem, and of all Israel near and far off, but with the most earnest intercession, is precisely the one that, as he prayed, received from God a prediction in some respects the most striking and important of any in scripture. Here even rationalism cannot but own that the promised blessings of verse 24 belong to the Messianic hope, when the 490 years really close. Thus it shares, with every other prediction in the book, the mark of going down to the end of the age; when the times of the Gentiles are fulfilled, and God sets up His kingdom in Christ by judgments executed on all lawlessness, Jewish or Gentile. But here, where Jeremiah's seventy years are referred to, with the provisional return of a remnant from Babylon to rebuild the city and the sanctuary, we have not only Jehovah the Lord God of Israel addressed, but also Messiah's first advent and cutting off. This interrupts the thread of the seventy weeks, as it naturally must; and an undated vista of desolation follows. For it clearly includes Messiah's rejection, and leaves nothing but the destruction of the city and temple, and a flood of troubles on the Jews. There evidently comes the break. Messiah's death was "after" the sixty-ninth week = 483 years. Then follows the desolation determined, and to the end war, outside the course of the "weeks" altogether, as it is hardly possible for a serious man to deny.

The last week remains for the close, without fixing any connexion or starting-point, save that the Roman "prince" (whose "people" came and destroyed Jerusalem) will, at the time of the end, make covenant with "the many", or mass of faithless Jews, for a week or seven years, and will in the midst of it cause the sacrifice and the oblation to cease. That is, he will put down the Jewish religion, contrary to his covenant; and "because of the protection" [rather than the overspreading] "of abominations" or idols, which take its place, a desolator shall be, even until the consumption and that which is determined to be poured on the desolate, *i.e.* Jerusalem. The desolator seems to he the last north-eastern enemy, as the Roman prince is he who is so prominent in Daniel 7, where we saw the times and laws given into his hand for the same last half week, or three and a half times.

Instead of this plain, worthy, and homogeneous interpretation, what do the neo-critics say? "There can be no reasonable doubt that this [the cutting off of Messiah] is a reference to the deposition of the high priest, Onias III, and his murder by Andronicus (B.C. 171)"; while the rest is turned to Antiochus. Of course, all is chaos among these critics. The design is to pervert the prophecy, from Christ's death and the burning of their city and the flood of desolation, to those murderers. The precise scope is clear if the interruption of the series is observed in the text, with the future bearing of the last week. If this be true, it is a death-blow to the "higher critics", and an unanswerable proof that the true Daniel wrote it; who here distinctively brings in the awful truth of Christ's rejection, which has deferred the world-kingdom till His second advent; while the disasters of the poor Jews are shown, not only till the Romans destroyed their city and temple, but at the end of the age when they meet their worst tribulation, before deliverance comes for the godly in that day, as it surely will.

Chapter 10 answers to the earlier portion of chapter 9 when the power of Babylon was broken, and a new dynasty reigned with favour toward the Jews. Daniel was in no way deceived as to the moral state of the Jews, but led into humiliation and prayer more than ever before. As the vision of chapter 9 was given him, and the violent rejection of Messiah its most notable fact within a measured period, so in chapter 10 Daniel beheld One of surpassing glory, and had an angelic communication (inscribed in the scripture of truth) of what should befall his people at the end of the days. And so we find that a prophecy follows in chapters 11, 12 remarkable beyond any in scripture for details, especially for the persecution which befell the Jews in the land for their religion. Thence it turns with plain intimation to "the time of the end", when the similar spirit of unbelief among the Jews, which had long before cut off the Messiah, will receive the Antichrist at the end of the age, bringing in the conflicts of Gentile powers, and the unparalleled tribulation that precedes the deliverance of the righteous remnant, and the blessed rest of that day.

The last three chapters are also a particular prophecy, chapter 11 being exceedingly minute, to the fierce dislike of such as think for God, and would dictate to Him if they could. There is a rich variety in scripture, and not least in the prophetic word. Our place is to bow to God and learn of Him. Unbelief sits in judgment of Him Who is worthy of all trust and adoration. Now chapter 11, peculiar as it may be, demands and deserves our fullest confidence, whatever say the scorners. It was in the third year of Cyrus that the revelation came to Daniel. Three more kings were to arise in Persia— Cambyses, Pseudo-Smerdis, and Darius Hystaspis; then the fourth, richer than them all, Xerxes, who, when waxed strong by his riches, should stir up the whole against the kingdom of Javan or Greece. This gives the fitting gap, which necessarily must be, unless an uninterrupted thread were inserted: a thing unprecedented in such cases, for the gap we have seen to be regular.

The next personage is the Macedonian chief, who repaid the blow intended by Persia. No unprejudiced man can avoid seeing Alexander the Great in verse 3, or his divided kingdom in verse 4, which introduces two of those divisions, the kingdoms of the north and the south, and their conflicts which follow. Again, it is clear and certain that in verses 21-32 we have a full account of him who more than any hated the Jews and their religion. The sceptical theory is, that a patriotic Jew in his day personated Daniel of ancient renown in the exile, and converted the past history into professed prophecy up to that time. But the fact stands opposed that, when Antiochus Epiphanes is dropped, verses 33-35 give a protracted state of trial which ensued long for the Jews, when their old foe had ceased from troubling; and that the text expressly declares their trial was to go on to "the time of the end". Here, therefore, is the great gap implied in accordance with the other predictions of the book, and even with the same principle on a smaller scale between verses 2 and 3 of this very chapter as already pointed out and undeniable.

Then from verse 36 we find ourselves confronted with the last time. We are told, not of a king of the north or of the south as before, but of "the king", that final wicked one whom a prophet so distinguished and early as Isaiah presents in chapters 11:4, 30:33, 57:9 under the same ominous phrase. He is the Anointed's personal rival reigning in the land according to his own pleasure, and thus fully contrasted with Him who only did His Father's will. It is an energetic sketch of one exalting himself against every god; whereas Antiochus Epiphanes was devoted to the gods of Greece and Rome. Though speaking impious things against the God of gods, he is to prosper "till the indignation be accomplished"—God's indignation against His guilty people (as Isaiah also spoke), another proof of days still to come. The Palestinian prince (which Antiochus Epiphanes was not, but king of the north) will have no regard for the God of his fathers, namely, Jehovah (for *he* is an apostate Jew), nor the desire of women (Messiah, the hope of Israel), nor any god (*i.e.* of the Gentiles); which last it is absurd and false to say of Antiochus Epiphanes. In truth it is the long predicted and then present Antichrist, supplanting Christ, denying the Father and the Son, coming in his own name, and received by those that refused Him who came in the Father's. His and their destruction is shown elsewhere. But here the prophet turns to the old struggle of the kings of the north and of the south, both being as opposed to "the king" as to each other: an incontestable proof of the folly, first of fancying Antiochus Epiphanes here, and next of denying that these events, believed or disbelieved, are set forth as the prophet's prediction of the last future collision.

Observe, finally, what accumulation of proofs Daniel 12 affords of these events to come, which of themselves refute the petty scheme of seeing only Antiochus Epiphanes up to the end. For when the last king of the north perishes by divine judgment, a divine intervention on behalf of Israel is assured "at that time". Sorely will the Jews need it, for they will be passing through this their last and severest tribulation. But, unlike their calamitous history for long centuries, "at that time thy people shall be delivered, every one that shall be found written in the book." It is no mere policy nor prowess, but mercy for the righteous. Hence the appropriate figure of many of the sleepers in the dust awakening, some to everlasting life, and some to shame and everlasting contempt. So Isaiah (26) and Ezekiel (37) employed the same figure of resurrection for the uprising of Israel nationally, but with the rejection of the unrighteous, as our prophet plainly indicates.

The result, then, of this brief survey of the book, assailed by neo-critical unbelief, is to show that their scheme is unfounded from first to last; and that it overlooks the grand scope of Gentile empire, both exoteric (2) and esoteric (7). In this so inconsiderable a ruler as

Antiochus Epiphanes could have no place, still less be the culmination of all in bringing on the divine extinction of the entire system of Gentile empire, and hence in restoring Israel under conditions of blessing and glory which will change the world's history.

Plainly no such time is arrived. When Christ came, the fourth empire was in power; which will also play its part against Him at His second advent, as the New Testament carefully and clearly reveals. His cross laid the basis for reconciling, not believers only, but all things also in due time. Meanwhile in the world "the times of the Gentiles" proceed, and "the indignation" against faithless Israel. The gospel is indeed sovereign grace *toward* all, and *upon* all that believe, and the church is Christ's body for heavenly glory. But the world-kingdom of our Lord and of His Christ is not yet come, nor can it come till the seventh trumpet is blown. Even in the particular prophecies of Daniel, where Antiochus Epiphanes is referred to (chapters 8 and 11), the book itself teaches us to look on from his evil to a greater and worse antitype expressly bound up with "the time of the end", which in no way applies to the Seleucid king.

5.27 Minor Prophets

Does the group of the so-called Minor Prophets differ from all the other component parts of Holy scripture? or is each of them characterised by its own special aim, and a peculiar contribution to the sum of divine revelation? Let us examine them, however briefly, one by one, though in time they were gathered for convenience into a single volume by the Jews.

5.27.1 Hosea

The drift of Hosea, though in style terse and abrupt to obscurity, is sufficiently clear in the main to any attentive believer. He announces in chapter 1 the fall of Jehu's house and of Israel's kingdom under the symbolic children Jezreel and Lo-ruhamah. A still more awful doom was intimated by Lo-Ammi, when the ruin of Judah should leave Jehovah without a recognisable people. Yet the chapter does not conclude without the assurance, (1) that in the place where Lo-Ammi was said, sons of the living God should be said (which Romans 9 applies to the call of the Gentile and to privileges higher than Jewish); (2) that the two houses of the divided people shall be gathered together with one head (Messiah without doubt in a day yet to come). Is not this so? 1 Peter 2 applies the end of chapter 2 to the Christian Jews even now. It is plain however that the end of both chapters contemplates as a whole what is not yet in terms fulfilled. Chapter 3 fills up the gap with a graphic sketch of the long interval during which the people abide without privilege, civil or religious, and yet without idolatry, before their blessed restoration at the end of the days. Such is the first section, as sure for the future, as for the present.

The second part is a series of expostulations, entreaties, menaces, and lamentations over the beloved but guilty people, distinguishing the sons of Israel from Judah's in danger; and testifying not only the loss of priestly place as a whole (4:6), but priests, people, princes, all objects of divine displeasure and judgment (chapter 5). Chapter 6 breaks out into a touching appeal, that they might repent; as chapter 7 has to pronounce woe, because even when they howled, they cried not to Jehovah in heart. Chapter 8 therefore is the trumpet blast of coming destruction on Israel and Judah. Yet in chapter 9 what tender pleading over Ephraim, about to become a wanderer, wherein the prophet was a snare! It was no new evil, but since Gibeah: what could be but cutting off Israel's king and the Assyrian their king (chapters 10, 11)? What a contrast with Jacob, as chapter 12 draws out! Nevertheless He declares that He will ransom them from the power of Sheol, and redeem them from death (chapter 13).

Accordingly the last chapter (14) provides words of confession, and of return to Jehovah from iniquities and creature help, with His own blessed and blessing promises, which shall be made good as surely as He spoke them through the prophet.

5.27.2 JOEL

Joel remarkably differs from the general sweep of Hosea; for he concentrates attention, from a then famine (chapter 1), on the northern army in spite of its menaces to perish between the eastern and the western seas. After that will come not only fulness of outward blessing but the divine Spirit poured out upon all flesh, and in Jerusalem shall be, no ruin nor danger more, but deliverance in every sense (chapter 2). For in those days Jehovah will enter into judgment with all the nations in the valley of Jehoshaphat on account of Israel (chapter 3). The apostle Peter was beyond controversy justified in vindicating the effusion of the Spirit at Pentecost as of this character, and in no wise creaturely excitement (Acts 2:16). But he is far from intimating that it was the fulfilment of the prophecy; which did not contemplate the formation of the church, or the going forth of the gospel to all the creation, but the earthly glories of the Messianic kingdom for Judah and Jerusalem, as shall follow in the due season. So the apostle Paul applies it in Romans 10 to the salvation of Jew or Gentile now, stopping short of citing the promised deliverance in mount Zion and in Jerusalem.

5.27.3 AMOS

Who can fail to discriminate the work assigned to the herdman or sheep-master Amos of Tekoa? No competent person can deny the beauty and force of his style, or the fresh originality with which he pronounces Jehovah's punishment on the nations which surround His people, and the surprising fact that Judah and Israel fall under it also (chapters 1, 2). Indeed chapter 3 lets them together learn that, because they were known as none else, therefore He should visit them for their iniquities. But He would do nothing without revealing it to His servants the prophets. Do professing Christians believe either of those words of His? "Hear this word" begins 3, 4, 5, all of them warnings to His guilty people, whose false worship was the mother sin of all other sins. Chapter 6 is a woe on their self-security and luxury, like Gentiles who know not God. Now would the Lord Jehovah, who repented of destroying judgments at the prophet's intercession, take the measuring-line in hand and desolate the people and king (chapter 7); as in chapter 8 the end is shewn coming on Israel, and the land darkened in the clear day. Chapter 9 reveals the Lord standing (not on a wall) but on the altar for judgment still more overwhelming. Yet, while He declares that He will shake the house of Israel to and fro among all the nations, He says not the least grain shall fall. Nay more, He will raise up David's fallen tabernacle, and build it as in days of old to the downfall of their spiteful foes; He will pour on them earthly blessing without stint; and when He plants them in those days on their land, they shall no more be plucked up. These glorious realities await repentant Israel.

5.27.4 OBADIAH

Obadiah calls for few words, not only because it is so short, but because its distinctive aim is most unmistakeable. Edom is the object before him, and the judgment which the Lord Jehovah would inflict on its jealous and rancorous hatred of His chosen people. Their pride had deceived them; their fastnesses should not screen them: Jehovah will bring them down. Their boasted wisdom is in vain, as well as their might. Their malice was aggravated, as against "thy brother Jacob", and "in the day of his disaster". But in the day of Jehovah upon all the nations shall be deliverance on mount Zion, and it shall be holy; and the house of Jacob shall possess their possessions. Can any thing be plainer than the speciality of our prophet? or that he looks onward to the triumphs of the last days, when saviours shall come upon mount Zion to judge the mount of Esau, and the kingdom shall be Jehovah's in a form and fulness never yet known on the earth?

5.27.5 JONAH

He who does not see Jonah's distinctive place must have singularly little perception. Indeed it is the man or what befell him that is the prophetical sign, though the prophetic message, short as it is, must strike us as addressed to the Gentiles in Nineveh. The history is a great and instructive type throughout; and this is no mere idea but truth taught by our Lord.

Chapter 1 tells us of Jonah charged to cry against the great city because of its wickedness. Strange to say, he a true prophet flees west when bidden to go east. But Jehovah sent a mighty tempest on the ship sailing to

Tarshish; and Jonah slept below, while the mariners cried each to his god, and vainly struggled on. At length they cast lots, and the lot fell on Jonah, who, as they knew, fled from Jehovah's presence; and he frankly bade them cast him overboard as their only safety. This reluctantly and with prayer to Jehovah they did; and the sea ceased from raging to their deeper fear, which issued in a sacrifice to Him and vows. But Jehovah prepared a great fish to swallow Jonah, who was in its belly three days and nights, the sign of Christ (Matthew 12).

There he prayed as in chapter 2 owning salvation to be of Jehovah, Who commanded the fish to vomit out Jonah on the dry land. And the word of Jehovah came to him the second time, bidding him to go and preach to Nineveh what He should say. Jonah both despised the Gentiles, and feared that Jehovah might repent Him of judgment if they sought His mercy; and where then would be the glory of a prophet of Israel, when his Yea became Nay? The figure of death and resurrection opens the door of grace to the lost. If Christ for the time be lost to the Jew who rejected Him, grace works to save Gentiles. Jonah does his errand now (chapter 3); and they repent at his preaching from the king downward, the very beasts covered with sackcloth being denied food and drink that they might cry out; and God repented of what He threatened.

This even now Jonah resented (chapter 4) and wished to die rather than *his* word should fail and Nineveh abide. But here was the truth so needed by Israel as well as Jonah. Hence the gourd (that sprang up under the hand of Jehovah Elohim to shelter the narrow-hearted and self-occupied prophet) withered under the worm He prepared to this end, so that Jonah fainted under the heat, and again wished to die. Then said Jehovah, "Thou hadst pity on the gourd ... and I, should not I have pity on Nineveh, the great city, wherein are more than 120,000 persons that cannot discern between their right hand and their left hand; and also much cattle?" Yes, He is the God of all grace, the God not of Jews only but of Gentiles also, whose mercies as the faithful Creator are over all His works. What Jew, what Rabbi, had ever allowed such a book within the sacred canon, if God had not written it for the purpose?

5.27.6 MICAH

Next comes a still more brilliant seer: the word of Jehovah that came to Micah the Morasthite, a contemporary of Isaiah, concerning Samaria and Jerusalem. It is composed of three chief divisions, ushered in by a call to listen, "Hear, ye peoples, all of you; hearken, O earth, and all that is therein" (1:2); "And I said, Hear, I pray you, ye heads of Jacob, and princes of the house of Israel" (3:1); and "Hear ye now what Jehovah saith", &c. (6:1). Can the least discerning of believers fail to apprehend its distinctive character?

It opens with the imminent fall of the northern kingdom because of its transgression, but goes on to the punishment of Judah also and Jerusalem. "Of late my people is risen up as an enemy." "Arise ye, and depart; for this is not the rest, because of defilement that destroyeth, even a grievous destruction" (chapter 2:8, 10). The people and their prophets were alike wicked and rebellious. As chapter 1 has a predictive sketch of the Assyrian foe coming against Jerusalem, so does the end of chapter 2 present Him Who will effectuate Jehovah's purpose of deliverance and blessing for the remnant of Israel at the end.

In the next section he appeals to the chiefs, warning them against the prophets that cause Jehovah's people to err. If they cried, Peace, without a vision or light from God, Micah could say that he was filled with power by the Spirit of Jehovah to declare unto Jacob his transgression and unto Israel his sin. Heads, priests, prophets were only building up Zion with blood and Jerusalem with unrighteousness, while veiling iniquity under the privilege of His name. Zion and Jerusalem should come to utter desolation (chapter 3:9-12). But this is followed in chapter 4 by the glowing picture with which Isaiah begins his chapter 2. Only Micah, instead of going on to the overwhelming judgment of the day of Jehovah as there, predicts the going to Babylon as Isaiah does in his chapter 39. Thence he turns to the closing scenes where many nations gather against Zion, which is told to arise and thresh many peoples: a judgment awaiting its sure fulfilment, when the first or former dominion shall come to her.

This gives occasion for announcing a still deeper reason for putting off blessing and the giving up His people for a season. Awful to think and say, they should smite the Judge of Israel with a rod on the cheek (chapter 5:1)! And a parenthesis reveals Him born at Bethlehem, whose goings forth are from of old, from everlasting. His rejection was their own rejection, till God's counsel comes to birth; when the residue of His brethren, instead of merging in the church of God as now, shall return unto the children of Israel, and the kingdom be displayed in power and glory before all the world. And the prospect is beautifully described to the end of this part.

The third section is a most affecting call to hear Jehovah's controversy with His people, in spite of His goodness to them from the beginning and through the wilderness into Canaan. It is not offerings but righteousness He values. In the face of iniquity, deceit, and violence, of family bonds turned to enmity all the more evil and destructive, the prophet waits on Jehovah with confidence of deliverance and vindication. And he looks through the desolation that must intervene because of Israel's sins to the restitution of all things in the latter day, when the nations shall be ashamed of all their might, and lick the dust. "Who is a God like Thee, that pardoneth iniquity, and passeth by the transgression of the remnant of His heritage? He retaineth not His anger for ever, because He delighteth in mercy. He will turn again and have mercy upon us; He will tread under foot our iniquities. And Thou wilt cast all their sins into the depths of the seas. Thou wilt perform truth to Jacob, loving-kindness to Abraham, which Thou hast sworn unto our fathers from the days of old" (chapter 7:18-20). In denying God's faithfulness to Israel and monopolising the earthly promises, Babylon has shown herself, as in all else, faithless to the true place of His church, in present suffering and future glory with Christ. But we speak not of her that occupied the plain of Shinar, but of the more guilty woman that sits on seven hills, mystery written on her forehead, the corrupt counterpart of the bride, the Lamb's wife.

5.27.7 NAHUM

As Micah on a small scale noticed both Babylon and the Assyrian which Isaiah presented much more fully, Nahum is occupied only with Nineveh and its chief before the world-powers were ordained. For such was the order historically, as prophetically it will be the inverse. (Compare Isaiah 13 and 14 with Micah 4, 5). For what answers to Babylon, the imperial Beast or fourth empire revived for judgment at the consummation of the age, will meet its doom before the Assyrian comes up with the external nations for final destruction when Israel shall be owned of Jehovah; but the reign of righteousness and peace is not yet fully established. Who can deny the special place designed for Nahum as to Nineveh, any more than the peculiar task given to Obadiah as to Edom?

Nahum was a Galilean like Jonah; and if the latter was sent long before to warn the haughty Gentile, and on repentance to defer the judgment in divine mercy, the former was given, on its raising its head still more proudly, to pronounce Jehovah's indignant vengeance, however slow to anger; for He is as great as He is good. In vain went forth out of Nineveh one that imagined evil against Jehovah, a counsellor of Belial. He will make a full end—trouble shall not rise a second time; as Sennacherib proved, his yoke broken, His people's bonds burst, out of the house of the Assyrian's gods graven and molten images cut off, and his grave prepared. The scourge finally past is followed by the enduring peace of His people (chapter 1).

What more superb than the lifelike graphic sketch of the dashing in pieces (chapter 2)? But all ends, not in Jerusalem taken, but in Nineveh and its palace melting away in its own rivers which burst the gates, the converse of Babylon's later fate. The lair of the lions would be an utter ruin, instead of a terror (chapter 3). Nineveh was no better than Thebes, or No-Amon; there is no healing of her breach.

5.27.8 HABAKKUK

Habakkuk begins by complaining of the evil in Jehovah's people, when he is reminded of the marvellous work He wrought in using the Chaldeans in their proud self-seeking energy to chastise them. This turns his complaint against the wicked swallowing up one more righteous, and withal sacrificing to his net and burning incense to his drag (chapter 1). Can any hesitate to own distinctive design here?

The prophet waits for His word, and Jehovah's answer comes so plainly that its reader may run. The just shall live by his faith, before public deliverance is given. If God is patient, His people may well be. All the iniquity was seen and felt: retribution would come at an appointed time. The peoples labour for the fire, and the nations weary themselves in vain. For the earth shall be filled with the knowledge of the glory of Jehovah (not of the gospel, which appeals to faith now for heaven), as the waters cover the sea. The Babylonian capturing would be to no purpose any more than their famous building; and their intoxication of others for deceit as of themselves would end in shame, like their idolatries: Jehovah is in His holy temple above, whatever the state of His house on earth. Silence! (chapter 2).

His prayer follows in chapter 3 and the power that will make itself seen, heard, and felt, rises for his soul, as he recalls His deliverance of old, though but partial, as He had only Israel in view, not yet Messiah and the new covenant. He anticipates the triumphant lot of Israel, as is already seen, no less than the downfall of their foes; but he ends with the faith that waits, though not a sign meanwhile appears (chapter 3).

5.27.9 ZEPHANIAH

Is Zephaniah one whit less distinctive? Is he not beyond mistake occupied from first to last with the day of Jehovah on Jerusalem? But the land and the Jewish remnant are fully in view for that day. The reign of the last pious king did not hinder or defer it; for the general advance in evil revolt would be all the surer when that check vanished. Divine judgment must clear away all offences, that righteousness by grace may flourish. Hardly any truth is more repulsive to haughty and lawless Christendom than the Lord's unexpected dealing with the living, though every one in word confesses that He is coming to judge the quick as well as the dead. Who can wonder that idolatrous Jews decried it? It is the becoming answer of our prophet to all questions. If Jehovah must judge His people, all the world must bow, no nation can escape. What Nebuchadnezzar did was but the earnest of a great and complete judgment; yet Jehovah could not but begin with His land, people, and city, as in chapter 1.

In chapter 2 a remnant is looked for, the meek, that they may be hidden in that day which overtakes the guilty mass. There is indeed and for the same reason the doom of the Philistines, of Moab, and of Ammon. But not the neighbours only; He will famish all the gods of the earth: and Assyria with its great city Nineveh shall fall into desolation.

Chapter 3 returns to Jerusalem unsparingly. But from verse 8 he shows Jehovah rising to pour His indignation upon the nations and kingdoms in all the earth. Then will He turn to the peoples a pure language that they may all call on Jehovah's name and serve Him with one consent. And His dispersed shall return, suppliant and accepted, afflicted and poor, but unrighteous and deceitful no more. Assuredly it is a day yet future, when none shall make them afraid. From verse 14 he calls on the daughter of Zion to exult, Israel to shout. Jehovah is their king and in their midst, having taken away their judgments and cast out their enemy. "He will rejoice over thee with joy; he will rest in his love; he will exult over thee with singing." Praise and fame He will make in all the lands of their shame when He gathers and turns again their captivity before their eyes. It is wholly distinct from the gospel or the church.

5.27.10 HAGGAI

The three prophets that remain were after the Return, and thus differ from all before. The house of God, lowly as it might be, was a great test for their lukewarm state. Haggai was sent to awaken their zeal: not God's providence, however it might work, but Jehovah's word. Difficulties arose; and they left off to build. It was not the time, said they. "Is it time for you to dwell in your wainscotted houses, while this house lieth waste?" replies the prophet, as he points out how their efforts came to failure under His hand Who bade them, "Consider your ways." But there were who heard Zerubbabel and Joshua, and others of opened ear; and Jehovah's messenger declared on His part, I am with you, saith Jehovah; and they came and worked for Jehovah's house (chapter 1).

Near a month after, the word came to such as had ears to hear, abating any disappointment from comparison with the house in its former glory: Be strong, for I am with you. "For thus saith Jehovah of hosts: Yet once, it is a little while, and I will shake the heavens, and the earth, and the sea, and the dry [land]; and I will shake all nations, and the desire of all nations shall come; and I will fill this house with glory, saith Jehovah of hosts. The silver is mine, and the gold is mine, saith Jehovah of hosts. The latter glory of this house shall be greater than the former, saith Jehovah; and in this place will I give peace, saith Jehovah of hosts" (verses 6-9). Could any answer be more assuring or glorious? Some believed it then, we may trust, to their blessing: do men who call themselves Christians believe it now? Whatever measure of application it had when Christ came the first time, Hebrews 12 leaves no doubt that its fulfilment awaits His second advent.—It may be observed how carefully the house is viewed as one till then. Render therefore as in the Septuagint, "the latter glory of this house", not "the glory of this latter house". It has unity in His eyes.

The third message turns on holiness according to the law. Things ordinary are not sanctified by the touch of what is holy; though the holy becomes unclean by contact with defilement. Such the prophet declares this people and every work of theirs—unclean. Yet they are told to consider from this day that, instead of smiting as before, Jehovah would bless them (verses 10-19).

On the same day came a fourth word, in which Jehovah says, "I will shake the heavens and the earth, and I will overthrow the throne of kingdoms, and I will destroy the strength of the kingdoms of the nations, and I will overthrow the chariots and those that ride in them, and the horses and their riders shall come down, every one by the sword of his brother", verses 21, 22. It is the judgment of the quick, or at least that part which relates to the nations that gather against Israel; it is after the destruction of the Beast and his vassal kings and armies whom the Lord destroys by His appearing. Zerubbabel seems taken as a shadow of great David's greater Son in the verse following. A strange critic would he be who fails to discern Haggai's special place, and a faithless one who questions his divine inspiration.

5.27.11 ZECHARIAH

No less distinctive is the work given to Zechariah, who alone approaches in his earlier visions to the apocalyptic character of Daniel among the four so-called greater prophets. But unlike Daniel he is occupied with Jerusalem, and launches out in his later visions to the open and magnificent scenes of universal glory under Jehovah-Messiah for all the earth. If all peoples and all the nations assemble against Jerusalem even in the day of Jehovah, He will go forth and fight with them and smite all the adversaries; and it shall be that all that are left of all the nations which came up against her shall go up from year to year to worship the King, Jehovah of hosts, and to celebrate the Feast of Tabernacles. It is the day of His manifested supremacy in the midst of Israel, and clearly as yet to be fulfilled. What circumstances among the returned remnant gave the prophet an existing groundwork? Did the book come from God? or is it a human dream? That the writer could begin with prose, and rise later to poetical style when called for is no great marvel.

After aggrieved appeal in the preface of chapter 1:1-6, the youthful prophet saw (as in the rest of the chapter) the vision of the administering powers of the three empires under the symbol of red, bay, and white horses; for the first empire had passed away and the provisional return to the land had already been a fact for some 18 years. Next he saw four horns, powers which had scattered Judah, Israel, and Jerusalem, as well as four smiths to cast out those Gentile horns. Chapter 2 presents a man with a line to measure Jerusalem; for if Jehovah was jealous over the feeble remnant, He also looks on to the time when He would be the glory in their midst; and a song quite as lofty as any afterward follows. In chapter 3 is solved by grace the question of fitness for His presence, though the high priest represents also their responsibility meanwhile. But the Branch or Sprout is promised, Who will be the true Stone of Israel, when their iniquity shall pass away, and communion shall abound. The vision of order and of holy power in testimony follows in chapter 4, in its measure of light then, but complete only when He reigns Who combines royalty and priesthood. Chapter 5 gives two visions of judgment which must be: the flying roll against iniquity in Israel toward man and toward Jehovah; and the ephah with the woman (this is wickedness, or demoralising idolatry) carried off to Shinar, its source, for its dwelling-place. After the vision of the four chariots in chapter 6, representing the external powers in divine providence, comes the word of Jehovah, on the occasion of gifts from those of the captivity, to make crowns, one of which was to be set on Joshua, again looking on to the Branch Who should build the temple of Jehovah emphatically, bearing the glory, sitting and ruling upon His throne, a priest thereon, when the counsel of peace should be between Them both. What believer can mistake the special design of this?

Chapters 7, 8 seem transitional. Such fasts as those in the captivity would not do: Jehovah claimed righteousness and mercy, not oppression and evil-mindedness, for which He had scattered them. Returned to Zion He would restore and bless to the full, as He will yet. Fasts will yield to feasts; and peoples come to Jerusalem as they never yet have done, whatever the application of intermediate condition then.

Then we have "the burden of the word of Jehovah" in chapter 9. Not only will He defend His house against surrounding foes, but Zion's King will come in humiliation, notably and to the letter fulfilled, but going on to the day when Ephraim, as well as Jerusalem, shall behold His judgments issuing in peace to the nations and dominion everywhere. How could such a future be before the prophet without kindling the fire of hope so assured? And this is pursued through chapter 10.

But in chapter 11 comes a change to pathos and grief, as Christ's rejection passes before his spirit, and the retributive usurpation of Antichrist. Then another "burden" is heard concerning Israel; and beseiged Jerusalem becomes a burdensome stone, as never yet, "to all peoples" (chapter 12:3); and David's house and Jerusalem's inhabitants shall be objects of grace in true repentance; and a fountain to cleanse those who may look to Him Whom they pierced shall be opened in that day (chapter 13). Then shall the very names of idols, and prophets with the unclean, pass out of the land; and Christ is again recalled, wounded in the house of His friends, albeit Jehovah's Shepherd, the Man Who is His fellow. Scattering is thence justly predicted, though not without protection for the little ones. But again we are in presence of the final crisis (8, 9), which is too plain in chapter 14 save for obstinate unbelief. There is a final capture of Jerusalem in part when all the nations join to assail it; but Jehovah then decides all. (Compare Psalm 48, Isaiah 29, 66). Subjection of all to Him is the glorious and blessed result.

5.27.12 MALACHI

The brief prophecy of Malachi has its specific moral traits, exactly suited to Jehovah's final call to the Jew in view of His messenger to prepare the way, and of the Lord suddenly coming to His temple. He denounces irreverence, corruption, fraud, and profanity in the returned, but looks for a remnant, and is sure of divine faithfulness to purpose and promise. Jehovah's name shall be great among the nations when His kingdom comes. What is Israel now? What the priests are as in chapter 2. All hung on Jehovah's coming; but He will judge as well as purge (chapter 3). Meanwhile those that fear Him have the resource of His name and shall be His peculiar treasure; as He will discern the wicked too. For His day comes as a furnace for the wicked, but with healing for those that are His, who also shall tread down the wicked. It is for Israel in that day, not the heavenly church, though we should profit by all the word (chapter 4). Thus He recalls the law of Moses, and promises Elijah before that day, to turn the hearts of the fathers to the children, and of the children to their fathers, lest His coming should bring not blessing but curse, as the first man entails.

Here, as all know, closes the great volume of Old Testament inspiration. There only is found the authentic account of creation and of early mankind; there of the deluge, and of nations and tongues subsequently, of the promises given to the fathers, and of Israel, their offspring, the people chosen of God, but failing under trial, and worst of all (as the prophets predicted) when they rejected their Messiah. But the prophets as certainly predicted that He will surely restore them penitent and believing in the latter day.

New Testament

A new language, the characteristically Gentile one *i.e.* the Greek, marks outwardly a still deeper inward distinction in what is commonly called the New Testament. Its basis is the Son of God come, who has given all who believe, Jew or Greek, an understanding that we should know Him that is true. The gospel therefore goes out freely to every creature, and the children of God are gathered in one by the Holy Spirit; whilst the Lord, ascended to heaven, promises to come and receive His own, before the day of His appearing when the kingdom shall be set up over the earth in visible and indisputable glory, and Christ's supremacy be manifested over all creation heavenly and earthly, which the church shall share as His bride. Hence God is revealed as He is in light and love; man is laid bare as wholly evil and lost; provisional dealing and probation yield to grace and truth come in Jesus Christ, Who, rejected of man and the Jews especially, accomplished redemption, and brings in the new things according to the hidden but eternal counsels of God, before He will resume His relations with Israel in fulfilment of His promises to the fathers and the blessing of all families of the earth in the restitution of all things, of which God spoke by the mouth of His holy prophets since time began.

5.28 Matthew

In the first Gospel the Holy Spirit has for the distinctive object, as shown in its contents, to set forth Jesus as the Christ or Messiah, according to promises and prophecy; Son of David, Son of Abraham, in an especial sense; yet rejected by the Jew no less but more than by the Gentile, and so proclaiming Himself Son of man to suffer for mankind, and be exalted to heavenly and universal glory. The mysteries of the kingdom of the heavens meanwhile are disclosed to faith, and the church, part of a mystery still greater, is built on Him, the Son of the living God, before He returns as Son of man in power and glory.

Hence chapter 1 furnishes His genealogy in the Messianic point of view, down from the roots of promise and royalty in three series of fourteen generations, in which the few women named carry the manifest significance of grace to Gentiles and the grossest of sinners. It is Joseph's line from Solomon, which was legally essential; though due care is taken to mark His birth of "the virgin" of that house by the Holy Spirit, according to Isaiah 7, Emmanuel, and Jehovah or Jah in His very name.

In chapter 2 magi from the east are seen coming to pay homage to the born King of the Jews; but they learn Bethlehem to be the birthplace, as Micah had predicted long before. An Idumean under Roman authority then ruled Jerusalem; and king and people were troubled at the tidings. But the strangers are angelically warned as well as Joseph, to defeat the designs of Herod, and thus also to accomplish Hosea 11:1 and Jeremiah 31:15. The return to dwell at Nazareth, despised as it was, fell in with the prophecies that such was to be Messiah's lot.

Chapter 3 presents the voice of one crying in the wilderness, Prepare ye the way of Jehovah. It is John the Baptist saying, Repent, for the kingdom of the heavens hath drawn nigh: a testimony to Christ's coming to baptise with the Holy Spirit and fire. But Jesus stoops to be baptised, and is owned as Son by the Father, while the Spirit descends on Him visibly. The Trinity now revealed.

In chapter 4 we have Jesus tempted by the devil forty days and after that in three special ways, but victorious. Then when John was delivered up, the Lord's Galilean ministry begins, as in Isaiah 9:1, 2, and the call of the earlier disciples, with a general summary of His teaching and preaching which attracts from far beyond that province, as of His healing all sickness and disease, and of His power over demons.

Then in chapters 5-7 He on the mount lays down authoritatively the principles of the kingdom in contrast to the law, with the manifestation of the Father's name and the suited word, concluding with the security of the obedient, but the sin and vanity and ruin of mere profession.

Chapter 8 displays the reality and character of Jehovah's presence in Christ here below: (1) the Jewish leper, (2) the Gentile centurion, (3) Peter's wife's mother, (4) the fulfilment of Isaiah 53:4, (5) scribes and disciples tested, (6) the tempest rebuked, and (7) the demoniacs delivered. In chapter 9 is shown the growth of unbelieving hatred and blasphemy brought out by (1) the paralytic forgiven, (2) the tax-gatherer called, (3) the question of fasting, (4) the ruler's child raised, (5) and on the way the flux of blood healed, (6) the two blind given to see, and (7) the dumb demoniac to speak.

Thereon, deeply pitying the distressed and scattered sheep of Israel, He bids His disciples pray the Lord of the harvest to send forth labourers; and in chapter 10 *He* sends forth the twelve with authority like His own over unclean spirits and diseases, but as yet only to the lost sheep of the house of Israel (not to Gentiles or Samaritans), preaching the kingdom, as John had preached and Himself. He prepares them for enmity and tells them that their task will not close till the Son of man be come, while He assures them, not only of the Spirit's grace, but of honour and reward before His Father.

In chapter 11 Christ testifies to John, instead of getting due testimony from him; shows that the kingdom calls for decision at all cost but is well worth while; reproves the caprice of "this generation"; and warns the cities unrepentant in the face of the powers displayed. Yet He bows with gracious confession to the Father, Who hid these things from wise and understanding men, yet revealed them to babes. He not only sees but announces a higher glory and a deeper grace opening out than if Israel had received Him after the flesh.

After the rest given to faith, chapter 12 opens with the lesson of the sabbath perverted to deny His glory Who is Lord of the sabbath as of all, and with the resolve of the Pharisee to destroy Him. The Lord retires, heals still, but charges them not to make Him known. He bows to His rejection. In another and deeper way would the divine counsel be made good, as Isaiah 42 declared. So, when a blind and dumb demoniac was healed and the Pharisees attribute His power to Beelzebub, He warns of the blasphemy against the Spirit that shall not be forgiven, pronounces the last state of "this evil generation" to become worse than the first, and owns His true relationship henceforth to be, not with mother and brethren after the flesh, but with such as shall do the will of His Father Who is in heaven.

Accordingly in chapter 13 the Lord expounds in seven parables (beginning with His new work as the Sower of the word and in six following similitudes) the mysteries of the kingdom consequent on His rejection and going on high. The first took in His work before the kingdom was set up in the heavens, and was spoken outside like the next three. The interpretation of the wheatfield spoilt by darner was given within the house like the last three. But, whatever His words or works, the Jews stumbled at the stumbling-stone, His person.

In chapter 14 we see the state morally no better but rather worse. Yet if the Lord withdraws, His compassion to Israel is unabated. He heals their diseases, satisfies the poor with bread as the true and royal Son of David, dismisses the multitude, and goes up the mountain to pray, the picture of His present work on high. But when the disciples are tempest-tossed with the winds contrary, He rejoins them, and the wind ceases, and those in the ship pay Him homage as God's Son. And now He is recognised and welcomed in His beneficent power.

Chapter 15 is the Lord's judgment of earthly religion proud in the poverty of tradition, with an unclean condition inwardly, whatever the zeal in washing of hands. On the other hand, if a Canaanite under curse cried for mercy against a demon's oppression, would Jesus deny her? He vindicates her faith, while He renews His labour of love in despised Galilee, and abundantly blesses the provision of the poor as David's Son.

In chapter 16 none the less does the Lord denounce the hypocrisy of a generation seeking after a sign, while blind to those set before them so fully. None more should be given but that of Jonah's death and resurrection, opening the door to Gentiles. If men said this or that, Simon Peter confesses Him Christ, the Son of the living God, as revealed of the Father. And the Son also gives him a new name, declares that on this rock He will build His church, and confers on him the keys of the kingdom: two distinct, yet connected, systems of blessing to replace Israel. Thereon He announces His suffering, death, and resurrection, and calls on the one that owns Him to deny self, take up his cross, and follow Him.

Chapter 17 is a miniature though divine display of the kingdom, but Christ meanwhile declared Son of God, Who is to be heard, not law and prophets. Yet here below the disciples fail through unbelief; whereas Christ, proving Himself Lord of all, takes as yet no glory here, but associates His own with Himself in grace meanwhile.

Next in chapter 18 He enforces humiliation in love as befitting His own in the kingdom; and in the church grace to win the wrong-doer with the sanction of heaven on their acts rightly done. The parable from verse 23 teaches that such as professedly had forgiveness, but outraged its spirit, have all their guilt renewed to their ruin.

Chapter 19 tells us that, while God's constitution of man is right, grace reveals better things to those that share Christ's rejection, and that God encourages fidelity by due reward. It ought to be plain that there are no thrones for the apostles till the regeneration when the Lord comes in glory. Those "enthroned" meanwhile are not genuine successors, but merely affect Gentile grandeur.

Chapter 20 begins with the other side of God's rights in a parable maintaining His sovereignty. But the Son of man's path lies through shame and death, and there is no other way to glory, though the disposal is His Father's. The danger is from a fleshly mind, which is no better than a Gentile's: the Son of man on the contrary came to serve, and to give His life a ransom for many.

The Lord had now entered on His last journey to Jerusalem; and the healing of the two blind men near Jericho begins the final presentation of Himself Who knew the end before He began (20:29-34). In chapter 21 He accomplishes Zechariah 9:9, purges the temple, and defends the children's Hosannas with Psalm 8. The curse on the fig-tree was the sentence on the people, full of show but without fruit; and when the religious chiefs ask for His authority, He puts a question to their conscience. When they shirk the answer, He sets out one parable that proves them to be worse than the tax-gatherers and the harlots; and in another He describes God's dealings with the rebellious people, even to His own rejection in death. They themselves must own (verse 41) their just destruction; on which He cites Psalm 118:22, and connects with it not only the removal of the kingdom of God from them but the effect of both His advents, now their stumbling on Him to be broken, by-and-by His falling on them to be scattered as dust. They knew what He meant, but as yet feared to do their will.

So in chapter 22 the Lord adds in a parable what grace has done and is doing, with the effects for the unbelieving, not only providential judgment which fell on Jerusalem, but that for each at the end and for ever. Then come the Pharisees with the Herodians about the tribute, and the Sadducees about the resurrection, and the lawyer about the commandments, all answered to their confusion; after which the Lord puts the question of questions for a Jew (as indeed for any). Faith alone answers; but they had none; and there they are to this day.

In chapter 23 the Lord, while owning the law's authority (spite of the falseness of those who administered it), calls His disciples to the lowly position He had taken as their pattern; and He Who began with "Blessed, blessed", now ends with "Woe, woe." How their evil did not cease with His cross but went on against His servants, we know too well. But even here in declaring the inevitable retribution, He cannot close without a door of hope in the last verse (39).

Chapters 24 and 25 are His great prophecy on the mount, beginning with the Jews, and ending with the Gentiles in 25:31 to the end. Between these two (from 24:45 to 25:30) is the part that deals with the Christian profession. This takes therefore the general unrestricted form of three parables, since the link is with Christ Himself, not with the land or the people of Israel: the house-bondman faithful and prudent, or evil, respectively characterising Christendom in comprehensive responsibility; the ten virgins, foolish or prudent, manifested by the reality or unreality of the hope when judgment falls; and the bondmen trading with His goods, good and faithful on the one hand, or wicked and slothful on the other, in individual responsibility. The sheep and the goats represent the true and the false, not in Christendom, but among all the nations in the end of the age, tested by the testimony of the King's "brethren" during that crisis, while the heavenly saints are with Christ on high before He appears, and they with Him, in the same glory (verses 31-46).

In chapters 26, 27 we have the unutterably solemn and touching scenes of the Lord's earthly close. The Lord announces it; the chief priests and their associates plot; the last anointing is done for His burial; the traitor covenants; the Lord directs the paschal feast and eats it with the disciples; He institutes His supper; He goes out to Olivet, and He enters on His agony in Gethsemane; and then becomes the willing Captive, as later the Victim. The mock trial before Caiaphas follows; and Peter denies, and Judas in remorse casts down his silver in the sanctuary, and commits suicide. Pilate condemns the Holy One and releases Barabbas. Jesus is crucified, "the King of the Jews": for this alone is Pilate firm. All rail, even the robbers. He dismissed His spirit; and the veil of the temple was rent, and the earth quaked, and the rocks rent, as there had been supernatural darkness around the cross when the Messiah made sin was abandoned by His God. But if men designed otherwise, He was with the rich in His death, as the prophet said so emphatically.

Chapter 28 tells of Him risen. What availed the keepers or the seal? And the angel, before whom the guard trembled, bade the women not fear, but tell the disciples He was risen and would meet them in Galilee, the familiar ground of His ministry. And so it was amid fear and joy and doubt: He Himself appeared and confirmed it, whatever lying Jews and bribed Gentiles pretended. There too He gave them His commission. "All authority is given to me in heaven and on earth. Go ye, disciple all the nations, baptising them unto the name of the Father and of the Son and of the Holy Spirit; teaching them to observe all things, whatsoever I have commanded you. And lo! I am with you all the days, even unto the consummation of the age." Here may be seen what supersedes Israel till the age is ended. When the new age comes, they will be owned and blessed as the head of the nations. The first dominion will be Zion's. Even during that period (for such is the consummation of the age, not a mere epoch) there will be a suited state of transition. Till then discipling proceeds; and disciples are to be baptised to the name, not of Jehovah, but of God fully revealed as now—the Father, and the Son, and the Holy Spirit. Observance of Christ's injunctions follows, with the assurance of His constant presence: a condition quite distinct from His millennial reign in manifested power and glory.

5.29 MARK

The second Gospel has for its design the setting forth of the service "of Jesus Christ, the Son of God". He who at first failed but at length was pronounced "profitable for ministry" was just as suitable in the power of the Holy Spirit for that task, as Matthew called from the receipt of customs to be an apostle was for the first Gospel. Christ Himself serves in the gospel, and does mighty works accompanying it, as Mark describes.

Before proceeding farther, the precision which Mark furnishes, partly by his characteristic "straightway" that so often occurs, partly by a perhaps still more definite specifying of time *e.g.* in chapter 4:35, enables us to clear up some difficulties in the different order of the events related in the three Synoptic Gospels. From a careful comparison it results, that of the four inspired writers, two were led to preserve save in a rare exception the chronological order, two from their respective designs subordinate that order where requisite to a grouping of events or discourses independently; and of the two in each case one was an apostle, the other not. Matthew and Luke were from time to time not bound to simple historic sequence; whereas Mark and John as the rule adhere to it.

None can be justly called "fragmentary"; for each has a specific design impressed on his work, and all that is inserted or omitted may be accounted for on this principle. Where an incident illustrates that which belongs to the scope of all four, they all introduce it, as for instance the miracle of the five loaves and the two little fishes. Where it falls in with the province of one only, there it is given and nowhere else; as the temple tax in Matthew 17, the deaf stammerer in Mark 7, the penitent woman in Luke 7, and the Samaritan woman in John 4, to mention but one of the many facts, signs, and discourses peculiar to each, to John most abundantly. In some cases three give the same subject matter, in others but two.

But this is not all; whilst there are notable phrases and words common to all, there are quite as notable differences in the mode of communication. Hence speculative minds are tempted to irreverent cutting of the knot they cannot untie; whilst unexercised souls fail to gather the profit intended of the Spirit through every shade of difference. For it is a perversion of the truth, that the writers were inspired, but not the writings. If 2 Peter 1:21 warrants the former, still more explicit and distinctly applicable is the claim for the latter in 2 Timothy 3:16. In the verse preceding we have the "sacred" title of the Old Testament; but in verse 16 the Spirit of God pronounces for "every" thing that falls under the designation of "scripture". It is not a question of human infirmity but of God's power. Every scripture is inspired by God (θεόπνευστος). Not only were the men inspired, but so according to the apostle Paul is the result. Ordinarily their writing, like their words, would have been liable to the imperfections of human speech and the limitations of human thought; but every scripture, every writing that comes under this category, is God-breathed, and in no way "left" to the mere accidents of human faculties. To mix up with inspiration the manifold errors of copyists in the lapse of ages is illicit and illogical, not to say dishonest; for this is quite another question. All we contend for is the divine character of indisputable scripture.

Differences then there are; but instead of being the discrepancies which unbelief hastily and improperly calls them because of ignorance, they are the beautifully instructive effect and evidence of God's varied design. Take Matthew 8 as an instance: "a solemn assembly of witnesses", as one justly calls it. The leper came in fact long before what is called the sermon on the mount. "And, behold", in verse 2 ties us down to no date. But as the Holy Spirit had already given a summary of the Lord's deeds of gracious preaching and power in Matthew 4:23, 24, so He presents details of His teaching in chapters 5, 6, 7, and of His miracles in chapter 8, and again in another way in chapter 9 where the date yields to deeper considerations, and selected proofs are grouped together designedly. In Mark 1:40-45, where no such purpose operates, we see its place historically. Luke confirms the fact that it was on "one of those days" when Christ was in Capernaum, and before the healing of the paralytic, which in Matthew is reserved for the first case in chapter 9.

But, to look into details, the leper's cure fitly attested the present power of Jehovah-Messiah which opens Matthew 8. And as this proved His grace toward the Jew that came in his uncleanness and faith (however faltering), the Gentile centurion's great faith next follows, and here only is connected thus. In the Gospel of Luke it has a different place; in Mark it has none. The third fact in chapter 8, the healing of Peter's mother-in-law, so interesting to a Jew and assuring that grace to the Gentile did not turn Messiah's heart from Israel, seems here inserted with that design; whereas historically it preceded both the previous miracles in date, as shown in Mark 1 and Luke 4. So of course did the healing of many demoniacs and sick on that evening after the sabbath, in fulfilment of Isaiah 53:4. It is not in the least difficult to believe that the Holy Spirit led Matthew to introduce at this point what Luke presents in quite a different connexion (chapter 9:57), and with an addition too. The harmonists who imagine "duplicates" are no more faithful than the commentators who tax the inspired with "discrepancies". The conversation whenever it occurred seems given in the first Gospel to mark the great vessel of divine power and grace (*i.e.* the Messiah) consciously rejected, the Son of man having nowhere to lay His head, yet claiming from a disciple to be followed, even if a father lay dead. We know too for certain that both the storm which He rebuked, and the deliverance of the demoniacs took place after the parables of chapter 13 were heard and explained.

The septenary of chapter 9 is a similar collection of witnesses, following that of chapter 8 which indicates not only His divine power displayed in Israel, but the growing hatred and jealousy which it excited in the Scribes, till it culminated in the Pharisees who sought to poison the multitude with their blasphemy, "By the prince of the demons he casteth out demons." But no more evidence is needed, that Matthew was led, where it was required, to state facts and words so as best to give dispensational order; as Luke was led in no less a degree to present moral order. Take the Lord's genealogy as a clear proof, not in chapter 1 but in chapter 3 *after* the statement of John put in prison, and of the wondrous scene of his baptism following, though of course it long preceded what is here recounted. Take again the temptation where Luke puts the third act in the second place, as the moral order; whereas the actual fact as represented by Matthew coincided with dispensational order which it was his function to make known. This necessitated the remarkable omission which the true and ancient text testifies, as distinguished from the common error introduced by copyists, harmonists, and the like, whose clumsy assimilations provoke the rather more evil doubts of their opponents.

How full of interest, as bearing on divine purpose, to observe that in the Gospel of Mark there is no account of the Lord's reading of Isaiah 61 and preaching in the synagogue at Nazareth, any more than Matthew or John gives it. For Luke 4 it was reserved, as Christ's grandly suited introduction to public witness, as we shall see more fully in its place. The introduction for Matthew's Gospel was the striking but wholly different application of Isaiah 9 where the light shining in despised Galilee was promised. Mark was not given to state this, but only Matthew, whose also it was above all to point out the fulfilment of prophecy in the still more despised Messiah; as he only had mentioned the visit of the Magi, and the flight into Egypt, and the slaughter of the babes, all bearing in the same direction.

Again, Mark was not led to present the remarkable healing of the centurion's servant, which has so prominent a position in the First Gospel, and at still greater length in the Third. Mark does give the leper's cleansing, followed by the healing of the paralytic, and very graphically in both cases; but there was no design by him to bring in the witness that Jehovah's power would call in Gentiles when Israel should be cast out, as in Matthew 8, any more than to blazon, as in Luke 7, the faith of the Gentile, not so seen in Israel, which recognised the power of God in Jesus to command sovereignly and in love; and this in a soul so humbled by grace as to discern His people in the degenerate Jews, loved and honoured for His name' sake.

So further in the First Gospel and the Second we have no account whatever of the widow's son raised from the dead outside Nain. It had no connexion with their scope in particular, and we may presume that it was therefore here omitted. But it had the utmost importance for illustrating divine power in the highest form united in our Lord Jesus with the fullest human sympathy; and so it is exactly in accord with the special aim of Luke's Gospel where alone it is found.

On the same principle we may account for a vast deal of intermediate matter given in the central parts of the First and Third Gospels, which does not appear in the Gospel of Mark. We are thus delivered from the theories which have occupied many learned men to the hurt of themselves and of those who trust them. For they have sought on human grounds to explain the different phenomena of the Synoptic Gospels, some advocating a common document, others only a general apostolic tradition. Again, a supplemental intention has been attributed to those that followed successively the first, for his own contribution, to the sum as it gradually appeared and grew. Had they believed in the special design imprinted by the Holy Spirit on each and every one of them, erroneous speculation had been spared to the honour of God's word, and to the spiritual profit of His children. The differences which undoubtedly occur would then have been known to be in no case discrepancy, but springing from God's wisdom, not man's weakness, and adding incalculably to the witness of Christ, and consequently to the spiritual intelligence of him that accepts all from God in faith of His truth and love.

Mark 1 presents neither genealogy nor early history, as we have in the accounts of Matthew and Luke. Yet this is not due to his abridging previously well-known facts, but to the divine design which made a genealogy here out of place: the service even of such a Servant did not call for it. Here as every where none so much abounds in striking details. The forerunner is briefly introduced preaching and baptising. Jesus too is baptised, and then tempted of Satan; here without the details given by Matthew and Luke, yet only Mark speaks of His being with the wild beasts. When John is imprisoned, Christ begins His public service, saying, "The time is fulfilled." Calling certain disciples to follow Him, He promises to make them fishers of men. His words and works attest the truth. The unclean spirit is cast out publicly. Simon's mother-in-law is healed of fever, and forthwith ministers to them. Sick and demoniacs are alike set free in numbers. He goes to preach; for this He is come forth. He prays without seeking fame; and a leper is cleansed with His touch as benignant as His word in divine power, love, and compassion.

In chapter 2 are given minute details of the paralytic, not healed only but forgiven (for sin is the root of evil), and made to walk, that they might know the Son of Man's title on earth to remit sins: a title which causes the Scribes to blaspheme. He goes on in grace to call a despised tax-gatherer to follow Him, eats with those whom the Pharisees branded as sinners beyond others, and vindicates it as His mission: "I came not to call righteous but sinners." What a Saviour for guilty man! Any truly righteous were already called: He came to call sinners. Those who believed were to rejoice in His presence there: let John's disciples and those of the Pharisees fast in unbelief of Him; full soon should His own have reason to fast. Besides, the new truth and power of the kingdom cannot without loss mix with old things. The sabbath itself was made for man, and the Son of Man is its Lord, not its slave as Pharisees wished.

Hence in chapter 3 He on the sabbath heals a man with a withered hand. He was here, sabbath day or not, to do good and save; but the orthodox counselled with their time-serving adversaries how to destroy Him. If He withdraws, it is to heal and deliver more abundantly; and after being alone on the mountain, He calls and appoints twelve, whom He would, to carry on the work of grace in power like His own. For He did all in the Spirit; but such was His unflagging zeal that His relations called Him deranged; and such His power, that the scribes from Jerusalem imputed it in their malice to Satan. Thereon He pronounces sentence, and announces His relationship, not after the flesh, but with him, whoever he be, that does the will of God.

Accordingly in chapter 4, seated on board ship, He teaches the new departure, contingent upon the people's apostasy, and takes the place of the Sower in the world, such that three parts of the seed come to nothing, and only a fourth by grace takes effect in varying measure where conscience works before God. Light is to shine in service; the veil no longer hides; and he that has gets more, as he that has not loses all. A parable follows peculiar to Mark, and emblematic of the Lord's ways in service, Who works throughout and produces all, yet hiddenly now till the harvest is come when *He* reaps. The parable of mustard seed illustrates the outward rise from little to a great show on the earth. Such would be the abnormal result of service in man's hand. The evening closes with the storm on the lake, Jesus asleep in the boat now filling, and the alarmed disciples awaking Him Who in two words made a great calm.

In chapter 5 we see Him met by the fiercest of demoniacs, Legion; for many spirits were there. Jesus, expelling them from the possessed, let them enter a great herd of swine which bore witness to their evil power in rushing at once to destruction; while the man sat clothed and in his right mind, beseeching to be with Jesus. The time however is come, not yet for this, but to testify to his friends what great things the Lord, even Jesus, had done for him; while those who heard alas! besought, not Legion, but the Lord to depart from their borders. And Jesus departs. On the other side Jairus beseeches Him to come and lay His hands on his dying daughter. As He went, a woman touches Him secretly and is healed of her issue of blood; the Lord will have her too in the light and without fear. The damsel now dead is restored to life, as the Lord will do for Israel by-and-by. This closes the first part.

Then chapter 6 lays bare the unbelief that could not deny His word or work, yet stumbled at His humiliation in the grace which escaped them. So the Lord before His departure began to send forth the twelve with power over unclean spirits, but without resources of their own; He could control men's hearts as He pleased. Meanwhile Herod is shewn as troubled in conscience because of

John as well as Herodias, dreading the report of Jesus as a resurrection of John. And the Lord gives the disciples, full of their great work, their needed quiet with Himself, while He waits on man's wants and satisfies the poor with bread. Then sending away the multitude and the disciples by ship to Bethsaida, while He went on high to pray, He appears to them toiling in vain against contrary wind, and walked the water as if He would pass them, but immediately rejoins them on their crying out in fear; and the wind ceased. When they reached land, those who once wished Him to depart bring their sick, earnestly seeking that they may be healed.

Chapter 7 manifests the superficial worthlessness of the religious chiefs and their tradition. Man's heart was a spring of evil; but grace reveals God's heart, even to the Syro-Phœnician, and His power to deliver her demoniac daughter; whilst the deaf stammering one, like the Jewish remnant, is led apart and healed, that he may hear and speak to the praise of God.

In chapter 8 a fresh pledge, in the seven loaves multiplied, is given of divine compassion to the poor of His people, as also of His power to make the blind, again led outside, see clearly. The leaven of the Pharisees and of Herod was evil; yet the disciples, though ill-affected by it, had no uncertainty as to the Messiah, but like Peter confessed Him. This however must yield to the deeper glory of the Son of Man in His rejection and death; but it was too much for Peter, who deprecates it and is rebuked of the Lord, even insisting on a path like His own for His followers and at all cost.

In chapter 9 His glory as Son of Man and Son of God is presented to witnesses on the hill, while below even His own failed in faith to use His name against Satan. How painful to the Lord! How humbling to the disciples! "O faithless generation, how long shall I be with you, how long shall I suffer you?" Only His presence in a coming day will deliver the people from Satan's power. Meanwhile it is a question of faith for individual deliverance. Power depends on faith; the ability is in the believing. Jesus acts by His word in power. But He goes on to be slain and to rise the third day, whilst they understanding nothing dispute who should be greatest, and have a little child set before them as their right example. Even John is jealous for "us" rather than for Christ; but the Lord in grace owns all He can. Woe to the despiser of the little ones that believe! Woe too, when hand, foot, or eye causes to stumble! It is not earthly judgments, but unquenchable fire that awaits the unbelieving; as believers are to have salt (the preservative power of the truth) in themselves, and peace with one another.

Chapter 10 shows our Lord vindicating the relationships as God ordained from the beginning! He insists on the purity of marriage, and blesses babes. Yet while appreciating the blameless young man, who sought everlasting life (*not* to be saved), He denies goodness in man, and lays bare love of means and position, which is ruin, as he left Jesus to go away in sorrow. The Saviour thereon dwells on the danger, not blessing, of wealth, to the astonishment of His own; and when Peter boasts *their* self-denial, the Lord declares the sure remembrance of every loss for His sake (and the gospel's, peculiar to Mark), not only spiritual gain now but life everlasting beyond, with the caution that many first shall be last, and the last first. Then His death and delivery to the Gentiles are announced, and the ambition of Zebedee's sons, as well as the displeasure of the ten, corrected by the cross as God's pattern in a lost world.

The last presentation from verse 46 begins with blind Bartimæus appealing to David's Son and receiving his sight, as Israel will in due time. In chapter 11 He is presented as the anointed King, and owned with hosannas; He pronounces on the barren fig-tree which is seen withered next morning, cleanses the sanctuary, and exposes the incompetence as well as insincerity of the officials who demand His authority.

Chapter 12 sets forth in a parable Israel's rebellion and Messiah's rejection but exaltation, and in few words the hypocrisy of the question as to Cæsar, to whom they were no more subject than to God. Then the Sadducees (who talked of resurrection to undermine it and Him) hear the truth which refutes their error; and the intelligent scribe has the moral sum of the law laid down for his encouragement. Jesus puts the question how David's Son is David's Lord, which is life to him that answers it according to God. But alas! religious show and pretensions with selfishness end in more severe judgment; while the widow and her mite have everlasting record.

In the brief form of the prophecy in chapter 13 the special aim of the Spirit is evident from the fulness given to service past or future; so it is, not only in the centre, but near the end. Hence in that character "the Son" does not know; yet He gave to His bondmen their authority, and to each his work. Nowhere else is service so distinctly noticed.

The end approaches in chapter 14, His final rejection, His death, resurrection, and ascension, yet "working with them" still as the Lord. The chief priests plot, but God's will is done. Love anoints the Lord's body for His burial; the traitor makes his sad bargain with the rejoicing chief priests; the last passover is eaten, and the Lord's supper instituted. Peter is warned, and all three sleep while the Lord goes through the agony in Gethsemane. Judas then leads the band that takes Jesus, and the high priest condemns Him, not for the false witness of others but for His own confession of the truth, while Peter denies Him thrice and with oaths.

Chapter 15 shows us Jesus delivered to Pilate, the Gentile judge, who owns Him guiltless and knows the chief priests' envy, but gives Him up to be crucified. Thereon ensues the scene beyond all before or to come. The Messiah, the righteous Servant, forsaken by all, even by God (for so it must be for our sins), expires on the cross; the centurion in charge confesses Him Son of God; and Joseph, an honourable councillor, lays His body in his own rock-hewn sepulchre.

In chapter 16 we have His resurrection briefly told by an angel to the women that saw the sepulchre open and empty. They were too fearful and amazed to say anything. In the second part of the chapter, of which some unreasonably and unbelievingly doubt, we have the Lord appearing to Mary of Magdala who is disbelieved; then manifested to the two going to Emmaus, as afterward to the eleven at table, with reproof of their unbelief. Yet did He give their great commission of the gospel to all the creation, with signs following those that believed. And if He risen and ascended is styled "Lord", none the less true to the design is He said to be "working with them" and confirming their words, as His servants went forth and preached everywhere. Here only in the New Testament have we the fact historically stated, however briefly. Can specific purpose be clearer first and last?

5.30 Luke

The third Gospel is distinguished by its display of God's grace in man, which could be only and perfectly in the "Holy Thing" to be born and called the Son of God. Here therefore, as the moral ways of God shine, so is manifested man's heart in saint and sinner. Hence the preface and dedication to Theophilus, and the evangelist's motives for writing; hence also the beautiful picture of Jewish piety in presence of divine intervention for both forerunner and Son of the Highest to accomplish promise and prophecy, as announced by angels (chapter 1). The last of the Gentile empires was in power when the Saviour was born in David's city, and Jehovah's glory shone around shepherds at their lowly watch that night when His angel proclaimed the joyful event and its significant token, with the heavenly host praising as they said, Glory to God in the highest, and on earth peace, in men complacency (or, good pleasure). God's Son, born of woman, was also born under law, the seal of which He duly received; and the godly remnant seen in Simeon and Anna, that looked for Jerusalem's redemption, testified to Him in the spirit of prophecy; while He walked in the holy subjection of grace, with wisdom beyond all teachers, yet bearing witness to His consciousness of divine Sonship even from His youth (chapter 2).

In due time, marked still more explicitly by the dates of Gentile dominion and of Jewish disorder, both civil and religious, John comes preaching, not here the kingdom of the heavens, nor yet the kingdom of God, but a baptism of repentance for remission of sins. Here alone and most appropriately is quoted from Isaiah's oracle, "All flesh shall see the salvation of God"; here only have we John's answers to the enquiring people, tax-gatherers and soldiers; and here too is stated anticipatively his imprisonment, but also the baptism of our Lord; and here only is given His praying, when the heaven was opened and the Holy Spirit descended on Him, and the Father's voice, "Thou art my beloved Son; in thee am I well pleased." And the genealogy is through Mary (as she throughout is prominent, not Joseph as in Matthew) up to Adam, as becomes the Second Man and Last Adam (chapter 3). It may help if it be seen, that "being, as was supposed, son of Joseph" is parenthetical, and that "of Heli, of Matthat", &c., is the genealogical line from Mary's father upward.

Then follows His temptation viewed morally, not dispensationally as in the first Gospel; the natural, the worldly, and the spiritual. This order necessarily involved the omission in chapter 4:8, which ignorant copyists assimilated to the text of Matthew. The critics have rightly followed the best witnesses, though none of them appears to notice the evidence it renders to plenary inspiration. Divine purpose is clearly in it. Thereon He returns to Galilee in the power of the Spirit, and at Nazareth in the synagogue He reads Isaiah 61:1, 2 (omitting the last clause strikingly), and declares this scripture fulfilled today in their ears. In that interval, or within the acceptable year, Israel as it were goes out, and the church comes in where is neither Jew nor Gentile, but Christ is all and they one new man in Him. Then when His gracious words were met by unbelieving words on their part, He points out the grace of old that passed by Israel and blessed Gentiles. This kindled His hearers to murderous wrath even then, whilst He, passing through the midst of them, went His way. At Capernaum He astonished them publicly with His teaching and cast out an unclean spirit in the synagogue, as He brought Peter's mother-in-law immediately to strength from "a great fever", and subsequently healed the varied sick and demoniacs that were brought, while He refused their testimony to Him. And when men would detain Him, He said, "I must announce the kingdom of God to the other cities also, for therefore was I sent" (chapter 4). It is a question of the soul yet more than of the body.

In connection accordingly with preaching the word of God, we have (chapter 5) the Lord, by a miracle that revealed Him, calling Simon Peter (who judged himself as never before) with his partners, to forsake all and follow Him: an incident of earlier date, but reserved for this point in Luke. The cleansing of a man full of leprosy follows, and after the healing of multitudes He retires and prays; but as He afterwards was teaching in presence of Pharisees and law-doctors, He declares to a paralytic the forgiveness of his sins, and, to prove it, bids him arise, take up his couch, and go to his house, as the man did forthwith. Then we have the call of Levi, the tax-gatherer, and a great feast with many such in his house; but Jesus answers all murmurs with the open assertion of His coming to call sinners to repentance, as He defends the actual eating and drinking of His disciples by their joy in His presence with them: He once taken away, they should fast. In parable He intimates that the old was doomed, and that the new character and power demand a new way; though naturally no one relishes the new, but likes the old.

Chapter 6 shows first, the Son of Man Lord also of the sabbath, and secondly the title to do good on that day, which filled them with madness against Him. Next, going to the mountain to pray all night to God, He chose twelve and named them apostles, with whom He came down to a plateau, healing all that came under diseases and demons. Then He addresses them in that form of His discourse which falls in perfectly with our Gospel. The great moral principles are there, not contrast with law as in Matthew, but the personal blessedness of His own, and the woes of such as were not His but enjoy the world. Another peculiarity is that Luke was led to give our Lord's teaching in detached parts connected with facts of kindred character; whereas Matthew was no less divinely given to present it as a whole, omitting the facts or questions which drew out those particulars.

Then in chapter 7 He entered Capernaum, and the healing of the centurion's slave follows. Luke distinguishes the embassy of Jewish elders, then of friends when He was near the house; but the dispensational issue was left to Matthew. The raising of the widow's only son at Nain yet more deeply proves the divine power He wields with a perfect human heart. It was high time for John's disciples to find all doubts solved by Jesus, Who testifies to the Baptist's place instead of being witnessed to by him. Yet was wisdom justified of all her children, as the penitent woman finds from the Lord's lips in the Pharisee's house. Everywhere it was divine grace in man; and she tasted it in the faith that saved, and in the grace that bade her go in peace.

In chapter 8 we see Him on His errand of mercy, followed not by the twelve only but by certain women healed of wicked spirits and infirmities, who ministered to Him of their substance. And the Lord addresses the crowd in parables, but not of the Kingdom, as in

Matthew; after that He designates His true relatives to be those that hear and do the word of God. The storm on the lake follows, and the healing of Legion in the details of grace, as well as of the woman who had a flux of blood, while He was on the way to raise the daughter of Jairus.

Chapter 9 gives the mission of the twelve empowered by and like Himself, and sent to proclaim the Kingdom of God, with its effect on Herod's bad conscience. The apostles on their return He leads apart, but, being followed by a hungry crowd, He feeds about 5,000 men with five loaves and two fishes multiplied under His hand, while the fragments left filled twelve hand-baskets. After praying alone, He elicits from His disciples men's varying thoughts of Him, and Peter's confession of His Messiahship (Matthew recording much more). For this He substitutes His suffering and His glory as Son of Man: they were no more to speak of Him as Messiah. Deeper need had to be met in the face of Jewish unbelief. The transfiguration follows with moral traits usual in Luke, and the centre of that glory is owned Son of God. When the Lord and His chosen witnesses come down, the power of Satan that baffled the disciples yields to the majesty of God's power in Jesus, Who thereon announces to them His delivery into men's hands, and lays bare to the end of the chapter the various forms that self may assume in His people or in pretenders to that place.

Then we have in chapter 10 the seventy sent out two and two before His face, a larger and more urgent mission peculiar to Luke. On their return, exultant that even the demons were subject to them in His name, the Lord looks on to Satan's overthrow, but calls them to rejoice that their names were written in the heavens. To this our

Gospel leads more and more henceforth. His own joy follows, not as in Matthew dispensationally connected, but bound up with the blessedness of the disciples. Then the tempting lawyer is taught that, while those who trust themselves are as blind as they are powerless, grace sees one's neighbour in every one that needs love. The parable of the Samaritan is in Luke only. The close of the chapter teaches that the one thing needful, the good part, is to hear the word of Jesus. It is not only by the word that we are begotten; by it we are refreshed, nourished, and kept.

But prayer hereon follows (as He was praying), (chapter 11), not only because of our need, but to enjoy the God of grace Whose children we become through faith; and in His illustration He urges importunity. Here again we have an instructive example of the divine design by Luke as compared with that in chapter 6 of Matthew. His casting out a dumb demon gave to some occasion to blaspheme, whereon He declares that he that is not with Him is against Him, and he that gathers not with Him scatters: a solemn word for every soul. Nature has nothing to do with it, but the grace that hears and keeps the word of God. So did the Ninevites repent, and the Queen of Sheba come to hear; and more than Solomon and Jonah was there. But if light is not seen, it is the fault of the eye; if it is wicked, the body also is dark. Then to the end the dead externalism of man's religion is exposed, with the woe of such as have taken away the key of knowledge, and their malice when exposed.

Chapter 12 warns the disciples against hypocrisy, and urges the sure revelation of all things in the light, with the call to fear God and to confess the Son of Man, trusting not in themselves but in the Holy Spirit. It is no question now of Jewish blessing; and He would be no judge of earthly inheritances. They should beware of being like the rich fool whose soul is required when busy with gain. The ravens and the lilies teach a better lesson. The little flock need not fear, but rid themselves rather of what men covet, and seek a treasure unfailing: if it is in the heavens, there will the heart be. And thence is the Lord coming Whom they were habitually and diligently to wait for. Blessed they whom the Lord finds watching! Blessed he whom the Lord finds working! To put off His coming in heart is evil, and will be so judged. But the judgment will be righteous, and worst of all that of corrupt and faithless and apostate Christendom. Whatever His love, the opposition of man brings hate, and fire, and division, not peace meanwhile. His grace aroused enmity. Judgment came and will come; as on the other hand He was baptised in death that the pent up floods of grace might flow as they do in the gospel.

With the Jews on the way to the judge, and about to suffer from God's just government (at the end of the chapter before), the Holy Spirit in chapter 13 connects the question of what had befallen the Galileans. Here the Lord pronounces the exposure of all to perdition, except they repented. The parable of the fig tree tells the same tale; respite hung on Himself. In vain was the ruler of the synagogue indignant for the sabbath against Jehovah present to heal; it was but hypocrisy and preference of Satan. The kingdom about to follow His rejection was not to come in by manifested power and glory, but, as under man's responsibility, from a little seed to wax a great tree, and to leaven the assigned measure, wholly in contrast with Daniel 2, 7. Instead of gratifying curiosity as to "those to be saved" (the remnant), the Lord urges the necessity of entering by the strait gate (conversion to God); seeking their own way they would utterly fail. So He would tell them He knew them not whence they were, in the day when they should see the Jews even thrust out, and Gentiles sitting with the fathers, last first, and first last, in the Kingdom of God. Crafty as Herod was, it was Jerusalem He lamented, the guiltiest rejector alike of God's government and of His grace, yet not beyond His grace at the end.

Hence chapter 14 points out unanswerably the title of grace in the face of form, and its way of self-renunciation, which will be owned in the resurrection of the just, not by the religious world which is deaf to God's call to the great supper. But if the bidden remain without, grace fills it not only with the poor of the city but with the despised Gentiles. Only those that believe God's grace are called to break with the world. Coming to Christ costs all else: if one lose the salt of truth, none more useless and offensive.

In chapter 15 the Lord asserts the sovereign power of grace in His own seeking of the lost one, in the painstaking of the Spirit by the word, and in the Father's reception and joy when he is found; as self-righteousness betrays its alienation from the Father and contempt for the reconciled soul.

Then chapter 16 describes parabolically the Jew losing his place; so that the only wisdom was, not in hoarding for self but in giving up his master's goods, to make friends with an everlasting and heavenly habitation. Practical Christianity is the sacrifice of the present (which is God's) to secure the future (which will be our own, the true riches). Pharisees, being covetous, derided this; but death lifts the veil that then hid the true issue in the selfish rich tormented, and the once suffering beggar in Abraham's bosom. If God's word fail, not even resurrection would assure. Unbelief is invincible, save by His grace.

As grace thus delivers from the world, so it is to govern the believer's walk, who must take heed to himself, rebuke a sinning brother, and, if he repent, forgive him even seven times in the day (chapter 17). Faith is followed by answering power. But the yoke of Judaism, though still existing, is gone for faith, as the Lord shows in the Samaritan leper, who broke through letter of the law, rightly confessed the power of God in Christ, and went his way in liberty. The kingdom in His person was in the midst of men for faith. By-and-by it will be displayed visibly and judicially; for such will be the Son of Man (now about to suffer and be rejected) in His day, as in those of Noah and Lot, far different from the indiscriminate sack of Jerusalem by Titus.

Chapter 18 shows prayer to be the great resource, as always, so especially when oppression prevails in the latter day, and God is about to avenge His elect, and the question is raised if the coming Son of Man shall find faith on the earth. After this the Lord lets us see the spirit and ways suited to the kingdom in the penitent tax-gatherer contrasted with the Pharisee, and in the babes He received, not in the ruler who, not following Jesus because he clave to his riches, lost treasure in heaven. Yet he that leaves all for His sake receives manifold more now, and in the coming age life everlasting. Lastly the Lord again announces His ignominious death but His resurrection.

Then (verse 35) begins His last progress to Jerusalem and presentation as David's Son; and the blind beggar, invoking Him so, receives his sight, and follows Him, glorifying God.

Zacchaeus in chapter 19, chief tax-gatherer and rich, is the witness of yet more—the saving grace of God. But the Lord is not going to restore the Kingdom immediately, as they thought; He is going to a far country to receive it and to return; and when He does, He will examine the ways of His servants meanwhile entrusted with His goods and He will execute judgment on His guilty citizens who would not that He should reign over them. Next He rides to the city from the Mount of Olivet on a colt, given up at once by the owners; and the whole multitude of the disciples praise God aloud for all the powers they had seen, saying, Blessed the coming King in Jehovah's name: peace in heaven, and glory in the highest. It is a striking difference from the angels' praise at His birth; but both in season. Pharisees in vain object, and hear that the stones would cry out if the disciples did not. Yet did He weep over the city that knew not even then the things for its peace, doomed to destruction because it knew not the time of its visitation. The purging of the temple follows, and there He was teaching daily; yet could not the chief priests and the chiefs of the people destroy Him, though seeking it earnestly.

Then in chapter 20 come the various parties to judge Him, really to be judged themselves. The chief priests and the scribes with the elders demand His authority; which He meets with the question, Was John's baptism of heaven or from men? Their dishonest plea of ignorance drew out His refusal to tell such people the source of His authority. But He utters the parable of the vineyard let to husbandmen, who not only grew worse and worse to their lord's servants but killed at last his son and heir, to their own ruin according to Psalm 118:22, 23, adding His own solemn and twofold sentence. Next, we have His reply to the spies who would have entangled Him with the civil power; but as He asks for a denarius, and they own Cæsar's image on it, He bids them render to Cæsar Cæsar's things, and to God the things that are God's; and they were put to silence. The heterodox Sadducees followed with their difficulty as to the resurrection; whereon He shows that there was nothing in it but their ignorance of its glorious nature, of which present experience gives no hint. Resurrection belongs to the new age, to which marriage does not apply. Even now all live to God, if men cannot see. The Lord closes with His question on Psalm 110, how He Whom David calls his Lord is also his Son. It is just Israel's stumbling-stone, ere long to be Israel's sure foundation. Then the chapter concludes with His warning to beware of those that affect worldly show in religion, and prey on the weak and bereaved, about to receive, spite of long prayers, judgment all the more severe.

Chapter 21 begins with the poor widow and her two mites of more account than the richest in the offertory. Then, in correction of those who thought much of the temple adorned with goodly stones and offerings, the Lord predicts its approaching demolition, though the end was not to be immediately. But He cheers and counsels His own meanwhile. From verse 20 to 24 is the siege under Titus, and its consequences to this day. Verse 25 and the following look on to the future. The Gentiles are prominent; whence we have, "Behold the fig tree and all the trees" in verse 29. Observe also "this generation", &c. in 32, is in the future part, not in what is fulfilled. Lastly, verses 34-36 give moral appeal. Here again we find Him teaching in the temple by day, and every night lodging at Olivet.

The last Passover approaches (chapter 22) and found the chief priests and the scribes plotting, when Judas Iscariot* gave them the desired means. On the day of sacrifice He sent Peter and John to prepare, and the Lord instructs them divinely when and how: for as He said, "With desire I have desired to eat this passover with you before I suffer", and its cup He bade them take and divide it among themselves. Then He institutes His supper. As yet He had given no sign to mark the traitor, though He had long alluded to the fact. But alas! they were even then contending which of them would be accounted greatest; whilst He explains that such is the way of the Gentiles and their kings, whilst they were to follow His example—"I am in the midst of you as he that serveth." Yet He owns their continuance with Him in His temptations, and appoints to them a kingdom. He tells Simon of Satan's sifting, but of His supplication that his faith should not fail, and bids him, when turned again, or restored, to stablish his brethren. After further warning Peter, He clears up the change from a Messianic mission to the ordinary ways of providence in verses 35-38, and then goes out to the mount and passes through His agony with His Father (39-46) while the disciples slept. Then a crowd comes, and Judas drew near to kiss, and the Lord laid all open. He heals the high priest's bondman, whose right ear was cut off; but remonstrates, yet allows Himself to be taken Who could have overwhelmed them with a word. Peter denies Him thrice.

---

* It is quite general here in verse 3: "And [*not* Then] Satan entered into Judas." The precise time is shewn in John 13:27, where *then* is expressed; here the statement is general, as often in the third Evangelist. So in 24:12 it should be And or But, not *Then*.

The men revile the Lord with mockery and blows; and as soon as it was day, He is led to the Sanhedrin, and when asked if He were the Christ, He tells them of the place the Son of Man will take, and owns Himself Son of God.

Before Pilate in chapter 23 the effort was to prove Him a rival of Cæsar; but though confessing Himself the King of the Jews, Pilate found no fault in Him. The connection with Galilee gave the opportunity for a compliment to Herod, who got not a word from the Lord; but, after with his soldiers insulting Him, he sent Him back, when Pilate again sought to release Him, as neither he nor yet Herod found evidence against Him. But the Jews only the more fiercely demanded a seditious murderer to be released, and Jesus to be crucified. Still Pilate made a last effort. But their voices prevailed. And Pilate gave sentence that what they asked for should be done. Such is man; and such is religious man, even more wicked: "Jesus he delivered up to their will." Simon of Cyrene had to prove the violence of that hour; and Jerusalem's daughters lamented with wailing. But the Lord bade them weep for themselves and for their children, and proceeds to Calvary where He was crucified, and the two robbers on either side. There He prayed His Father to forgive them as rulers scoffed and soldiers mocked. Even one of those crucified kept railing on Him; but the other became a monument of grace, confessing the Saviour and King, when others forsook and fled. The centurion too bore testimony to Him; and if they made His grave with the wicked, the rich was there in His death, and with Pilate's leave laid His body in a tomb hewn in stone where never man had yet lain. It was Friday, growing dark, and sabbath twilight was coming on. And the Galilean women who saw Him laid there returned and prepared spices and unguents. Little did they know what God was about to do; yet they loved Him in Whom they believed.

On the first day of the week at early dawn the women came (chapter 24) but found the stone rolled away from the tomb and the body gone; and two in dazzling raiment stood by them to their alarm, who asked, "Why seek ye the Living One among the dead? He is not here, but is risen"; and they recalled to their minds His words in Galilee now fulfilled in His death and resurrection. Even the apostles disbelieved. And Peter went, and saw evidences and wondered. Then we have the walk to Emmaus with all its grace and deep instruction from the scriptures, not for those disheartened men only, but for all time and all believers. Next the Lord makes Himself known in the breaking of bread (the sign of death), and at once vanishes. For we walk by faith, not by sight. On returning to Jerusalem they hear how He had appeared to Simon; and as they spoke, the Lord stood in their midst, bids them handle Him and see (for they were troubled), and even eats to reassure them of His resurrection. He speaks further and opens their minds to understand the scriptures; a distinct thing from the power of the Spirit they were to receive in due time. No going to Galilee is introduced here; it was exactly suited to Matthew's design. Here Jerusalem is prominent, which was avowedly most guilty. So repentance and remission of sins "were to be preached in his name, unto all the nations, beginning with Jerusalem." There too they were to tarry till clothed with power from on high. But thence, when the day arrived, He led them out over against Bethany, and blessed them with uplifted hands; and, while blessing them, He parted from them and was borne up into heaven.

5.31 JOHN

Can it be doubted by any serious reader that the fourth Gospel presents the Lord pre-eminently in His divine aspect? He is the Word Who in the beginning was with God and was God. In Him was life, and the life was the light of men. He was made (or became) flesh; but none the less the Only-begotten *is* Son in the bosom of the Father, as we hear in the wonderful opening (chapter 1:1-18) of the three introductory chapters. Indeed most of chapter 4 is before His public ministry commences in Galilee after John was put in prison.

Chapter 1 is striking in its enumeration of His various titles, and in setting forth the work which on earth (verse 29) or from heaven (verse 33) none but a Divine Person could do. Chapter 2 prefigures the bridal joy He will usher in at His coming, and the judgment which is to cleanse the temple in Jerusalem; but it is as risen from the dead, as He announces. Man, however, was quite unmeet. Hence chapter 3 insists on his being born anew as indispensable even for the earthly things of the kingdom. But the Son of Man lifted up on the cross opens the way for heavenly things and life eternal, being in truth also the Son of God given in love to the world that the believer might be fully blessed. And the chapter closes with John's witness to His glory as above all, Whom the Father loves and has given all things to be in His hand.

To the woman of Samaria (chapter 4) the Lord opens the free giving of God in the Son stooping to the uttermost, yet giving not life only but living water, the Spirit, as a fountain within; as He goes on to the hour when the true worshippers worship the Father in spirit and truth. Not only does she own Him as the Christ, but many of the Samaritans believed because of her word, and many more because of His, confessing Him the Saviour of the world. When at Cana, the dying son of the courtier is healed by His word, though the father's faith at first was short and corrected by the Lord.

In Jerusalem (for this Gospel tells of His often working there), at the pool of Bethesda, He brings out His quickening and raising power, with a resurrection of judgment for unbelievers, in a discourse which grew out of a man long infirm being immediately made well. The latter part of chapter 5 points out man's responsibility because of the ample testimonies afforded.

Chapter 6 opens with the five loaves in His hand feeding five thousand men, and the Lord owned as the Prophet, refusing at present to be King, goes as Priest on high but will return to His own, tempest-tost as they may be, so that the ship at once reaches the land. The discourse follows, or rather discourses (see verse 59), in which He speaks of Himself coming down from heaven as the bread of God; next, giving His flesh to be eaten and His blood drunk; lastly, the Son of Man ascending where He was before: the Incarnation, the Redemption, and the Ascension, the "common faith".

Chapter 7 completes this portion by the disclosure that, though the time was not yet come to show Himself to the world as He surely will when He comes in His kingdom, He would give the Spirit when glorified, like rivers flowing out. It is the Spirit for bearing witness, as in chapter 4 for worship. Judaism is in all these chapters set aside for Christ, Who is really and in power what it was in figure, not to say much more.

In chapter 8 we have Christ, the Son, yea God, manifested by His word, but rejected; in chapter 9 manifested by His work, and equally rejected by those unbelievers who pretended to see, while the once blind from birth believed, saw, and worshipped Him. Chapter 10 closes this section by the Good Shepherd service of the Son, one with the Father, Whose word and work are the resting-place of His sheep, not Jews only but Gentiles, and even now one flock, one Shepherd.

The next portion gives the testimonies borne to the Lord Jesus; and first in chapter 11 as Son of God in power of resurrection shewn on Lazarus, already not dead only but buried, "for the glory of God, that the Son of God might be glorified thereby." The Jews, dead to all but self and present interests, are only afraid of the Romans; and Caiaphas, more wicked than Balaam, prophesies the expediency of one man (albeit Son of God!) dying for the people. Yes, grace in God sent Him, grace in Himself came, to die; but what blind and blasphemous iniquity in that expediency, whereby the whole nation morally speaking did perish, and their priesthood notably! In chapter 12 Mary's anointing Jesus' feet with the costly unguent is told, censured by the heartless covetousness of Judas about to betray Him. But the testimony is next given to Him as King of Israel, Son of David, when entering Jerusalem. Here the Greeks desire to see Jesus, Who answers, "The hour is come that the Son of Man should be glorified", and announces in His solemn formula the necessity of His death to bear much fruit. Thus could Gentiles be fellow-heirs as well as Jews in God's rich grace. But if man was insensible, the Lord realised the sacrifice; and the Father answered the trouble of His soul with the assurance of glorifying His name again, as He had already, to wit in resurrection. The Lord, no longer in figure but in open speech, explains the judgment of the world and of its prince, because of His rejection on the cross; whereby He becomes the centre for all, whether Jew or Gentile, the One by Whom alone the believer comes to God. From verse 37 the evangelist ponders on the situation of Jewish unbelief, as owned in Isaiah 6 and 53, putting God's seal on the prophet. It is the more awful because many even of the rulers did believe, but feared to confess through loving the glory of men rather than of God. From verse 44 it is Jesus in His last charge publicly laying bare the root of things. It was not Himself only come as light and to save: the word He had spoken should judge in the last day. The Father Who had sent Him, and Whose commandment is life eternal, was behind and above all.

Then in chapters 13-17 we have the communications that open out the coming association with Christ in heaven, which was a wholly new thing after the breach with the Jew, chapter 17 completing it by giving us to hear His communion with His Father thereon. The first of these presents Christ in the significant act of washing the disciples' feet, with (not blood but) water. It is His advocacy for us now in heaven with the Father, interceding for us, as we on earth are called to do for one another (14). Advocacy is not to form relations, but to restore communion when interrupted by sins: as generally misunderstood now as by Peter then, to the shame of those who have the Holy Spirit given them. Judas is excepted, whose betraying Him He most touchingly discloses after supper; "and he went out immediately; and it was night!" Thereon, in terms of infinite depth, the Lord says, "Now is the Son of man glorified, and God is glorified in him. If God is glorified in him, God also shall glorify him in himself, and shall straightway glorify him." There is the ground and the display of the righteousness of God in its highest character. The blessing proclaimed in the Gospel is its result to us in His grace. Here we have all fully in Christ, where none as yet could follow. Yet all are exhorted to love one another as His disciples. If Peter trusted himself, he should learn what he himself was by denying Him thrice.

Chapter 14 follows, comforting the disciples on His departure by the blessed hope of His coming to receive them for the Father's house, whither He was going to prepare a place for them: a wonderful statement indeed of that wonderful hope. Next, He points out what the Father is Whom He had been showing while here, words and works alike the Father's; as they should do even greater works because of His going to the Father. Obedience was to be the witness of their loving Him; on His part, the Father at the Son's instance would give them another Advocate, the Spirit of truth, to dwell with them for ever, yea to be in them. Hence in that day they should know that Christ is in the Father, and they in Him, and He in them. But obedience should only be deepened, not of His commandments only but of His word. Here comes in the Christian's responsibility, and in the Father's government of our souls more enjoyment follows fidelity. Indifference to the Saviour's words would prove that one loves Him not. The Advocate, the Holy Spirit, Whom the Father would send in His name, should teach them all things, as well as recall all that Christ had said. He leaves them peace, and gives them His peace. Why then be troubled or fear? Love to Him would rejoice that He was going to the Father. Now that He is rejected, the enemy acquires the title of Prince or Ruler of this world; but his coming finds nothing in Christ, Who loves the Father and obeys, as Adam disobeyed, unto death. And what a death was His!

Chapter 15 treats of Christ as superseding Israel (fully proved an empty vine, and worse), and the disciples as branches, responsible to bear fruit, but this only done so by abiding in Him. Not life, still less unity of the members with the Head, is in question, but practical cleaving to Him in order to fruit. Those who do not are cut off as hollow professors. Keeping His commandments is to abide in His love; for here it is ours to Him in daily practice, not His to us as in the gospel. Even here His love to us is the spring and pattern of ours one to another; but it is as friends, who once were enemies; and He chose us to bear fruit abidingly, telling us all He heard from His Father, and assuring us that what we ask of the Father in His name He will give us. He urges mutual love in the face of the world's hatred, as of Him, so of those who must expect persecution for His sake, and are avowedly not of the world. Christ's words and works had only brought out hatred of Him and His Father—a sin outdoing all other sins. But the Advocate when come would testify of Him, as those also did who were with Him from the beginning.

In chapter 16 we have distinctly the presence of the Holy Spirit Whom Jesus sends; and He, when come, demonstrates to the world sin, righteousness, and judgment; as He guides the disciples into all the truth, and announces the things to come, thus glorifying Christ. It was but a "little while" in contrast with Jewish expectation. Meanwhile how wondrous to have the Father plainly revealed, and to be loved of Him ourselves, and to have peace in Christ with tribulation in the world!

Chapter 17 crowns all with the Son's spreading before the Father His person and His work as His double plea for glorification, but in order to glorify the Father in the objects of their common love beyond all thought of man. He requests that they should be associated with Him before the Father as well as before the world; and at length be with Him and behold His glory, and meanwhile yet more know the Father's name with its blessed consequences.

Chapter 18 commences the final scenes: the betrayal of Judas, the denial of Peter, the blasphemous unbelief of Annas and Caiaphas, the guilty yielding of Pilate against his conscience, and the guiltier clamour of the Jews who prefer Barabbas. In chapter 19 Pilate scourges Jesus, but vainly strives against spite till the chief priests disavow the Christ of God in the apostate answer, We have no king but Cæsar. The only One that shines with divine dignity and grace is Jesus, as this is the design of the Gospel: not His agony in the garden, but the prostration of the band at His name; not the forsaking on the cross, but, "It is finished", and the dismissal of His spirit; for He, and He only, had authority to lay down His life (soul) and to take it again. Here too is noticed the piercing of His side after death, and the blood and water that came out, as John testifies in the Gospel and applies in his First Epistle. Also Nicodemus reappears, and Joseph (whatever man designed)—"with the rich in his death". In chapter 20, early as Mary of Magdala came on the first day of the week, she found the stone taken away from the tomb. Peter and John run at her call, and see the evidence of His resurrection. They had not as yet known the scripture that He must rise. Such faith is powerless. Mary knew no more, but remained weeping; when first angels, then the Lord, ask her why she wept. All was known when He said, "Mary." He forbids her touching Him (not so was the Christian to know Him, but as glorified), and sends His message of full grace to His brethren, I ascend to My Father and your Father, and My God and your God. At evening within the shut doors they were assembled, when Jesus stood in the midst, announces peace to them, and gives them their mission of peace, with administrative remission and retention of sins. Thomas was both absent and unbelieving; but eight days after he was with them, and Jesus comes, though the doors were shut, and again salutes them, with full acceptance of Thomas' challenge to shame him into faith, so that he cries, My Lord and my God. The words that follow confirm the conviction that he typifies the Jew brought to see and believe, after the Christian is called to the better part—believing without seeing.

Chapter 21 appends typically the millennial haul of many great fishes from the sea of the nations, in contrast with the catch now (as in Luke) where the nets break and the boats are sinking. Peter is then probed, but reinstated before his brethren and entrusted with Christ's lambs and sheep. Besides, he is assured of that portion by grace which could not be in his self-confidence. Next John has his place defined enigmatically; not as the earliest tradition said, that he should not die, "but if I will that he abide until I come, what [is it] to thee?" All is left in suspense. John remained, when all the rest were gone, to point out the passing away of the churches, "the things that are", and to predict the judgments on the world which precede the Lord's return in visible glory, when He will take His great power and reign.

5.32 The Acts of the Apostles

What then is the aim of this book, the sequel of the third Gospel? As the title is human, one may draw from its own contents that we have in it the working of the Holy Spirit, rather than of the Twelve of whom we hear little save of Peter, and of Paul called extraordinarily, but of others too who were not apostles.

In the first chapter the risen Christ is seen ascending to heaven after forty days since His resurrection, and injunctions given to the apostles through the Holy Spirit Who was soon to baptise them. But instead of His restoring at this time the kingdom to Israel as they expected, they were to be His witnesses everywhere when they received power, whilst waiting for His return from heaven. Meanwhile they gave themselves to persevering prayer; and Peter takes the lead in filling up the vacant place of Judas Iscariot among the witnesses of His resurrection, according to Psalm 109.

On the day of Pentecost, as they were all together, the Father's promise was fulfilled with twofold outward signs: a blowing sound out of heaven that filled all the house; and parted tongues as of fire that sat on each, so that all were filled with the Holy Spirit and began to speak in other languages as He gave them utterance—the answer of grace to the judgment of Babel. While all were amazed and some mocked, Peter vindicated the wonderful work of God by citing the close of Joel 2, though he does not say it was its fulfilment yet till the great and gloriously appearing day of Jehovah. He then lays on the men of Israel the awful sin of crucifying, through lawless men's hand, Jesus, Whom God raised up (Psalm 16), the Christ yet to sit on David's throne (Psalm 132), meanwhile ascended to sit at Jehovah's right hand (Psalm 110). Pricked in their heart when they heard this, they were called to repent and be baptised in His name; when they too should receive the Holy Spirit. For to them and theirs was the promise. In that day about 3,000 souls were added, and such fellowship in joyous unselfish love and truth and in holy worship as earth had never seen; and the Lord kept adding day by day together those to be saved. It was the church's birthday (chapter 2), though there remained then, and for long, attachment to the institutions of the law.

Accordingly, while going up to the temple, Peter and John were asked alms by a notorious cripple. This was met by Peter's bidding him, in the name of Jesus, arise and walk; as he did immediately before all. And Peter proclaimed that it was the God of their fathers glorifying His Servant Jesus, Whom *they* delivered up and denied when even Pilate had decided to release Him. They denied the Holy and Just One, preferring a murderer to Him Whom God raised up as the apostles testified. It was the virtue of His name which in faith wrought that deed. He called them then (for grace would treat His rejection as ignorance) to repent and be converted for the blotting out of their sins, so that seasons of refreshing might come from the Lord's presence, and He would send Jesus, Whom heaven must receive till times of restoring all things according to the prophets. This will be the kingdom in power, as the church knows the kingdom in patience till then. But Jesus was the Prophet of Whom Moses spoke in Deuteronomy 18, as all others foretold of these days, for He was also the true Seed of promise for blessing (chapter 3).

But Saducean unbelief here opposed the risen Christ (chapter 4), as Pharisaic self-righteousness hated Him when here below. And the two apostles were put in ward unto the morrow, when the high priest and his party enquired and learnt distinctly from Peter that it was in the name of Him Whom *they* crucified, Whom God raised from the dead, that the infirm man stood before them whole. Psalm 118:22 was cited as the most irrefragable evidence and for declaring Jesus the only Saviour. Unable to reply they, after consultation, charged them not to utter a word nor teach in the name of Jesus, but received the bold reply whether they should be hearkened to rather than God, for themselves could not but speak what they saw and heard. These, let go, came unto "their own" (for so the Christians are now distinctly called), and reported all; when arose with one accord their cry to God, applying Psalm 2:1, 2, but with no thought at all that the following verses could be accomplished till Christ comes again. The Holy Spirit wrought in answer, and gave great power to their testimony of His resurrection and in all ways of grace, Barnabas then first shining conspicuously.

Chapter 5 opens with the sin and judgment of Ananias and Sapphira, deliberately guilty against the gracious working that characterised all at that time; but God turned it to great fear within and without, yet adding more than ever to the Lord, and working in mighty power on men's bodies. Hence the high priest was incensed beyond measure and put in prison all the twelve, who were brought out by an angel and sent to speak in the temple all the words of this life. Led thence by the captain of the temple with the officers, they openly answered that God must be obeyed rather than men, and asserted that the Holy Spirit was witness, as well as they, of what they set forth. This cut to the heart. Counsel was taken to slay them; but Gamaliel with a certain fear of God gave such sound advice, that they satisfied themselves with beating them and reiterated injunction not to speak in the Name. They however retired with joy that they were counted worthy of dishonour for the Name, which every day in the temple and at home they ceased not to teach and preach.

Another cloud gathered; again failure against the very grace that was so marked. Jealousy and mistrust came in, the Hellenists against the Hebrews, as if their widows were not duly cared for (chapter 6). The twelve cope with the danger in wisdom and grace, calling on the mass of the believers to choose seven men of good report, full of the Holy Spirit and wisdom, to relieve the apostles of this outward task and be set by them over the business. For what the church gave, the church was entitled to choose. It is the Lord only who gave spiritual gifts, which are therefore above man's choice. So when the seven were chosen (apparently all Hellenists), the apostles prayed and laid their hands on them. And great blessing followed, even a crowd of the priests obeying the faith. But as Stephen surpassed all in grace and power, so he soon became an object for deadly persecution, and false witnesses were set up, when he was brought before the council.

In chapter 7 he gave the striking testimony, which convicted them, like their fathers, of always resisting the Holy Spirit. Beginning with the call of Abraham (tardy in obeying wholly), he shows him to have been but a pilgrim in the land of promise, as his descendants were bondmen in Egypt, the sons of Jacob selling their brother Joseph to the Gentiles before that. But God, with wonders and signs, delivered them by Moses, whom they had rejected. Even so they went after idols, as the prophets long after testified, and were carried for it beyond Babylon. Law and prophets, Christ and the Spirit, made no difference: they opposed and forsook all. So now, exasperated by the truth, they stoned God's witness invoking the Lord to receive his spirit, and to lay not this sin to his murderers' charge.

A great persecution followed, and the greatest persecutor of the saints a young man named Saul (chapter 8). But grace used those scattered by it, not the twelve, to preach the gospel far and wide. Philip, clothed with power, proclaimed the Christ to the Samaritans to their great joy; so that even Simon the sorcerer, believing the miracles, professed faith and was baptised. The apostles sent Peter and John, who crowned the work with the gift of the Spirit in answer to their prayers and by imposition of hands. But Peter detected Simon's unreality; and while he and John returned, Philip is used to the salvation of the Ethiopian noble travelling home from Jerusalem, but was caught away by divine power for other work, so as to confirm the convert only the more who went on his way rejoicing.

The ninth chapter shows us the new step of sovereign grace in the conversion of Saul to be the witness of an ascended Christ, Who owns the saints as part of Himself, and calls the persecutor to be His chosen vessel to bear His name before Gentiles, kings, and children of Israel, the deepest in truth, the largest in heart, the most abundant in labour of all the apostles. No wonder the gospel of Christ's glory marked him, who first saw and heard the Lord thus; yet a simple disciple baptised him who forthwith, in the synagogues, preached Jesus as the Son of God. Even the disciples in Jerusalem were afraid; but Barnabas, having a deeper sense of grace, banished their fears by showing what the Lord had wrought. When here too menaced with Jewish violence, Saul is sent to Tarsus. The rest of the chapter recounts Peter's activity and power in the Spirit; the paralytic

Æneas healed, the dead Tabitha raised, and all around in the Sharon converted, with many in Joppa.

Chapter 10 presents Peter used to open the kingdom to the Gentile Cornelius and his friends, in spite of his own Jewish prejudice. Already converted and devout, Cornelius was yet without; and the law kept such there. The gospel brings them within, as well as converts those who were enemies, telling words whereby believers "shall be saved". For "salvation" means more than to be born again. In a vision seen by Peter, as well as by an angel sent to Cornelius, we see the way God took to call and gather the uncircumcision. Peter preached the gospel, and while he was yet speaking, the Holy Spirit fell on all those hearing the word, who were accordingly baptised at Peter's direction by the brethren that accompanied him from Joppa.

As this unexpected act of accrediting Gentile confessors, no less than Jewish, roused strong objection in Jerusalem (chapter 11), Peter set out the matter as originating in God's word and culminating in the fullest token of God's favour—the equal gift of the Spirit to those Gentiles as to themselves. They could only be still, and even glorify God for His grace. Concurrently with this we hear how God blessed the free action of the Spirit in the scattered preachers to many, not Hellenists but Greeks as the right reading tells us. And Barnabas is sent to Antioch where the work had been; as Peter and John went before to Samaria. He seeks Saul; and there both taught for a whole year, where the disciples were first called Christians. As a prophet predicted universal famine, love wrought actively and maintained sense of unity by sending relief to the brethren in Judea through Barnabas and Saul.

In Jerusalem the Spirit testifies (chapter 12) to the murderous hatred that animated the people and their king, who killed James the brother of John, and apprehended Peter with a like intent. But God answered the prayers of the saints, even to their own surprise, in delivering him the very night before the purposed execution. And ere long Jehovah's angel that brought the apostle out of prison smote the self-exalting king. The word of God grew. Barnabas and Saul returned from Jerusalem, as Peter left on his deliverance; but we hear no more of his active work, though he spoke to good purpose in Jerusalem (chapter 15) at the council.

The solemn and momentous mission of Barnabas and Saul for work among the Gentiles is recorded in chapter 13. It was from the Syrian Antioch (Antakieh), and by the Spirit through a prophet, their fellow-labourers fasting and laying hands on them as thus commended to God's grace. Going to Seleucia they sail to Cyprus and preached in the synagogues in Salamis. But at Paphos Jewish hatred to the gospel's reaching the Gentiles is judged by the infliction of blindness for a season, whilst the proconsul believed. But from Perga in Pamphylia, John Mark (not then profitable for service) returned to Jerusalem; and the apostles come to Antioch (Yalobatch) in Pisidia, where Paul, as he was now called, preached Jesus and the resurrection in the synagogue, dwelling on Psalms 2, 16, and Isaiah 55, with the warning of Habakkuk 1:5. On the next sabbath almost all the city flocked to hear; which filled the Jews with a jealousy that drew out the striking use of Isaiah 49 to the joy of the Gentiles, though the apostles were expelled.

At Iconium (Koniyeh), the capital of Lycaonia, the apostles had like experience (chapter 14) in the face of signs and wonders; and when worse was purposed, they fled to Lystra and Derbe and the surrounding regions, and preached. At Lystra a miracle of healing would have led to offering them sacrifice, had they not utterly refused it, exhorting them to turn to the one living and gracious God. Yet at the instigation of Jews that came and opposed they stoned Paul, who revived and departed next day to Derbe, where they preached and taught, but revisited the scenes of their labours on their return through Attalia (Adalia) in Pamphylia, from whence they sailed to their point of departure. On this journey they chose elders for the disciples in every church. At Antioch they related to the assembly what God had wrought among the Gentiles.

Chapter 15 records how the Judaising snare which would have put Gentiles under law was put down authoritatively in Jerusalem itself by the apostles and elders, with the whole assembly concurring. Peter testifies, as well as Barnabas and Paul; James sums up in the establishment of liberty for the Gentiles, but of course recognising those principles which prevailed from Noah's time before the law. Thence Paul and Barnabas return (Judas Barsabas and Silas being chosen to go with them), and read the letter at Antioch whence Judas returns, Silas remaining. But after a while the question of taking John Mark on their next missionary journey led Paul to sever himself from Barnabas and take Silas with him, recommended afresh to the Lord's grace (which is not said of Barnabas): ordination it clearly was not.

From chapters 16 to 20 we see the free power of the Spirit in the apostle's ministry, its character, and its effects. Compare his circumcising Timothy, and his refusal of it in the case of Titus; his use of the apostolic decrees in the cities passed through, and his solving the question independently of that letter in writing to the Corinthians. The Holy Spirit (for the book treats of His action rather than of the apostles') specifically calls him to fresh scenes. After visiting Phrygia, and working in Galatia and in Philippi of Macedonia, it is still "To the Jew first and to the Greek." Satan wrought by applauding the servants through a Pythoness; but Paul exorcised the spirit. A tumult ensued set on by those whose gain was stopped, and the colonial Duumvirs (for it was a Roman province) yielded for peace' sake and committed them to prison; where God (not the prisoners only) heard their praises and answered by such an earthquake as never was before or since: doors opened, bonds loosed, yet none escaped. The alarmed jailor received the gospel on the spot, and was baptised, he and all his, immediately. But the magistrates, wishing to hush up things, are compelled by Paul to own their wrong: and Paul and Silas depart at their request.

In chapter 17, at Thessalonica, we see the more usual religious opposition to the gospel; and some converts are brought before the Politarchs, who take security and no more. The brethren send away Paul and Silas to Berœa, where the Jews prove more noble than those in Thessalonica, being such as received the word of God readily, and searched the scriptures too. But when Jewish enmity pressed here also, Paul went off, Silas and Timothy abiding. At Athens the apostle reasoned in the synagogue and in the market place; and, when attacked by Epicurean and Stoic philosophers, made a speech at the Areopagus, which refuted alike Chance and Fate by a Creator Who is misrepresented by idols, the work of men's hands, and Who will judge the habitable earth, having given proof to all in raising from the dead Jesus Christ the righteous.

From that inquisitive seat of art and letters, where the fruit was small, the apostle goes to dissolute Corinth (chapter 18). There after Jewish opposition the Lord assured him of His protection, as He had much people in it: and there he stayed a year and a half teaching the word of God. Even the proconsul Gallio's indifference to Jewish plots and to contemptuous Gentile violence shielded him. After a visit to Ephesus where the Jews were willing to hear, he goes to Jerusalem to pay a vow as well as salute the assembly, and revisits Galatia and Phrygia. From verse 24 we have the interesting account of the Spirit's way with Apollos at Ephesus.

After that while he was at Corinth (chapter 19), Paul comes to Ephesus; and finding a dozen disciples, who, like Apollos at first, only knew the word of the beginning of Christ, he sets the truth of the gospel before them; and they are baptised unto the name of the Lord Jesus. We may profitably compare Ephesians 1:13, 14. He preached for three months in the synagogue; when conflict came, he separated the disciples, discoursing daily in the school of Tyrannus; and this for two years, so that all in the province of Asia heard the word of the Lord. There the wiles of the enemy in profane Jews bowed before the power of the Lord Jesus, even when great gain through sorcery was in question. Here again Satan raised an uproar against His servants, by which the Jews sought to profit. Yet in fact it was the mingled pride of local idolatry and their interests which agitated men; and some of the Asiarchs who were friendly dissuaded the apostle from taking part in the scene. But after much outcry the town-clerk pointed out the futility and disorder of the proceedings, and dismissed the meeting.

The next chapter (20) opens with Paul's departure for Macedonia, where he exhorted much, and then came to Greece for three months; but when Jewish plots threatened, he resolved to make his way to Jerusalem through Macedonia. At Troas we have the instructive account of a Lord's-day; and Eutychus suffers for his drowsiness, but is restored through the apostle to the comfort of all. From Miletus the apostle sent to Ephesus for the elders of the church, and gave them that really edifying charge which fills the latter part of the chapter. He feels as if his work was closed, dwelling on its character for their profit. He does not doubt that bonds and afflictions await him; and as he was clean from the blood of all, he calls on them to take heed to themselves and to all the flock wherein the Holy Spirit set them overseers, to feed God's assembly. He knows of a sad change after his departure, not only grievous wolves coming in, but from among themselves men rising up, speaking perverse things to draw away the disciples. Not a hint of succession as a safeguard, but a sure declension. Yet he commits them to God and to the word of His grace. This is the resource in perilous times. And in the spirit of His grace had Paul laboured, as they ought, remembering the words of the Lord Jesus, the reflex of Himself. No wonder that they wept, especially at the word that they were to see his face no more.

As far as the inspired history speaks, the active service of the apostle was closed. His latest Epistles give evidence that he wrought freely between his first and second imprisonments in Rome. But his visit to Jerusalem (chapter 21), against which he was cautioned, issued in his arrest, and the book terminates with Paul a prisoner. It was thus the fellowship of Christ's sufferings, rejected by the Jews whom he loved, and the Gentiles urged by them not only to imprison but to kill him.

On his way he enjoys Christian communion at Tyre; then from Cæsarea he goes on in the face of warning, and in Jerusalem yields to Jewish feeling, which brought on the opposition it was meant to allay: all Jerusalem in uproar, and the multitude demanding his death.

In chapter 22 he addresses his defence in Hebrew to the excited Jews, who hear the wondrous tale of his conversion, but are convulsed afresh. Mission to the Gentiles they would not endure; as he should have learnt from the Lord's words to him in a previous trance. As the Jews raged murderously, so the Roman tribune or chiliarch violated law in his haste; and in Jerusalem the apostle did not display the power which marked him in his own proper field outside.

Nor in chapter 23 do we see the same superiority to circumstances, as usual, before the council, where he set the Pharisees in his favour against the Sadducees. But the grace of the Lord was as perfect as ever to cheer him, when he needed it sorely: he was to bear witness in Rome, as in Jerusalem. Then we find the Jewish plot discovered, and Paul conveyed to Cæsarea under a characteristic letter from the tribune to the governor or procurator, Felix.

Five days after, the high priest and the elders, with an orator they had retained, accused the apostle of that which he refuted with simple truth and dignity, pointing out the resurrection as the occasion of offence. Felix, conversant with Jewish prejudice, gives latitude to Paul till Lysias came down and all was known. But after an interval he and his wife Drusilla, a Jewess, sent for Paul, who, instead of discussing the faith, dealt with the conscience, so that Felix trembled and closed the interview. The "convenient season" to hear more never came. Disappointed of a bribe from Paul, and willing to gratify the Jews, Felix left him bound when Porcius Festus succeeded (chapter 24).

The new procurator (chapter 25) was equally unscrupulous. For at Cæsarea he proposed to send Paul to Jerusalem, which he had before refused to the Jews; thereon Paul appealed unto Cæsar, which compelled Festus to act on it. But the arrival of king Agrippa with Bernice furnished a new occasion for testimony before the dignities of this age; and Festus was glad, not only to give these members of the Herod family a hearing of interest, but to gather matter for a report to the emperor.

In chapter 26 Paul before all again lays stress on the resurrection as the basis of the promised hope, and tells how he, as determined a foe of Jesus as any, had seen His glory from heaven and heard His voice constituting him a witness, and taking him out of the people and the nations, to which last he was now sent. And this was to turn them from darkness to light and the power of Satan to God, that they might receive remission of sins and inheritance among those that are sanctified by faith in Christ the Lord. Not disobedient to the heavenly vision, he was standing to this day to the call of God everywhere, which drew on him the hatred of the Jews; yet was it in full accord with what Moses and the prophets said should be. Festus broke out as an incredulous heathen; but Paul calmly appealed to the king as one cognisant of the prophets; and his answer proved that he was not unmoved, though seeking to hide it. This drew out from the captive apostle the expression of a heart filled with a happiness he desired for them all, except his bonds. They admitted his innocence: only his appeal sent him to Cæsar.

Then in chapter 27 we have his voyage as far as Malta where the shipwreck occurred. We hear not of evangelising; but the proof is plain that faith saw clearly in circumstances so novel where no other eye did. It was reserved for a naval man, a Christian in our day, to clear up terms and facts misunderstood by all previous translators ignorant of things marine. Yet the great feature was unmistakable: the reality of God's mind and care enjoyed here by the believer.

The last chapter is also full of interest. Paul practically proves the truth of Mark 16:18 (first clause and last); and many honours and kindnesses followed for the Christians from the heathen islanders. In another ship, of Alexandria, the rest of the voyage was completed; and they slowly made their way from Puteoli to Rome, met on the road by the brethren at Appii Forum and Tres Tabernae. This cheered even the apostle. Arrived at the great city Paul was suffered to abide by himself with the soldier that guarded him, and after three days called together the chief of the Jews, and explained the strange fact that for the hope of Israel he was a prisoner through Jewish accusation. On a subsequent day he testifies the kingdom of God, and sets forth Jesus from the law and the prophets, some being persuaded while others disbelieved. So that Paul could but show them now the sentence finally of the Holy Spirit, as of the Son on earth (John 12) and of Jehovah of old (Isaiah 6). But if Israel cut themselves off, save a remnant (the pledge of future restoration), the salvation of God is sent to Gentiles who hear.

Such is the bearing of this book first and last. Only it is well to add that the apostle's charge in chapter 20 is no less clear that after his departure evil would prevail in the church, as previously in Israel. And we know from Romans 11 that the Gentile, if not continuing in God's goodness (as he surely has not), must also be cut off, and thus make way for the recall of Israel to the universal joy and blessing of the world under the Redeemer.

5.33 THE EPISTLE OF PAUL TO THE ROMANS

It is scarce possible to overlook or mistake the divine aim. For herein, on the proved failure of man, God's righteousness is revealed, by or of faith unto faith, with its resulting deliverance (1-8). Yet sovereign grace like this is conciliated with special mercy and unfailing promises to Israel (9-11). The practical consequences of God's mercies are urged in devotedness as a living sacrifice to Him personally, as well as in subjection to the world's authority, and in grace one toward another (12-16).

In chapter 1 the inspired writer presents himself as bondman of Jesus Christ, a called apostle, separated unto God's gospel, which He promised before through His prophets in holy scriptures. It is now fulfilled; for it is concerning His Son, Who came of David's seed according to flesh, and also marked out Son of God in power according to the Spirit of holiness by resurrection of the dead—Jesus Christ our Lord. Thus He is heir of promise, and conqueror of death. It is not yet the day when to Him shall the obedience of the peoples be; but He is sending out witnesses of Himself, as here *He* was God's faithful Witness. Through Him Paul received grace and apostleship, not for law but for faith-obedience among all the nations, in behalf of His name; among whom were also they called of Jesus Christ, all that were in Rome beloved of God: they saints, as he apostle, not by birth or merit but called respectively by divine grace. He wishes them grace and peace from God our Father and the Lord Jesus Christ, as he did to all saints. It was not only that he thanked his God for them, always at his prayers beseeching that he might be prospered in God's will to come to them, for joint comfort as he graciously said; but he was hindered hitherto. He is not ashamed of the glad tidings, for God's power it is (not promise merely) to every one that believes, both to Jew first and also to Greek; for God's righteousness in it is revealed, and therefore by faith unto faith. Thus the gospel is about God's Son; and therein God's righteousness is revealed, in contrast with His law in vain claiming human righteousness. Hence as faith is the way or principle (so wrote the prophet), it was open to every believer, Jew and Greek (as wrote the apostle). Such is the introduction (verses 1-17).

Then follows from chapter 1:18 to 3:20 the overwhelming proof of man's dire need of the gospel. For God's wrath is revealed from heaven (in contrast with earthly judgments under law) upon all impiety and unrighteousness of men holding fast the truth in unrighteousness. As this embraces both Gentiles and Jews, he from verse 21 to the end of chapter 1 shows the shameless departure of mankind from God: first, ignoring the testimony of creation (19, 20); secondly, abandoning what they knew, especially by the public demonstration of moral government given in the deluge. Professing to be wise they were befooled, and changed the truth of God into falsehood; and as they gave up God for idolatrous images, God gave them up to vile lusts and a reprobate mind. Such were the heathen for ages before, and when the gospel went forth, morally as bad or worse (21-32).

But had there not been philosophic moralists who judged those unspeakable enormities and religious follies (chapter 2)? Yes, but they did the same things; and their fine words could not screen them from the judgment of God. For they despised His long-suffering goodness, which leads to repentance, and thus treasured up wrath in a day of wrath. Then God will render to each according to his works, Jew and Greek (for with Him is no favouritism, though He considers privilege or the lack of it), in a day when He will judge the secrets of men through Jesus Christ (1-16).

From 2:17-29 the Jew is weighed, and his rest on the law, and boast in God, and superiority in light to others; but how about his own ways? Was not the name of God blasphemed among the nations on their account, as it is written? Unrighteousness made circumcision uncircumcision, as righteous uncircumcision will be reckoned for circumcision. Shadows are gone with God, Who insists on reality; and he only has the praise of God who is a Jew in what is secret, and heart-circumcision is in spirit, not in letter.

Are divine privileges nothing? Much every way, says the apostle in chapter 3 (1-19); and in nothing so much as having the scriptures. Yet the unbelief of some cannot invalidate either the faith of God or His right to judge. Was not the Jew then better than the Greek? In no wise. Jews and Greeks are alike under sin. This is shewn in Psalm 53, &c., Isaiah 59, &c. "Now we know that whatever things the law saith, it speaketh to those under (or, in the scope of) the law, that *every* mouth may be stopped and all the world come under judgment to God." The Jew, who would readily allow the Gentile to be hopelessly evil, is expressly condemned by the scriptures. All then were guilty beyond dispute. "Wherefore by deeds of law shall no flesh be justified in his sight; for through law is knowledge of sin" (verse 20).

From verse 21 God's mouth is open to declare His grace, and how it can be righteously, now that every mouth of man is stopped. It is God's righteousness manifested apart from law, witnessed by the law and the prophets; God's righteousness by faith in (literally of) Jesus Christ unto all, and upon all that believe: its universal direction, and its actual effect (confounded in the Revised Version, because of trusting the blunder of some old manuscripts, but right in the Authorised Version). For there is this distinction. All in fact sinned, and come short of the glory of God; for this becomes the standard, when Adam's paradise was lost. Hence there is "no way" but being justified freely through the redemption that is in Christ Jesus, Whom God set forth a propitiatory through faith in His blood for showing His righteousness in the present time, that He might be just and justify him that is of faith in (literally of) Jesus. What can be plainer or more precise? Behold boasting excluded. If law can be said, it is faith-law, apart from works of law; and God is of Gentiles as well as of Jews— one God justifying Jews by faith only, and Gentiles through the faith which they have (and hence only in this case the article is used). Thus is law established, not annulled, through the faith of Jesus Who paid the penalty to the utmost.

Did the Jew plead the cause of Abraham for favour to his seed? The apostle answers in chapter 4:1-5 that Abraham *believed* God, and it was reckoned for righteousness. David's case (6-8) equally and quite as evidently proves that all depends on God's grace through faith. For how else is a transgressor to have blessedness? We see again, how circumcision contributed nothing; for Abraham was reckoned righteous by faith when uncircumcised (9-12). Faith secures the promised heirship of the world in the face of all natural disabilities; not law, which works wrath through man's transgression (13-19). Faith on the contrary gives glory to God, and reaps its fruit (20-22). And the Christian has more even than Abraham, fully persuaded as he was that what God had promised He was able also to do; whereas we believe on Him Who actually raised from among the dead Jesus our Lord Who was given up for our offences and was raised for our justification (23-25). Thus as the latter part of chapter 3 brought in propitiation through Christ's blood, chapter 4 adds the intervention of God in justifying us by His raising Him from the dead, though not without our faith.

Chapter 5:1-11 draws the blessed consequences: peace with God in view of the past, His grace for the present, and His glory in the future. Not only do we boast this, but also in tribulations, as the allotted experience of Christians now, knowing the invaluable result to which God turns them, in breaking the will, and severing from the world, and lifting above things seen; so that faith, love, and hope are all strengthened by better learning God's love. Not only are we so, but "boasting in God through our Lord Jesus Christ, through whom now we received the reconciliation." Beyond this "boasting in God" it is impossible to rise. One may learn the glories of Christ in God's purpose and our own union with Him in them; but to boast in God Himself is of unequalled depth and joy, and we are called to it now.

Yet a profound discussion forms the needed supplement to that which we have already had, dealing not with our sins, but with sin in the flesh, and deliverance in Christ learnt experimentally and enjoyed by the power of the Holy Spirit in the believer. Hence from Romans 5:11 (closing the former part) the apostle is no longer occupied with the evils we had done, and the grace of God in justifying the guilty by faith. He now lays bare the root of all that we are, and so goes up to Adam, the figure of Him that was to come. For as to man there are two heads, of whom scripture speaks: as of sin and death in him who transgressed where all was good, so of obedience and life eternal in the face of nothing but self-will and ruin here below; the first man, and the Second. For, as we know, no Jew doubted that one man's sin brought those dreadful consequences on the human race.

If this were just on God's part, as they allowed, was it not worthy of God to bring in the gift by grace through one man, Jesus Christ? Adam was under *a* law, and the Jews had *the* law; and transgression followed for both. But the nations who had not law were none the less sinners, and thus obnoxious to death like the Jews; for in fact death reigned universally. But shall not the act of favour be as the offence? And shall not the gift be as through one that sinned? Accordingly, as the bearing through one offence was to condemn all men, so is it through one righteousness toward all men for justification of life. For as through the one man's disobedience the many were constituted sinners, so through the One's obedience the many shall be constituted righteous (verses 12-19).

Thus grace far outstript sin; and if the Adam family were obnoxious to death through sin, the Christ family in spite of manifold sins shall be justified and reign in life. The law came in by the way, that the offence might abound and so crush Jewish self-righteousness; but where sin (and not transgression only) abounded, grace exceeded far; that as sin reigned in death, so also grace might reign through righteousness unto life eternal through Jesus Christ our Lord (verses 20, 21).

Chapter 6 meets the cavil that grace tends to license sinning. This, the apostle shows, contradicts the truth that we died to sin, and by baptism unto Christ Jesus were baptised unto His death; in order that as Christ was raised up from the dead by the glory of the Father, so we too should walk in newness of life. He that died has been justified from sin; for it is a question not of sins forgiven, but of sin and of continuing in it, which death with Christ denies. Hence this also is the meaning of our baptism (verses 1-14). But there is the further reply that being under grace, not law, is the way of holiness for those set free from sin and become bondmen to God. For the wages of sin is death, but God's act of favour is life eternal in Christ Jesus our Lord (verses 15-23).

Then in chapter 7 Christ dead through Whom we were made dead is deliverance from law, as in chapter 6 from sin. Law provoked lust and condemned those under it. The Christian belongs to Christ dead and risen, in order that he might bear fruit to God (verses 1-4). When we *were* in the flesh, fruit was borne to death; but now even Jewish believers have been discharged from the law through having died thus, so as to serve in newness of spirit (verses 5, 6). Thereon follows the detailed case (which the apostle personates, as he often does) of one converted yet still struggling under law with its powerlessness and misery; till, experimentally learning that we have flesh unchanged along with a new nature, one looks to God for deliverance, and finding it in Christ (as truly as before for the remission of our sins), he thanks God for it; though the old man is as bad as ever, but with the mind he serves God's law (verses 7-25).

Lastly, chapter 8 is the blessed conclusion of this appendix on indwelling sin through death with Christ, as chapter 5:1-11 was of pardon of sins through Christ's blood. We are in Christ where *all* condemnation is gone, as fully treated in verses 1-4 (the latter half of verse 1 being spurious, but right in verse 4). We are not in flesh but in Spirit, if so be that God's Spirit dwells in us—the distinct privilege of the Christian; and therefore we put to death the deeds of the body. For the Spirit we have received is of power, love, and sobriety, as the apostle reminds Timothy. Hence as He is a spirit of adoption, so He groans in us who are delivered, yet with our bodies awaiting redemption which we now have only in our souls. Thus the Spirit, Who gives us joy, helps our weakness, interceding for us according to God. For we are called, as well as predestinated, and being justified, the apostle can say, "glorified": so sure is God's purpose (verses 5-30). Then comes the final triumph even now: God for us, who against us? A series of unanswerable challenges of grace and truth in Christ follows, in the face of all opposing circumstances; and as "no condemnation" began the high argument, "no separation" from God's love closes it in verses 31-39.

We have now to consider the bearing of chapters 9-11. They are the divine solution of the question, how to reconcile the indiscriminate grace of God in the gospel (as already seen in chapters 1-8) with the special promises made to the fathers in favour of the children of Israel. Here all is cleared to the opened eye. The scriptures, which the Jews owned to be of God, are here also clear and decisive.

First, the apostle shows how far he was from lowering his interest in Israel; they on the contrary were shutting out their highest privileges by their unbelief. Moses loved them no more than he; but how blind were they in not recognising the Christ, not more truly of David according to flesh than One Who is over all, God blessed for ever! Psalms 45, 102; Isaiah 9, 50 (9:1-5). Next (in 6-13), he denies that the word of God had fallen through, for it is certain that not all are Israel that are of Israel. This he proves from the family of Abraham and of Isaac. Fleshly descent, or "seed", is not all: witness Ishmael and Esau. If the Jews must, as they would, repudiate the title of both lines, they must also admit God's sovereignty: a principle plainly shewn in Isaac, still more in Jacob where the mother and father were the same, and the children twins. It was God's purpose according to election as Jehovah indicated before their birth, in the first book of the Pentateuch (Genesis 25:23), and sealed it by the last of the prophets (Malachi 1:2, 3). Is anyone ready to charge God with unrighteousness? The unrighteousness was in Israel beyond doubt, when they made and adored a calf of gold, and must have been justly destroyed but for that sovereignty in God which unbelief criticises and rejects: "I will be gracious to whom I will be gracious, and I will show mercy on whom I will show mercy" (Exodus 33:19). How would pretension to righteousness have suited Israel then? But God is no less sovereign in judgment, as the apostle cites Pharaoh's case (Exodus 9:16). God is judge, not man, who has no right to reply against Him. For has not the potter power of the same clay to make one vessel unto honour and another unto dishonour? In effect however He endured with much longsuffering vessels of wrath fitted unto destruction, and vessels of mercy which He fore-prepared unto glory. The evil is man's, the good is of God's grace, whether of Jews or also of Gentiles, as Hosea declares (2:23; 1:10). On any other ground all was lost for Israel, but if God fell back on His sovereignty, the prophet shows he would use it for Gentiles who believed; and this at the very time He executes judgment on Israel, guilty not of idolatry alone but of rejecting their own Messiah, His Messiah, as is plain from Isaiah 1:9; 8:14; 10:22, 23; 28:16 (verses 14-33).

In chapter 10 the apostle reiterates his earnest love for their salvation. Zealous for God, they ignored His righteousness in the gospel and sought to establish their own. For Christ is end of law for righteousness to every believer. Deuteronomy 30 furnishes the proof; for there, when Israel lost their land by apostasy, God holds out His testimony for believers to lay hold of, though exiles from the land where alone the law could be carried out. Under the law they were ruined, where the word of faith (pointing to Christ) can alone avail, as Isaiah 28:16 confirmed. But being the word of faith, not law, it is for Gentiles as much as Jews, and calls for preachers according to the principle of Isaiah 52:7; 53:1; Psalm 19:4; and, as a fact, Jews needed it no less than Gentiles. Nor could Israel deny that God had made this known. Moses (Deuteronomy 32:21) and Isaiah had warned, not only of God's provoking Israel to jealousy, but of being found by a nation that sought Him not, while Israel was perverse and disobedient.

This raises the enquiry in chapter 11 if God thrust away His people (Israel), as indeed Christendom had long dreamt. Of this three disproofs follow. (1) The apostle cites himself as witness of a remnant, and refers to Elijah who erroneously thought himself alone; whereas God had and has a remnant, the fruit and pledge of grace, the rest blinded and for judgment (1-10). (2) Their fall, far from being definitive, is but to provoke Israel to jealousy, as already stated. Theirs is the olive tree, so that they are the natural branches, and the breach of some was because of their unbelief. The Gentiles, now grafted in, were but wild olive; and if they continued not in God's goodness, they too should be cut off (11-24). (3) The prediction is sure, that after the solemn dealing of God with His guilty people, and when the complement of Gentiles shall have come in during the partial blindness of the Jews as now, "All Israel shall be saved; as it is written, There shall be come out of Zion the Deliverer; He shall turn away ungodliness from Jacob." According to the gospel the Jews are enemies for the Gentiles' sake, according to election beloved for the fathers' sake. God does not change His mind as to His gifts and calling. "For as ye once disobeyed God, but now were objects of mercy by their disobedience, so also they disobeyed your mercy that they too should be objects of mercy. For God shut them all together into disobedience that He might show mercy on them all." No wonder that the apostle breaks forth into a transport of praise. For thus the special promises are fulfilled, while all pride of the law and pretension to righteousness vanish: again, Gentiles who boast, instead of enjoying all as mercy, like the Jews before them, must be cut off; whilst all Israel returning to His mercy are saved.

After the episode of the three chapters preceding, the direct course of the Epistle proceeds. The apostle beseeches the saints by the compassions of God, so fully shewn, to present their bodies (for they are now vessels of the Spirit) a living sacrifice, holy, well-pleasing to God, their intelligent service (or one governed by the word). Outwardly they are not to be conformed to this age, yet not by mere externalism, but changed by the renewing of the mind unto their proving the will of God, good, well-pleasing, and perfect. They were to be lowly, and obedient to God in the Spirit, each acting according to the place God chose, many members in one body, but each in his own function. The gifts pass from those in the word to moral and gracious service in the varying circumstances of saints on earth, blessed with all good and its expression to all, in a spirit of humble and holy sympathy. Such is chapter 12.

In chapter 13 the saints are set in their due relation to higher authorities of the world. Every soul was to be subject. For there is no authority but of God; and the existing authorities have been ordained of God. To resist authority is to oppose God's ordinance; and they that do shall receive judgment (not "damnation", which is an extravagant mistake here as in 14:23); but a chastening (compare 1 Corinthians 11:29-32). Conscience therefore acts, and not merely dread of punishment. The Christian is to pay honour as every other debt—love alone the due that can never be paid off. And love works no ill, and is the law's fulfilment. Besides, it is already time to wake up: salvation, our deliverance for glory, is nearer than when we believed. As in day-light let us walk becomingly, not as the dissolute world, but putting on the Lord Jesus Christ, and making no provision for lusts of the flesh.

From chapter 14 to 15:7 is the great seat of brotherly forbearance as to things above which "the strong" rose in liberty, but which burdened "the weak" with scruple. Many Jewish saints did not realise their deliverance from meats forbidden, or from days enjoined by the law; which Gentile believers knew to be outside Christianity. This led to friction and trial: to judging on the one side; and to despising on the other. The apostle does not hesitate to declare for freedom, but urges receiving the weak, not for discussions of such points. Conscience, though uninstructed, must not be forced: doing, or not doing, "to the Lord" is a great peace-maker. Each shall give account of himself to God. We are therefore now if strong to bear the infirmities of the weak, and not to please ourselves, receiving one another, as Christ received us, to God's glory.

This question, to which the union of Jew and Gentile naturally gave occasion, leads on to the apostle's explaining God's ways from verse 8 and onward. Jesus was minister of circumcision for God's truth to stablish the promises of (*i.e.* made to) the fathers, and that the Gentiles (who had not promises) should glorify God for His mercy. And proofs are produced not only from the Psalms 18:49, 117:1, but from the law (Deuteronomy 32:43) and the prophets (Isaiah 11:10). He appeals to the God of hope to fill the saints in Rome with all joy and peace in believing, and give them to abound in hope; and the more so, as he had no doubt of their actual blessing and ability to admonish each other. But he does not hide from them the grace given him by God to do Christ's public service toward the Gentiles in the sacred work of the gospel of God, that the offering up of the Gentiles might be acceptable, sanctified by the Holy

Spirit. What a difference from Israelitish holiness with its fleshly mark of circumcision!

Then he speaks of the extensive work he had already wrought in might of signs and wonders, in power of the Spirit, preaching the gospel of the Christ from Jerusalem to Illyricum round about, and this where He was not named (as in Isaiah 52:15). This had been the hindrance; but as he had no more of this work in those parts undone, and had long desired, he would visit them on his way to Spain. He was going now to Jerusalem in remembrance of the poor saints, as those of Macedonia and Achaia wished with their contributions; after which he would set off by them into Spain, assured to come with the fulness of the blessing of Christ (omit "the gospel of"). But he beseeches their earnest prayers for him that he might be delivered from the disobedient in Judea, and that his service in Jerusalem might be acceptable to the saints. The Acts of the Apostles shows how he got to Rome, not free but a prisoner.

Chapter 16 is very full of personal commendations and salutations to individuals, though he was as yet a stranger there. But what associations of love and faith! What comfort to Phœbe going to Rome! What joy to Prisca and Aquila in such a mention from him! and to the assembly in their house! It is a notice of much interest. Then follows a roll of brothers and sisters with the distinctive marks of honour which a single eye does not forget, closing with a call to them all to salute one another, and to receive the salutation of the churches of Christ. It is the mind of heaven on earth. In verse 17 he is equally earnest in warning against those that make divisions and stumbling-blocks contrary to the doctrine learnt. If they formed divisions, they were to be avoided; for such serve their own belly (he says with disgust), whatever their fair speech to deceive the hearts of the harmless. The obedience of the Roman saints was known: but they should be wise unto the good, and simple as to the evil. And a second time he commends them to the God of peace, yet more fully and triumphantly. Then he adds the names of Christians saluting with him, and of the scribe of the epistle, Tertius; and after more salutation prays that the grace of our Lord Jesus Christ may be with them all. Lastly he himself ascribes glory to Him that was able to strengthen them according to his gospel and the preaching of Jesus Christ, according to the revelation of the mystery as to which silence had been kept in everlasting times, but now manifested, and by prophetic scriptures according to the eternal God's command made known for obedience of faith to all the Gentiles; to an only wise God, through Jesus Christ, to whom be the glory for the ages. Amen.

5.34 1 CORINTHIANS

We now enter on a very different theme from that developed in the Epistle to the Romans, where the foundation of the gospel is in question, and the individual privileges and walk of the saint. The same apostle writes on the corporate walk of Christians, of the church. The difference of the divine aim is made evident in their respective addresses.

To those in Corinth he writes, but to more; "to the assembly of God that is in Corinth, to those sanctified in Christ Jesus, to called saints, with those that in every place call on the name of our Lord Jesus Christ, both theirs and ours". It is a remarkable superscription, and, as written by the Holy Spirit, surely means to warn against an imminent danger to which the new institution of His grace, His assembly, was to be exposed. The work of grace in each is of course presupposed. That they were saints by God's calling is not forgotten in addressing them in their corporate position. Further, there is care taken from the start to guard against all independency, "with all that in every place", etc. (verses 1-3). No countenance is given to the assumption that the church is free to change or innovate; it has to walk everywhere, and, we may add, always obedient to the word and in holy fellowship.

The usual thanksgiving follows for the grace of God given them in Christ Jesus, which assuredly from the apostle was no mere form. But we may observe that it is not said for faith as he speaks of the Roman believers, but for gifts of grace, while waiting for the revelation of our Lord Jesus Christ, Who also would confirm them as blameless in His day. Solemn responsibility with encouragement he thus awakens: "God is faithful, by whom ye were called unto fellowship of his Son, Jesus Christ our Lord" (verses 4-9).

Thence he turns to their state, and reproaches them with their divisions. They had set up schools of thought among themselves, like the Jews and the heathen, saying, I am of Paul, and I of Apollos, and I of Cephas, and I of Christ. Assuredly Christ was not divided, nor was any servant of His crucified for them. The apostle thanks God that, as things were at Corinth, he had baptised only a few of them, lest any should say that he had baptised unto his name. His repudiation shows the mistaken place assigned to baptism. For he presses the superior dignity of evangelising, which Christ sent him for, and the contempt which God puts on the world's wisdom by that which is its foundation, Christ crucified, to Jews a stumbling-block, and to Gentiles folly, but to those that are called, both Jews and Greeks, Christ the power of God and the wisdom of God. Far from choosing the wise, powerful, and well-born, God had chosen the foolish, the feeble, the vile and despicable, yea things that are not to annul those which are, that no flesh should boast before Him. But he adds the position and blessing too: "Now are ye of him in Christ Jesus, who was made to us wisdom from God, and righteousness, and sanctification, and redemption; that, according as it is written, He that boasteth, let him boast in the Lord" (verses 10-31).

Hence when Paul first testified at Corinth, it was not the world's wisdom he urged, but Jesus Christ, and Jesus Christ crucified. No truth makes less of man, and more of God, when those who heard were men, yea, guilty and lost sinners. But when believers can bear, they indeed need more; when they are not infants but grown men ("perfect" here as elsewhere), he could, and in fact did, lead them to learn of Him everywhere, incarnate, risen, glorified, and coming again. Then he goes on to make known that all hangs for the truth on the Spirit of God, Who now does far beyond what the Old Testament had revealed. We have Christ and redemption accomplished for the soul; and hence, as He is on high, the Holy Spirit is sent down here, God revealing by Him what had previously been reserved. Thus the all-important relation of the Spirit to Christ comes fully out. Revelation, communication by words, and reception, are alike and only by the Spirit of God. So foolish was it to cry up man's mind or the spirit of the world (chapter 2).

The Corinthians addressed were not "natural" as once; nor were they "spiritual" as they ought to have been. They were "carnal". They falsely estimated their state, and, in fact, needed the food of babes rather than of men in Christ. The proof of their carnality, of their walking "as men", was their setting up Paul and Apollos, as rival leaders with the saints as followers to each. The servants thus shrouded the Master to their loss, fleshly as they were. God gives the increase. The most honoured fellow-servants are but God's journeymen; while the saints are God's building. If Paul was given as a wise architect, the sole foundation is Jesus Christ; and hence the serious question of what one builds on Him. Happy he who builds things precious that stand the fire! Sad is he, who, though saved, loses his building of what the fire consumes. Terrible is his lot who corrupts God's temple and is himself destroyed. Here the world's wisdom only ensnares. Besides it is real folly: for all things belong to the saints, not only Paul, Apollos, and Cephas, but world, life, death, present things and future: "all are yours, and ye Christ's, and Christ God's" (chapter 3).

The apostle then in the beginning of chapter 4 exhorts that he and others like him should be accounted as servants or officials of Christ and stewards of God's mysteries. These last are the Christian truths, previously hidden as being incompatible with the restricted object and the earthly character of Judaism, but absolutely essential to the gospel and the church. They have nothing to do with the notion of sacraments, which superstitious men have fancied. Now fidelity is requisite in a steward, and the Lord is the One that examines; not the saints, who have neither the place nor the power, but are responsible in matters of discipline as we shall see in chapter 5. When the Lord comes, He will make manifest the hidden; and then shall be to each the praise from God. He had applied the case to himself and Apollos, not to set man up but to humble him and exalt the Giver (6, 7).

In fact God appointed apostles to the extreme place in suffering at the grand spectacle that Christianity affords to the world, both to angels and to men. The light-minded worldliness in Corinth adds point to the comparison: "*we* fools for Christ, but *ye* prudent in Christ; *we* weak, but *ye* strong; *ye* glorious, but *we* in dishonour". And as he had opened this in verse 8 by saying that they "reigned without us", so in 11 he continues, "to the present hour we both hunger and thirst, and are in weakness and buffeted, and wander homeless, and labour working with our own hands. Reviled, we bless; persecuted, we endure; blasphemed, we entreat; we became as the world's offscouring, refuse of all, until now." How withering is the contrast, not for the Corinthians then only, but for the still more selfish and vain development in our day, as in fact ever since!

Yet he tenderly assures them, that it was not as chiding, but to admonish them as his beloved children, he writes (verse 14). "For if ye had ten thousand child-guides in Christ, yet not many fathers; for in Christ Jesus I begot you through the gospel. I entreat you then, become mine imitators." "Teachers" is not the word in verse 15, but a servile term expressly. And in his love had he sent to them one so beloved and faithful as Timothy, "who shall remind you of my ways that are in Christ, according as I teach everywhere in every assembly" (verse 17). The church, as the Christian, stands in liberty; but it is the liberty of Christ, never the liberty of differing as we like, or to oppose others. The Spirit of God dwells there to maintain the glory of the Lord Jesus, Whose mind is one. Petty man sets himself up. The apostle lets those know who said he was not coming, that he was, and quickly, the Lord willing; then he would know not the word of the puffed up, but the power. It was love, and to spare them, that he did not come sooner (18-21).

In the next division we have the apostle availing himself of evil rumours which had reached him, not about their general party spirit on which he had dwelt so fully from chapters 1 to 4, but on special evils, the abominable case of incest as yet unjudged in their midst (chapter 5), their worldliness in going to law before the unjust (chapter 6:1-11), and their abuse of liberty, or licentiousness, denounced and corrected (12-20). As the portion is short, we may dilate the more.

Desperately evil as were these disorders, general or special, the apostle did not lose confidence in the words of the Lord during the early days of his work at Corinth: "Fear not but speak ... because I have much people in this city" (Acts 18:9, 10). With these evils of theirs weighing on his heart he wrote to them as "the assembly of God that is at Corinth", sanctified (as they were) in Christ Jesus, saints called (or, by calling). The inconsistency of their practical state with their standing, individually and corporately, was extreme; but he remembered the Lord's assurance, and pressed home their responsibility. There is no sufficient ground for assuming a lost epistle from chapter 5:9 of this Epistle, any more than an unrecorded visit from 2 Corinthians 13:1, 2, though not a few have argued for both. The worst enormity may glide into the church through its light state or individual pravity; and thus Satan incessantly seeks to dishonour the Lord and destroy those who bear His name. Then comes, as here, the testimony of the Holy Spirit to judge the evil and deliver the saints. It is the rejection of His testimony, and the maintenance of the evil notwithstanding, for which they forfeit their place as God's assembly. From heinous evils, as here, the church may be restored, as the second Epistle proves; for incomparably less, if not judged, the church may have its candlestick removed, as we read in Revelation 2:5.

What a grief for the apostle to write about the common rumour of fornication among the Corinthian believers, "and such as is not even among the Gentiles, so that one should have his father's wife" (5:1)! But it was a great aggravation that they, the saints generally, were puffed up, and did not rather mourn, in order that he who did this deed might be taken away from among them (2). Though not on the spot, the apostle could and does pronounce on the case. "For I, absent in body but present in spirit, have, as present, already judged him that hath so wrought this, in the name of our Lord Jesus, ye and my spirit being gathered with the power of our Lord Jesus Christ,—to deliver such a one to Satan for destruction of the flesh, that the spirit may be saved in the day of the Lord" (2-4).

Thus did it seem good to divine wisdom that we should have the extreme act of excommunication fully left on record. If the Corinthian assembly had known and discharged its duty, we could not have had it in so solemn a form. For in this instance the apostle joins the exercise of his own official authority and power with the duty of the church to put away the offender. He could deliver to Satan, and thereby to sore trial of mind and body, though with the good and holy aim of the flesh destroyed in order to the spirit's salvation eventually; as we learn in 1 Timothy 1:20 that he could act similarly in cases demanding it without the church. But, with or without apostle, the church is bound not to tolerate but to remove the wicked person from themselves (6-13).

In order to explain the principle further, and to show its application fully, the apostle uses the figure of leaven, intelligible to everyone familiar with its working, and especially to such as knew the care to get rid of it required at the paschal feast, which bore typically on the redeemed. Leaven represents corruption—evil in its tendency to spread and in its character of contaminating. "Your glorying is not good: know ye not that a little leaven leaveneth the whole lump? Purge out the old leaven that ye may be a new lump, even as ye are unleavened. For our passover also, Christ, was sacrificed: wherefore let us keep the feast, not with old leaven nor with leaven of malice and wickedness, but with unleavened things of sincerity and truth." Clearly Christ's sacrifice, set forth in the paschal lamb, is the ground and means by which Christians are unleavened. The feast of unleavened bread that follows figures the hallowed condition that attaches to them imperatively.

We who believe in Christ are now celebrating this feast during our earthly sojourn as pilgrims and strangers, if we rest on His redemption. But the Corinthians in their levity had ignored it; and the apostle most instructively rebukes them with the authority of that word which abides for ever. If they did not yet know God's mind about discipline, divine instinct left them inexcusable. Granted that they had no elders, nor experience; but they had gifts, and if they had life eternal in Christ, they should have felt rightly. Instead of mourning, they were puffed up and boasting: never a becoming state, but how shameful at such a crisis! The will of God was now declared; theirs was to judge themselves and obey. Here we have authoritatively the fullest light from on high to guide us, and to guard from like error.

"I wrote [or rather "write", the epistolary aorist] to you in the epistle not to mix with fornicators; not altogether with the fornicators of this world, or the covetous and rapacious or idolaters, since then ye must go out of the world. But now I write [same aorist as before] to you not to mix, if any one called a brother be a fornicator or covetous or idolater or a reviler or a drunkard or rapacious; with such a one not even to eat. For what have I [to do] with judging those outside? Ye, do ye not judge those within? But those without God judgeth. Remove the wicked [person] from among yourselves."

Here the scope is shown to embrace not only the immoral but the evil generally, though in no way to give an exhaustive list; for other scriptures duly denounce other sins. As a plain instance, false and wicked doctrine does not here find a place; whereas in Galatians 5 it is treated as "leaven", no less than immorality. In 1 John also fundamental error as to Christ's person is dealt with more stringently still as "antichrist", or even not bringing Christ's doctrine. Thus is the church preserved from legislation and called to be true in this respect as in all others to Christ's glory. We have only to do God's will, as He did it perfectly.

In chapter 6:1-11 the apostle insists on the incongruity of the saints appealing to the tribunals of that world which they are destined to judge, yea, to judge even angels. Yet at Corinth, instead of bringing a difference before the saints, they like men who had no faith appealed to "the unjust"! Even those of no account in the assembly could well judge such matters; for he speaks to make them ashamed. Why did they not rather suffer wrong? Alas! they did wrong, and to brethren, forgetting that wrongdoers (and he enumerates more than in chapter 5) shall not inherit God's kingdom.

Their past evil was no excuse; seeing that they were washed, sanctified, justified (a very observable order), in the name of the Lord Jesus and by the Spirit of our God.

This introduces the abuse of liberty. It is not Christian to be under the power of anything. Even now the body is for the Lord; and as God raised Him up from the dead, so will He raise us. We shall be conformed to Him in that glorious change, and are to act now in faith of it. Our bodies are Christ's members. How shameful and disloyal to be joined to a harlot! For this was the habit, one might say the religion, of the old Corinthian community. Hence the enormity of fornication in a saint, who is "one spirit with the Lord". Our body is the temple of the Holy Spirit Who is in us, and this of God. We are not our own, but bought with a price, and therefore to glorify God in our body. The rest of the verse in the Authorised Version and others is a spurious addition from bad manuscripts.

In this section of the Epistle we have answers to questions which seem to have been submitted to the apostle on marriage and meats, with a notice of the detraction of his authority.

There is a spiritual energy which raises one to whom it is given above ordinary conditions; but the institution of God, as here marriage, remains all the same. If Paul was a witness of the former, none the less does he maintain the latter. Marriage is the rule as laid down of God; but the Holy Spirit may and does exceptionally lift up this one or that for worthy reason above the need of marriage. It was a question of God's gift; so that he who marries does well, and he does better who does not marry. The contrast of this holy wisdom is seen in the world-church, which turns the exception of grace into an ecclesiastical rule of corruption, and builds up thereby a city of confusion hateful to God and ruinous to man. The apostle calls for mutual consideration in married life, as well as for prayer, as having to do with God and the adversary.

This leads him, in an interesting and instructive way, to draw the line between what he counselled, and what the Lord commanded by revelation, though the apostle was inspired to give both. He deals also with mixed marriage, and, looking at position and occupation, reminds us that God has called us in peace. Hence too, if one were called as a bondman, it was not to be a concern; but if one could become free, to use it rather. For the bondman called in the Lord is His freedman; likewise the called freeman is Christ's bondman. Bought with a price, they were not to be bondmen of men, but abide with God in that wherein they were called. He presses also the time as straitened, and the passing away of this world's fashion, as reasons for not setting the heart on change. Such is the outline of chapter 7.

In chapter 8 he speaks of eating of animals sacrificed to idols; and, quite allowing the nullity of an idol, he points out the danger for conscience in those who lacked that knowledge seeing a Christian at table in an idol-temple. Gracious thought for another is better than knowledge empty, selfish, and sinning against Christ.

This largeness of heart in the apostle exposed him to the false charge of looseness and self from those really guilty, and brings in the parenthetical chapter 9 in which he vindicates his apostleship, and glories in its grace. He maintains title to eat and drink and lead about a sister-wife, as also the other apostles, specifying the

Lord's brethren and Cephas. "Or I only and Barnabas, have we not a right not to work?" Yet he draws the plain title to support for all labourers—from the soldier, the husbandman, the shepherd, and the herdman. Nevertheless he used no such title, supported though it was by the clear case of those that served the altar in the law. While asserting the right, he refused to use it for himself (not "abuse") in the gospel. It was God's grace in it that filled his heart and led his course, free from all yet making himself bondman, so inexplicable to man and hateful to the worldly mind, becoming all things to all that he might save some. A fellow-partaker with the gospel, he was living what others only preached, lest he, after preaching to others, should himself be rejected or reprobate.

This warning, though transferred to himself (as he says in chapter 4:6, "to himself and Apollos for their sakes" who were in danger), he follows up in chapter 10 by pointing out the ruin of so many in Israel of old, who all were baptised unto Moses in the cloud and in the sea, and all ate the same spiritual food, and all drank the same spiritual drink (10:1-4). Is the Christian to be more indifferent, because privilege is now greater? Idolatry is a great danger for the professing Christian, as it was for the Jew. Yet what condemns it more than Christ's death? What more inconsistent with the Lord's table? For demons were behind the idols; and those a serious reality. True liberty is profitable and edifies; it cannot be at the expense of God's glory, unto which we as Christians are called to do all things, giving no occasion of stumbling to Jews or Greeks or God's assembly. So it was that the apostle pleased all in all things, not seeking personal advantage, but that of the many that they might be saved; and he called them again to imitate him, as he did Christ (11:1).

We have here another section of the Epistle, as distinct, or nearly so, from what precedes as from its concluding two chapters. Before coming to the assembly which was compromised in more ways than one at Corinth, the apostle regulates the relative place of the man and the woman in themselves. The importance of this is the more evident from the humanitarian liberalism of our own day which leaves out God's mind and order. Paul wished them to know that the Christ is the head of every man (ἀνδρὸς), but woman's head is the man, and the Christ's head is God. Hence not men but women, in praying or prophesying, were to have their heads covered before others in token of subjection, as the act otherwise seemed to deny it. For woman was created because of man and as of him, so also the man by her; and angels looked on who should see godly decorum. Neither is without the other, but all things of God, which unbelief forgets or takes no account of. For woman to act like a man is to her shame, and that of the contentious person who ignores God's will (2-16).

Nor was it in private only. The Corinthians publicly were coming together for the worse. Schisms already existing would surely lead to heresies or sects, which in effect deny the one body of Christ, the church, though the approved are thereby made manifest. How sad too at such an occasion as the Lord's Supper the dishonour put on the poor! It was really on the church of God; so that such a supper was not the Lord's. Therefore as he emphatically received the Supper from the Lord, he here also delivered it to them in all its grace and holy solemnity for the remembrance of Him, the centre of the church's worship. The Lord's death makes selfishness in any form most hateful, yet fills the heart purified by faith with thanksgiving and praise, and claims vigilant self-judgment, lest any slight might bring on the Lord's chastening now, that one be not condemned with the world by-and-by. So the apostle rules the severance of a meal, even were it that called the love-feast or Agape, to hinder such disorder in future (17-34).

Thereon follows the greatest unfolding which scripture furnishes of the presence and working of the Holy Spirit in the assembly with the love so essential to right and worthy operation, and the Lord's regulation of it accordingly against abuse, in chapters 12-14. It is designedly apart from the Lord's Supper, though that Supper was in fact the most indispensable aim on the most important occasion for which the assembly met, the Holy Spirit acting in all holy freedom. But it seemed good to the Lord to treat of His Supper separately, and before entering on "the spirituals" (or manifestations of the Spirit) which are here explained. The apostle opens it by guarding against the imitative intrusion of demons, whose aim is to debase Jesus, the Son of God, as the power of the Spirit works in exalting Him. Now there are distinctions of gifts, but the same Spirit; as there are of service, but the same Lord; and of operations, but the same God that worketh all in all (12:1-6).

It is a question here, not of souls saved but of discerning spirits who sought to dishonour the Lord, and deceive if it were possible the very elect. None the less but the more is the Holy Spirit sent down, and here in the church, to glorify the Lord and bless His own as His witnesses of Jesus in glory. The presence of the Spirit is more momentous than even the gifts He distributes and directs. It is that which constitutes the one body; and the assembly is bound to own and act thereon; which is exactly what Christendom has in effect denied since the apostles, perhaps the most perverse of the perverted things the apostle warned of as at hand. There was but one Spirit, as also but one body; as faithfulness means walking by faith, so it is the shame of any to confess truth which they do not seek to carry out at all cost. The Corinthians were light and carnal, and their failure is turned to everlasting profit by the inspired instruction and corrective (7-13).

The gifts are manifestations of His power Who dwells in the church and works, though sovereign, to the Lord's glory; the one Spirit's baptism at Pentecost established that unity, which unbelief overlooks and virtually denies. Every true assembly is Christ's body, as the apostle told the Corinthians they were, though their state was bad enough to draw out the gravest rebuke. But it is the refusal to bow to the word and judge the evil which forfeits the title of God's assembly; whilst the Corinthians did bow to their restoration, as the Second Epistle shows. Again it is in the assembly as a whole that God set, first apostles, secondly prophets, thirdly teachers, etc. (14-28). Ministry therefore (that is, gift in exercise) is set in *the* church. The gift in every variety is for all. There is no such idea in scripture as *the* minister of *a* church; which supposes and generates all sorts of error. The edifying gifts are on the same principle and from the same source as the sign gifts (miracles, healings, tongues, etc.), but far more important and permanent and set in the higher place, whatever Corinthian vanity might prefer.

There was however a quality higher than all, and of deep necessity for the right working of every gift, as indeed for the well-being of every saint, to the Lord's praise. It was love: a sad word among the Greeks, who readily claimed the most refined place of the first man; but how blessed and blessing and divine as heard and seen and proved to death and deeper still in the Second! And this is essential both for the individual Christian (who alone loves, as begotten of God), and for the assembly. Again, it accounts for its place here, between the presence and the operations of the Spirit in chapter 12, and the order of His action (for which every member is responsible) in chapter 14. It is striking to observe how the passive characters of love take precedence of the active, while the intermediate dwell on that joy in good which is truly godlike, as it well becomes the children of God now on earth. Again love never fails and abides for ever.

It is well to note in chapter 14:3 that we have no definition of prophecy here, only its description in contrast with "a tongue". Edification is the great criterion for the assembly, as comely order is due to Him Who dwells there, and to the Head. Revelation, now complete in scripture, is distinguished from knowledge; and power is subject to the Lord's authority Who gives rules which bind even prophets who might plead divine impulse, as they impose silence on women in the assembly. These might use their gifts at home, though as subject to order, like Philip's four daughters who prophesied. The word of God did not come out from the assembly, nor does it come to one only. Through a called and inspired channel it is for all the church, being the Lord's commandment. "But if any be ignorant," it is his withering rebuke of the independent, "let him be ignorant." God has not only spoken but written, and His word abides for ever. May we be subject to the Lord, not in word only but in deed and truth!

Next comes the great unfolding of Christ's resurrection and its consequences. Some of the Corinthians doubted that the saints rise. They had no question as to the soul's immortality, but ventured to deny that the dead rise. The apostle treats the matter from its root in Christ, and thus decides it for the Christian, being associated with Him, as man is with the head of the race. It is for the apostle fundamental, bound up not only with God's counsels but with the gospel itself, which announces the glad tidings of Christ dead and risen. With this accordingly he begins, proved by the weightiest and fullest testimonies, his own closing them (15:1-11). Then (12-19) he reasons on Christ's resurrection out of (or, from among) dead men as the incontrovertible truth which utterly destroyed their speculation. "How say some among you that there is no resurrection of the dead?" For this denies Christ's, and if so Paul's preaching, and their own faith; nay, it would make them false witnesses of God Who in that case had not raised Christ, and themselves be yet in their sins: so those put to sleep in Christ must have perished, and Christians alive be the most pitiable of all men.

This he interrupts with a sort of parenthetical revelation, terse, pregnant, and profound. "But now hath Christ been raised from out of the dead, first-fruits of those that are asleep. For since through man [is] death, through man also [is] resurrection of the dead." Two heads have thus their families respectively characterised, dying, and made alive. "But each in his own order (or, rank): Christ first-fruits; then, those that are Christ's at his coming; then the end, when he shall give up the kingdom to the God and Father, when he shall have annulled all rule and all authority and power. For he must reign till he put all the enemies under his feet. Death, last enemy, shall be annulled. For he subjected all things under his feet. But when he saith, All things are subjected, it is evident that he is excepted who subjected all things to him. And when all things shall be subjected to him, then shall the Son also himself be subjected to him that subjected all things to him, that God may be all in all" (20-28). The resurrection of those that are His is at His coming, and to reign with Him. The end is, when He judges those that are not His, yet raised; and He delivers up the kingdom, all enemies put down, for the everlasting scene, when not the Father only but "God" (Father, Son, and Holy Spirit) shall be all in all.

Next he renews the reasoning, and refers in 29 to 18, and in 30 to 19, which clears up the sense. Why by baptism join such a forlorn hope, why share such a life of danger, if dead men are not at all raised? Paul's life was in view of resurrection; as theirs denied it who merely eat and drink. Let such not be deceived, but wake up righteously and sin not. Ignorance of resurrection is ignorance of God and holiness, to the shame of those that speculate. And why raise curious questions? God surrounds us with even natural facts of analogous character: wheat and other grain, after death of what perishes, spring up, not what was sown, but of its own kind and not a different, yet in a new condition. There are also heavenly bodies and earthly. So too is the resurrection; and here again and yet more richly the last Adam, the Second Man, is contrasted with the first. We too who believe are styled heavenly, for we shall in due time bear that image, as now we bear the image of the earthly (or rather dusty) man, Adam (29-49).

Christ's life (and in resurrection, if men were to be His associates) alone suits God's kingdom and incorruption (50). This introduces a mystery or secret of God not revealed in the Old Testament: "We shall not all sleep, but we shall all be changed, in a moment, in an eye's twinkling, at the last trumpet; for trumpet it will, and the dead shall be raised, and we shall be changed" (51, 52). And this new Christian truth he connects with Isaiah 25:8 and Hosea 13:14, the heavenly things with the earthly; for the Kingdom of God, as our Lord shows (John 3:12), comprehends both. All is wound up with a call to his beloved brethren to be firm, unmoveable, abounding in the work of the Lord always, knowing that their labour is not vain in Him.

This is fitly followed by the various details of chapter 16. As he directed the assemblies of Galatia to collect for the poor saints in Jerusalem, so he wished those in Corinth to do. Each first of the week is a most proper day for the Christian, in the sense of his blessing and of that infinite grace which is its source, to lay by him in store as he may have prospered. The apostle would not use personal influence when he came; but whomsoever they should approve, these he would send with letters to carry their bounty to Jerusalem; and if well for him also to go, they should go with him. How incomparably better is God's way than man's societies and their machinery or devices! Christ with His work is the centre of all. It was only when restoration wrought, that in his Second Epistle he explains why he did not then visit them. But while tarrying at Ephesus, he would have no despising of Timothy if he came. And he lets them know how much he besought Apollos to go to Corinth, who, though not now, would come when he had good opportunity (1-12).

The apostle then charges them to watch, stand fast in the faith, play the man, be strong. "Let all ye do be done in love." They had failed in all: he despaired in nothing (13, 14). They knew the house of Stephanas, that it was the first-fruits of Achaia, and that they devoted themselves to the saints for service; so he besought them to be subject to such, and to every one working together and labouring. This is the more notable, as we never hear of elders in the two Epistles to the Corinthians; for if there had been, they must naturally have incurred special blame. Apart from elders (who needed appointment by those who had discernment and full authority) there were, as we learn, labourers to whom the subjection of the saints was due, as we also find in other Epistles: a fact of the utmost importance for the present circumstances of the church. Any unbiassed reader may satisfy himself of this, who will consider the import of Romans 12:6-8; of 1 Thessalonians 5:12, 13, 19, 20; of Hebrews 13:17; of James 3:1; and of 1 Peter 4:10, 11. Elders or no elders, it is clear that the door was open for ministrations to edification where gift existed without official designation of any kind. Ministry in the New Testament is the Lord's service, and far more varied than what has been so called since the apostles, who sanctioned it to the largest extent if exercised in the fear of God and in love of the saints.

Further, he speaks of Stephanas with two others, whose names are subjoined, coming and by their practical love refreshing his spirit "and yours" he graciously adds. "Own therefore such" (15-18). Salutations of assemblies and individuals follow, as he affixes his with his own hand (19-21). But while desiring the fullest flow of holy affections with one another, he pronounced an unsparing curse on any one that loved not the Lord [Jesus Christ]: "Let him be anathema Maranatha" (our Lord cometh). This assuredly was no licence for such to be in their midst (22). Not content, in the face of much he had suffered from them, with the prayer "The grace of the Lord Jesus Christ be with you", he concludes with "My love be with you all in Christ Jesus, Amen" (23, 24). What more Christlike!

5.35 2 Corinthians

The Second Epistle does not admit of sections so defined as in the First, being less ecclesiastical and dogmatic. It is restorative rather than corrective, and overflows with the sense of God's compassion and encouragement in the midst of tribulation and sufferings. The address here, "to the church of God that is in Corinth", adds (not "with all that in every place call on the name of our Lord Jesus Christ, both theirs and ours", but quite appropriately) "with all the saints that are in all Achaia". It is less external and more intimate: not thanks for gifts and power, but blessing for delivering grace.

The apostle's heart was full. He had drunk deeply of Christ's sufferings; but now his encouragement also abounded through Christ; and both, he assures them, were for their encouragement and salvation. If they had passed through sufferings, he would have them know what had been his in Asia, "when excessively pressed beyond power, so as to despair even of living". Having the sentence of death within to trust in the God of resurrection, he yet confides, counting now on their prayers for thanksgiving also. And as conscience had begun its good work in them, he can speak of his own, and explain, as he did not in the First Epistle, why he had not gone to Corinth. Their state forbade it, not his levity, nor aught of fickleness, as some said. This leads on to a wondrous assertion of God's immutable word of grace in His Son, and the no less power of our establishment and enjoyment by the Holy Spirit, with which he ends chapter 1, assuring them now of his love in desiring to see them at Corinth only with joy.

Little did the Corinthians conceive his grief and earnest desire for joy from them (chapter 2). Not only had he and they grieved, but sufficient to the one who had caused it by his evil was "this punishment" by the many. They should show grace now, lest he should be swallowed up with grief, and their obedience too in confirming love as they had in judging. In blessed grace and ungrudging maintenance of the church's place the apostle says, "To whom ye forgive anything, I also; for what I also have forgiven, if I have forgiven anything, [it was] for your sakes in Christ's person, that no advantage be gained over us by Satan; for we are not ignorant of his devices." What a contrast with either the assumption or the indifference of worldly religion! What a defeat he anticipates of Satan's aim! This again gives occasion for their learning how his heart yearned over them right through. At Troas, though a door was opened in the Lord and he came for the gospel, he had no rest for his spirit at not finding Titus, but went on to Macedonia where he met him, and got good tidings of Corinth. Was this a loss? "Thanks be to God who always leadeth us in triumph in Christ and manifesteth through us the savour of his knowledge in every place." The apostle identifies himself with the gospel, a sweet savour to God in the saved and in the perishing. And who is competent for these things? He was not as the many, trading with the word of God; he gave it as purely as he received it from God.

Chapter 3 contrasts the law with the gospel, and in particular exposes the mixture of the two, the favourite device of those who misread Christ. For did he begin to commend himself? Did he need letters of commendation to them or from them? *They* were his letter, written on his heart, manifested that they were Christ's letter.

What grace for the apostle so to write of them! What an honour for them so to hear! His competency was from God Who made us competent as new covenant ministers, not of letter but of spirit; for letter kills, but spirit quickens. Then, in a parenthesis which includes from verse 7 to the end of verse 16, he sets out the law graven on stones, as a ministry of death and condemnation, introduced with glory but annulled; whilst the ministry of the Spirit and of righteousness is the surpassing glory, and the abiding in glory. The Lord is the spirit of what in the letter only kills; but where His Spirit is, there is liberty. Law was a veiled system like Moses' face; whereas in the gospel "we all with unveiled face looking on the glory of the Lord are being transformed according to the same image from glory unto glory as by the Lord the Spirit."

Therefore having this ministry, and being shewn mercy, we faint not. Grace banished fear and dishonesty, and gave by manifestation of the truth to commend oneself to every conscience of man in the sight of God. So chapter 4 begins. All is out in the light of the knowledge of the glory of God in the person of Jesus Christ. Man is lost, man under law most guilty and blinded by the god of this age; God in the glory of His grace has the believer face to face without a veil. Self is not our object, but Christ Jesus as Lord, and ourselves your bondmen for Jesus' sake. But we have this treasure yet in earthen vessels, that the surpassingness of the power may be of God and not out of us; in everything afflicted, but not straitened, always bearing about in the body the putting to death of Jesus that the life also of Jesus may be manifested in our body. Such is the principle; then comes the fact: "For we that live are ever delivered unto death on account of Jesus, that the life also of Jesus might be manifested in our mortal flesh." This life works in others: we believe, and therefore speak, knowing Him Who raised up the Lord Jesus and will raise and present us with those we serve for His sake. Far from our fainting, the inward man is renewed day-by-day. Our momentary light affliction works for us a surpassingly eternal weight of glory, looking as we do at, not the seen, but the unseen and eternal things.

In chapter 5 we have the power of life in Christ tested not only by death but by judgment. The Christian is shewn more than conqueror thereby, as, if dead, rising like Christ, and if living, mortality swallowed up of life (verses 1-4). Nor does Christ's judgment-seat abate the constant confidence; for our manifestation before Him will only prove the perfectness of His redemption, though there may be loss also. The glory begun abides. Then the love of Christ constrains, besides the sense of the terror of the Lord for such as meet judgment in their nakedness, so that we persuade men to receive the gospel. The judgment of charity is, that "One died for all: therefore all died"; and He died for all "that the living [which is only by faith in Him] should live no longer to themselves but to him who died and was raised." Even Christ after the flesh is known no more, but dead, risen, and glorified. So if one be in Christ, there is a new creation; the old things are passed, behold, they are become new; and all things are of the God Who reconciled us to Himself by Jesus Christ and gave us the ministry of the reconciliation. This he explains to the end, characterised by God in this way and now based on Christ's work.

Chapter 6 describes this ministry of God's grace; not only in its source and distinctive properties and glorious end, but in its irreproachable character and its deep exercises through all circumstances. Assuredly the Corinthians were not straitened in Paul, as he could now freely tell them; it was in their own affections. But true largeness of heart goes with thorough separateness from all evil. The exhortation follows against any incongruous yoke with unbelievers. What has a Christian to do with helping to draw the world's car? Righteousness, light, and Christ forbid such a part. What agreement too has God's temple with idols? The saints are a living God's temple, more deeply than the Old Testament expressed; wherefore the call to come out of their midst and be separate and touch no unclean thing was the more imperative. How they knew themselves received, God's Fatherhood, and their own sonship, the gospel had already proved. "Having then these promises, beloved, let us cleanse ourselves from every pollution of flesh and spirit, perfecting holiness in God's fear" (chapter 7:1) is the real close of the chapter.

In chapter 7:2-16 the apostle concludes what had been interrupted by the marvellous exposition of the Spirit's ministration of the gospel, the matter of grief which grace had turned into blessing. He enlarges on what chapter 2 only touched, and lets them know what his letter cost him, when he knew its effect on them. It was grief according to God working out repentance to salvation unregrettable. Love is of God, and creates happiness rising above self, sorrow, sin, and Satan. The grief of the world works out death. The teaching is highly valuable, not only in a moral way but in the light of God cast on the assembly's clearance of itself from the evil which it is bound to judge in the last resort. "In every thing ye proved yourselves to be pure in the matter." Thus it is not by any means enough, if we desire God's will, that the offender be truly penitent, but that also the saints, having to do with a grievous case, should humble themselves and in grace bear the shame as if it were their own. How awful the state of such as rebel against the Lord in refusing its judgment, and in shameless sympathy that tends to harden and destroy the guilty one! No wonder that party spirit is so odious to the Spirit of God, and so destructive of true unity.

The way was now clear for the apostle happily to treat fully of that collection for the poor saints at Jerusalem, which he had briefly introduced in the last chapter of his First Epistle. Now that grace was doing its work, he can speak of the grace bestowed on the Macedonian assemblies in their own deep poverty and trial. And beyond hope it was; for they gave themselves first "to the Lord, and to us by God's will." Taking nothing himself from the rich Corinthians, Paul was the more earnest for others; not as commanding, but, through the zeal of others, proving also the genuineness of their love. As they abounded in much, let them abound in this grace too. What a motive and pattern is the grace of our Lord Jesus Christ! He simply gave in this his mind—he would not say more. It was expedient, or profitable, for those who purposed a year ago, to perform. A willing mind was the great thing without burdening any. Titus too was jealous for them; and Paul sent with him the brother whose praise was in the gospel through all the assemblies and chosen by them as "our fellow-traveller with this grace". For the apostle was careful to provide things honest not only before the Lord but also before men. Hence he sent a second unnamed brother (22) of oft proved diligence, but now much more diligent "through his [not, I think, Paul's] great confidence as to you." They were to show the proof therefore (chapter 8).

Yet another chapter (9) is devoted to the theme. He knew their ready mind, of which he boasted to the Macedonians, that Achaia (of which Roman province Corinth was the metropolis) was prepared a year ago; and he would not that "we, not to say, ye", should be put to shame. Nor does he fail, in awakening their souls to the joy of grace practically, to remind them that God loves a cheerful giver, and would have us abound to every good work, with thanksgiving to God as the result. Thanks be to God for His unspeakable gift, the spring of all grace by us.

In the later chapters (10-13) he vindicates his authority, entreating them by the meekness and gentleness of Christ; let others boast of natural appearance or of fleshly arms. His arms were powerful according to God for overthrowing strongholds, and leading captive every thought unto the obedience of Christ. He was ready to avenge all disobedience when their return to it was fulfilled. If boasting somewhat more abundantly of what the Lord gave him, he would not be put to shame. As strong by letters when absent, so he would be present in deed. He had not gone beyond the measure God had apportioned, but hoped, their faith increasing, to be enlarged among them, and yet more to evangelise beyond them, instead of boasting in another's rule as to things ready. He that boasts, let him boast in the Lord; for not he that commends himself is approved, but whom the Lord commends (chapter 10).

Jealous over the beloved Corinthians, whom he had espoused (he says in chapter 11) as a chaste virgin to Christ, he fears lest their thoughts should be corrupted from simplicity as to Christ. In the most touching way he asks if he committed sin in abasing himself that they might be exalted, and in every thing kept himself from being burdensome to them, though Macedonian brethren supplied his wants. God knew whether it was lack of loving them; but so he did to cut off occasion from some wishing it, against whom he thunders as deceitful workers. To speak of his own devotion, labours, and sufferings, he counts to speak as a fool; but we are indebted to that unworthy occasion for details of the deepest interest. They had compelled him in their folly. Was there any heroism in being let down in a basket through a window by the wall?

In chapter 12 he glories in what "a man in Christ" he knows (without saying who, for flesh had no part in it) experienced when caught up to the third heaven. Otherwise he gloried, not in any thing man loves to attach to his name, but "in his infirmities". He knew not even whether it was in the body or out of the body; so completely was it apart from all living associations or nature, before God in the glory of His Paradise. Yet was it as a check to this unequalled distinction (of the deepest moment to all subsequent life and service), lest he should be exalted by the exceeding greatness of the revelations, that there was given a thorn in the flesh, a messenger of Satan to buffet him. Nay more, he tells us that he prayed the Lord thrice for its removal, but had the answer, "My grace sufficeth thee, for power is perfected in weakness." It is dependence in faith, the true and signal secret of all Christianity in practice. "Behold, this third time I am ready to come to you." He had been at Corinth once and long. Only their state, and his desire to come when they were restored, hindered him when ready to come a second time. This is the true force of coming a "third time". How painful to such a heart to rebut the imputation of craft, when they could not deny his personal unselfishness! or of their supposing he was excusing himself to them! All was really in love for their edifying; but he feared lest perhaps on coming he should find them not as he wished, and be found by them such as they did not wish.

Chapter 13 closes this part and the entire Epistle with an overwhelming appeal, not only spoilt by false punctuation in the Authorised and Revised Versions, but making way for wrong doctrine at issue with the gospel. " Since ye seek a proof of Christ speaking in me (who is not weak toward you but is powerful among you,* for he was crucified of weakness, yet he liveth of God's power; for we too are weak in him, but we shall live with him by God's power toward you), try yourselves whether ye be in the faith, prove yourselves. Or recognise ye not as to yourselves that Jesus Christ is in you? unless indeed ye be reprobate" (3-5). As *this* alternative was the last thought which could occur to the carnal vanity which

---

* Any person of intelligence ought to see the impossibility of the sentence ending here, as in the version of 1611. An answer to the "since" or "seeing that" is required, in order to make any tolerable sense. As this is not furnished by the close of verse 3, nor by verse 4, we have it really supplied by verse 5. And this answer is not only simple and satisfactory but full of gracious force and a serious rebuke to their ungrateful and thoughtless vanity. The version of 1881 yields evidence that the Revisers perceived the lameness of the sense afforded by the Authorised Version, but of their own total failure to seize the true connection. For they hang verses 3 and 4 on to verse 2, though there is no trace of a link with what goes before to warrant it. Verse 2 appropriately follows verse 1, as both do the closing verses 19-21 of chapter 12. But 13:3 opens a fresh and distinct appeal to the hearts of those who ventured to question his apostleship. "Seeing that ye seek a proof of Christ that speaketh in me, ... try your own selves, whether ye be in the faith; prove your own selves. Or know ye not as to your own selves that Jesus Christ is in you? unless indeed ye be reprobate." The Revised Version is purposely cited to show how excellent is the sense, when the erroneous punctuation is corrected, and the true connection is allowed. Otherwise the appeal is robbed of power, and a spurious meaning is suggested, to the injury of souls ever open to man's mistake rather than God's truth.

questioned Paul's apostleship, the application turns on their own standing in the faith. As surely as they were in it, he was an apostle to them. If Christ were not in them, they were reprobates and not entitled to speak on such a question. Where was their vapouring now? But his prayer was that they might do nothing evil, and his joy to be weak if they were powerful, praying also for their perfecting, and writing thus when absent that when present he might spare severity. He adds a farewell message of suited tenderness and care, with a commendation which speaks to the hearts of all believers ever since. Who, accepting it from God, has not profited?

5.36 GALATIANS

Who can doubt the special aim of the Holy Spirit in this characteristic letter? It is not, like that to the Roman saints, a systematic establishment of God's righteousness in the gospel, on the plain and full proof of man's universal failure. Here we have the vindication of Paul's apostolate and of the gospel of grace against the Judaisers. It is a standing witness, on the one hand, how quickly the professing Christian is apt to surrender even the foundations of his blessedness to legalism; and on the other, of the Holy Spirit's care to raise the divine standard against the enemy, and rally men of faith around it. For God has here given us His own refutation of that early encroachment, so ruinous to the enjoyment of His grace, of Christ's work, and of the believer's standing and power. The Epistle is characterised by unusual severity of warning from first to last, and a total absence of those individual salutations in brotherly kindness which abound wherever it was possible. Not even the loose levity of the Corinthians troubled the apostle's spirit so profoundly, as the fall of the Galatians from grace.

Chapter 1 opens with Paul, "apostle not from men nor through man, but through Jesus Christ, and God the Father who raised him out of the dead, and all the brethren with me". The legal party objected that he was not of the twelve, nor yet ordained by them in due succession. The apostle confronts this with the fact, that the Lord Jesus and God the Father expressly called him to the apostleship in an immediate way and with resurrection's associations; and that all the brethren with him joined in his words now. Even his wonted form of general salutation has the stamp of the truth the Galatians were imperilling. "Grace to you and peace from God the Father, and our Lord Jesus Christ, who gave himself for our sins, that he might deliver us out of this present evil age according to the will of our God and Father, to whom be the glory unto the ages of ages." In verses 6-10 he bursts like lightning on their central error. "I wonder that ye so quickly change from him that called you in Christ's grace unto a different gospel, which is not another: only there are some that trouble you and desire to pervert the gospel of Christ." Such as preached aught else, were it himself or an angel or any, he anathematises. It were but pleasing men, which would make him not to be Christ's bondman as he was.

Next, he asserts direct revelation for the gospel he preached, affirmed already for his apostolic authority. It had shone on him, when devoted to the law and a persecutor of the church of God. But His grace revealed His Son in him, that he might preach Him among the Gentiles. The essential design was that he should not take counsel with flesh and blood, not even with the apostles before him. So he went elsewhere, and even when he did go up to Jerusalem, it was but for a short visit to Cephas, and seeing only James the Lord's brother, as he solemnly averred. Afterwards he went to Syria, and Cilicia; so that he was only known in Judea by the report, to God's glory by him, that the persecuting Saul now preached the faith he once ravaged.

In chapter 2 the apostle furnishes fresh light in this connection on his memorable visit with Barnabas to Jerusalem, when he took Titus with him. Assuredly it was to receive neither authority nor truth. He went up by revelation, which is nowhere else intimated, but characterises his special place. Nor was it apostles who laid before him the gospel, but he before the chiefs privately what he preached among the Gentiles. Could any say he was running or had run in vain? Nor was it entertained to circumcise Titus, whatever bondage false brethren might desire to impose. Add to the gospel, and its truth continues no more. It was seen by the reputed pillars that He, who energised Peter for the apostleship of the uncircumcision, energised Paul also for the Gentiles. God's order for both and grace given to Paul being recognised, James and Cephas and John gave Paul and Barnabas right hands of fellowship, only with due remembrance of the poor, in which Paul was zealous too.

But from verse 11 he goes farther, and recounts his open resistance of Peter at Antioch because he was condemned. What a rock for the church, if Christ had really resigned His place to His servant! Away with a pretension so blasphemous, ignorance so deplorable. Christ alone was and is the Rock. Peter shilly-shallied when certain came from James; "and the rest of the Jews dissembled likewise with him, so that even Barnabas was carried away with their dissimulation." How solemnly instructive for the Galatians, for all other Christians, for ourselves also! "They did not walk uprightly according to the truth of the gospel" is the unsparing censure of the apostle. What a withering rebuke of their own folly in listening to the adversaries of him and the gospel! His argument is unanswerable, and stands in abiding record. "If thou being a Jew livest Gentilely and not Jewishly, how forcest thou the Gentiles to judaise?"

It was grievous inconsistency in Peter, who on a most critical occasion proved himself not only feeble as a reed, but false to the Lord's charge in Acts 10 and his own faith, afraid of those he ought to have fed and guided aright. It was flinching from the common standing of justification by faith, and not by law-works even for born Jews. But the worst of all remained; for he had left law for grace in Christ to justify him, and, in turning his back on this now, he not only made himself a transgressor, but in effect Christ a minister of sin! Paul on the contrary for the Christian says, Through law I died to the law, for all was met in Christ crucified. The sinner was in Him condemned, that he should go free, the flesh only and utterly dealt with by God for him who believes; and himself living, no longer the old I, but a new life, Christ living in him: a life in faith of the Son of God "Who loved me and gave Himself up for me." Adding law makes void the grace of God; for if righteousness be through law, Christ in this case died gratuitously.

As chapter 2 ends with the great truth of Christ living in the Christian by faith in the Son of God, in contrast with the law, so chapter 3 shows that the reception of the Spirit was not by works of law but by report of faith. How senseless then to perfect in flesh, with which law deals, what they began in Spirit! Thence he turns in verse 6 to Abraham who believed and had not the law but the promise, "In thee all the nations shall be blessed", but solely by faith. For as many persons as are by works of law are under the curse; for which Deuteronomy 27 is cited. There, when the two mountains were taken by six tribes on each for blessing and curse, only Ebal had the curses, and not a word of the blessings on Gerizim! Granted that in fact the blessings were pronounced on the appointed mountain; in effect, as God knew, it must fail; and hence the silence of that inspired book. On the principle of law there is no blessing but curse for sinful man. "The just shall live by faith", as Habakkuk 2:4 testifies when all was ruin; where in vain law held out life to him that shall have done its demands. But Christ has redeemed from out of the curse by having become a curse, as elsewhere Deuteronomy attests ([chapter] 21); that the blessing might come unhindered, the promise of the Spirit through faith (1-13).

Then in a deep unfolding the notion of annexing law to promise is excluded. For the promises were addressed to Abraham, and to his seed, 430 years before the law, and hence cannot be annulled by it. The promise was in grace. Law was added for the sake of transgressions till the Seed came to Whom was made the promise, which has no mediator like the law with Moses between God and man. There are two parties in law, one of them sinful; there is but one in promise, God, and therefore all is sure in the end. They are not against each other, as they must be if joined: each serves its proper aim. There is no righteousness by law; but the promise by faith of Jesus Christ is given to believers. Law was but a servile childguide; but we are all, Gentiles as well as Jews, God's sons by faith in Christ Jesus; and Him it is, not law, we put on in baptism, in Whom there can be no distinction in the flesh; and if of Christ, we are Abraham's seed, heirs according to promise (14-29).

In chapter 4 the apostle points out the immense change wrought for the saints through Christ's work and the sending of the Spirit. Previously the heir, a child or infant, did not differ from a slave under the elements of the world; but now he was redeemed by the Son and became a son. And so were the Gentile believers sons, with the Spirit in their hearts crying, Abba, Father. Such is the true relationship of the Christian (1-7). For Gentile saints, after being known of God, to turn to the weak and beggarly elements (*i.e.*, of the law) was really a return to their idolatry in principle. "Ye observe days, and months, and times, and years. I am afraid of you lest I bestowed upon you labour in vain. Be as I [am], for I [am] as ye, brethren, I beseech you: ye have not injured me at all" (8-12). He was freed from law by Christ's death. They as Gentiles had nothing to do with law. They inflicted no wrong in saying so of Paul. Compare Romans 7:6 and Galatians 2:19. How the new delusion had alienated them from him! Had he become their enemy by telling them the truth? Their zeal should not be only in his presence (13-18). They needed that he should travail again in birth to have Christ formed in them (19).

"Tell me ye that desire to be under law, do ye not hear the law?" Then he speaks of Abraham's two sons: one by a bondwoman, the other by a free woman, one born after the flesh, as the other by promise, allegorising the two covenants, and answering respectively to Jerusalem in bondage, and to free Jerusalem which is above, our mother, entitled to rejoice after desolation. We then, as Isaac, are children of promise, and persecuted by him born after the flesh as of old. "Nevertheless what saith the scripture? Cast out the bondwoman and her son; for the son of the bondwoman shall not be heir with the son of the free woman. So then, brethren, we are not children of the bondwoman, but of the free" (21-31). How convincingly the tables were turned on these retrogradists from grace to the law!

The beautiful use, which the apostle drew according to divine design from the story of Sarah and Isaac on the one hand, and on the other of Hagar and Ishmael, leads into the teaching of chapter 5, the freedom with which Christ freed us. So, therefore, is the Christian to stand, and not be entangled again in a yoke of bondage—the enemy's effort. To receive circumcision was to become debtor to do the whole law and to fall from grace: Christ would profit nothing in that case. We, believers, are justified by faith; and by the Spirit on the same principle of faith we await, not righteousness but its hope, even the glory into which Christ is gone. For in Him neither circumcision nor uncircumcision avails aught, but faith working through love; as of God it ever does. Who stopped them when running well, that they should not obey the truth? The persuasion was not of Him that called them. It was a corruption tainting the lump as a whole. For his part, his confidence as to them was in the Lord, that they would have no other mind; and their troubler whosoever he be shall bear the judgment (or, guilt). "And I, brethren, if I yet preach circumcision, why am I yet persecuted? Then is done away the offence of the cross." For Judaism was ever the sleepless foe. Indignantly he adds, "I would that those who unsettle you would even cut themselves off" (verses 1-12).

"For ye" he says emphatically, "were called for liberty"— on that condition. "Only [use] not liberty for occasion to the flesh, but through love serve one another"—the gist of the whole law. Were they fulfilling it in biting and devouring one another? To walk in the Spirit (which grace gave, not law) is to fulfil in no way flesh's lust. No doubt the flesh opposes, but so does the Spirit, that we may not do the things which we would: a scripture perverted in the Authorised Version. But if led by the Spirit, they are not under law: grace is the spring. "Now manifest are the works of the flesh, which are fornication, uncleanness, licentiousness, idolatry, sorcery, enmities, strife, jealousies, angers, contentions, divisions, sects, envyings, [?murders,] drinkings, revels, and such like; of the which I forewarn you, as I forewarned you, that they who do such things shall not inherit God's kingdom." Could they not recognise these sad traits of late? Law acting on flesh provoked them. "But the fruit of the Spirit is love, joy, peace, long-suffering, kindness, goodness, fidelity, meekness, self-control against such things is no law." Did they really know this fruit familiarly? "And they that are of Christ Jesus crucified the flesh with its passions and its lusts. If we live by the Spirit, by the Spirit let us also direct our steps. Let us not become vainglorious, provoking one another, envying one another." What can approach these burning words which close the chapter? The Spirit is the power of good, not the law, moral any more than ceremonial. Law's power is to slay sinners.

The next chapter (6) follows it up. Even if a man be overtaken in some fault, does the remedy lie in the law? In nothing but grace. "Ye that are spiritual restore such a one in a spirit of meekness, considering thyself lest thou also be tempted." The general rule is to bear one another's burdens, and thus fulfil the law of the Christ, if they desired a law. The flesh boasts, and only deceives itself while burdening others. Faith proves its own work without claiming that of another. Each shall bear his own burden. Meanwhile there is ample room for love, as for the learner in the word toward the teacher in all good things (verse 6). God holds to His order: whatever a man sows, this shall he also reap,—corruption from the flesh, from the Spirit life eternal. Let us not be faint-hearted then in well-doing, for in due season we shall reap if we faint not. So then as we have opportunity (season), let us work good toward all, and specially toward the household of faith.

The conclusion is touching. "Ye see in how great letters I write to you with my hand." He habitually employed an amanuensis, as was usual in those days. To the Galatians he would write himself; and so in large uncouth letters he wrote the entire Epistle. (Contrast with the aorist here the present in 2 Thessalonians 3:17). Once more he thunders against those who would revive flesh and restore law and circumcision to the denial of the cross of Christ. Only would he glory in that cross which put shame on the world; and he accepted its shame with Christ. In Him is new creation. This is the rule for our steps; and peace be on such and mercy, and upon those of Israel who are really God's. Let none trouble him henceforth: he bore in his body the marks of suffering for Christ, whose grace, he prays, to be with their spirit. It is controversial throughout, yet with the deepest feelings of love underneath.

5.37 Ephesians

In writing to the Ephesians the apostle takes his stand on ground wholly different from the Epistle to the Galatians. There he combats return to law in every shape, ceremonial or moral, and insists on grace in

Christ crucified and risen, on promise before the law and accomplished only in Christ, so that blessing should flow even to Gentiles, and the promise of the Spirit be received by faith. But to the Ephesians he shows divine and eternal counsels.

The Christian is blessed with every spiritual blessing in the heavenlies in Christ (1:3); and this by the God and Father of our Lord Jesus Christ, Who was both man and Son of His love. The same God and Father chose us in Him before the world's foundation, far above earthly ways and beyond promise. He chose us that we should be holy and blameless before Him in love (4). If He would have us there, He could not but have us like Himself. But He was pleased to fore-ordain our relationship, even for adoption or sonship, through Jesus Christ to Himself, according to the good pleasure of His will (5) for the praise of the glory of His grace, which He freely bestowed on us in the Beloved (6). In Him (for we were evil) we have redemption through His blood, the forgiveness of offences according to the riches of His grace (7), which He made to abound toward us (not like Adam for the earth) in all wisdom and intelligence (8). He also made known to us the mystery of His will according to His good pleasure which He purposed in Himself (9) for administration of the fulness of the fit times: to head up the universe in Christ, the things in the heavens, and the things on the earth; in Him in Whom we also were given inheritance, for if sons of God, we were heirs. We were thus fore-ordained according to the purpose of Him Who works all things according to the counsel of His own will, that we should be to the praise of His glory. "*We*" are the believing Jews that had pre-trusted in the Christ (12). In Him *ye* too (Gentile saints), having heard the word of the truth, the gospel of your salvation, in Whom, having also believed, ye were sealed with the Holy Spirit of promise, Who is earnest of our inheritance for the redemption of the possession, for praise of His glory (14). Jew and Gentile are alike thus blessed in the highest degree, far beyond the promises to the fathers.

So delicate and precious and rich is the apostle's preamble, that one does best to give it just as it is. The glory of His grace embraces the whole sweep of the purposed blessing; the riches of His grace, what more than meets all our need now; the praise of His glory, when we enter on the inheritance. But the choice of God and foreordaining go back into eternity before there was a universe to inherit with Christ. The summing or heading up in Him of the whole heavenly and earthly will be administered when the various seasons run out, and the inheritance, heavenly and earthly, will be displayed; and we, of all others, share Christ's glory over all, and have the earnest as well as seal already in the Holy Spirit given to us.

Then we have from verse 15 and at least to the end of chapter 1 the apostle's prayer for them, founded on the God of our Lord Jesus Christ, the Father of glory (17), of Whom he desires the enlightenment of the eyes of their heart to know what is the hope of His calling, what the riches of the glory of His inheritance in the saints, and what the exceeding greatness of His power toward us that believe, according to the working of the might of His strength which He wrought in the Christ, when He raised Him out of the dead and seated Him at His right hand in the heavenlies, far above the most exalted of creatures now and ever, and subjected all under His feet, and gave Him [to be] head over all things to the church which is His body, the fulness of Him that filleth all in all (23).

The prayer almost imperceptibly passes into the teaching of chapter 2. To the hope of God's calling as in chapter 1:3-6, with its accompaniments in verses 7, 8, and the riches of the glory of His inheritance in the saints (for He takes it in them as in the Christ) in verses 9-11, with the way Jews and Gentiles come in, and the Holy Spirit's relation to both blessings, he adds the wondrous power displayed in raising and exalting Christ. Now in chapter 2:1-10 he shows it to be the same power that wrought in the Ephesian saints, and so in all Christians, quickened with the Christ, raised up together, and made sit down together in the heavenlies in Christ Jesus, that God might display in the coming ages the exceeding riches of His grace in kindness toward us in Christ Jesus. Thus were and are they saved by grace through faith, His workmanship, created in Christ Jesus for good works which God before prepared that we should walk in them. All were alike dead in offences and sins. God thus wrought to bring believers into this new estate of living association with Christ on high.

From verse 11 the apostle would have those once Gentiles remember their then far off condition, without one of Israel's privileges. Now they were made nigh by the blood of the Christ; and in the same nearness were the believing Jews. For Christ, our peace, not only took away all obstacles, but made both one, forming the two in Himself into one new man, one body. Though Jews had once been outwardly nigh, and Gentiles afar off, through Him we both have access by one Spirit to the Father. Strangers and foreigners the Gentile believers were no more, but fellow-citizens with the saints and of

God's household, all alike being built on quite a new foundation—that of the apostles and prophets (of whom he speaks in chapter 4:11), Jesus Christ Himself (not Peter) being the corner-stone. In Him all the building framed together increaseth unto a holy temple in the Lord; "in whom ye also", he says, "are builded together for God's habitation in the Spirit."

Thus we have the church viewed as Christ's body, and God's house, in which distinct respects Paul's Epistles often regard it. The article seems necessarily wanting in verse 21, though excellent old manuscripts insert it; but according to correct usage, as the building is not complete, it could not be there. Yet this does not warrant "each several", as in the Revised Version. For though as the ordinary rule πᾶσα without the article requires "every", there are known exceptions, as "all Jerusalem" (Matthew 2:3), "all the house of Israel" (Acts 2:36), "all Israel" (Romans 11:26). It is not a proper name that really accounts for this; a whole viewed in its parts excludes the article, yet means "all". The mistranslation is therefore not only superficial, but directly upsets the unity of the building on which the apostle here insists as everywhere else.

Chapter 1 revealed the counsels of God in Christ risen and seated on high, followed up by the apostle's prayer to the God of our Lord Jesus; and chapter 2 showed us how grace has brought us in, not only as individuals but collectively, and the temporary setting aside of Israel, believing Jews and Gentiles alike to be Christ's body and God's habitation in the Spirit. Chapter 3 connects with the subject Paul's special administration of this mystery or secret.

Therefore are the Gentiles the objects of grace in a way wholly unheard of in other generations, as now revealed to His holy apostles and prophets in the Spirit—the same power which builds all the saints together for God's dwelling. It was by revelation made known that the Gentiles should be fellow-heirs, fellow-members of the body, and fellow-partakers of His promise in Christ through the gospel, of which Paul was become minister according to the gift of His grace given him according to the working of His power. This of course could not be, nor be revealed, till the cross had closed the Jewish system and opened the door in Christ ascended for the Creator of all things to make known heavenly counsels and ways in Him to any and everybody that believed. Equally clear is it that when Christ comes for His own to be with Him in the Father's house, and subsequently appears to execute judgment on the Beast and his vassals, on the Antichrist and all other enemies, He will restore Israel specially and bless the Gentiles in general under His blissful reign over the universe, even Egypt and Assyria being conspicuous.

Meanwhile the gospel where these distinctions are obliterated and unknown goes forth, and the unsearchable riches of the Christ announced, as Paul did pre-eminently and far beyond all prophecy. This was in order that now to the principalities and the authorities in the heavenlies might be made known through the church the manifold wisdom of God according to a purpose of the ages (or, eternal) which He purposed in Christ Jesus our Lord, in Whom we have boldness and access in confidence through the faith in Him. The apostle would not have them discouraged at his tribulations for them: it was their glory, which roused the enemy (3:1-13).

"For this cause" (repeating the phrase which opens the chapter, and carrying out the parenthesis into a new prayer founded on its wondrous intimations) he bows his knees to the Father [of our Lord Jesus Christ, an addition favoured by many manuscripts, Versions, etc.] of Whom every family in heaven and on earth is named. Here, however, it is not as in chapter 1 that a spirit of wisdom and revelation might be given to the saints to know the hope of His calling and the glory of His inheritance and the greatness of His power in Christ risen and exalted. It is to be strengthened with power by His Spirit in the inner man, that Christ might dwell in their hearts through faith, rooted and grounded in love, that they might be able to apprehend with all the saints what is the breadth and length and depth and height (he does not say of what, but evidently of the mystery), and to know the love of the Christ which surpasses knowledge; that they might be filled unto all the fulness of God. This is not for spiritual intelligence of God's counsels and of what God had wrought in Christ to give them effect, but for present power of the Spirit in realising Christ dwelling in their hearts, and thus entering into fellowship with all the saints into the boundless glory, and His love deeper than the glory which will display it another day. Now to Him that is able to do far exceeding above all we ask and think, according to the power that worketh *in* us (and not only *for* us), to Him be the glory in the church in Christ Jesus unto all generations for ever and ever. Amen (verses 14-21).

Paul, the prisoner in the Lord, beseeches the saints on the ground of all he has made known, to walk worthily of the calling wherewith they were called, with all lowliness and meekness, with long-suffering, forbearing one another in love, using diligence to keep the unity of the

Spirit in the joint bond of peace. This leads him fully to set forth unity: "one body and one Spirit, even as also ye were called in one hope of your calling; one Lord, one faith, one baptism; one God and Father of all, who is over all and through all, and in you [or, us] all" (4:1-6). The relationship determines the duty: what then must be ours, so blessed of God? It is easy to see that verse 4 sets out the vital, as verse 5 the professing, unity; while verse 6 is universal in its early clauses, yet the most intimate grace in the last. We are exhorted to be faithful in every case.

Next, the various workings in each for the blessing of all to Christ's glory are shewn in verses 7-16. All is founded on Him ascended on high, as this depended on His descending into the lower parts of the earth, and also ascending to the highest, that He might fill all things. He it is Who gave some apostles, and some prophets, and some evangelists, and some shepherds and teachers, for the perfecting of the saints, unto work of ministry, unto edifying of the body of Christ. What is the term of this? Until we all arrive at the unity of the faith and of the knowledge of the Son of God, at a fullgrown man, at the measure of stature of the fulness of Christ. For His gracious aim is that we be no longer babes, tossed and carried about by every wind of the teaching [that is] in the sleight of men for the spread of error; but, holding truth in love, we may grow up into Him in all things, Who is the head, the Christ; from Whom the whole body, fitted and compacted together by every joint of supply, according to the effectual working in measure of each one part, works for itself the increase of the body unto its own edifying in love.

It is not here, as in 1 Corinthians 12, the Holy Spirit testifying in this creation (and hence by tongues, healings, etc.) to God's glory in Christ, Who has defeated Satan before the universe. It is Christ in His love to His own, sending down from His heavenly seat the gifts of His grace to His body and to every several member. Thus here only we have the assurance that, while His members are on earth, His supplies of grace cannot fail. The foundation has been laid so well that it were folly to expect it relaid; but all that perpetuates and edifies, it were unbelief to doubt till He come. With this goes the promise of the other Paraclete, the Holy Spirit, to abide for ever in and with us (John 14), Who guides into all the truth. Hence the very babes in Christ are said (1 John 2:20) to have unction from the Holy One. No Christian need distrust.

Thereon the general exhortations proceed. They are warned against any allowance of their former walk as Gentiles, alienated from God's life in every way, inward and outward. Not so did they learn the Christ, if albeit they heard Him and were taught in Him according as truth is in Jesus. What is this? Their having put away as to their former behaviour the old man corrupt as to its lusts of deceit, and their being renewed in the spirit of their mind, and their having put on the new man which according to God was created in righteousness and holiness of the truth. Therefore putting away falsehood (this goes beyond lying) they were to speak truth, as being members one of another. They were not to allow continued anger. Instead of stealing they were to give, and to speak what was good for edifying, and not to grieve the Holy Spirit of God by Whom they were sealed for redemption's day. So all bitterness and heat, wrath, clamour, and abusive language, with all malice, must be put away from them; and they were to be kind one to another, compassionate, forgiving each other, even as God also showed them grace (verses 17-32).

Grace toward faultiness, however, is not all. Chapter 5 opens with the more positive call to be imitators of God as children beloved, and walk in love; as Christ also loved us and gave Himself up for us, an offering and sacrifice to God for an odour of sweet smell. It was perfection in Him—for us, but to God; and it is our express pattern of love. But the danger of uncleanness is as carefully urged as of violence just before; and this in the levity of speech as in lust. Thanksgiving is a great antidote; as is our sense that those who so indulge are incompatible with the kingdom of the Christ and God. Grace to believers in no way precludes God's wrath on the sons of disobedience. We, who were once darkness but now light in the Lord, should be far from such partnership, and walk as children of light, the fruit of which is in all goodness and righteousness and truth. The Spirit comes in, not in verse 9 but later in verse 18 as power, after love and light have been fully treated as the source, principle, and character of the walk for the new creation, proving what is agreeable to the Lord. Are any disposed to sleep? The Christian is therefore to awake and rise up from among the dead, and Christ shall shine upon him: an evident allusion to Israel's portion by-and-by. Hence the need of walking carefully as wise, buying up the fit time, intelligent in the Lord's will, and filled with the Spirit in songs of praise of a Christian sort, certainly not with the world's dissolute excitement. Entitled as we are always and in all things to give thanks to Him Who is God and Father in the name of our Lord Jesus Christ, let us not fail in doing thus, submitting ourselves to one another in Christ's fear (5:1-21).

This leads to the application of the same principle in our relationships; where the subject one is regularly first exhorted in each pair, wives to husbands, children to parents, and slaves to masters (verses 22—6:9). The wife and husband give occasion to a grand unfolding of Christ's love for the church or assembly as the model. He "loved the church and gave himself up for it, that he might sanctify it, purifying it by the washing of the water in virtue of the word, that he himself might present to himself the church glorious, not having spot or wrinkle or any of such things; but that it might be holy and blameless." Christ thus loved the church before He gave Himself up for it; and not content with this infinite self-surrender to sanctify it, He purifies after a divine fashion, as He will consummate His love in the glorious issue. His love sees to it all, and He uses the word now, as He will personally at length present it to Himself according to His own perfectness. So is the husband to love his own wife, and the wife to fear the husband.

Children are not only to submit but to "obey" their parents in the Lord. If the law bade them pay honour, how much more the gospel? But fathers are not to irritate their children, but bring them up in the Lord's discipline and admonition. So were slaves to obey their masters according to flesh, but "as to Christ". What a privilege, and beyond all other emancipation! Masters were to do the same things, in the equity they expected, forbearing threat, and knowing they had a common Master in the heavens.

Then follows (verses 10-20), after the call to be strong in the Lord and in the power of His might, the whole armour of God we are to put on. It is not the righteousness we become in Christ, but practical as against the enemy. The sword of the Spirit, being God's word, is our one offensive weapon. That panoply we need that we may be able to stand against the schemes of the devil. "For our wrestling is not against blood and flesh, but against principalities, against authorities, against the world-rulers of this darkness, against the spiritual [hosts] of wickedness in the heavenlies." We are contrasted with Israel arrayed against the Canaanites. Wherefore he bids us to take up the whole armour of God that we may be able to withstand in the evil day, as it is now till the Lord take His great power and reign. First, we are to be girt about our loins with truth, the inward movements thus braced before God; then, to put on the breast-plate of righteousness, the confidence of an irreproachably right course; next, the walk animated by the gospel's peaceful spirit; besides (or, in) all, we must take the unwavering faith in God, which is the shield to quench all the inflamed darts of the wicked one; and receive the helmet of salvation in the assurance of what God wrought for us.

But even God's word will not avail against the foe unless the Spirit guide us in wielding it. Thus all demands simple and constant dependence on God. Hence "praying at all seasons with all prayer and supplication in the Spirit, and watching thereunto in all perseverance and supplication for all the saints, and for me," added the blessed apostle, "that utterance may be given me in the opening of my mouth with boldness to make known the mystery of the gospel, for which I am ambassador in a chain, that I may be bold in it as I ought to speak." In what a place of nearness to God stand the faithful—in common interest with Him, and hence with the greatest of apostles as with the weakest of saints, for Christ's glory! Hence as the apostle shared Christ's love to them all, so he was assured they in their love would delight to hear all particulars of him; he sent Tychicus therefore to comfort their hearts, as a joint and band in the body.

The salutation is in keeping: "Peace to the brethren, and love with faith, from God the Father and the Lord Jesus Christ. Grace with all that love our Lord Jesus Christ in incorruptness." Without the Father and the Lord, what is anything else? Without incorruptness, even the love, or rather what is called love, were vain.

5.38 PHILIPPIANS

No where is special aim more evident than in this Epistle. In saluting the Philippian saints the apostle associates Timothy with himself as "bondmen of Christ Jesus", and them "all", with overseers and deacons (1:1, 2). For the assembly there was not immature like that in Corinth; it possessed those local charges, for which experience was due, such as apostolic authority set over the saints in due time. But the absence of the apostle, a prisoner in Rome and object of their loving remembrance, gave occasion to much that is characteristic in it for the Christians, soon to lack that care altogether. No epistle breathes so distinctively of confidence in God and joy in all his remembrance of them; and this, not founded on the enriching powers of the Spirit as to the Corinthians, nor on the heavenly counsels of God as to the Ephesians, nor on the fulness of the Head as to the Colossians, nor yet on the broad and deep foundations of the gospel as to the Romans. This letter surveys and reciprocates what Christ is for every day's communion, conduct, worship, and service. It is therefore in reality, and in all forms, and in the highest sense, Christian experience from first to last. Their state warranted, as it called forth, the full opening of his heart to them.

In verses 3-11 he thanks his God because of their uninterrupted fellowship with the gospel, that He Who began a good work in them will complete it till Jesus Christ's day. It was right for him to think thus as to them all because they had him in their hearts. Both in his bonds, and in the defence and confirmation of the gospel, were they not all partakers in his grace? For God was his witness how he longed after them all in the bowels of Christ Jesus. And he prayed that their love might abound yet more and more in knowledge and all discernment, unto their proving the things that are excellent, that they might be pure and without a stumble for Christ's day, being filled with fruit of righteousness that is through Jesus Christ unto God's glory and praise. He looked for the due result of Christ and His work in them, not merely that they should be kept from inconsistency and failure.

Then from verse 12 to the end of the chapter he speaks of his bonds and how God had thereon wrought in His good way, as man in his evil. He would have them know that his matters, sad as they looked, had come rather for furtherance of the gospel; so that his bonds became manifest in Christ in the whole prætorium and to all the rest. Nor was this all. For the most of the brethren, trusting in the Lord by his bonds, dared more abundantly to speak the word without fear. It was not without alloy. Some indeed also preached Christ for envy and strife, and some too for goodwill: these of love, knowing that he was set for the defence of the gospel; but those out of faction announced the Christ, not purely, thinking to arouse affliction for his bonds. But grace prevailed, and his heart had joy in Christ.

"What then? Notwithstanding [or, Only that], in every way, whether in pretence or in truth, Christ is announced, and in this I rejoice, yea and will rejoice. For I know that this will turn to me for salvation through your supplication and the supply of the Spirit of Jesus Christ, according to my earnest expectation and hope, that in nothing I shall be ashamed, but in all boldness, as always, now also, Christ shall be magnified in my body, whether by life or by death. For to me to live [is] Christ, and to die gain; but if to live in flesh [is mine], this [is] to me worth while. And what I shall choose I know not. But I am pressed by the two, having a desire for departure and being with Christ, for [it is] very much better; but to remain in the flesh [is] more necessary for your sake. And having this confidence I know that I shall abide and continue with you all for furtherance and joy of faith, that your boasting may abound in Christ Jesus in me through my presence again with you" (verses 18-26).

How clearly faith by grace made him, bondman though he was, master of the situation! His desire drew him away to Christ: the need of the saints detained him. God gave him, as it were, the decision for their sake. "Only behave worthily of the gospel of Christ, that, whether coming and seeing you or absent, I may hear of your affairs, that ye stand in one spirit, with one soul striving together with the faith of the gospel, and not frightened in anything by the adversaries; which is to them evidence of destruction but to you of salvation, and this from God; because to you was granted on behalf of Christ not only to believe on him but also to suffer for him, having the same conflict as ye saw in me and now hear of in me." Living the gospel, living worthily of it, was his earnest desire for them, yea, suffering for Christ.

Chapter 2. Zeal was not wanting in Philippi, yet does it not endanger unity, lowliness, and love? Where is the corrective but in Christ? "If then any comfort [be] in Christ, if any consolation of love, if any fellowship of the Spirit, if any bowels and mercies, fulfil ye my joy, that ye have the same mind, having the same love, joined in soul, thinking one thing, nothing in faction or vainglory, but in lowliness of mind esteeming one another better than themselves, regarding not each his own things, but each those of others" (verses 1-4). This brings in the image of Christ. "For let this mind be in you which was also in Christ Jesus, who subsisting in God's form did not count it an object for seizing to be on equality with God, but emptied himself, taking a bondman's form, having come in likeness of men; and, when found in fashion as a man, he humbled himself, becoming obedient unto death, even death of the cross. Wherefore also God highly exalted him and granted him the name which is above every name, that in the name of Jesus should bow every knee of [beings] heavenly and earthly and infernal, and that every tongue should confess that Jesus Christ [is] Lord to God the Father's glory" (verses 5-11).

For the Philippians were in contrast with the Galatians (Galatians 4:18), and obeyed, not as in his presence only, but now much more in his absence. They are exhorted accordingly to work out their own salvation with fear and trembling, now that they had not the apostle's care; for it is God that was working in them both the willing and the working for His good pleasure. What source of confidence so great, along with distrust of self! Murmurs and disputes were to be far from them, that they might be blameless and simple, God's children irreproachable in the midst of a crooked and perverse generation, among whom they appeared as lights in the world, holding forth life's word for a boast to the apostle against Christ's day that he ran not nor laboured in vain. Again he refers to death before him, but here as a libation poured on the sacrifice and ministration of their faith to his joy, and theirs also. Yet he hoped in the Lord to send Timothy to them, as he graciously felt for his refreshment by knowing how they got on; for only he shared Paul's care genuinely. Alas! even then all were seeking their own things, not those of Jesus Christ. They knew Timothy's service with Paul in the gospel work. Whatever the cost to himself, he would send one so dear to him and them, when he could report matters.

Meanwhile he sent Epaphroditus, his fellow-worker and fellow-soldier (what links of honour!), but their messenger and minister to his need (what communion!), not only as longing after them all, but distressed at their hearing of his sickness. So he was, adds the apostle, nigh to death; but God had mercy not on him only but on Paul also, that he might not have sorrow on sorrow. Yet him he had sent, that they seeing him might rejoice, and he himself be the less sorrowful. What unselfish love all round, the mind that was in Christ Jesus! Him therefore they were to receive in the Lord with all joy, and to hold such in honour; because for the work's sake (whether Christ the Lord, or God, were in question) he came nigh to death, risking his life to supply what lacked in their service toward Paul (verses 12-30). Truly this is Christian experience.

Chapter 3 presents our Lord in a way quite different from that of chapter 2. It is not the uttermost humiliation in obedience of the Son's Person become man, emptying Himself and humbling Himself to the death of the cross: that service of love beyond compare, which creates, fashions, and maintains Christian devotedness in the saints. Here the central truth is Christ glorified, as the object set before the believer to detach him from every idol, to shine on the path with sure and heavenly light, to fill the heart with His own excellency, and to keep the glorious goal before him, whatever the trials of the way.

The apostle exhorts his brethren for the rest to rejoice in the Lord. *He* deserves and desires it; and well may we. Did any complain of sameness? To write so was not irksome to this wondrously endowed soul; for them it was safe. Yet he finds room with energetic contempt to denounce the Judaisers, as the dogs, the evil workers, and the concision, of whom they had to beware. He declares that the circumcision are we who worship by the Spirit of God, and boast in Christ Jesus, and have no confidence in the flesh; though if any had such ground of confidence, the apostle had more. It is of fleshly religion he speaks here and throughout, not of fleshly licence (verses 1-5).

Next, he states his own case. Was he not circumcised the eighth day, of Israel's race, of Benjamin's tribe, a Hebrew of Hebrews? as to law, a Pharisee; as to zeal, persecuting the church; as to righteousness that is in or of law, found irreproachable? But the Christ he had seen in glory made him regard this gain as a loss. Nor was it a hasty estimate, but so he counted all things because of the excellence of the knowledge of Him, his Lord, for whom he suffered the loss of all things. He was still counting them dung, that he might win Christ and be found in Him, not having his own righteousness which is of law, but that which is by faith in Christ, the righteousness of God on condition of faith. The same Paul in Romans 9 would have the Jews know that, far from disparaging, he exalted the privileges of Israel beyond their estimate; here he shows that the Christian has in Christ far better things than Israel's hopes (verses 5-9). And so he continues, "that I may know Him, and the power of His resurrection, and the fellowship of His sufferings, being made conformed to His death, if by any means I might attain to the resurrection from out of (the) dead" (verses 10, 11).

Nothing then satisfied him short of that portion. Flesh and earth are quite left behind. Therefore he adds, "Not that I already attained, or have been already perfected, but I pursue, if I may apprehend (or, get possession of) that for which also I was apprehended by Christ." We shall then be like Him and in the same glory. Yet he carefully tells his brethren that, as this was not true of him yet, "one thing" (he does); "forgetting the things behind [not past evils, but present progress], and stretching forth toward those before, I press unto the mark for the prize of the calling upward of God in Christ Jesus" (12-14). All the fullgrown should have this mind; and, if in any thing they were otherwise minded, God would reveal this also to them; but whereto they were arrived, let them walk alike. How wholesome even for saints in good estate! Nor does the apostle hesitate to bid them imitate him and mark those that followed his example. Others alas! did very differently, enemies of Christ's cross, and earthly-minded, whose god is the belly, whose glory is in their shame. For our citizenship subsists in the heavens, whence also we await the Lord Jesus Christ as Saviour, who shall change the body of our humiliation and conform it to the body of His glory, according to the working of the power He has to subject even all things to Himself (verses 15-21). Salvation here looks on to that final change.

Chapter 4 opens with strongly expressed affection, and the call to stand fast in the Lord. Two sisters he exhorts severally by name to the same mind in Him; and he beseeches his true yoke-fellow, Epaphroditus probably, to help those women in that they shared his own conflicts in the gospel, with Clement too and the rest of his fellow-workers whose names are in the book of life. How sad their lot whose names were not there! They did not love the Lord, whatever their labours (verses 1-3).

The saints in general here again he calls on to rejoice in the Lord "always", and again would say, "Rejoice." How blessed from Paul the prisoner in Rome under Nero to saints at Philippi suffering in Christ's behalf! Yet he would have their gentleness known to all (in view of the Lord at hand), their anxiety in nothing, their requests to God in everything by prayer and supplication with thanksgiving; and he assures them that the peace of God (and it is constant), which surpasses all understanding, should guard their hearts and their thoughts in Christ Jesus (verses 4-7). For the rest, he urges brethren to think, not on the dark side but on whatsoever things are true, honourable, just, pure, lovely, and of good report, if any virtue or any praise: what they both learned and received and heard and saw in him, let them do; and the God of peace, which is yet more than the peace of God, blessed though it be, should be with them. This indeed would be Christian experience—to live Christ (8, 9).

Then, as we easily see from verses 10 to 20, he speaks of his joy in the Lord at their renewed thought for him, though he spoke not of want, having learnt to be content in whatsoever state he was. For he knew both to abound and to be in want, and declares he can do all things through Him that empowers him. But he appreciated their fellowship with his affliction, which they only had shewn him thus in the early days of the gospel: not that he sought the gift, but the fruit that increased to their account. He could say that he had all things and abounded, that he was filled, having received from Epaphroditus their things, which he does not hesitate to call "an odour of a sweet smell, a sacrifice acceptable, well-pleasing to God." On their part or on his, it was to live Christ. "And my God", he adds, "shall fill up your every need according to his riches in glory in Christ Jesus. Now to our God and Father [be] the glory unto the ages of the ages, Amen." Then he salutes "every saint" in Christ Jesus, as he unites withal that of the brethren who were with him, and indeed of all the saints there, specially those of Cæsar's household; for so did Christ work in His own. "The grace of the Lord Jesus Christ be with your spirit" is the suited close.

5.39 Colossians

The distinctive aim is as legible here as elsewhere. It is not Christian experience as in the Epistle to the Philippian saints, nor the blessedness of the saints in the heavenlies in Christ as to those in Ephesus, but the glories of Christ in respect of both earth and heaven, as man and as God. Nor is any notion more contrary to truth than to conceive that to the Ephesians an amplification of this to the Colossians, even if both were admitted to be genuine. That they are in the closest mutual relation is apparent; for the body of Christ is as prominent in the Ephesian letter as is the Head in the Colossian. But for this very reason each has its own special object; and both are of the highest interest and importance, as giving the truth in question fully and without confusion. Why they were severed by the Epistle to the Philippians it is hard to say; for internal considerations point to the writing of the Epistles to the Ephesians and to the Colossians about the same time; whereas that to Philippians has no such link, and while it may have preceded them as Bishop Lightfoot contends, it rather seems from its tone to have been the later of the three.

However this be, which is comparatively immaterial, here we have the complement of the letter to the Ephesians, as it appears evidently written at nearly the same time. Here we learn the fulness of Christ for the saints, Christ in them; as there were revealed the privileges in Christ for the saints and the church. They thus lend one another the most necessary and remarkable help. But they also differ quite as strikingly; for to the Colossians the apostle dwells on Christ our life, even where the word may not be used, and only once (1:8) speaks of the Spirit; whereas to the Ephesians he unfolds the Holy Spirit's functions as he does nowhere else.

The apostle did not write alone as to the Ephesians, but joins with himself "Timothy the brother to the holy and faithful brethren in Christ that are in Colosse". After the usual wish but curtailed, thanks are here given at once to God the Father of our Lord Jesus Christ, continually praying for them, having heard of their faith and love on account of the hope that is laid up for them in the heavens (1-5), "of which ye heard before in the word of the truth of the gospel which came to you as in all the world, bearing fruit and growing, even as also among you since the day ye heard and rightly knew the grace of God in truth; even as ye learnt from Epaphras our beloved fellow-bondman, who is a faithful servant of Christ for you, that also declared to us your love in [the] Spirit."

The rich unfolding of God's call and inheritance found in Ephesians 1:3-14 has no counterpart here, because of the dangers which menaced those addressed. Nor here is it only "for the hope". "For this reason we also, since the day we heard, do not cease praying and begging that ye may be filled with the right knowledge of his will in all wisdom and spiritual understanding, to walk worthily of the Lord unto all well-pleasing, bearing fruit in every good work and growing by the right knowledge of God; strengthened with all strength unto the might of his glory unto all endurance and long-suffering with joy; giving thanks to the Father that made us meet for sharing the portion of the saints in light; who rescued us out of the power of darkness, and translated us into the kingdom of the Son of his love, in whom we have redemption the forgiveness of sins" (9-14).

Before proceeding into the setting forth of the glories of Christ's person that follow, remark that the walk, power, and thankfulness are directly, not of Paul and Timothy that prayed for them, but of the Colossian brethren. Thus then, while present fruit and growth are sought, thanks were to be that the Father qualified "us", not the writer nor those written to only but all Christians, for sharing His presence in the light. The Vulgate, followed by Roman Catholic theologians, &c., is utterly wrong in the perversion "made worthy"; as are most Protestants too in blotting out to faith this actual standing to make it a gradual process.

"Who [Christ] is image of the invisible God, firstborn of all creation, because by (or, in virtue of) him were all things (or, the universe) created that are in the heavens and that are on the earth, the visible and the invisible, whether thrones or lordships or principalities or powers; they all have been created through him and for him; and he is before all and by (or, in virtue of) him all things hold together. And he is the head of the body, who is [the] beginning, firstborn out of the dead, that he in all things might be pre-eminent" (15-18).

"Image" observe, not likeness. The Word *was* God. Like would be only resembling; "image" represents, as Christ perfectly represented here below the invisible God. "He that hath seen me hath seen the Father", as He said to Philip. So, when born of woman, He was firstborn of all creation. Even Solomon, His type, was by sovereign grace "made" firstborn, though younger than many of David's sons. The glorious reason follows for Christ— because He created all. How conclusive! No matter when born, He was chief of creation. The Authorised Version is right: the Revised Version dangerously wrong in giving "*in* him were all things created". It expresses not the instrumental means as near the end of the verse, but the intrinsic power by which the work was done, here of universal creation. The mystical idea of the Revisers, for which there is no ground, seems refuted also by the tense which points to historical fact, as distinguished from the abiding continuance of the past act in the latter clause. Besides, it opens the door for universalism in opposition to all truth. Nothing can be clearer than the universality of creation here attributed to our Lord, heavenly and earthly, visible and invisible: they, the whole of them, have been created "through" Him, and not only so but "for" Him as the end in view. And as He existed before all, so does the universe hold together by, or in virtue of, His power.

But a wholly new glory succeeds, on which the church specially depends, and from which she derives her being and character. "And he is the head of the body, the church; who is [the] beginning [which is distinctive here, and not said of Him either when a divine person only, or when the Word became flesh, but only as risen], firstborn out of the dead." He rose the conqueror over sin and death to be the Beginning, and the suited Head of the body, that in all things He might become chief in rank. Anything short would have dishonoured both Him and the Father.

Next comes His work of reconciliation in its future scope for the universe, and in its actual and complete application to the saints, due to the glory of His person. "Because all the fulness was pleased in him to dwell, and through him to reconcile all things to him- (or it-) self, having made peace through the blood of his cross—through him, whether those on the earth or those in the heavens. And you, once alienated as ye were and enemies in the mind by wicked works, yet now he reconciled in the body of his flesh through death, to present you holy and unblemished and unimpeachable before him, if at least ye abide in the faith grounded and steadfast, and not moved away from the hope of the gospel which ye heard, that was preached in all the creation under heaven, of which I Paul became servant. Now I rejoice in the sufferings for you, and fill up that which is behind of the tribulations of Christ in my flesh for his body, which is the church, of which I became servant according to the dispensation (or, stewardship) of God that was given me unto you to complete the word of God: the mystery that had been hidden from the ages and the generations, but now was manifested to his saints, to whom God would make known what [are] the riches of the glory of this mystery among the Gentiles; which is Christ in you the hope of glory, whom we announce, admonishing every man and teaching every man, that we may present every man perfect in Christ; whereunto also I labour in conflict, according to his working which worketh in me mightily" (19-29).

Here we have a twofold reconciliation (answering to His twofold personal supremacy over creation as a whole, and of the church), of which last not even His incarnation, however blessed and essential, but His death was the basis; for not till His cross was sin for ever judged before God. Again, the apostle mentions his twofold service, corresponding to Christ's person and reconciling ministry of the gospel in its unrestricted extent, ministry of the church in filling up the blank (left in the word of God) by the revelation of the hidden mystery, or secret unknown in Old Testament times. It here emphasises the Gentiles having part in it, not you in Christ, but "Christ in you, the hope of glory" on high, instead of Christ reigning over the earth, with Israel His centre and all the nations blessed according to the promises and the prophecies. For that the apostle toiled mightily, as he also endured afflictions for the sake of Christ's body, the church (atonement His only, but those afflictions of holy love left for His own to share), that he might present every man full-grown in Christ, of which toil He was not only the object but the power, being Head.

So above man, so opposed to fallen nature, is the truth of Christ, as to involve conflict as well as toil, in such as serve Him. What can one do better than transcribe the apostle's burning words? "For I would have you know what conflict I have for you and those in Laodicea and as many as have not seen my face in flesh; that their hearts may be comforted, being knit together in love, and unto all riches of the full assurance of understanding unto right knowledge of the mystery of God, in which are the treasures of wisdom and of knowledge hidden. And this I say that no one may delude you by persuasive speech. For though in the flesh I am absent, yet in the spirit I am with you, rejoicing and seeing your order and the firmness of your faith in Christ. As therefore ye received Christ Jesus the Lord, walk in him, rooted and being builded up in him, and confirmed in the faith, even as ye were taught, abounding in [it] with thanksgiving. See lest there shall be one that leadeth you astray through philosophy and vain deceit according to the tradition of men, according to the elements of the world and not according to Christ. For in him dwelleth all the fulness of the Godhead bodily; and ye are filled full (or, complete) in Him, who is the head of all principality and power; in whom also ye were circumcised with circumcision not done by hand, in the putting off of the body of the flesh, in the circumcision of Christ; buried together with him in baptism, in which ye were also raised together, through faith in the working of God that raised him out of the dead. And you being dead in the offences and the uncircumcision of your flesh, he quickened you together with him, having forgiven us all the offences, having blotted out the handwriting in ordinances that was against us, which was contrary to us, and hath taken it out of the way by nailing it to the cross; having stripped he made show of the principalities and powers, openly triumphing over them by it. Let none therefore judge you in eating or in drinking, or in respect of feasts, or new-moon, or sabbaths, which are a shadow of the things to come; but the body [is] of Christ. Let no one cheat you, in a voluntary humility and worship of the angels, intruding into things which he had not seen, vainly puffed by the mind of his flesh, and not holding fast the head, from whom all the body, being supplied and knit together by the joints and bands, increaseth with the increase of God" (chapter 2:1-19).

None on earth knew as the apostle how all the treasures of wisdom and knowledge are hid in the mystery, or secret, God now reveals in Christ. Philosophy which flatters men's minds was as vain to penetrate and unfold it as the law which condemned his unrighteousness and left God in the dark. Man was thus exposed to worship of the angels, not those who beheld by faith all the fulness of the Godhead dwelling in Christ bodily, and themselves made full in Him Who is the head of all principality and power; and this in virtue of a redemption which gives in Christ the fullest force to the old rite of circumcision and the actual sign of baptism. For the truth goes farther than His death and resurrection, and declares that God quickened ourselves together with Him, having forgiven us all our offences. Hence the reflected light of ancient ordinances, as but shadow, passes away for such as hold fast the Head unfailing in His gracious supply.

Hence he thus applies it:—"If ye died with Christ from the elements of the world, why as alive in the world do ye subject yourselves to ordinances (Handle not, nor taste, nor touch, which things are all for corruption with the using), according to the injunctions and teachings of men: things such as have indeed a show of wisdom in will-worship and humility and unsparingness of the body, not in a certain honour, unto satisfaction of the flesh" (verses 20-23). But more, "If ye then were raised together with Christ, seek the things above where Christ is sitting at God's right hand: mind the things above, not those on the earth. For ye died, and your life is hidden with Christ in God. When Christ, our life, shall be manifested, then shall ye also be manifested with him in glory" (3:1-4) The Christian is not only quickened, but quickened and raised together with Christ; and thus he has new life in its highest character. It is hidden because Christ is hidden, hidden with Christ in God. When

Christ our life shall be manifested, then shall we too be manifested with Him in glory. How close and blessed is the association!

Practical consistency is doubly pressed. "Put to death then your members that [are] upon the earth, fornication, uncleanness, passion, evil lust, and covetousness, which is idolatry, on account of which things cometh the wrath of God upon the sons of disobedience; among whom ye also walked once when ye lived in these things. But now ye put off also all the things, wrath, anger, malice, blasphemy, shameful speech out of your mouth. Lie not to one another, having put off the old man with his deeds, and having put on the new that is being renewed into knowledge, according to his image that created him; where there can be no Greek and Jew, circumcision and uncircumcision, Barbarian, Scythian, bondman, freeman, but Christ [is] the all, and in all" (5-11). Thus Christ and His work, and our association with Him dead and risen, become the standard of every-day walk for the Christian. Higher there cannot be, if our union with Him on high be added; lower is not acceptable to God Who thus blessed us in Him, but a slight to His grace.

Nor is it only deliverance from the corruption and the violence of the flesh, as we already had from its philosophy and its religion; the positive is not omitted. "Put on then, as elect of God, holy and beloved, bowels of compassion, kindness, lowliness, meekness, long-suffering, forbearing one another and forgiving each other, if any should have a complaint against any; even as Christ forgave you, so also [do] ye. And over all these [put] love, which is the bond of perfectness; and let the peace of Christ rule (or, arbitrate) in your hearts, to which also ye were called in one body, and be thankful. Let the word of Christ dwell in you richly in all wisdom, teaching and admonishing each other, with psalms and hymns, spiritual songs, singing with grace in your hearts to God. And every [thing] whatever ye do in word or in deed, do all things in the name of the Lord Jesus giving thanks to God and [the] Father through him" (12-17). It will be noticed that the peace and the word are Christ's: all here is to exalt Him, and detach from every rival.

Then from verse 18 follow special relationships on earth, but in the Lord: wives and husbands, children, and fathers; bondmen, and masters; (the first verse of chapter 4 being strangely dislocated from the close of chapter 3). The Lord, the Lord Christ, is the key-note. He is the masters' Master in heaven.

From verse 2 is the call to perseverance in prayer and watching with thanksgiving, and prayers for Paul that he might speak the mystery of Christ, to which he attributes his bonds, that he might manifest it as he ought to speak. He exhorts that we walk in wisdom toward those without, redeeming the fit time; and that their speech be always with grace, seasoned with salt. Tychicus and Onesimus would make known to them all about Paul and things at Rome; and the former would report their matters to him. Then follow from verse 10 the salutations of many fellow-labourers by name, with instructive comments, greeting to the brethren in Laodicea and the assembly in the house of Nymphas, direction as to the Epistle and a companion one, and a charge to Archippus not to be slighted. And as in his early letters, so in this late one, Paul's salutation is with his own hand. He reminds them of his bonds, and prays that grace be with them. It is altogether a needed and noble Epistle.

5.40 1 Thessalonians

This Epistle has an interest peculiar to itself, as being the first inspired writing of the apostle. It is addressed to an assembly gathered a short time before by his (with others') labours, fresh in zeal and all due spiritual affections, but necessarily immature in knowledge. This led, it would seem, to the remarkable character of the inscription, "Paul, and Silvanus, and Timotheus, to the assembly of Thessalonians in God the Father and the Lord Jesus Christ." There they are viewed in the closest and highest association, babes in the Father and the Son (1 John 2:24). The workmen used toward them were giving thanks always for them, with mention in their prayers.

Could it be otherwise with those who remembered unceasingly, not their "work" only but its "faith", their "labour of love", their "endurance of hope of our Lord Jesus Christ, before our God and Father"? All the great springs of power wrought in their souls and ways, and this in God's sight: what a testimony, as brethren beloved by God, to their election (verses 1-4), and to the power of the gospel, truly in the Holy Spirit and much assurance, according to the life of those who preached it (verse 5)! Hence they became imitators of them and of the Lord, having accepted the word in much tribulation with joy of the Holy Spirit, so as to become a model to all the believers in Macedonia and in Achaia (verse 7). Nay, more: the word of the Lord had sounded out from them, not only in these two Roman provinces, but in every place their faith God-ward had gone forth; "so that we have no need to say anything, for they themselves report concerning us what manner of entering in we had unto you." What a wonder then, or at any time! "And how ye turned unto God from idols to serve a living and true God, and to await his Son from the heavens, whom he raised up from the dead, Jesus the deliverer from the wrath to come" (8-10). Yes, it is the faith, the walk of love and truth, and the hope.

In chapter 2 the apostle depicts the true workman in guileless suffering and unselfish love, as pleasing God, seeking no glory from men, but gentle as a nurse and faithful as a father, that they should walk worthily of God, "who calleth you unto his own kingdom and glory" (verses 1-12). "And for this cause also we give thanks to God unceasingly that, having received God's word reported from us, ye accepted, not men's word but even as it is truly, God's word, which also worketh in you that believe." This only brings into living relationship with Him, and keeps there; proved by endurance of suffering for it, as the assemblies in Judea, and the apostles, yea, in the highest degree the Lord Himself, from the envious hatred of the unbelieving Jews on whom is come wrath to the uttermost (13-16). It is true that Satan may hinder, and grace may call us elsewhere; but he presents the Lord's coming as the unfailing joy when all the fruits of love shall, without fail, bloom in His presence Who produced them. "For ye are our glory and joy" (17-20). We all then should look thus to His coming, which more than makes up for every drawback.

From chapter 3 we learn that as persecution followed the apostle, so it pressed on the young saints in Thessalonica; and Timotheus was sent by him to them, that none might be moved by these afflictions, though he had forewarned of all, and thus the tempter might be foiled (verses 1-5). But Timotheus on his return filled the apostle with good tidings of their faith and love (6-8), as the apostle attests his joy before God, and prays "our God and Father himself and our Lord Jesus to direct our way unto you; and the Lord make you to increase and abound in love toward one another, and toward all, even as we also toward you, unto the establishment of your hearts unblameable in holiness before our God and Father at the coming of our Lord Jesus with all his saints" (9-13). When He comes *with* His saints, not before, will be manifested in perfection that holiness which flows from and is maintained by love.

In chapter 4 the apostle presses purity and love, proper to the disciples of the Lord Jesus, and called for by habits which ignored both. Not only is He the avenger of unclean wrongs, but God gave us His Holy Spirit as power in sanctification (verses 1-8). So the saints are themselves God-taught to love one another, ambitious of being quiet and doing their own affairs, and working with their own hands in order to a reputable walk and need of nobody. Not till here does the apostle correct the fancy that the dead saints would lose much at the Lord's coming (13-18). The Thessalonians were so absorbed by that hope as to conceive that only those who survived till then would be in its full blessing. Had they overlooked His own death and resurrection? Did they leave out of His triumph Stephen, James (John's brother), and many another fallen asleep, to say nothing of the Old Testament saints? The apostle assures that God will bring with Jesus those put to sleep through Jesus: so mistaken was it that we, the living that remain to His coming, shall anticipate those put to sleep. Then he explains as a new revelation how this is to be effected. "For the Lord himself with a shout, with archangel's voice, and with trump of God, will descend from heaven; and the dead in Christ shall rise first; then we, the living that remain, shall be caught up together with them in clouds to meet the Lord in the air; and so shall

GOD'S INSPIRATION OF THE SCRIPTURES

we ever be with the Lord." What cheer so great, and all together too?

Chapter 5 takes up the manifestation of the Lord with His own when He judges the world; that is, His day, which was no new truth but familiar in all prophecy. His day so comes as a thief in the night, and with sudden destruction. It does not so overtake Christians who are sons of light and of day. Such then should watch and be sober, putting on suited armour; because God set us not for wrath but for obtaining salvation through our Lord Jesus Christ, that, whether we wake or sleep, we may live together with Him. "Wherefore encourage one another", etc. (verses 1-10). Then follow short but precious exhortations: to recognise those labouring and taking the lead; to be in peace among themselves; to admonish, encourage, sustain, and be long-suffering; none to render evil for evil, but always to pursue the good mutually and toward all. "Always rejoice; unceasingly pray; in everything give thanks, for this is God's will in Christ Jesus concerning you. The Spirit quench not; prophesyings despise not; but prove all things; the good hold fast; from every form of wickedness hold aloof. Now the God of peace himself sanctify you wholly, and your spirit and soul and body be preserved as a whole blamelessly at the coming of our Lord Jesus Christ. Faithful is he that calleth you, who will also perform" (11-25).

Then the brethren are asked to pray for the apostle and those with him; as all the brethren were to be greeted with holy kiss. With remarkable solemnity he adjures them by the Lord that the Epistle be read to all the [holy] brethren, and wishes the grace of our Lord Jesus Christ to be with them. None thought less of himself than the apostle; yet none had so deep a sense of the all-importance to the saints, everyone, of these special communications from the Lord as the Epistles; and the first from Paul implies this in the highest degree. Compare also 2 Thessalonians 3:17.

5.41   2 THESSALONIANS

Here the address is in substance as in the First Epistle, but a little modified to meet the need. Hope was enfeebled by a Judaising error intended to alarm (2:2). Hence after the salutation the apostle with his two fellow-labourers says, "We ought to thank God always for you, even as it is meet, because your faith groweth exceedingly, and the love of each one of you all toward one another aboundeth." But there is nothing now to mark in their endurance of hope as before, though it is added that "we ourselves boast in you in the churches of God for your endurance and faith in all your persecutions and the tribulations which ye sustain." They were still faithful, though their hope was darkened. Apprehension of the day of the Lord had displaced their longing joy in His anticipated coming.

Hence he thus early in this letter points out that those afflictions they were enduring had nothing to do with that day, but were an evident token of the righteous judgment of God, to the end of their being counted worthy of the kingdom of God for which they were suffering. That day is, on the contrary, to destroy the wicked and usher in the kingdom of God, when those that suffer now shall reign with Christ. So he appeals to its indisputable principle: "If at least it is righteous with God to requite tribulation to those that trouble you, and to you that are troubled repose with us at the revelation of the Lord Jesus from heaven with angels of his power, in flaming fire rendering vengeance to those that know not God, and to those that obey not the gospel of our

Lord Jesus [Christ]." For that day is directed against not one class but two, not only the nations ignorant of God, but the Jews who rejected the glad tidings of our Lord Jesus.

Why then fear? It was for both so described, who were such as should pay penalty in "everlasting destruction from the Lord's presence, and from the glory of his might, when he shall have come to be glorified in his saints, and to be wondered at in all that believed ... in that day." Can anything be plainer than that here we have the retributive character of that day in correction of unfounded alarm? "To which end we also pray always for you that our God may count you worthy of the calling, and fulfil every good pleasure of goodness and work of faith in power; so that the name of our Lord Jesus may be glorified in you, and ye in him, according to the grace of our God and [the] Lord Jesus Christ" (verses 1-12). It will be apparent, the more the words are examined, that he does not speak thus far of our Lord's coming to meet the saints caught up, but of His judicial revelation (or, His day), when He and they shall be seen together in glory, as to which they had been misled.

In chapter 2 the apostle directly refutes the false teaching; for this it was: not ignorant and mistaken inference about the Lord's coming or its issues, as in 1 Thessalonians 4:13-15. Here it is a spurious notion for which the highest claim was made, bringing terror on the living saints; there it was a hasty deduction of their own as to the dead saints. "Now we entreat you, brethren, by [or, for the sake of] the coming of our Lord Jesus Christ, and our gathering together unto him, to the end that ye be not quickly shaken in [or, from] your mind, nor yet be troubled, neither by spirit, nor by word, nor by letter as from us, as that the day of the Lord is present" (verses 1, 2). Thus the blessed hope of His coming to gather them to Himself is the motive for asking them not to be disquieted by the groundless notion, not without fraud, that His day had arrived with its terrors.

How could it be? The saints were still here, not gathered up to Him; and the frightful evils which His day is to avenge were not yet manifested. "Let not any one deceive you in any manner; because [it will not be] unless there have come the apostasy first, and there have been revealed the man of sin, the son of perdition, he that opposeth and exalteth himself above every one called God, or object of veneration, so that he sitteth in the temple of God, showing himself that he is God. Remember ye not that while yet with you I told you these things?" (verses 3-5).

Before that day there must be, first the falling away, or the abandonment of the truth, next the revelation of the lawless one, in contrast with the mystery or secret of lawlessness at work in the church even when the apostle wrote. These three must not be confounded. The man of sin is the future adversary of the Lord, the Man of righteousness, the Antichrist of the First and Second Epistles of John, the wilful king of Daniel 11:36-39, and the second Beast of Revelation 13, identical with the False Prophet of [Revelation] chapter 19, as he is the antithesis of the true Prophet of Deuteronomy 18, if we heed the apostle Peter (Acts 3). The restraining power and person (for both are true) is the Holy Spirit in His governing action providentially, not limited to the Roman empire (for He still restrains, though the empire exist not); and when it reappears under the dragon's influence, it is exactly when the Spirit ceases to restrain. Till then the powers are ordained of God; after it, Satan will be allowed to set up the lawless man as God even in His temple, whom the Lord Jesus will slay (or, consume) with the breath of His mouth and annul by the manifestation of His coming, having already gathered His saints to Himself on high.

No solid ground appears for regarding either the apostasy or the man of sin as successional, like the mystery of lawlessness. They are both future at the consummation of the age, the former preparing the way for the latter. Nor is it well founded to view the "consuming", if that word were read, as gradual through the word: compare Isaiah 11:4, 30:33. The Lord's antagonist is unique and arrayed with portentous power and signs and wonders of falsehood, according to Satan's working retributively to deceive and destroy those who refused the love of the truth and had pleasure in unrighteousness (verses 6-12).

In contrast with such, it drew out thanksgiving always that God chose the brethren from the beginning unto salvation in sanctification of the Spirit and faith of the truth. This was shewn when He called them "through our gospel" to obtaining our Lord Jesus Christ's glory. So they are exhorted to hold fast what they were taught, whether by word or by "our epistle"; and as in closing chapter 1, so here in chapter 2 he prays that our Lord, and our God and Father Who had so loved and blessed, might encourage their hearts and stablish them in every good work and word.

Chapter 3 opens with asking their prayers that the word of the Lord might run and be glorified, even as also with them, and for deliverance from unreasonable and evil men, for faith is not of all. But the Lord is faithful; what a strength to stablish the saints and keep from evil! And hence it was that the apostle trusted that what he enjoined they both were doing and would do, and prays that the Lord would direct their hearts into the love of God and into the patience of Christ. He was waiting above; let them wait here below.

But the act of withdrawing from disorderly idlers, serious as it is, should not be confounded with purging out the wicked person in 1 Corinthians 5, which last only is excommunication. They were therefore not to esteem one that shirked work as an enemy, but rather to admonish as a brother. Leaven, on the contrary, has to be peremptorily purged out as unclean. Again, he prays the Lord of peace Himself to give them peace through everything in every manner, and Himself be with them; for such things are apt to disquiet and lead to errors if not judged. As he adjured them by the Lord to read the First Epistle to all the holy brethren, so here he salutes by his hand as the mark in every epistle, and wishes the grace of our Lord Jesus Christ to be with them all.

5.42 1 Timothy

That the Pastoral Epistles should have a common character distinct from those to the saints is easily understood; and that each has its own peculiarity is a plain matter of evidence to the attentive reader. The difference is conspicuous in the two letters to Timothy; for the first is as careful to insist on order as the second is to provide for a state of disorder, that the godly might even then have divine directions for their walk, bound as they were and we are, to take account of so sad a change. That to Titus comes in character between the two extremes.

[Chapter] 1. "Paul, apostle of Christ Jesus according to command of God our Saviour and of Christ Jesus our hope, to Timotheus, genuine child in faith; grace, mercy, peace from God the Father and Christ Jesus our Lord." The prefatory words, as usual, give a clear insight into the scope of what follows. The apostolic title is as important for authority here as for the truths of the gospel and of the church to the Roman and to the Corinthian saints, to the Galatians, Ephesians, and Colossians. "According to command" assimilates this letter and that to Titus, while it differentiates both from the second Epistle to Timothy. "God our Saviour" is also very notable here and to Titus, bespeaking the universal testimony of God's grace in the gospel, and strongly contrasted with Judaism. God in love goes out actively to man in the death of the Mediator. Christ is the hope, and unfailing if cherished. The exhortatory injunction to Timothy was first and foremost to guard the truth from all alien teaching, and specially fables and interminable genealogies which are such as yield questionings rather than God's dispensation that is in faith (3-7), the end of it being love out of a pure heart and a good conscience and unfeigned faith. It is inseparable from Christ.

These then are the substantial blessings of the gospel, and missed by such as turned aside to vain discourse, wishing to be law-teachers. Therein was the early plague of imagination, and of legalism which assails grace as antinomian while itself tending to that evil, whatever its own contrary claim. It is not that the lawful use of the law is denied, which is to convict lawless and insubordinate persons (8-11). The gospel alone witnesses of Christ to save sinners, of whom the apostle specifies himself as first, to whom, in his ignorant unbelief, mercy was shewn—Christ's whole long-suffering (12-16). This draws out his praise, after which he repeats the injunction laid on Timothy, that he might war the good warfare, maintaining faith and a good conscience. For such as put away the latter make shipwreck of the former; of whom he holds up Hymenæus and Alexander, whom he had delivered to Satan for their dishonour to God (18-20). How practical and personal it all is! And what is there but a sham and a shame if it be not so?

[Chapter] 2. Here we find the public attitude of Christianity. All should breathe of loving goodwill toward man and the chiefs of the world, even if heathen and persecuting. "I exhort therefore first of all that supplications, prayers, intercessions, thanksgivings be made for all men; for kings and all that are in authority, … for this is good and acceptable before God our Saviour, who wisheth that all men be saved and come unto full knowledge of truth. For there is one God, one mediator also of God and men, a man Christ Jesus who gave himself a ransom for all, the testimony in its own times; to which I was set preacher and apostle (I speak truth, I lie not), teacher of nations in truth and love" (1-7). Grace rises above all natural thoughts, feelings, and ways, and calls on those who believe to bear a living witness of "God our Saviour", Who is willing to save all that bow to Jesus, the ransom for all. Such is the testimony; and now that the cross on man's side proves the guilt of all (Jews and Gentiles), the same cross on God's side proclaims salvation to all that believe.

Paul was herald of this grace, but moreover apostle in full authority, and teacher in patient wisdom, that even besotted Gentiles might believe and know the truth. Yet reverence and divine order become those who profess the truth. "I will therefore that the men pray in every place, lifting up pious [or, holy] hands, without wrath and disputation." All the faithful were holy brethren;

and it was no longer the question of a Jewish sanctuary any more than of a Gentile high place. They were free and invited to pray elsewhere. The women were to cultivate modesty and discretion (instead of fashion and finery), with good works their true ornament. To learn is their place, not teaching nor authority, but quiet subjection; for which he cites the case of Eve, who, deceived, brought in transgression, whatever mercy may do even in her chief natural sorrow.

[Chapter] 3. Then Timothy has directions for the local charges of bishops (or, overseers) and deacons. "Faithful is the saying: if one is eager for oversight, he desireth a good (or, comely) work." The requisite qualities (2-7) are moral or spiritual, rather than the possession of an express gift. Free from reproach, husband of one wife, sober, discreet, orderly, hospitable, apt to teach; not quarrelsome over wine, not a striker, but gentle; not fond of money; ruling his own house well, having children in subjection with all gravity (for how could one command respect in God's house who had it not in his own?). And again, not a novice, nor one destitute of a good report without. All this is of so much the more moment as it has been slighted habitually by the greatest systems down to the least. But we cannot wonder where the office itself is turned to ecclesiastical and even worldly show. Those to be entrusted with the diaconate are briefly described in 8-13, and in this case the women or wives, who might be useful or a hindrance.

Occasion is given, not here to a doxology, but to a solemn presentation to that church in which the apostle, Timothy, elders, and deacons, and indeed all saints, each called in his special place, have to walk. "These things I write to thee, hoping to come to thee rather soon; but if I delay that thou mayest know how one ought to behave in God's house, which is a living God's assembly, pillar and support of the truth. And confessedly great is the mystery of godliness: He who was manifested in flesh, was justified in Spirit, was seen of angels, was preached among nations, was believed on in [the] world, was received up in glory." Godliness depends on and is the fruit of the truth in Christ, the secret no longer hidden but revealed; which as a whole, therefore, is in ways wholly distinct from and above a Jewish Messiah reigning in visible power, but known as we Christians know Him. Compare 2 Corinthians 5:16-18.

[Chapter] 4. With this the apostle draws a dark contrast. "But the Spirit speaketh expressly that in latter times some shall fall away from the faith, giving heed to seducing spirits and doctrines of demons by hypocrisy of legend-mongers branded as to their own conscience, forbidding to marry, [bidding] to abstain from meats which God created for reception with thanksgiving by those faithful and well acquainted with the truth; because every creature of God [is] good, and nothing to be rejected if received with thanksgiving, for it is sanctified through God's word and prayer" (1-5). Asceticism is no more Christian than moral laxity, though it assumes a fairer form. It is a pretentious assault on the Creator and Preserver of man by setting up a superior sanctity, which ends in turpitude against nature. Monachism is unconscious war against God. Timothy was called to be a good servant of Christ Jesus by laying the contrary good teaching of benign and faithful providence before the brethren, and avoiding what he calls profane and old wives' fables. For piety or godliness is profitable for everything, having promise of the present life as well as of that which is to come: our God is

Preserver of all men, especially of the faithful. He must not be deterred by such as objected to his youth, but meet the reproach by an example in word, in conduct, in love, in faith, in purity. Reading, exhortation, and instruction are enjoined till Paul came. The gift that was conferred on him he was not to neglect, but to be diligent in these things, and wholly in them, that his progress might be manifest to all. A divided heart ruins the service of Christ. Self-vigilance, too, is imperative, to save both himself and others.

[Chapter] 5. Here we have the proprieties of that work, which cannot be slighted without danger and harm. An elder he was not to rebuke but exhort as a father, younger ones as brethren, elder women as mothers, and younger ones as sisters, with all purity (1, 2). Widows were to have special and careful consideration (3-10), and younger ones to be shunned, in which case suited directions are laid down (11-16). Elders or bishops were to rule, and those who ruled well to be counted worthy of double honour, especially those labouring in word and teaching: a scripture important to bear in mind; as it is also to receive no accusation against one, save with two or three witnesses. Those that sin should be convicted before all, that all the rest too should fear. He adjures Timothy solemnly to observe these duties without prejudice and without favour, cautious against haste in sanctioning others, lest it might compromise him. He even deigns to counsel liberty where his scruples might injure health, before he closes the warning he had begun, lest he should unwarily be a partaker of other men's sins.

[Chapter] 6. Christian slaves are not forgotten, as to whom grave and gracious counsels are given, in the face of different teaching, which is exposed sternly, though the last clause of verse 5 is a spurious accretion. Godliness or piety with contentment, the reverse of making it a means of gain, *is* great gain. For as we brought nothing into the world, neither can we carry anything out. Having food and covering, we will be, or let us be, content therewith. How true that those who will be rich fall into temptation, and a snare, and many foolish and hurtful lusts, such as drown men in destruction and perdition! For the love of money is a (not exactly "the") root of every evil, after which some, too eager, wandered from the faith and pierced themselves with many sorrows. Timothy is then urged, as God's man, to flee these things and to pursue righteousness, godliness, faith, love, endurance, meekness, to combat the good combat of faith, to lay hold on eternal life, according to the good confession he confessed. Then follows a deep and lofty injunction which crowns this Epistle, and urges his keeping it spotless and irreproachable till the appearing of our Lord Jesus Christ, which in its own seasons the blessed and only Potentate shall show, the King of those that reign and the Lord of those that rule, Who only hath immortality, dwelling in light unapproachable; Whom none of men hath seen or can see, to Whom be honour and might everlasting. Amen.

Thereon Timothy is told to charge the rich to rest, not in uncertain wealth, but on the living God; to be rich in good works, laying up for themselves a good foundation for the future, that they may lay hold of what is really life. Timothy, in fine, is to keep the entrusted deposit, avoiding profane vain babblings and oppositions of falsely named knowledge. How trenchantly and in all moral earnestness the apostle speaks before he wishes him grace!

5.43 2 Timothy

The second Epistle to Timothy assumes a deeper character because of the grave disorder of a general kind which was before the eyes of the Holy Spirit. The regular means would not meet that which already and most seriously disclosed departure from God. Hence in the address it is no longer "according to command", &c., but "by God's will according to promise of the life that is in Christ Jesus", anticipating in measure that on which the apostle John falls back for the last time. Individual fidelity is the more required, yet in no way giving up but maintaining the divine association of saints, which the Spirit forms here below.

[Chapter] 1. The value of unfeigned faith rises before the apostle's heart in this last word of his to his beloved child, to whom he again wishes grace, mercy, peace. He thanks God whom he serves from his forefathers in a pure conscience, with increasing remembrance of Timothy and his tears, and longing to see him that he might be filled with joy. He speaks even more decidedly of the faith which dwelt first in Timothy's grandmother and in his mother, as in his child also. He puts him in mind to stir up the gift of God in him through the imposition of the apostle's hands, and bids him not be ashamed of the Lord's testimony, nor of Paul His prisoner, but suffer evil with the gospel according to God's power. He it was who saved us with a holy calling, not according to our works, but according to His own purpose and grace that was given us in Christ Jesus before everlasting ages, but now manifested through the appearing of our Saviour Christ Jesus, annulling death as He did and bringing to light life and incorruption through the gospel, unto which Paul was appointed herald and apostle and teacher of Gentiles. For this cause he was suffering thus, but not ashamed; "for I know whom I have believed and am persuaded that he is able to guard for that day my deposit." Hence he says, "Have an outline of healthful words which thou heardest from me in faith and love that is in Christ Jesus; the good deposit guard through the Holy Spirit that indwelleth in us." Scripture alone is reliable, as afterwards expressly said; not human tradition, of all things the most uncertain. Timothy knew the cowardice of many—that all those in Asia, specifying two, had deserted Paul. How different Onesiphorus, for whom and whose house he asks mercy, because he often refreshed him, and when in Rome the more diligently sought him out when a prisoner, besides his loving service in Ephesus!

[Chapter] 2. Faithful as Timothy had been, the apostle is now most earnest, "Thou therefore, my child, be strong in the grace that is in Christ Jesus. And the things thou heardest from me among many witnesses, these entrust to faithful men, such as shall be able to teach others also. Thou therefore take thy share of suffering evil as a good soldier of Christ Jesus. No one on service entangleth himself with the businesses of life, that he may please him that enlisted [him]. But if one also contend [in the games], he is not crowned unless he have contended lawfully. The labouring husbandmen must first partake of the fruits." These maxims need only to be correctly represented to carry their weighty sense. It was no rite, but truth which had to be communicated; yet suitably an earnest devotedness is pressed, and subjection to the Lord's will; and, as the labourer, first to share the fruits.

"Remember", says he, "Jesus Christ risen from the dead, of David's seed, according to my gospel, wherein I suffer evil unto bonds as a malefactor; but the word of God is not bound." Royal rights gave Him no exemption. On the contrary, death was His portion, and what a death! Him Paul followed and imitated as far as this could be, as he urges on all in verses 11-13, and on Timothy to put them in remembrance of these things, instead of wordy fights worse than profitless. His earnest zeal cut straightly the word of truth, warned by two others whom he names as samples who had strayed in asserting the resurrection as past, overthrowing faith under so spurious an exaggeration.

This gives occasion to an instruction of great and general value. "Nevertheless the firm foundation of God standeth, having this seal, The Lord knoweth those that are His; and, Let everyone that nameth the Lord's name depart from unrighteousness." From individual comfort and responsibility he goes on to corporate condition and duty. "Now in a great house are vessels, not only of gold and silver, but also of wood and of earthenware, and some to honour and some to dishonour. If one therefore purge himself from these, he shall be a vessel to honour, sanctified, serviceable for the Master, prepared unto every good work. But flee youthful lusts, and follow after righteousness, faith, love, peace, with those who call on the Lord out of a pure heart." If the Lord's secret is with Himself, responsibility is mine as calling on His name: I am bound to have done with iniquity. No presumed usefulness can justify my persevering in wrong.

But does not God's house abound in anomalies? Am I to leave it? No, I dare not cease from the public profession of the Lord's name with all the baptised; but I am here to purge myself from the vessels to dishonour in that house, and, instead of isolation, to follow every Christian duty with those that call on the Lord out of a pure heart. It may cost much, but it is plain and obligatory in all times and places. And while moral care is ever incumbent, He claims my soul also, with a peaceful and gentle bearing, "in meekness instructing those that oppose, if haply God may give them repentance unto acknowledgment of truth, and that they may wake up out of the snare of the devil, taken as they are by him, for His will."

[Chapter] 3. Next comes a solemn warning of the outlook in Christendom, for many would expect progressive good on earth. "But this know that in the last days difficult (or, grievous) times shall be there. For men shall be lovers of self, lovers of money, boastful, haughty, blasphemous, disobedient to parents, unthankful, unholy, without natural affection, implacable, uncontrolled, fierce, haters of good, traitors, headstrong, puffed up, pleasure-lovers rather than God-lovers, having a form of piety (or, godliness) but deniers of its power; and these turn away from." One might have shrunk from a course so peremptory, had the apostolic charge been less plain. It was direct to Timothy, but for every Christian also. The evil was at work even then, and the apostle severely characterises not only the corrupt misleaders, like Jannes and Jambres, but the misled as silly women laden with sins, led by various lusts, always learning and never able to come to right knowledge of truth.

As the false or senseless teachers have their limit set, Timothy is told how he had closely followed Paul's teaching, course, purpose, faith, long-suffering, love, patience, persecution, sufferings. Such is the ministry of Christ the Lord, with persecution endured, and the Lord delivering out of all! What is more, the apostle assures that all who desire to live piously in Christ Jesus shall be persecuted, but wicked men and impostors shall advance for the worse, deceiving and being deceived. How sad, yet how true! What is the resource or safeguard for Timothy and for all saints? "Abide thou in those things which thou didst learn and wast persuaded of, knowing of whom thou didst learn them [they were no mere traditions of unknown source]; and that from a babe thou knowest the sacred letters [those of the Old Testament] that are able to make thee wise unto salvation through faith that is in Christ Jesus. Every scripture [of New Testament or of Old] is God-inspired, and profitable for teaching, for conviction, for correction, for instruction that is in righteousness; that the man of God may be complete, furnished thoroughly unto every good work."

[Chapter] 4. Not less solemn is the apostle's direct charge. "I testify earnestly, before God and Christ Jesus that is about to judge living and dead, both His appearing and His kingdom: preach the word, be instant in season, out of season; convict, rebuke, encourage with all long-suffering and doctrine. For the time will be when they will not endure sound teaching, but according to their own lusts they will heap up to themselves teachers, having an itching ear, and will be turned aside unto fables. But be thou sober in all things, suffer evil, do evangelist's work, fully perform thy ministry." Be it observed that Christ's appearing, not His coming as such, is though distinct connected with His Kingdom. He comes to receive His own to Himself and for the Father's house; He appears and establishes His kingdom, when all shall see Him and them in the same heavenly glory. "For I am already being poured out, and the time of my departure is all but come. The good combat I have combated, the course I have finished, the faith I have kept: henceforth is laid up for me the crown of righteousness, which the Lord, the righteous judge, will award to me in that day; and not to me only, but also to all that love [have loved and do love] His appearing." Here again, as His coming is the expression of sovereign grace, His appearing is the display of His righteous remembrance of faithfulness, or, of course also, marks the want of it.

Then the apostle bids Timothy be diligent to come unto him quickly; he valued his loving presence, and knew that Timothy reciprocated it. He speaks of Demas with grief. Whatever he might be as known to God, he deserted the apostle through love of the present age. Crescens and Titus had their work, and only Luke was with the apostle. He wished Timothy on his way to take up and bring Mark with him. There indeed he had joy, if sorrow over Demas. For Mark, says he, is useful to me for ministry. He had no longer Tychicus whom he sent to Ephesus. How interesting in these ministerial solicitudes, to have the apostle—while writing an inspired pastoral epistle—telling Timothy to bring the cloak which he left behind in the Troad with Carpus, and the books, especially the parchments! Hence we learn of the Christian liberty the apostle exercised as to these outward things of body and mind. He preferred to have the cloak brought than to buy another, and he asked for his books there, which had their interest or use for him, though looking for death he knew not how soon. He would not so speak of the scriptures. If he put special stress on "the parchments", or unwritten material of a costly and durable nature, was it to have his Epistles correctly copied and multiplied?

Next, he alludes to the hostility of Alexander the coppersmith, not in a prayer, but in the grave conviction that the Lord would render to him according to his works; for he showed much evil against the apostle, who warns Timothy also to beware of him. He pathetically names how all deserted him on this repeated imprisonment when his first defence came on; but the Lord stood by him, turned it for all the Gentiles to hear, and delivered him from most imminent danger, as He surely would from every evil work, and preserve him for His heavenly kingdom. He wishes salutations to his old friends Prisca and Aquila, and to Onesiphorus' house. He tells of Erastus at Corinth, and Trophimus left sick at Miletum; for a sign of healing (as the rule) did not apply to a Christian, who came under the Lord's government. He gives the greeting of Eubulus, Pudens, Linus, Claudia, and all the brethren; he prays that the Lord should be with the spirit of Timothy, and grace be with him and others there.

5.44 Titus

There does not appear to be enough of external marks to decide when the apostle wrote this Epistle to his genuine child and fellow-labourer. But internally we may gather that it was after the First Epistle and before the Second to Timothy, with which letters it has closer links of connection than with any others. For on the one hand it treats like 1 Timothy of official government; on the other it speaks like 2 Timothy of the hope of life eternal which the God that cannot lie promised before times everlasting. As in the former, it is our Saviour God who commands; it is not the law, but faith of His elect, a common faith.

[Chapter] 1. "Paul, bondman of God, and apostle of Christ Jesus according to faith of God's elect and acknowledgment of truth that (is) according to godliness in hope of life eternal, which the God that cannot lie promised before times everlasting, but manifested in its own seasons his word in a preaching wherewith I was entrusted according to our Saviour God's commandment, to Titus genuine child according to a common faith: grace and peace from God [the] Father and Christ Jesus our Saviour" (verses 1-4). Truth according to godliness is to be acknowledged.

National or birth privileges, so prized in Israel as in the world, vanish before a revealed and believed Christ, in whom was life eternal before all ages, but now in virtue of His word preached in its own due time, as authoritatively entrusted by a God of saving love to the apostle, who writes to Titus with his usual Christian salutation. "For this cause I left thee behind in Crete that thou mightest thoroughly set right things remaining, and appoint city by city elders, as I directed thee: if one is unimpeachable, husband of one wife, having children faithful, not accused of excess or unruly. For the overseer must be unimpeachable as God's steward, not self-willed, not passionate, not a wine-sitter, not a striker, not a base-gainer: but hospitable, loving good, discreet, just, pious, temperate, holding to the faithful word according to the doctrine, that he may be able both to encourage with the healthful teaching and to rebuke the gainsayers. For there are many unruly vain-speakers and beguilers, chiefly those of circumcision, who must have the mouth stopped, who upset whole houses, teaching what they ought not for the sake of base gain. Said one of themselves, a prophet of their own, Cretans, always liars, evil wild beasts, lazy gluttons (or, bellies). This witness is true; for which reason rebuke them severely, that they may be healthful in the faith, not heeding Jewish fables and commandments of men turning from the truth. All things (are) pure to the pure; but to those that are defiled and faithless nothing [is] pure, but both their mind and their conscience are defiled. God they profess to know, but in works deny him, being abominable, and disobedient, and for every good work worthless" (verses 5-16).

Thus we see that elders (not gifts) required apostolic establishment, direct or indirect; and that moral weight was sought, and a good report in themselves and their households, to cheer those who valued healthful teaching and to rebuke adversaries. For already disorder was at work largely, and evils had entered within like the world's without. Epimenides is cited as a prophet, not of God but of their own, frankly and unsparingly denouncing what Titus was to rebuke severely, helped on as it was by Jewish professors who set Jewish fables and human ordinances before them, not the truth. Thus man and his deceits cover impurity, while our souls are purified by obeying the truth unto unfeigned brotherly love. To the pure all things are pure; to the defiled and faithless is nothing pure, yea, both their mind and their conscience are defiled. Professing to know God only aggravates the case of those who deny him in their works, being loathsome in themselves, disobedient to God, and for every good work reprobate. What a picture of the Christian confession before the first generation passed away! How like that which we have to face today! Alas, there is yet more now and worse.

[Chapter] 2. Titus, however, was not only to appoint elders, such as the apostle describes, and so to carry out the moral government which the Lord enjoins suitably to the need of souls; he is instructed also in his own charge to the same end. Hence his duties are laid down toward elder men and elder women, young women and young men. Bondmen have a large place: and it is after dealing with them that the apostle speaks so grandly of the saving grace of God that appeared for all men, and its all-important teaching for such as received it meanwhile and await the blessed hope and appearing of the glory of our great God and Saviour Jesus Christ. Separateness and zeal for good works become those redeemed to Himself, a people purified. He was to deal out exhortation and rebuke with all authority.

"But speak thou the things that beseem the healthful teaching, that elder men may be sober, grave, discreet, healthful in faith, in love, in patience; that elder women in like manner [be] in mien beseeming sacred things, not slanderers, not enslaved to much wine, teachers of comeliness, that they may train the young women to love husband, to love children, discreet, chaste, home-workers, good, subject to their own husbands, that the word of God be not reviled. The younger men in like manner exhort to be discreet, as to all things affording thyself a pattern of comely works; in the teaching incorruption, gravity, sound word not to be condemned, that he who is opposed may be abashed, having no evil to say about us; bondmen to be subject to their own masters, to be well-pleasing in all things, not gainsaying, not purloining, but showing all good faithfulness, that they may adorn the teaching of God our Saviour in all things. For the saving grace of God appeared to all men, teaching us that, having denied ungodliness and worldly lusts, we should live discreetly, and righteously, and godlily in the present age, awaiting the blessed hope and appearing of the glory of our great God and Saviour Jesus Christ, who gave himself for us, that he might redeem us from all lawlessness, and purify for himself a people for his possession zealous for comely works. These things speak and exhort, and rebuke with all command: let no one despise thee" (verses 1-15).

Here we learn how momentous it is, that those who are the objects of God's grace in the gospel should be to its praise by a walk in every relation of this life formed, strengthened, and guided according to Christ; and how inconsistency or disorder in these respects gives occasion for the enemy to blaspheme. How touching is that grace which is developed in its rich and direct bearing immediately after the exhortation as to slaves! Beyond doubt it was for all the faithful, and for every relation among them; but how considerate our Saviour God's care to tell it out at that point in the chapter! The law of God was imposed on one people; *the grace of God appeared* with its saving character to all men, as it teaches "us" who believe that, having denied ungodliness and worldly lusts, we should live discreetly as to ourselves, righteously toward others, and godlily in the highest respect. Nor is this all; but awaiting the blessed hope and *appearing of the glory* of our great God and Saviour Jesus Christ. And how assuring for the heart to remind us here, that He gave Himself for us that He might redeem us from all lawlessness and purify for Himself a people for His own possession, zealous for works good and comely!

[Chapter] 3. But there are other relations more external which are not overlooked. The self-will, which breeds emulation and strife in the homes and in the assembly, is not less disorderly, evil, and destructive in the world. "Remind them to be subject to rulers, to authorities, to be obedient, to be ready for every good work, to revile no one, to be uncontentious, gentle, showing all meekness toward all men." It was not so always in our case. Grace it is that makes the difference in us that believe.

"For ourselves too were once senseless, disobedient, going astray, slaves to various lusts and pleasures, spending our time in malice and envy, hateful, hating one another. But when the kindness and the philanthropy (or, love to man) of our Saviour God appeared, not from works in righteousness which ourselves did, but according to his mercy he saved us through washing of regeneration and renewing of Holy Spirit, which he poured out on us richly through Jesus Christ our Saviour; that, justified as we were by his grace, we should become heirs according to hope of life eternal. Faithful [is] the saying; and as to these things I would have thee insist that those that have believed God be mindful to maintain comely works. These things are comely and profitable to men; but foolish questions and genealogies and strifes and legal contentions shun, for they are unprofitable and vain. An heretical man after a first and a second admonition shun, knowing that such a one is perverted and sinneth, being self-condemned" (verses 1-11). It is sect-making, heterodox or not.

How mighty and worthy of admiration is the goodness and the special affection of our Saviour God that appeared in Christ! What a contrast with man's philanthropy, which might be in Jew, Heathen, or Islamite, of whom either gives a little out of his abundance, or compounds for sins by a superstitious and self-righteous poverty to enrich the priesthood! The Christian was proved in himself utterly evil and ruined, when God's love wrought in saving goodness according to His mere and sovereign mercy: wherein He saved us through washing of regeneration, which totally changed our state from that of fallen Adam to the risen Christ, and renewal of Holy Spirit, not only in a sinless life given which loves holiness, but in the Spirit's power which He poured out on us richly through Jesus Christ our Saviour. But thus it could not be till He wrought redemption and was glorified; and thus it was that, being justified by His grace as well as purified, we should be heirs according to hope of life eternal. "Hope" it is, for that life has not its full consummation till the body is as instinct with it at Christ's coming as the inner man is already by faith; for only thus has hope its glorious fruition. The apostle would have Titus occupied with these things, which deliver from evil and give us communion, not only in the good and comely ways of divine mercy, but with God Himself. The conscience too is exercised that there might be moral conformity in good or comely works, the fruit of love, shunning the idle and barren speculations of gnostic philosophy and legalist battles, where peace with God is unknown.

But there is another evil to be avoided, not only "heresy", as a split from the unity of the Spirit is called (see also 1 Corinthians 11:19, Galatians 5:20), but any sanction of him who is self-condemned in leaving the church of God.

The close follows. "When I shall send Artemas or Tychicus unto thee, be diligent to come unto me at Nicopolis, for there I have decided to winter. Zenas the lawyer and Apollos zealously forward, that nothing be lacking to them; and let ours also learn to maintain comely works for necessary wants, that they be not unfruitful. All that are with me salute thee. Salute those that love us in faith. Grace [be] with you all" (verses 12-15). Paul desired the presence of Titus, but not at the expense of the saints and the work in Crete whither he was sending his fellow-labourer, Artemas or Tychicus. But jealousy of other workmen not so connected was alien to his heart; nay, he would have all learn to maintain comely works to help on this and other fruitful ways for the necessary wants. He gives the salutation of all, and wishes it to those who dearly loved them if in faith, and that grace should be with all, which all needed.

5.45 PHILEMON

Here we have a letter of marked distinctiveness, placed after the pastoral Epistles though clearly written about the time when the great communications were made to the saints in Philippi, Ephesus, and Colosse. Its occasion was the return of Onesimus, a runaway slave, now a Christian brother, to his master Philemon; which calls out by the Spirit the most admirable application of grace and truth in Christ. It stands in full contrast with law, and exemplifies the gospel in its practical power and effect, turning a once worthless man's wrong into the exercise of divine affections in consonance with redemption, the holy fellowship of the faithful, and the deep and delicate proprieties withal of their social relations.

"Paul, prisoner of Christ Jesus, and Timotheus the brother, to Philemon the beloved and our fellow-workman, and to the sister Apphia and to Archippus our fellow-soldier, and to the assembly at thy house. Grace to you and peace from God our Father and [the] Lord Jesus Christ" (verses 1-3). Each word and the entire scope alike express grace, not official authority. It is as Christ's prisoner Paul introduces himself, as farther on he appeals. Timothy figures simply as "the brother". Philemon is addressed as "the beloved" according to his known character (verse 1), and honoured as a fellow-labourer in the Lord's work. And, what is most unusual, his wife is associated in the address, not "the beloved" as in the Authorised Version and the later copies, but "the sister" as in the ancient and best manuscripts. That she should be addressed was most fitting in the circumstances, and the mode is no less becoming. Next is Archippus, designated as "fellow-soldier" in sharing the conflicts of the truth; and lastly the church at Philemon's, which the apostle includes in the address to fill up the communion his heart desired with the usual benediction.

From verse 4 he lays the ground for his appeal with thanksgiving. "I thank my God, always making mention of thee at my prayers, hearing of thy love and the faith which thou hast toward the Lord Jesus and unto all the saints, so that thy fellowship in the faith may become effective in acknowledgment of every good work that is in us Christward. For I had [the true reading] much joy and encouragement over thy love, because the bowels of the saints have been refreshed through thee, brother." He puts forward Philemon's love, but in no way omits to add his faith, so that his sharing in the faith might work every good, not "in you", which though true is commonplace and feeble, but "in us" according to the best authorities, that is, in other Christians from Paul to Onesimus as regards Christ, owning his joy and cheer in what Philemon had been shewn to be in refreshing the affections of the saints.

Then in the body of his letter (8-20) he tenderly presses his suit. "Wherefore, having much boldness in Christ to enjoin on thee what is fitting, for love's sake I rather exhort, being such a one as Paul, aged and now too prisoner of Jesus Christ, I exhort thee for my child whom I begot in my bonds, Onesimus, that was once of no use to thee, but now of use to thee and to me, whom I send back to thee* in person, that is, mine own bowels; whom I would have kept with me, that for thee he might minister to me in the bonds of the gospel. But apart from thy mind I wished to do nothing, that thy good might not be as of necessity but of willingness. For perhaps for this reason he parted for a time, that thou mightest have him back for ever, no longer as a bondman, but above a bondman, a brother beloved, specially by me, but how much more by thee, both in flesh and in [the] Lord. If then thou holdest me as partner, receive him as me; but if aught he wronged thee or oweth, put this to mine account. *I* Paul write with mine own hand, I will repay: that I say not that thou owest me besides even thyself. Yea, brother, I would have profit of thee in [the] Lord: refresh my bowels in Christ. Being confident of thine obedience I write to thee, knowing that thou wilt do even more than I say."

"But withal prepare me also a lodging, for I hope that through your prayers I shall be granted to you. Epaphras, my fellow-prisoner in Christ Jesus, saluteth thee; Mark, Aristarchus, Demas, Luke, my fellow-workmen. The grace of our Lord Jesus Christ [be] with your spirit."

The apostle in no way denies or forgets his position, but he prefers to exhort for love's sake, on one side as Paul aged and now also prisoner of Christ, on the other for his child begotten in his bonds, Onesimus. Grant that he was once a useless slave to Philemon, was he not now of good use to both Philemon and Paul, and sent back to his master himself, as it were Paul's very heart, though he would have kept him with himself to do him service on Philemon's behalf in the bonds of the gospel? Only

---

* The common text here reads, "Thou therefore [receive] him", &c.

apart from Philemon's mind he would do nothing, that his good might be of free-will, not of constraint. And how beautiful the turn that grace gives! "Perhaps for this reason he was parted for a time, that thou mightest have him back for ever, no longer as a bondman, but above a bondman, a brother beloved, specially by me, but how much more by thee, both in flesh and in the Lord." So simply is it urged in all its power that one can but repeat rather than explain. Then follows the point of fellowship. "If then thou holdest me a partner, receive him as me; but if aught he wronged thee or oweth, put this to mine account. *I* Paul write with mine own hand, I will repay: that I say not to thee, that thou owest me besides even thyself." For it would seem that Philemon too was indebted to the apostle for receiving the truth.

"Yea, brother, I would have profit of thee in the Lord," he says, referring to the name of Onesimus, "refresh my bowels in Christ." Would he refuse to Paul what he had done hitherto to the saints in general, as in verse 7? "Being confident of thine obedience I write to thee, knowing that thou wilt do even more than I say." Who can doubt that Philemon would receive Onesimus lovingly, and set him free to the joy of all? But it is on no ground of human rights, or natural benevolence, but showing him "the kindness of God", the grace of Christ, the fellowship of the faith. It is the counterpart of the riband of blue on the fringe of the garment, the heavenly ornament in our character on earth, grace governing in our relationships here below, as it reigns in God's dealings with us for eternity.

5.46 Hebrews

The distinctive character of this Epistle is at least as plain and as important as that of any other. It is expressly anonymous; for he who wrote it, though himself an apostle, did so as a teacher, resting its authority on the Old Testament, supplemented by the Son of God come and deigning to be Apostle in the highest sense and rank. This gives a divine and heavenly character to the communications, which were to Israel, represented now by a believing remnant, and sanctified for glory with Him on high, till the new age arrive, when the then remnant shall become a strong nation, and the new covenant formally and fully comes into force with the two houses of Israel as such. Then the Lord Jesus, Who was Apostle and Prophet on earth, and is the Great Priest in the heavens and above them, shall reign as King not only in Zion but over all the habitable earth. It may be observed that even this Epistle, like the rest, says nothing of that royal position so amply revealed by the Old Testament Prophets. It dwells on the present and intermediate place of Christ above, and thence passes to the heavenly calling of the saints.

Chapter 1 opens with His personal glory as Son of God, abundantly attested by the Psalms and the Prophets; as chapter 2:5 and onward follows with His glory as Son of Man, according to Psalm 8, in answer to His work of redemption, qualifying Him to be a merciful and faithful High-Priest as none else could be. Hence in chapter 3 the believers, addressed as holy brethren, partakers of a heavenly calling out of the chosen nation, are exhorted to consider Jesus the Apostle and High-Priest of our confession, before Whose worth, dignity, and power, Moses and Aaron were but shadows. The saints, like Israel, are passing through a wilderness of temptation and danger. Profession may be only profession, and thus many not only slip but fall and perish. Living dependence on God is essential; and the beginning of confidence to be held fast firmly unto the end. Unbelief is the great snare. Chapter 4 pursues this: we, who have believed are not in God's rest of glory but going on to it. Adam did not enter, though God sanctified the sabbath as its sign; Joshua did not lead into it, but only into a Canaan that typified it; for long after, David spoke of it as still future. Meanwhile we have to fear even seeming to come short; and we need to give diligence, for the time still calls for this. The rest remains. And God has provided two invaluable means to bring us through: His word (answering to the apostleship); and Jesus the Son of God, a great High-Priest before God as He went through the heavens. Thus we may approach the throne of grace with boldness, that we may receive mercy and find grace for seasonable help.

In chapter 5 the Aaronic priesthood is compared to show the incontestable superiority of Christ's. He Who erst commanded learnt obedience, not only as man, but in suffering beyond all. Perfected through death and resurrection, He is addressed or saluted of God as High-Priest after the order of Melchizedek. The danger for the saints here is of remaining babes, instead of growing to full age (or, perfection) by receiving the solid food of Christ. Chapter 6 solemnly warns against not pressing on to this status of majority, lest, even after great privileges were known, the mere elements* expose to falling away and irretrievable ruin. But the writer was persuaded better things of those who had shewn life in love, as he desired for them full assurance of hope, for God had laid indefectible ground for strong consolation. Then chapter 7 expounds the surpassing

---

* It is an unhappy rendering to say "first principles": for these we never "leave". It is really "the word of the beginning of Christ"—what was known before His death, resurrection, and ascension.

excellence of Christ's office as Melchizedek priest, not in exercise (which is set forth as Aaronic) as it will be, but in its order. For this answers fully and now to what His prototype was in figure, His being one sole intransmissible priesthood in contrast with Aaron's order.

Chapter 8 gives a summary of the aforesaid, and adds the greater excellency of Christ's ministry as Mediator of a covenant better than the Mosaic; not man's failing to obey, but God's effectual work in grace, the very title of "new" writing death on the "old". In the earlier verses of chapter 9 is shewn that under the law the way into the holies was not yet manifested: man could not go in, as God had not come out. Christ has verified both. In Him God came out, in Him man is gone in. How transcendent is the Christian's blessedness who reaps the fruit of both by His sacrifice and priesthood! In this chapter the fact of a testator and "testament" is turned to good account (verses 16, 17); everywhere else it is "covenant", as the context proves. Christianity is not man tested, but God who has wrought for His own glory in saving grace toward man. Chapter 10 applies the blessing fully to those who believe, and this on the basis of Christ's one perfecting sacrifice. Hence He sat down in perpetuity at God's right hand, as He has perfected in perpetuity the sanctified. Why wonder? It is God's will, Christ's work, and the Holy Spirit's witness. The believers, with whom the inspired writer joins himself, are exhorted to act now on these precious privileges in verses 19-25, and warned of the peril of apostasy in slighting or abusing Christ's sacrifice by sinning wilfully, as they were in chapter 6 of not going on to full growth. But they are again reminded of better things, and told not to cast away their confidence, though they had need of endurance. It is not all the truth that the once unjust are justified by faith (Romans 4:5); for "the just shall *live* by faith."

Hence in chapter 11 we have the roll of faith differently but invariably displayed in God's noble army of confessors long before Israel, of whom the Lord Jesus is the Leader and Completer (chapter 12:2). As to chastening, they were neither to despise it nor to faint under it. The danger here is failing from, or lacking, the grace of God (*i.e.*, losing confidence) through unbelief in His love; and Esau's profanity stands as a beacon. Then we have a grand contrast of what Israel came to at Sinai, with our having come by faith to the entire scene of blessing flowing out of Christ and His redemption: first Zion the highest point of royal grace on earth; then the heavenly city, not the old but new Jerusalem; next the indigenous dwellers on high, myriads of angels, all their assemblage; further the assembly of firstborns enregistered in heaven; and God Himself Judge of all; then we come down to the spirits of just men made perfect (the Old Testament saints), and to Jesus with fullest mercy and joy for the earth as Mediator of a covenant that is not only "new" but as "fresh" as ever; and lastly to the blood of sprinkling in contrast with Abel whose blood brought curse, this Christ's everlasting blessing. He changes even a warning into a promise to faith. But let us have grace by which to serve God acceptably with reverence and awe. For our God is a consuming fire. What has not *His* grace done and given!

Chapter 13 closes the Epistle with urging that brotherly affection abide, hospitality, and kindness to sufferers; that marriage be honourable in all (or, every way), and conduct be free from love of money. Next departed guides are to be remembered; but if they were gone, Jesus is the same yesterday, and to-day, and for ever.

Hence they were to be set against various and strange doctrines. Grace confirms the heart, not meats which profit not devotees even. Jesus that suffered without the gate, Whose blood avails within the holiest, is the key of the Christian position. "Therefore let us go forth to Him without the camp, bearing His reproach." The middle place, beloved of Judaisers and philosophers, is the place of apostate Jews, and now of effete Christendom. "By Him, therefore, let us offer the sacrifice of praise to God continually"; yet sacrifices in doing good have also their real place. Again living guides are to be obeyed. This is their use, to lead others who might not readily see the path of Christ. They shall give account, not of the souls led, but of how they led them. No one valued the prayer of saints more than he who here asks it, after his first imprisonment and before the second. With Timothy set at liberty he hoped to see them again. How suited is the prayer in verses 20, 21, not only to them and the writer, but to this Epistle! It seems to be beyond just question what Peter in his second Epistle refers to (3:15), as written by Paul to Christian Jews, to whom Peter addressed both of his (1 Peter 1:1, and 2 Peter 3:1).

5.47 James

The peculiarity of the Epistle before us is evident. The address marks it plainly and indelibly, "to the twelve tribes that are in dispersion". The entire breadth of the chosen people is brought before us, and this in the largest spirit of faith; for in fact there was no such people since the Assyrians executed judgment on the idolatrous ten tribes, first rent away from Rehoboam. Faith did not give it up, as we see in the Old Testament when Elijah testified for Jehovah against Baal (1 Kings 18:31, also 2 Chronicles 30:1; and Daniel 9:7); and so we see in the apostle Paul (Acts 26:7). Here only is it the direct address of an inspired Epistle. It is expressly far wider than the apostle Peter's word inscribed to the "elect sojourners of the dispersion", not only because these were limited to a part of Asia Minor, "Pontus, Galatia, Cappadocia, Asia [proconsular], and Bithynia", but still more deeply and restrictedly by the spiritual character notified, which excludes all but Christians like those contemplated in the great Epistle to the Hebrews.

Here it is not so, though such as had the faith of our Lord Jesus Christ are distinctly recognised (2:1); and the writer describes himself from the beginning as "bondman of God and of the Lord Jesus Christ" (1:1). But the peculiar condition that still obtained in Jerusalem is here supposed—at any rate till the Epistle to the Hebrews was written. The synagogue was frequented as yet (2:2), and the haughty bearing is not overlooked of the rich toward the poor (rich in a faith which those had not). Oppressive they themselves were in a worldly sort, nay also disposed to blaspheme the excellent Name that was called on the heirs of the Kingdom.

Hence we see already the plain traces of an unreal profession of faith, which in the apostle John's much later Epistle appears after a yet more solemn guise. But James takes up its earlier shape when faith was becoming a creed, intellectual and traditional. So it naturally would where Christians abounded in close connexion with their unbelieving brethren, not only in social but religious life also. For there seemed no such urgent reason to require separation as idolatry necessitated for the Gentile confessors among the heathen.

This goes far to explain the denunciations in chapters 4, 5. The Epistle from its nature according to its address deals directly with open fleshly and worldly wickedness in a way unexampled among the other apostolic writings. Here it is in keeping with the direction of the writer; which is as singular in the New Testament as the book of Jonah in the Old. Both are exceptional, for the latter has for its object the testimony and mercy of God to a Gentile power, in a circle of holy writ pre-eminently if not exclusively occupied with Israel; as the former is God's testimony still to the twelve tribes, in a volume which opens and goes through with the incredulous Jews stumbling at the Stumbling-stone, and His message of grace sent meanwhile to the Gentiles who were to hear. Yet the end of the Lord is that He is full of pity and merciful; so that, as Old and New Testaments bear witness, all Israel shall be saved at His purging judgment, and the nations shall rejoice with His people, when the rejected Christ shall arise to rule as Jehovah, King over all the earth, as the like never was, nor shall ever follow, though absolute rest and righteousness will be the worthy result for all eternity.

Chapter 1 after greeting those in view calls them to count it all joy when they fall into various temptations or trials. This presumes faith practically, looks for patience or endurance as the fruit, and exhorts that it have a perfect work, that they might be perfect and complete, lacking in nought. But if any of them lack wisdom, let him ask of God, who gives to all freely (or, liberally) and upbraids not, [as He well might]; and it shall be given to him. Hence he is told to ask in faith, as this is due to God, nothing in doubt. For the doubter is like surge of the sea wind-driven and tossed (for let not that man think that he shall receive anything from the Lord), a double-minded man unstable in all his ways (verses 1-8).

In Christ alone here as everywhere else we see the perfection of patience and of communion with God. Present circumstances are of such small account, that the brother of low degree is to glory in his elevation by grace, and the rich in his humiliation, as passing away like flower of grass. No sooner did the sun rise with its scorching, than it withered the grass, and its flower fell, and the comeliness of its look perished: so also shall the rich fade in his ways. Emphatically therefore is it added, Blessed the man (not that stands high in the world but) that endureth temptation; for, having been proved, he shall receive the crown of life which He promised to those that love Him (9-12). Worldly feeling is in no way spared. We are called by glory and virtue.

Next, we are warned of a wholly different temptation from within. "Let none say when tempted, I am tempted of (or, from) God. For God cannot be tempted by evils, and himself tempteth none. But each is tempted when drawn away and enticed by his own lust; then lust having conceived beareth sin; and sin when completed bringeth death. Err not, my beloved brethren. Every good giving and every perfect gift is from above, coming down from the Father of lights with whom can be [or, is] no variation nor shadow of turning. Of his own will he brought us forth by the word of truth, that we should be a certain first-fruits of his creatures" (13-18). It is not redemption which is here applied, but the new life by divine and sovereign grace; and suitable practice is demanded earnestly.

Confidence in our Father is inculcated as well as dependence, no less than distrust in self; consistency too as now having by grace a new and divine nature, and watchfulness against our own lusts. Hence the word from 19 to the end of chapter 1. "Ye know [it], my beloved brethren; but let every man be swift to hear, slow to speak, slow to wrath, for man's wrath worketh not God's righteousness. Wherefore, putting away all filthiness and abundance of wickedness, receive in meekness the implanted word that is able to save your souls. But be ye doers of the word and not hearers only, beguiling yourselves: because if one is a word-hearer and not a doer, he is like a man considering his natural [or, birth-] face in a mirror; for he considered himself and hath departed and immediately forgot what he was like. But he that looked into the perfect law of liberty and remained there, being not a forgetful hearer but a work-doer, he shall be blessed in his doing. If one think to be religious while not bridling his tongue but deceiving his heart, his religion is vain. Pure and undefiled religion before our God and Father is this, to visit orphans and widows in their affliction, to keep oneself unspotted from the world."

Who could possibly set forth more plainly truth so clear, pithy, and needed day by day? We want readiness in receiving from God, vigilance against haste of speech and the high spirit, to be consistent with our relationship to Him. Self-judgment greatly helps us to profit by the word which, meekly received, enters in power, and reproduces itself in action. Where it is merely hearing, all is forgotten speedily, instead of being blessed in one's doing. But where by grace the word fixes the heart's heed, it is a perfect law of liberty, and God's will is loved for its own sake and His. The tongue is bridled because it is ours; and its licence is just the opposite of pure and undefiled service whether in active care for the sorrow-stricken, orphans and widows, or in true and holy separateness from the world which seeks self and slew the Saviour.

Chapter 2 confronts the faith of our Lord—Lord of glory, with respect of persons. A graphic sketch of their synagogue, where the grandee was as honoured as the lowly was despised, convicts them of partiality with evil thoughts (1-4). What a contrast between God's choice and promise, and the natural effect of wealth, toward God and man (5-7)! The royal law was thus set at nought by such transgressions, yea, the whole law compromised; for whatever may be in this way, thus to offend in one point is to be guilty of all. And the law of liberty (the renewed soul going heartily as he was bidden) is alike right, given to enjoy mercy, while the judging spirit will meet the judgment it measures out (8-13).

This introduces the withering exposure (in 14-26) of faith boasting without moral reality. Such faith condemns a man instead of saving him. In vain are kind words without corresponding ways. If one say, Thou hast faith, and I have works, the answer is, Show me thy faith without works, and I from my works will show thee my faith. Need it be pointed out that Romans 3, 4 expounds how the ungodly is justified before God? Here it is the fruitless confessor condemned before man. The point here is, Show me. The demons believe; but there is no life, only ruin. Faith without works is idle; whereas the cases of Abraham and Rahab were works so truly of faith that without living faith they were evil. For at God's word one was ready to sacrifice his son, the other to betray king and country: faith quickened and transfigured them. From opposite sides, how blessedly the two scriptures agree!

In chapter 3:1-12 is a full warning against speech without dependence on God or His grace; and first in public teaching. "Be not many teachers, my brethren, knowing that we shall receive greater judgment. For we all often offend. If one offend not in word, he is a perfect man, able to bridle the whole body too." Bits in horses' mouths, rudders of ships, are small but of great power: so yet more with the tongue, more untameable than any animal of land, air, or sea. It is apt to be, not inconsistent only, but hypocritical.

Instead of things so unworthy, the exhortation is to show out of a good course of life one's works in meekness of wisdom, the reverse of bitter emulation and strife with the result of disorder and every other evil. But the wisdom from above (and what else is of moment?) is first pure, then peaceful, gentle, yielding, full of mercy and good fruits, uncontentious, unfeigned. And righteousness's fruit in peace is sown for those that make peace (13-18).

The contrast of wars and fightings is traced in chapter 4 to the self-pleasing and lust of the natural heart, and the corruption which flows from that friendship with the world which is enmity with God. "Think ye that the scripture speaketh in vain? Doth the Spirit that abode in us desire enviously?" Rather "He giveth more grace; wherefore he saith, God setteth himself against haughty ones and giveth grace to lowly." Submission to God is urged, and resistance of the devil who will flee, but drawing near to God: all as settled things (aorists). Then we have the remarkable call to "sinners" for cleansed hands and purified hearts in humiliation before the Lord, with true mourning and heaviness for His lifting them up (1-10).

Evil-speaking one of another is next (11, 12) reprehended as judging the law and the law-giver; to judge it is not to be its doer, but setting up against God Himself.

Like self-will appears in forgetting our entire dependence on God from day to day, and in the affairs of this life (13-17). The simple yet divine motto closes, "To him therefore that knoweth to do good, and doeth it not, to him it is sin." The law no doubt is generally characterised by what is negative, as Thou shalt not do this or that; Christianity, just as manifestly, by the positive exercise of doing good, the life of God in man. Here it is insisted on.

Chapter 5 brings in the coming of the Lord to warn the rich oppressors, and to comfort the suffering Jewish remnant that believed. The labourer awaiting harvest is made a homily of patience; and the prophets and Job still more (1-11).

Profanity is denounced, prayer prescribed to the evil entreated, singing to the happy. Again, we see how the elders intervened where any fell under a sickness inflicted governmentally, and the sick one confessed such sins and was forgiven. Indeed the general principle is pressed of confessing one to another (not a word about this to elders even while there); and the value of fervent supplication, of which Elijah was so signal an example. We also learn the privilege of restoring those who err from the truth or the right ways of the Lord, leaving it to shallow, hard, and proud men to pique themselves on putting away (12-20).

5.48 1 Peter

As the address in the Epistle of James differs from that of Peter, whose two Epistles are directed to the same Christian Jews, elect sojourners of the dispersion in part of Asia Minor, so the character of both is most distinct, as may be now seen in the first of the two. They were as he says "elect according to God the Father's foreknowledge in [virtue of] sanctification of the Spirit unto obedience and blood-sprinkling of Jesus Christ". Thus does the apostle contrast their standing with Israel, who had only a fleshly and external separation to Jehovah, and were bound to obey the law under the sanction of the sprinkled blood of victims which kept death before them, as the sure penalty in case of their disobedience.

The opening is like that of the Epistle to the Ephesians, yet with a marked difference from the first and throughout. Here it is not "with every spiritual blessing in the heavenlies in Christ, according as he chose us in him before the world's foundation that we should be holy and blameless before him in love", etc. It is, "Who according to his much mercy begot us again unto a living hope through resurrection of Jesus Christ out of the dead, unto an inheritance incorruptible and undefiled and unfading, reserved in the heavens for you that are guarded by God's power through faith for salvation ready to be revealed in the last time" (1:3-5). It is not "the mystery", but the "heavenly calling", for saints who pass through the wilderness and await their heavenly inheritance at Christ's appearing; it thus far resembles the Epistle to the Hebrews. Exultation meanwhile should be, as grief for a little through varied trials which terminate at His revelation. But we love Him, though we never saw Him; and though we do not see Him, we rejoice with joy unspeakable and full of glory, in distinctive contrast with Israel's faith and hope. We receive soul-salvation and wait for that of our bodies. The prophets predicted; the Holy Ghost now witnesses in the gospel; the Lord will be revealed to crown all in glory. Thus between the two, room is made for the gospel and Christianity. We therefore, cheered by what is accomplished, gird up our loins in the Spirit, and hope perfectly for the grace to be soon brought us in Jesus Christ's revelation (6-13).

He says then as obedient children, conforming not yourselves to the former lusts in your ignorance, but according to the holy One that called you, may ye be holy in all conduct; because it is written, Be ye holy, because I am holy. And if ye invoke as Father Him that impartially judges according to the work of each, pass the time of your pilgrimage in fear, (not because ye doubt your deliverance, but) knowing that not with corruptibles, silver or gold, ye were redeemed from your vain course of life handed down from fathers, but with Christ's precious blood as an unblemished and spotless lamb, foreknown before the world's foundation, but manifested at the end of times for you that through Him believe in God that raised Him out of the dead and gave Him glory, so that your faith and hope are in God (14-21).

The chapter closes with pointing out that having purified their souls by obedience of the truth to unfeigned brotherly love, they were out of a pure heart to love one another fervently, being born again not of corruptible seed but incorruptible through God's living and abiding word. It was not now a question of Israel's sons, but of God's. And as the new relationship was through His word received in faith, it was on the ground of His sovereign grace in presence of the total failure of His ancient people. Because all flesh is as grass, and all its glory as grass and its flower; but the Lord's word abides for ever. And this is the word which was preached unto them. Relationships to each other among believers follow these to God and Christ; they are most excellent, intimate, and enduring (22-25). Saints might suffer but ought to be of good cheer.

[Chapter] 2. Hence they were, putting away all malice, guile, hypocrisies, envies, and slanders, to long for the pure milk of the word as new-born babes, that they might grow thereby to salvation, if indeed they had tasted that the Lord is good: without this all was vain. As we see, salvation here as elsewhere is viewed as only complete when glory comes; but as by God's word we were born again, so are we nourished. He is the Living Stone, rejected by men but with God elect, precious; and they coming to Him as living stones were being built up a spiritual house, a holy priesthood, to offer up spiritual sacrifices acceptable to God through Jesus Christ. Isaiah 28:16 is cited; for the work of grace in Zion by-and-by is no less true for the believers now, to whom the preciousness belongs, while the nation stumbles in disobedience; whereas the faithful gain to the highest degree and are a chosen generation, a royal priesthood, a holy nation, a people for a possession, to set forth the excellencies of Him that called them out of darkness into His wonderful light. What Israel are to have when they believe is forestalled, and much more now (6-10). Christians as such are the sole priests whom the Lord now recognises.

As pilgrims and sojourners they are besought to abstain from fleshly lusts which war against the soul, with their behaviour seemly among the Gentiles, that wherein they slander them as evil-doers, they might, as witnesses, out of their good works glorify God in a day of visitation (11, 12). Christians are meant to be separate to the Lord, and ever waiting for Him and glory above, instead of being sown to Jehovah in the land, for great is the day of Jezreel.

Again, he lays down submission to the powers that be, closing with a pregnant summary: honour all, love the brotherhood, fear God, honour the king (13-17).

Domestics are next exhorted to subjection with all fear of their masters; and the Christian principle is enjoined, "If doing good and suffering ye shall endure, this is grace with God." Hence Christ in suffering every way and perfectly is set as model to us, who had gone far astray but now returned to the Shepherd and Overseer of our souls (18-25).

[Chapter] 3. Then wives and husbands are exhorted in the same strain of grace as objects of God's government at work morally (1-7). Finally, all were to be of like mind in sympathy, brotherly love, tenderness, and humility, not returning evil in deed or word, but contrariwise blessing in the sense that such is our calling and hope. The Psalms are freely used to confirm it, warning against self and assuring us of the Lord's care. Even if we should suffer for righteousness, how blessed! We need not fear or be troubled, but should sanctify Christ as Lord in our hearts, always ready to answer everyone that asketh a reason about the hope that is in us with meekness and fear, having a good conscience, that, wherein they slander us as evil-doers, those may be put to shame that calumniate our good behaviour in Christ (8-16).

Next he urges the manifest truth that it is better, if the will of God will it, to suffer well-doing than evil doing; for Christ also once suffered for sins, Just for unjust, that He might bring us to God, put to death indeed in flesh but quickened in Spirit, in [virtue of] which [Spirit] also He went and preached to the imprisoned spirits, heretofore disobedient when the long-suffering of God waited in Noah's days while the ark was a preparing, wherein few (that is, eight) souls were saved through water; which figure also now saves us, baptism, not putting away of filth of flesh, but a request of a good conscience Godward through Jesus Christ's resurrection, Who is at God's right-hand, having gone into heaven, angels and authorities and powers being subjected to Him (17-22). The notion of Christ's descent to Hades after death and there preaching to saints, sinners, or angels, is a mere dream, not only without scripture but contrary to it, and irreconcilable with revealed truth. The passage refers solely to His Spirit preaching to the antediluvians through Noah. As they then disobeyed the word, they are in prison, awaiting the still more solemn judgment for eternity; so must those be who refuse the gospel now preached.

[Chapter] 4. Christ suffering for us in flesh is here pressed on us, who also need it the more because of our having lusts, which He had not. The past surely should suffice those who are now renewed, and have lived with the unrestraint to which Gentile surroundings exposed. If now reviled, because they refused such vileness, those who did so should give account to Him that is ready to judge quick and dead. For therefore were glad tidings preached to dead also [of course while alive], that they might be judged according to men in flesh, but live according to God in Spirit. If they submitted to that judgment of themselves as guilty men, they emerged by faith with a new life whereby they lived according to God in Spirit. It is the other side of what the antediluvians experienced who disobeyed Noah's preaching of righteousness (1-6). They were dead now, who by faith bowed to the judgment of their condition and also laid hold of the promises to a life Godward.

This bringing before the apostle the end of all things as drawn nigh, he calls the saints to be sober and watch unto prayers; to cherish before all things fervent love among themselves, because love, instead of bruiting abroad, covers a multitude of sins; to be hospitable one toward another without murmurings. Even as each received a gift, they were to minister it to one another, as good stewards of God's manifold grace: if one speak, as God's oracles; if one minister, as of strength which God supplies; that in all things God may be glorified through Jesus Christ, Whose is the glory and the might unto the ages of the ages. Amen (7-11).

In verses 12-19 is the word not to take as strange the fire among them that cometh for their trial, as though a strange thing happened to them; but in communion with Christ's sufferings to "rejoice; that at the revelation of his glory also ye may rejoice exultingly. If ye are reproached in Christ's name, blessed [are ye], because the [Spirit] of glory and the Spirit of God rests on you." This is the highest suffering in God's sight, not merely for righteousness, but for Christ. Let none of you, he proceeds, suffer as murderer or thief or evil-doer or as overseer of other's affairs; but if as a Christian, let him not be ashamed but glorify God in this name. Because [it is] the time for the judgment to begin from the house of God; and if first from us, what [is] the end of those disobedient to the gospel of God? And if the righteous is with difficulty saved, where shall the ungodly and sinful appear? Wherefore also let those that suffer according to the will of God commit their souls in well-doing to a faithful Creator.

[Chapter] 5. The last chapter opens with exhorting the elders among them, himself a fellow-elder and a witness of the sufferings of Christ, who was also partaker of the glory about to be revealed, in exact keeping with the Epistle. Feed, says he, the flock of God that is among you, exercising oversight not by necessity but willingly, nor yet for base gain but readily, not as lording over your allotments but being models of the flock. And when the Chief Shepherd is manifested, ye shall receive the unfading crown of glory (1-4). How every word shines with the light and love of God, yet how forgotten in Christendom!

The younger he bids be subject to elders, and to bind on humility toward one another; for God sets Himself against proud ones, but gives grace to the lowly. "Humble yourselves therefore under the mighty hand of God that he may exalt you in season, having cast all your anxiety upon him, for he careth for you" (5-7). Again he says, Watch, be wakeful: your adversary the devil as a roaring lion walketh about seeking whom he may devour. It is not the wiles of a serpent here, still less the ruler of the authorities of the air, but the wilderness enemy. "Whom resist, stedfast in faith, knowing that the same afflictions are accomplished in your brotherhood in the world. But the God of all grace that called you to his eternal glory in Christ Jesus, after suffering a little, himself shall make perfect, stablish, strengthen, settle: to him [be] the glory for the ages of the ages. Amen." Did not the apostle remember and apply Luke 22:32? No doubt he was carrying out his charge over the circumcision that believed in the sphere where Paul laboured so much. And it is full of interest to note that the faithful Silvanus, the companion of the one, now conveyed this Epistle of the other, wherein he exhorts and testifies that this is the true grace of God "wherein ye stand, (or, in which stand)". Again "Mark my son" is now Peter's companion, quite restored to the confidence of the other apostle who had blamed him of old. "She that is joint-elect" appears to be the true force; but whether Peter's wife or another in Babylon whence he writes, we cannot say. He asks for a warm and holy greeting, and peace too mutually, to "you all that are in Christ".

5.49 2 Peter

Not less characteristic of the great apostle of the circumcision is his Second Epistle. They are both occupied with God's moral government; but the former is in view of saints now suffering for righteousness, and for Christ, waiting for His appearing; the latter in view of false and corrupt teachers (chapter 2), and of scornful philosophic adversaries (chapter 3), alike unrighteous, who shall not fail to meet His judgment in that day. Both are eminently practical and hortative, redemption and new risen life being the basis in the one case, as Christ's purchase aggravates the wickedness in the other.

[Chapter] 1. "Symeon Peter, bondman and apostle of Jesus Christ to those that obtained like precious faith with us by (or, in) righteousness of our God and Saviour Jesus Christ." These cited words of address are distinctive, notable, and instructive. He does not speak of their being reckoned righteous "through faith", as many misunderstand, but attributes their receiving faith such as the apostle had to God's faithfulness to His promise. For there is always a remnant of grace among Abraham's seed, and of none other. So it had been in the guilty history of Israel; and so it was then, after the Jews rejected their own Messiah. And the dispersed share like precious faith with those who by grace followed Him intimately. If the Blesser here, "our God", became our "Saviour Jesus Christ", it is the more impressive; as undoubtedly He was not Messiah only but the Jehovah God of Israel. To "Grace and peace be multiplied to you", he now adds "in the knowledge of God and of Jesus our Lord" (1, 2). The increasing stress called for it then and since.

Grace had already done so wondrously for them that he looks for growth accordingly and spiritual power (3-11). "As his divine power hath given us all things that pertain unto life and godliness, through the knowledge of him that called us by (or, by his own) glory and virtue, through which he hath given us the greatest and precious promises, that through these ye may become partakers of a divine nature, having escaped from the corruption that is in the world by lust. Even for this very reason too bringing in besides all diligence, in your faith furnish virtue, in virtue knowledge, in knowledge temperateness, in temperateness endurance, in endurance godliness, in godliness brotherly kindness, in brotherly kindness love. For if these things be and abound in you, they make [you] neither idle nor unfruitful as respects the knowledge of our Lord Jesus Christ; for he with whom these things are not is blind, shortsighted, having forgotten the purging of his old sins. Wherefore, brethren, give the more diligence to make your calling and election sure, for doing these things ye shall never stumble; for thus shall the entrance into the everlasting kingdom of our Lord and Saviour Jesus Christ be richly furnished to you." In the full provision of grace he would confirm their souls, but this in order to earnest diligence and the supply of all deficiency; that instead of questions through habitual negligence and short-coming, they should enjoy an unclouded sense of their election and calling, and their anticipated entrance into Christ's everlasting kingdom be supplied along the way.

Yet, glorious as the kingdom will be, Christianity has higher things in Christ to which our apostle but alludes. In view of speedily departing he casts on no apostle to succeed, still less on an imagined apostolic succession as men say, nor any safeguard but the word of God, as did Paul also. No cunningly devised fable do we follow to make known the power and coming of our Lord, but were sanctioned witnesses (not αὐτόπται only but ἐπόπται) of His majesty, and heard the Father's voice utter His delight in His beloved Son. This made the prophetic word more sure, to which those addressed did well to take heed, "as to a lamp shining in a squalid place, until day dawn and [the] morning star arise in your hearts." They were not to slight prophecy with which they were more or less familiar as Jews. But Christ now known by the gospel yields better and brighter things to which he encourages them. Hence he would have arise in their heart the heavenly light of the day of grace, and of Christ Himself the Star of the morning, the Christian hope before the day of Jehovah. Here they might be weak, as most have been even though not Jews previously. Prophecy is truly about the earth: our proper portion is with Christ in heaven. But they must not take prophecy of scripture as being of its own (or, isolated) interpretation. This might suit man's limitation; but God gave it as a whole converging on Christ and His glory. "For never by man's will was prophecy brought, but men spoke from God, borne on (or, moved) by the Holy Spirit" (12-21).

[Chapter] 2. Here the apostle sets out the ruin of the Christian confession by false teachers, as before it had been for Israel by false prophets. He allows no illusive hopes. Far from getting all the nations to the banner of Christ, there should be the "falling away", the apostasy, and worse still (as we read in 2 Thessalonians 2). "They shall bring in destructive sects, denying even the Sovereign Master that bought them, bringing on themselves swift destruction" (1). The Lord Jesus bought, not the hidden treasure only, but the entire field, the world. He tasted death for every thing. All are His not only by divine right of creation but by His death that purchased all with the utmost solemnity. This however does not mean redemption, which delivers the captive from the enemy, but simply that they are purchased. Believers are both bought and redeemed; all the rest are bought only, and among them those corrupters of whom the apostle speaks unsparingly as bringing the way of truth into disrepute. Their sure and exemplary judgment he confirms by varied instances.

"And many shall follow their licentiousnesses, because of whom the way of truth shall be blasphemed. And in covetousness with feigned words they will make gain of you; for whom the judgment from of old is not idle, and their destruction slumbereth not" (2, 3). The first witness of coming judgment he draws from sinning angels that were left till the Lord judges Satan at a later day; but God has already consigned them to pits of deepest gloom for that judgment. The next is the old world of ungodly on whom He brought a flood when He preserved Noah a preacher of righteousness. The third is the overthrow that consumed ungodly Sodom and Gomorrah when He delivered righteous Lot. Thus the Lord knows how to deliver the godly out of trial and keep unjust men for punishment in judgment-day, but chiefly those that go after flesh in lust of uncleanness and despising lordship (4-10).

A most energetic moral denunciation follows (11-17) of their audacity and self-will, corruption, luxury, and wanton licentiousness ensnaring unstable souls, and yet more. Forsaking the right way, theirs is the path of Balaam with no less folly; and for them the gloom of darkness is reserved. The plain proof is given from verse 18 to the end of the chapter. Their high-flown words of vanity only allured and ensnared others into their own slavery of corruption, however they might promise liberty. Their last state of return to evil was all the worse for a knowledge that gave a temporary escape from the world's pollution. It was as a dog turning back to its own vomit, and a washed sow to rolling in mud.

[Chapter] 3. This deals rather with scoffing unbelief of closing days against the promise of the Lord's coming. Peter would have them remember the words spoken before by the prophets, and the commandment of the Lord and Saviour through "your apostles". It was all foretold. Materialism would prevail, what is now called Positivism; not hypocritical corruption as in chapter 2, but philosophical or infidel materialism as the only truth and certainty (1-4). The apostle refutes it first by the inspired account of the deluge: things have not continued as they are from creation's start. The antediluvian world perished by the flood: whilst the now heaven and earth by His word are stored up, kept for fire unto a day of judgment and destruction of ungodly men (5-7). He intimates what is no small thing for understanding the coming day of the Lord, that one day is with Him as a thousand years and a thousand years as one day; though accomplishing immense change at once, it also extends through a long period. And it is His grace in now saving, not slackness, that defers it. But it will come unexpectedly as a thief; in which (day) the heavens shall pass away with rushing noise, and elements with fervent heat shall be dissolved, and earth and the works that are therein shall be burnt up (8-10). It is still the day, but its evening as it were, when this catastrophe shall come.

Hence his appeal to the saints. "All these things being thus to be dissolved, of what sort ought ye to be in holy ways and godliness, waiting for and hastening the coming of the day of God, by reason of which (day) heavens being on fire shall be dissolved and elements in fervent heat shall melt? But according to his promise we wait for new heavens and a new earth, wherein dwelleth righteousness. Wherefore, beloved, as ye wait for these things, use diligence, spotless and blameless to be found by Him in peace; and count the long-suffering of our Lord salvation, even as our beloved brother Paul wrote to you according to the wisdom given to him, as also in all [his] epistles, speaking in them of these things; in which (epistles) some things are hard to understand, which the untaught and unestablished wrest, as also the rest of the scriptures, to their own destruction" (11-16).

How weighty the application to holy and pious and devoted service! and how interesting in more ways than one the reference to "our beloved brother Paul"; who, while he mightily explained the prophets, went so far beyond as to divine counsels, hard to Jews especially, which the ignorant and unstable distorted to their ruin. It is clear that inspired Peter calls Paul's epistles "scriptures", all of which were so misused. And more than that; he speaks of Paul's having written to the Christian Jews, as Peter also in both his Epistles. What can this be, but the Epistle to the Hebrews? Compare Hebrews 12:26, 27: the one apostle referring to the morning, the other to the evening, of the same day of the Lord.

"Ye therefore, beloved, knowing beforehand, be on your guard lest, led away along with the error of the wicked, ye fall from your own stedfastness. But grow in grace and knowledge of our Lord and Saviour Jesus Christ: to him [be] the glory both now and unto eternity's day. Amen." All over it is Peter's fervour, but aged and mature, waiting for that death by which he should glorify God.

5.50 1 JOHN

The unique character of the Epistle before us cannot but impress every intelligent Christian, one might say any attentive disciple. Like that to the Hebrews, it has no formal address: like that of Jude, it is meant for, as that was addressed to, all saints everywhere, both too in view of the deepest evil among professing Christians; by Jude, of apostates who had crept in; by John, of many antichrists who had gone out.

But our Epistle is distinguished by the fullest development of the life eternal in Him who lived among men, in the closest intimacy with His own here below, the same life which was with the Father before He was manifested on earth.

"That which was from the beginning, which we have heard, which we have seen with our eyes, which we gazed on, and our hands handled, concerning the Word of life (and the life was manifested, and we have seen and testify and report to you the life eternal, the which was with the Father, and was manifested to us): that which we have seen and heard we report to you that ye also may have fellowship with us. And our fellowship too is with the Father and with his Son Jesus Christ; and these things we write that your joy may be filled full" (verses 1-4). This introduction is based on the grand one to the Gospel in John 1:1-18; but with the marked difference that there it was the Word *in* the beginning,

God with God before creature came into being; here it is "that which was *from* the beginning", the Word of life become flesh, that tabernacled among us in the most familiar love; that the chosen witnesses, and such as believe their report and like them have life eternal in Him, might have the same blessed fellowship, fellowship with the Father and with His Son in the fullest joy now and evermore. No higher joy than this fellowship will be in heaven; and it is our unbelief if it be not ours now on earth.

Then comes the divine nature, testing our reality in verses 5-10; it is "the message" that follows the manifestation.

"And this is the message which we have heard from him, and declare to you, that God is light, and in him is no darkness at all. If we say that we have fellowship with him and walk in darkness, we lie and do not the truth; but if we walk in the light as he is in the light, we have fellowship one with another, and the blood of Jesus [Christ] his Son cleanseth from all sin. If we say that we have no sin, we deceive ourselves, and the truth is not in us; if we confess our sins, he is faithful and just to forgive us our sins, and cleanse us from all unrighteousness. If we say that we sinned not, we make him a liar, and his word is not in us."

Thus having had the love of the Father and the Son, we must face God as light, as every converted soul proves. One following Christ walks no more in darkness but has the light of life. The question here is *where* we walk, not how. We are brought to God Who is light and therein walk henceforth, poor as the walk may be; but if that is so, we have fellowship one with another, all so walking (and no longer in the dark of an unknown God), with the assurance that the blood of Jesus cleanses us from every sin. Its efficiency is as great to purge as God's light to detect all sin, and this we now share with every saint. We confess, and God forgives and purifies. But if we pretend to walk in the light while still in the dark, our life is but a lie; if we say we have no sin, we deceive ourselves: else the truth would lay it bare. If we say that we did not sin, we go farther wrong still and make God a liar, for His word attests the contrary.

Verses 1, 2 of chapter 2 supply the resource if one should sin. "My little children, these things I write to you that ye sin not. And if one sin, we have an advocate with the Father, Jesus Christ the righteous; and he is the propitiation for our sins, and not for ours only, but for the whole world." His person and His work abide in unchanging value; but He meets our inconsistencies by His advocacy on our behalf on high. And we have "Father" here as in the introduction, not "God" as in the testing of our nature and ways by His light between the two paragraphs.

The question is then raised how to know that there is true knowledge of God. The first proof is obedience in 3-6, keeping His commandments, and yet more His word. All profession without obedience is false; while he that speaks of abiding in Him ought himself also so to walk as He walked. The second proof is love in 7-11. It was an old commandment without power when our Lord was here with His disciples; it became a new one when He died and rose. Always true in Him, it was then and thus "true in him and in you, because the darkness is quite passing, and the true light already shineth." Here too, claim to be in the light, while hating one's brother, proves that one is in nothing but the darkness of fallen nature. Christ must be our life, whether to obey or to love.

Next we have the family of God, all having their sins forgiven for Christ's name (verse 12), distinguished as fathers, young men, and babes ($\pi\alpha\iota\delta\iota\alpha$) in verse 13, and repeated with enlargement, save for the fathers, in verses 14-27, closed by verse 28 which unites them again as "little children" ($\tau\epsilon\kappa\nu\iota\alpha$) by the call to abide in Him, that when He shall be manifested, we (John &c., not "ye") may have boldness, and not be put to shame from before Him at His coming. The great principles and the details of this parenthesis are full of weight, beauty, and interest: the fathers characterised by knowing Christ as here, to which the apostle adds nothing; the young men by vigour in overcoming Satan and loving the Father, not the world; and the babes warned against the many antichrists, but knowing all as having unction from the Holy One, and as it abode in them, so were they to abide in Him.

Practical righteousness is touched in the last verse of chapter 2 as flowing from being born of God, when the apostle turns to another parenthesis in 3:1-3, where the Father's love, our present relationship as children, and the hope of Christ's manifestation are richly brought out in a few words. For indeed we need all grace to practise righteousness, which depends on the divine nature; but the hope too has purifying power. He then contrasts the sinner with Christ in Whom was no sin and Himself manifested to take away our sins: as every one that practises sin practises also lawlessness; for sin is a deeper and wider thing than transgressing the law. So whoever abides in Him sins not; whoever sins has not seen nor known Him. Thereon the family of God are warned against deceivers; and righteousness is insisted on, and the devil and the Son of God confronted as are the children of God with those of the devil, verse 10 being the transition to love, and Cain the ensample of hatred and unrighteousness.

Thus they were not to wonder if they were hated by the world which remains in unremoved death. We on the contrary know that we have passed out of death because we love the brethren; whereas hatred is in principle murder, and no murderer has life eternal abiding in him. But love must be real, not in the tongue only, from its utmost self-sacrifice down to little deeds of every day. We must also beware of a bad conscience, so as to have boldness toward God, and receive what we ask, in an obedient spirit, believing on the name of His Son and loving one another. "And he that keepeth his commandments dwelleth in him, and he in him; and hereby we know that he abideth in us by the Spirit which he gave us."

This leads into the unfolding of the Spirit in chapter 4 as to truth and love. "Beloved, believe not every spirit, but prove the spirits if they are of God; because many false prophets have gone out into the world. Hereby know ye the Spirit of God: every spirit that confesseth Jesus Christ come in flesh is of God; and every spirit that confesseth not Jesus [Christ come in flesh] is not of God; and this is the [spirit] of the antichrist whereof ye have heard that it cometh, and now it is already in the world" (1-4). *Ye* are of God, says he to the little children, and have overcome them; *they* are of the world, their all; *we* (the inspired like himself) are of God, as perfectly giving His word: a momentous thing then and ever since. "Hereby know we the Spirit of truth and the spirit of error." When the truth is thus clear and settled, we can freely speak of love.

"Beloved, let us love one another: for love is of God; and every one that loveth hath been begotten (or, is born) of God, and knoweth God; he that loveth not knew not God, because God is love." It is not standing here by faith, as Paul urges, which is also true, but participation in the divine by Christ as our life. "Herein was manifested the love of God in our case, because God hath sent his Only-begotten Son into the world that we might live through him. Herein is love, not that we loved God, but that he loved us and sent his Son as propitiation for our sins." Ought we not then to love one another? No one has ever beheld God; our love should now attest Him, as Christ when here declared Him (compare John 1:18). "Herein we know that we abide in him, and he in us, because he hath given us of his Spirit." For His Spirit is the power of all communion. Yet is the apostle careful to allege the surest fact, lest we should get lost in feeling. "And we have beheld and do testify that the Father sent the Son as Saviour of the world."

Hence the simplicity and the directness and the breadth of Christian truth. It is not only those who had beheld Him while here; nor was the deepest blessing the fruit of singular spirituality or attainment. "Whosoever shall confess that Jesus is the Son of God, God abideth in him, and he in God." How this strengthens the weak, and reproves the careless! Does it allow of doubt? "And we have known and believed the love which God hath in our case. God is love, and he that abideth in love abideth in God and God in him." Nor is this all: "Herein hath love been perfected with us, that we may have boldness in the day of judgment, because as he is, so are we in this world. There is no fear in love, but perfect love casteth out fear; because fear hath torment, and he that feareth hath not been made perfect in love. We love [?him], because he first loved us." Unreality is thus exposed. If one say, I love God, and hates his brother, he is a liar; for he that loves not his brother whom he has seen, how can he love God whom he has not seen? And this commandment have we from Him, that he who loves God love also his brother. The possession of a divine nature is the great contrast with the world in chapter 3; but here in chapter 4 we have the further and high privilege of God's dwelling in us, leading to our dwelling in Him, and His consequent dwelling in us as power spiritually.

With this chapter 5 connects itself. Who is my brother? "Everyone that believeth that Jesus is the Christ is born (or, begotten) of God; and every one that loveth him that begot loveth him also that is begotten of him." But John will not allow love apart from obedience: "Herein we know that we love the children of God when we love God and keep his commandments. For this is the love of God that we keep his commandments; and his commandments are not grievous." They unite in a new nature, life eternal, the substratum of the entire Epistle. "For all that is begotten of God overcometh the world; and this is the victory that overcometh the world, our faith. Who is he that overcometh the world but he that believeth that Jesus is the Son of God?"

Then he adds the work, or rather the person characterised by it. "This is he that came through (διά) water and blood, Jesus Christ; not by (ἐν) the water only, but by the water and the blood. And it is the Spirit that witnesseth because the Spirit is the truth. Because there are three that bear witness, the Spirit, and the water, and the blood; and the three are to the one (end)." Life is not in the first man, but in the Second, Who both atones and purifies. So blood and water came out of His pierced heart when dead; and the Spirit bore witness through

John who saw and knew its truth, that we might believe: three witnesses, yet one testimony. Full salvation is in Christ and in Him alone for the believer.

On this therefore the apostle reasons and appeals in 10-12. It is God's testimony about His Son; and he that believes on Him has the testimony in himself, if all else failed; for the life is in Him for security and association with Him, as we have it really for present exercise and fellowship every day. "He that hath the Son hath life; he that hath not the Son of God hath not life." Very weighty is the sum here: "These things wrote (or, write, epistolary aorist) I to you that ye may know ($εἰδῆτε$) that ye have life eternal, ye that believe on the name of the Son of God." It is conscious knowledge.

Then he urges confidence in prayer, and specifies it on behalf of a brother not sinning to death; if so, one should refrain. To suppose that the sin here in question is blasphemy against the Holy Spirit, and the death meant is eternal judgment or the second death, not only is unfounded but destroys the force of this scripture. It is the moral government which our Father carries on whilst we are here, as we may trace in 1 Corinthians 11:30-32, as also from the early time of the Old Testament (Job 33, 35). It may go beyond cleansing in order to one's bearing more fruit as in John 15:2; so both apostles teach.

The threefold assertion of "we know" in 18-20 grandly and with suitability concludes the Epistle. "We know that every one that [is] begotten of God sinneth not, but the begotten of God keepeth himself, and the wicked one toucheth him not. We know that we are of God, and the whole world lieth in the wicked one. And we know that the Son of God is come, and hath given us an understanding that we should know him that [is] true; and we are in him that [is] true, in his Son Jesus Christ." Here it is Christian knowledge, not objective only but conscious; and this next not merely in moral character as born of God, but of Him in the fullest contrast with the world as a whole lying in the wicked one. Then we have the conscious knowledge that the Son of God is come, the object of all blessing where all was evil and wretched, and He has given us an understanding that we should know the true One. And we are in the True, in His Son Jesus Christ, for they are inseparably one. Day of the worst evil as it was, what can match the calm confidence of victory over sin and Satan, of belonging to God and His nature above a lost world, of a spiritual understanding to know Him that is true, and to be in Him that is true, in His Son Jesus Christ? "This is the true God and eternal life. Little children, guard yourselves from idols." The deceptive power of the enemy in the evil day is recognised; and we need the divine safeguard. "But be of good cheer: I have overcome the world."

5.51 2 John

These two lesser Epistles of the beloved disciple could yield no such large or minute testimony to Christ as the first and longer one; but they are no less admirably suited to fulfil the work given him to do on our behalf, who face the dangers and difficulties of the last time. Each has from God its own special object. The Second Epistle is mainly to warn and direct where the doctrine of Christ was not brought; as the Third is to cheer and confirm those who zealously helped the true witnesses of Christ, and none the less but the more if self-seeking men sought to exclude and malign them. As in the First

Epistle, the truth, even Christ, is insisted on as of all moment in them both.

But the evident peculiarity of the Second is that the Holy Spirit addresses this inspired letter to "an elect lady and her children". This is so novel as to indicate an extraordinary crisis which called for it. And the crisis is that "even now are many antichrists". The lady and her children were exposed to danger in this respect: which is so great in itself, and so aggravated by the absence of a Christian head of the family, that it pleased the Lord to send them a solemn caution, and indeed a peremptory command. Nor do we hear of any assembly near at hand. We can easily understand that the antichristian may have been a friend, perhaps in former days used to preach and teach Christ, nay possibly to their conversion. In any case it seemed no small self-denial to close their door. Was she not a woman, and as such forbidden to teach, or to exercise authority over a man? Hers was but a private household. Why should she and her children be required to discharge so stern a duty? The apostle meets any such excuses.

"The elder to the elect lady and her children, whom I love in truth; and not I only, but also all who have known the truth, for the truth's sake which abideth in us and shall be with us for ever. Grace shall be with us (or, you), mercy, peace, from God the Father, and from the Lord Jesus Christ, the Son of the Father, in truth and love. I rejoiced exceedingly that I have found of thy children walking in truth, according as we received commandment from the Father. And now I beseech thee, lady, not as writing to thee a new commandment but that which we had from the beginning, that we should love one another. And this is love that we should walk according to his commandments. This is the commandment, according as ye heard from the beginning that ye should walk in it. Because many deceivers went out into the world, those that confess not Jesus Christ coming in flesh: this is the deceiver and the antichrist. Look to yourselves, that we* lose not what we wrought but receive a full recompence. Whosoever goeth forward and abideth not in the doctrine of Christ hath not God: he that abideth in the doctrine, he hath both the Father and the Son. If any one come unto you and bring not this doctrine, receive him not at home, and give him no greeting; for he that biddeth him greeting partaketh in his wicked works. Having many things to write to you, I would not with paper and ink, but hope to come unto you, and to speak mouth to mouth that our joy may be filled full. The children of thine elect sister salute thee" (verses 1-13).

All heterodoxy is evil; but not to bring the doctrine of the Christ, perfect man and true God in one person, is fatal and admits of no compromise. Neither a mother nor her children can plead innocence if they yield. It is high treason to admit friendly terms, if we own Christian ground. The lady might be ever so orthodox: but to welcome to the house one who, claiming to be a Christian teacher, denied Christ's deity or humanity (*i.e.* their union in one person), is to give up the foundation implicitly; and he or she who receives out of courtesy, liberal feeling, or any other human motive, becomes partaker of "his wicked works", even if the evil doctrine be declined. The truth of Christ admits of no neutrality. Truth, love, and obedience must be in those who, believing in Christ, have life eternal and the Holy Spirit.

---

* The various readings here in ancient and good manuscripts are due to a misunderstanding of the sense: "ye" was adopted to make it easier, Compare 1 John 2:28, which has the same sense; and here all agree to "we".

We go right as Christians only as the eye, the heart, is true to Christ. Not "transgressing" but going forward, instead of abiding in the doctrine, loses all. "Transgressing" is spurious: it was development rather, which cannot consist with the truth.

For the active mind of man confides in its own ability, loves to discover what is new, writhes against absolute subjection to the written word, and fails in reverence to Him, Who became not more truly man than He is the Son only known by the Father. To allow a lowering thought because the Lord deigned to become a bondman, and this also to be a propitiation for our sins, is to accept Satan's basest lie, and to affront God's love and truth in the tenderest point. This alone accounts for the peremptory command laid on a Christian woman and even her children, when exposed to such temptation from the evil one. And if it applied so unsparingly in the circle of private life, how much greater the guilt if the Christian assembly deliberately shrank from fidelity to Christ and His personal glory!

5.52 3 John

The Third Epistle deals with the good side in the evil day. We are entitled to have and enjoy it in the worst of times. As the lady and her children were appropriately warned not to yield through fear of being counted narrow, bigoted, and uncharitable, with no less fitness the apostle writes to the gracious Gaius that he might persevere in his loving care for all faithful servants of Christ, whatever be the party or personal opposition of any. John here too insists that it be love in truth and walking in it. One must have the truth intact before we can speak of love or exercise it: else we may be helping Satan against Christ under the name of charity. Even here truth has the first place; how indeed could it be otherwise?

"The elder to the beloved Gaius whom I love in truth. Beloved, I desire that in all things thou mayest prosper and be in health according as thy soul prospereth. For I rejoiced exceedingly when brethren came and testified to thy truth according as thou walkest in truth. Greater joy I have not than these things, that I hear of my children walking in (or, in the) truth. Beloved, thou doest faithfully whatsoever thou doest toward the brethren, and this strangers, who testified to thy love before the assembly; in sending forward whom worthily of God thou wilt do well; for they went out for the Name, taking nothing from the Gentiles. We therefore ought to receive such, that we may be fellow-workers with the truth. I wrote to the assembly; but Diotrephes that loveth the first place among them accepteth us not. For this reason when I come, I will bring to remembrance his works which he doeth, prating against us with wicked words; and not content with these, neither himself accepteth the brethren, and those that would he forbiddeth and casteth out of the assembly. Beloved, imitate not what is evil but what is good. He that doeth good is of God: he that doeth evil hath not seen God. Demetrius hath been testified to by all and by the truth itself; and we also testify; and thou knowest that our testimony is true. I had many things to write to thee, but I am unwilling with ink and pen to be writing to thee; but I hope soon to see thee, and we will speak mouth to mouth. Peace to thee; the friends salute thee. Salute the friends by name" (verses 1-14).

The hearty love of the apostle goes forth to Gaius, because his love was governed by truth. The right rendering corrects making his prosperity to be the prime desire, but that in or about all things it might be, and even his health too, as his soul was prospering. For how often, when the soul gets lax, God uses trial and sickness for good! His exceeding joy was brethren's testimony to Gaius' cleaving to the truth and walking in it; as he had no greater joy than to hear of this in his children. Nor does he fail to name Gaius' fidelity toward those labouring in the word, though strangers, not only in hospitality on the spot, but in setting them forward "worthily of God". And these labourers were worthy, for the Name was their motive; and they declined the world's favours. Even the apostle was glad to range himself as a fellow-worker with them and the truth.

But his writing to the assembly provoked the pride of Diotrephes who disliked these earnest witnesses for Christ, so as not to accept his words, and to go the length of babbling wickedly against an apostle. How soon the ruin came, and how audacious! Nor was it in word only, but in hostility to the stranger brethren and to those who honoured them for their work's sake. We discern here the spirit of the evil house-servant who beat his fellow-servants, and may be assured that Diotrephes was not (like John, Gaius, and these visitors) longing and looking for Christ; to him it would be an enthusiasm if not a delusion. For the Lord traced such misconduct to this very cause, to the heart saying, My lord delayeth. But his evil way should not be forgotten when the apostle came: for the church is holy ground. Gaius was to imitate not the evil but the good; so to do is of God.

Then he speaks of Demetrius as one testified by the truth itself and his own testimony, which he knew would have the greatest weight with Gaius. It was a green spot in the midst of ruin. If we have seen much of

Diotrephes that cannot be overlooked to our sorrow and shame, let us make so much the more of a Demetrius and a Gaius. All turns on the truth. Diotrephes no doubt assumed to respect order, but had no heart for the truth: else he had valued the working of the joints and bands in furthering and spreading it. His notion of order proved itself unsound, because of his indifference to the truth; for not content with opposing the visiting brethren, he ventured to despise the apostle's word on their behalf and ill-treated such as walked in truth and love. But be the declension ever so real and painful, the truth abides to walk in, and the love that is of God is its sure accompaniment. Such is the consolation in this the last Epistle of our apostle. If there was an elect lady with her children to warn gravely, a Gaius and a Demetrius were there to be encouraged, with devoted labourers who went out for the Name, taking nothing from the Gentiles. That evil too should rise more impudent than ever can surprise none who heed the solemn admonition of the Lord and His apostles.

5.53 Jude

The characteristic form and aim of this Epistle will become clear to every attentive believer. No other resembles it so closely as the Second of Peter; so much so, that many learned men have contended that the one must be copied from the other, and that the copy at any rate must be spurious. But this reasoning only betrays their spiritual ignorance and presumption. Both Epistles are not only of profound interest but evidently inspired of God; and each has its own specific object in the mind of the inspiring Spirit. Hence the distinctions graven by divine wisdom cannot fail to be seen to the great profit of him who reads in the dependence of faith which gives intelligence.

DIVINE DESIGN: JUDE

In the Second Epistle of Peter we have seen that the dominant truth is God's righteous government, not as in the First Epistle dealing with the saints in their daily path and with the house of God too, but with the unjust and the guilty world even to the day of the Lord, in which the now heavens and the earth, kept for fire unto a day of judgment and destruction of ungodly men, shall be burnt up. Jude was given to portray the same evil in the yet deeper and more solemn aspect of departure or apostasy from God, and so from the faith and holy will of God, rather than from righteousness. This gives occasion to the nicest points of difference which have escaped these carping critics, who, instead of admiring the perfect word in its astonishing consistency with the requisite variety, blindly turn it against the Holy Spirit to their own sin and shame and folly.

"Jude, bondman of Jesus Christ and brother of James, to the called, beloved in God, [the] Father, and kept by (or, for) Jesus Christ: mercy to you and peace and love be multiplied" (1, 2). There can be little doubt that "beloved" represents the true and certainly more ancient text. It is also singularly in keeping with the tried and perilous circumstances of His called ones exposed to evil within, which they are summoned to resist at all cost, and therefore need the comforting assurance of His love (compare 21), and of their preservation for Christ, as an abiding state. There is also the remarkable "mercy" in the address to all, as to Timothy in his delicate and difficult path: all the true-hearted have it here in the most emphatic way looked at as a state.

"Beloved, while giving all diligence to be writing to you of our common salvation, I was constrained to write to you, exhorting [you] to contend for the faith once for all delivered to the saints. For certain men got in privily that were of old prescribed unto this sentence (or, judgment), ungodly, turning the grace of our God into lasciviousness, and denying our only Master and Lord Jesus Christ" (3, 4).

It was the writer's joy to be writing of our common salvation, the blessed alphabet of the gospel; but the danger of the saints laid on him the necessary duty of exhorting them to contend earnestly for the faith. In days of apostasy the urgent call was to the converted, where shallower faith would be absorbed in the unconverted: the saints themselves were exposed to deadly peril. The faith itself once delivered to them, once for all, was not menaced only, but undermined within. For there had got in unnoticed certain men that of old were beforehand written of; and their ungodliness had the special trait of turning the grace of our God into licentiousness, and of denying the right of Jesus Christ as sovereign Master that bought all, and as our Lord that redeemed us who believe. Compare 2 Peter 2:1, who only speaks of the former; but Jude adds and specifies "our Lord" as well as their changing the grace of our God into dissoluteness.

"But I would remind you, though once for all knowing all things, that [the] Lord, having saved a people out of Egypt's land, in the second place destroyed those that believed not" (5). This is quite peculiar to the epistle before us, because it marks the doom of apostates. Peter does not allude to it, but speaks of "an old world" not spared, and Noah, preacher of righteousness, preserved with seven others, whilst a flood overwhelmed "a world of ungodly ones". Can we conceive of more exact thought and language in the two letters? Both draw warning from angels, but we readily see that even here each writes with exquisite propriety which unbelief overlooks. "And angels that kept not their own beginning (or, original state), but abandoned their proper dwelling, he hath kept in everlasting bonds under gloom unto [the] great day's judgment; as Sodom and Gomorrah and the cities around them, having in the like manner with them greedily committed fornication and gone after strange flesh, lie there an example, undergoing judgment of eternal fire" (6, 7). Jude points out departure from original position, whether of angels or of the cities in question. They went away from nature; and they suffered accordingly in a manner wholly uncommon. Peter, true to God's purpose there, writes of "angels having sinned", and of cities made an example to those that should live an ungodly life, and of "righteous Lot" saved (for the righteous man tormented his righteous soul from day to day), the Lord knowing how to deliver godly men out of trial and to keep unrighteous ones unto judgment day to be punished.

"Yet likewise these dreamers also defile flesh, and set at nought lordship, and rail at dignities. But Michael the archangel, when disputing with the devil he discussed about Moses' body, did not dare to bring against [him] a railing judgment but said, [The] Lord rebuke thee. But these rail at whatever things they know not; but whatever they understand naturally, as the irrational animals, in these things they corrupt themselves (or, perish)" (8-10). Here Jude depicts the apostate spirits of Christendom in their giving up all respect for authority, and railing against it; and cites Michael in particular, as Peter does angels generally with those that sinned, for marked contrast; and speaks of them as like irrational animals, receiving unrighteousness' reward, and so dilates on their grievous immoralities.

Then we have the awfully concise judgment which Jude pronounces on that which outwardly bears the Lord's name. "Woe to them! because they went in the way of Cain, and rushed greedily into the error of Balaam's hire, and perished in the gain-saying of Korah. These are spots (or, hidden rocks) in your love-feasts, feasting together, fearlessly pasturing themselves; clouds without water, carried along by winds; autumnal trees without fruit, twice dead, rooted up; raging sea-waves, foaming out their own shames; wandering stars for whom hath been reserved the gloom of darkness for ever" (11-13). Peter too alleged the way of Balaam who loved the hire of unrighteousness; but Jude prefaces that prolific error with Cain's apostasy from God, and finishes all with the rebellion of Korah against Moses and Aaron, the known types of Christ the Apostle and High Priest of the Christian confession. This is and will be perdition: ministry or service arrogating to itself what pertains to the Lord Jesus only, the closing apostasy, but carrying throughout the sad marks which show that the corruption of the best thing is the worst corruption.

Very striking too is Enoch's earliest warning against "these" who perish at the end of the age. "And Enoch, seventh from Adam, prophesied also as to these, saying, Behold, [the] Lord came amid his holy myriads, to execute judgment against all, and to convict all the ungodly [of them] of all their works of ungodliness which they ungodlily wrought, and of all the hard things which ungodly sinners spoke against him. These are murmurers, complainers, walking after their lusts, and their mouth speaketh swelling things, admiring persons for the sake of profit" (14-16).

Pretentious and ill-willed adversaries of scripture have availed themselves of the Book of Enoch in the

Aethiopic which was brought into Great Britain by Bruce and translated by Archbishop Laurence, as if the supposed original of that work could be the source of the quotation. They failed to observe that it yields conclusive proof that it is no prophecy but an imposture; for the concocter, trying to incorporate this very passage from the Epistle, could not even do his evil work correctly. He makes the Lord come in judgment of His saints: a false doctrine in direct antagonism to all scripture, which Jude of course in no way says or implies. It speaks only of condign judgment executed on the ungodly in works and words.

"But ye, beloved, remember ye the words that were spoken before by the apostles of our Lord Jesus Christ, that they said to you, In [the] end of the time shall be mockers walking after their own lusts of ungodlinesses. These are they that make separations, natural (or, soulish), not having [the] Spirit. But ye, beloved, building up yourselves on your most holy faith, praying in [the] Holy Spirit, keep yourselves in [the] love of God, awaiting the mercy of our Lord Jesus Christ unto life eternal. And some convict, when contending, but others save, snatching out of [the] fire, and others pity with fear, hating even the garment spotted by the flesh" (17-23).

The gracious encouragement in the darkest day is manifest and rich. Mockers, who set themselves apart like the Pharisees, are branded as natural men: the Spirit leads to, and in, fellowship as well as to faith and love. Therefore are saints to build themselves up on their most holy faith. Only here is it so designated. What a rebuke to such as would lower the standard and accept laxity to please a party, avoid decision, and shirk reproach! A loose time calls on us more strenuously to build ourselves up on our most holy faith, and for prayer in power of the Holy Spirit, that we may keep ourselves in the love of God, awaiting the mercy of our Lord Jesus Christ unto life eternal; for indeed we need both every step of the way through. This will the better enable us to help souls in slippery places such as are described in verses 22, 23, though the text is as tangled here in the copies as those whose well-being we should seek, imperilled as they are more and more.

The conclusion is in beautiful harmony with the Epistle. "But to him that is able to keep you without stumbling, and to set you with exultation blameless before his glory; to an only God our Saviour through Jesus Christ our Lord, [be] glory, majesty, might, and authority, before all time, and now, and unto all the ages. Amen" (verses 24, 25). It is not, as in 2 Peter, looking for new heavens and a new earth, wherein dwells righteousness, but that sovereign grace which will translate us into His presence like Christ Himself, associated with Him actually, yea bodily then and for ever, as now in spirit.

5.54 THE REVELATION

It needs little discernment to see that the characteristic design of this book is judicial beyond every other in the New Testament. Some may wonder that he who was inspired to present "the grace and truth which came through Jesus Christ" should also by the Spirit write the great book of divine judgments. But even the Gospel (chapter 5:27) prepares the way for it; for it reveals the Lord Jesus as the Son of God, the giver of life eternal to him who believes, but the same who as Son of man is the executor of judgment on all who disbelieve and dishonour Him. Hence He is seen as Son of man in the opening vision of chapter 1. There are exceptional words of grace, as we may observe where the saints at

His name break forth into a song of praise parenthetically in the preface of the book (1:latter part of verses 5, and all 6); and so again in the conclusion (22:17), where the Spirit leads the bride in welcoming Him, when He proclaims Himself the bright, the morning Star. How appropriate are both exceptions!

Yet government is the predominant truth, as even in the commencing address "to the seven churches that are in Asia", Grace to you and peace from Him that is, and that was, and that is to come; and from the seven Spirits which are before His throne; and from Jesus Christ, the faithful Witness, the Firstborn of the dead, and the Ruler of the kings of the earth. How different from the revelation we have in the Epistles! Christ's coming too, described in verse 7, is in view of judgment on the earth, without an allusion to the Christian hope as in John 14:1-3; 1 Thessalonians 4:16, 17; 2 Thessalonians 2:1, etc.

After the divine seal in verse 8, John carefully (as the prophets were wont) gives his name, but describes himself in strict keeping with the book, not as the disciple whom Jesus loved, but as their brother and fellow-partaker in the tribulation and kingdom and patience in Christ (or, Jesus), being in Patmos for the word of God and the testimony of Jesus. It was on the Lord's day, the first of the week or resurrection day, that he became in the Spirit; and he who knew so intimately the gracious tones of the Good Shepherd heard behind him a voice as of a trumpet, saying, What thou seest, write in a book and send to the seven churches, whose localities follow. A glorious vision truly, but judicial; for He walked Son-of-man-like in the midst of the golden lamps that represented the churches: the description of His clothing and person confirm it. It is not intercession nor supply from His fulness, still less cleansing their feet, but majestic scrutiny according to their standing in divine righteousness. He who erst lay on His bosom fell as dead at His feet; but the Lord laid His right hand on him, saying, Fear not: I am the first and the last, and the living One; and I became dead, and, behold, I am alive unto the ages of the ages, and have the keys of death and of hades. Write therefore the things which thou sawest, and the things which are, and what is about to take place after these things. The mystery of the stars and lamps is explained; the seven stars as angels of the seven churches, and the seven lamps as seven churches.

Chapters 2, 3 give "the things which are", as chapter 1 the things John saw. Briefly then, Ephesus is the church, though opposed to evil and zealous, yet declining from first love, and threatened, if not restored by repentance, with the Lord's removing the lamp out of its place (2:1-7). Smyrna suffers not from pretended apostles but from the blasphemy or reviling of Judaizers, Satan's synagogue, and tribulation even unto death (8-11). Pergamos dwells where Satan's throne is, and holds Christ's name and faith, yet has such as hold the doctrine of Balaam and that of Nicolaitans likewise. Hence, if not repentant, the Lord comes quickly to fight with them (12-17). With Thyatira is the change as to the call to hear, which thenceforward follows the promise suited to the overcomers in each. Then the personal coming of Christ is also presented appropriately, now that the state was characterised by the horrible yet pretentious Jezebel, though a remnant had not this doctrine (18-29). Sardis has a name of life but dead, with its works not complete, and threatened, as the world is, with Christ's coming for unwelcome surprise like a thief (3:1-6). Philadelphia has in their weakness Christ before them in spiritual power and liberty: they kept His word and denied not His name; and in particular kept the word of His patience, that is, as He patiently waited to come, so did they for Him (7-13). Laodicea is the saddest contrast of self-complacency, indifference, and lack of self-judgment, so that they lacked all that should distinguish the Christian; and therefore the Lord was about to spue them out of His mouth (14-22).

"The things that are" is a striking expression of these churches, and of itself suggests a protracted state. But see the wisdom of God, who would not allow any revelation inconsistent with constantly waiting for Christ as the hope. Hence their existence was a fact: but God took care to give light through their varying phases, and the Lord's estimate of all, when one looked back, and nothing was said of the future to put off the heavenly hope. For the elements were there from John's day, and any delay in fact only gave occasion to see more and more of developed display. They were seven, the known figure of spiritual completeness in good or evil. The first three do not express the future coming of the Lord as a terminus, like Thyatira and those that follow, save Laodicea which was the last; and these, though beginning successively on the protracted view, go on severally but together from the rise of each to His coming. "The things that are" last as long as there is any church-condition recognised by the Lord on earth. First, declension and threatened displacing; second, era of persecution and martyrdom by the heathen; third, worldly power, but false teaching; fourth, mediæval popery with faithful protests; fifth, formal Protestantism; sixth, return to Christ and the heavenly hope; seventh, fatal lukewarmness rejected with disgust. There is no other to follow on earth.

What stronger confirmation could be than that "after these things" the apostle in chapter 4 is called up by a door set open in the heaven to be shown "the things which must take place after these things", *i.e.* subsequent to "the things that are" or the church-state up to its end? "And straightway I became in the Spirit" for heavenly things, as in chapter 1:10 for the Lord seen judicially dealing with the churches, the sole corporate witness for God on earth. Here again he saw the throne, and the displayed glory of the Eternal Who sat on it, with a rainbow of emerald hue round about it, the emphatic pledge of covenanted mercy while He governed in providence.

But a wholly new sight too is there given to meet his eyes: round about that throne twenty four thrones filled by twenty four elders, mature in the mind of Christ. These symbolise the chiefs of the royal priesthood, not the courses but their chiefs, clothed with Christ as their meet robe, and on their heads crowns of divine righteousness. There they sit in peace, though out of the throne proceed lightnings and voices and thunders. It was no longer the throne of grace, to which Christians on earth approach boldly to obtain mercy and find grace for seasonable help. Nor was it the millennial throne of God and of the Lamb, with river of water of life clear as crystal proceeding out of it. It was unlike either; and, between both, manifestations of God's displeasure. But the enthroned elders, who had ever seen them before? Not even Stephen, nor Paul. John as the Christian prophet, who saw in the Spirit the church-state closed on earth, saw also the overcomers in heaven thus symbolised as the chiefs of the royal priesthood, and thoroughly at home in God's presence as if they had been there always. Their translation to heaven is thus implied by those seated on the thrones associated with the central throne of God; it is not described, because it was of sovereign grace, and so not falling under the judicial ways of this book. Already had it been announced by the Lord in John 14:1-3, with details given to correct the mistakes of the Thessalonian saints in 1 Thessalonians 4:16, 17, and 2 Thessalonians 2:1-8. Compare also 1 Corinthians 15:51-53.

This vision anticipatively sets before us what will be verified above when the heavenly saints are no more on earth but on high, and the earth becomes the object of God's providential judgments. Hence seven torches of fire burning before His throne, which are the seven Spirits of God: the Spirit not in His personal unity baptising the saints into one body, but in His varied powers governmentally and in consuming energy to deal with what opposed God's glory. Another remarkable proof of the great change at this time is, that before the throne was a sea of glass like crystal. While here below, these elders were cleansed by the washing of water by the word. A sea "of glass" attested that there was no need of purifying more: theirs was now fixed purity. And the cherubim or living creatures are prominent in the midst of the throne or around it, the emblematic agencies (whoever may be the agents) of God's government in power, firmness, intelligence, and rapidity, endowed with swift movement, and large and inward discernment, as suited to that critical time, seraph-like too in constant celebration of the thrice holy Eternal God Almighty. But the elders worship intelligently as knowing Him, prostrate themselves, and cast their crowns before His throne, owning His creative power and providence.

In chapter 5 it is plain that the sealed book is the question: who can open it? None but the Lamb so overcame to unroll its judicial announcements, in order to the reception and rule of His inheritance, now utterly alienated. Hence, when He takes it from the Sitter on the throne, "a new song" from elders and living creatures now united rises to Him who bought out the heirs with His blood from every nation and tongue. Nor this only; they are made to our God a kingdom and priests to reign over the earth. The key-note struck calls forth the anticipated deliverance of all creation, "all things" following the joint-heirs. See Colossians 1:20-23, as well as Romans 8:19-23.

On the Seals and Trumpets one may here be brief. They each reveal a complete course of judgments on the guilty world while Christ is still on high: the first comparatively ordinary and secret, but in the order prescribed; the second loudly sounding and severe up to the moment when Christ takes His great power and reigns. Each too has a striking parenthesis between the sixth and the seventh in its respective series; wherein we are given to see that God is active in goodness, not to gather into one body Jews and Gentiles, but to prepare out of Israel and out of the Gentiles distinct groups for blessing, when the Heir of all things enters triumphantly on His inheritance. Under the later series we hear the proclamation of the coming kingdom in its wide extent in chapter 10, and in 11 the connection with Jerusalem and its temple, inner worship, but as yet a sackcloth prophetic testimony, and the western enemy beginning to be descried. In a general way this ends what we may call the first volume of the Revelation.

The last verse of chapter 11 belongs as a sort of preface to chapter 12, the ark of God's covenant being first seen in His temple above, not yet found on earth, with even increased signs of His displeasure. But the sources of earthly change appear in heaven also, the sun-clad woman in travail, and the great red dragon in the forms of Roman power. The Son is born, but, instead of reigning now, caught up unto God and unto His throne; while she flees into the wilderness for 1260 days. But the great dragon with his angels is cast out of heaven, to the joy of the heavens and of those that dwell in them. But woe to the earth and the sea during the little while of his great wrath! Still the woman-mother, symbolising Israel (not the bride), is preserved.

But two great vessels of his hostile energy appear on the scene to do his worst (chapter 13): the Roman Beast or empire revived, for its deadly wound was healed to the wonder and worship of all the apostate earth; and the second Beast in the land imitating Christ's power as King and Prophet, the sign-making false prophet, each greatest in the sphere of the dragon's power. For the restrainer of 2 Thessalonians 2: 7 no longer acts: Satan is allowed his way for a short space, before judgment falls more openly.

Then in chapter 14 seven dealings of God come out in their order: 1, a special and large remnant of Jews, who follow the Lamb, seen with Him on mount Zion; 2, the everlasting gospel to every nation and tongue in view of His judgment; 3, the fall of Babylon declared; 4, as also the cup of God's wrath for any who worship the Beast; 5, the blessedness from henceforth of the dead that die in the Lord, for the tables are now turned; 6, the harvest of discriminating judgment; and 7, the vintage of unsparing vengeance on the vine of the earth, its religious falseness and evil.

Then in chapters 15, 16 the supplementary Bowls of God's wrath, the seven plagues the last. These are highly figurative like the Trumpets, but intense; and a parenthesis appears between the sixth and the seventh as before. Only here it consists of Satan's last efforts, with his two vassals also, to gather the kings of the whole habitable earth for the war of the great day of God the Almighty. Even here we may see an inner parenthesis of the Lord coming as thief: not as Bridegroom, for this had been after Revelation 3 and before chapter 4 for the heavenly saints, as that will be for those converted afterwards, as well as for His other purposes.

Chapters 17, 18 are devoted to the fuller description of Babylon, the great whore and the city that had kingship over the kings of the earth, the fall of which had been already announced in chapters 14 and 16. First, we have her relations with the Beast, ruling, or hated and destroyed; then, is her fall when the Lord God judged her; and all classes on earth were her mourners, but heaven called to rejoice, as we hear the loud Hallelujahs on high in the beginning of chapter 19, the last notice of the elders and the living creatures. For now the Bride prepared herself for the marriage of the Lamb; and we hear also of those that are called to the marriage supper, the Old Testament saints presumably, who with the Bride constituted the elders. Next, the heaven is seen set open; and the Faithful and True on the white horse comes to judge and war in righteousness, clothed now with a garment dipped in blood. His unmistakeable name is the Word of God. And the armies in heaven followed Him on white horses clad in pure white byss, the righteousnesses of saints (not of angels). But it was not theirs to wield the sharp sword against the nations; His it is to tread the winepress of the fury of the wrath of God the Almighty, though He with them will shepherd men inflexibly. But He alone has on His garment and on

His thigh a name written, King of kings and Lord of lords. And the carnage that ensues, what a supper for all the birds in mid-heaven! For if the Beast and the False Prophet were consigned alive to the lake of fire, the kings of the earth and their armies fall victims under the sharp sword. The symbols are obvious.

So it is in chapter 20 clearly: plain narrative prevails therein. The restraint of Satan is one of the marked traits of the age to come. Nothing like it has been since man was created; nor will it be again when he deceives and destroys for a little while after the thousand years' reign is over. He too will then be cast into the lake of fire. But the grand fact is, Christ then reigns over the earth; as He is the exalted and displayed Head over all creation, heavenly and earthly. It is the administration of the fulness of the times, He shining where all else had failed (Ephesians 1:10). Prominence is given to those who had suffered unto death, not only in the first half-week, but still more in the last when the Beast rose into supremacy during Satan's great rage. Only it is an oversight to leave out that John saw thrones with sitters on them, and judgment theirs, before he saw the souls of those who were martyred raised up to join them. The sitters were changed when Christ met them in the air and took them into the Father's house, seen above from Revelation 4 and on, till they follow the Lord out of heaven as His armies for His appearing and day. Two classes of martyrs here follow like them to reign, who now rise as we see. They all comprise the First Resurrection, and so reign with Christ for the thousand years.

Some wonder at the loosing of Satan after that; but why? The coming age, though immensely different from this evil age, is a dispensation; and men would not be tried adequately without the old tempter being allowed to assail them. But though the unconverted may long yield a feigned obedience, ever so long a reign of righteousness and power, peace and blessing, will not turn them to the living and true God. And they too, as men before, listen to the Serpent for their destruction, and muster from the distant quarters of the earth against the beloved city, and the camp of the saints who separate from the mass and congregate there, in marked contrast with the darnel and the wheat growing together in this age.

Nor is it the wicked of that age only that are consumed, but the earth and the heaven fled from His face Who next is seen, seated on a great white throne to judge the dead, the wicked now raised who had no part in the first resurrection. Having rejected Christ, they were judged each according to their works in the other books; and each was cast into the lake of fire, the second death. This was no coming of Christ, for there was no earth then to return to. It was the standing before the throne of those to be judged who had not eternal life, while earth and heaven had fled. Christ had come long before: these appear before Him for their doom.

Then comes in its due order the end of all, a new heaven and a new earth, not in the inchoate sense of Isaiah 65, 66 where it is applied to the renovation of Jerusalem, created a rejoicing and her people a joy, with the earth and the animals too and vegetable creation delivered. But 2 Peter 3 even and Revelation 21:1-8 go much farther, and show us the everlasting state, which is marked by the sea existing no more, a condition incompatible with natural life on the globe. All its former inhabitants who were saved, including the righteous during the millennial reign, were now in unchangeable blessedness for the ages unto the ages. The holy city, new Jerusalem, for so the Bride is designated, retains her pristine place and beauty. The mediatorial kingdom is closed, and God is all in all (1 Corinthians [15]:24, 28). Righteousness dwells now, above and below, in perfect peace; it is no longer righteousness ruling as in the kingdom till the last enemy be destroyed. Hence, apart from the church, God's tabernacle, we have simply God and men, they His people, and Himself (like His tabernacle) with them, their God, every tear wiped away, death no more nor grief, but all things made new absolutely. What a bright testimony to the water of life He freely gave! What an awful proof that He is not mocked, in all the wicked cast into the lake that burns with fire and brimstone, the solemn back-ground of the state without end!

It is plain that nothing can historically follow the vision of eternity in those eight verses. But just as there was a supplement to the series of judgments of earthly character about the corrupt city Babylon, so there is one now about the holy city, the Bride of the Lamb, during the millennium. As the city of confusion, full of idolatry, and murder of the saints, was shown in her illicit connexion with the kings and the Beast, so we have now the pure and blessed place she, the heavenly bride of the Lamb, is to fill during the millennium, with the homage paid her by the kings and the nations walking by her light; for the glory of God enlightened her, and the Lamb is the lamp thereof. Those who take these verses (Revelation 21:9-27, 22:1-5) in continuity with the eight before are involved among other errors in the folly of conceiving kings and nations throughout eternity. They fail to profit by the break with which verse 9 opens, and the plain analogy afforded with Revelation 17:1, etc. From 21:9 to 22:5 is a retrogressive vision, letting us see the relation of the heavenly to the earth, its nations, and its rulers, during the thousand years.

The rest of the last chapter (6-21) consists of both grave warning and divine cheer. Christ's coming, notwithstanding the predicted events, is declared to be soon, and the time near. Blessed those that wash their robes that they may have title to the tree of life, and through the gates enter the city: without are the dogs, and the sorcerers, and the fornicators, and the murderers, and the idolaters, and every one that loves and makes a lie. But how precious when the Lord Jesus provides for testifying these things in the churches: alas, how far from being duly done by His servants!

Here then Jesus presents Himself, not only as the Root and the Offspring of David, but as the bright, the morning Star. An outburst of faith is heard at the end, as we heard another suited to the beginning of the book. "And the Spirit and the Bride say, Come; and let him that heareth say, Come." It is the Spirit animating he church to welcome Christ's coming; nor only her that knows her bridal relation, but the simplest Christian—"and let him that heareth say, Come." The rest of the verse calls on him that is athirst to come (not to say, Come); yea, he that will, to take life's water freely. This is the call to the unconverted, the gospel call.

Again, after the gravest menace directed against adding to or taking from the words of this prophecy He that testifies responds, Yea, I come quickly. May we by grace join the apostle John in saying, Amen: come, Lord Jesus.

Chapter 6
Conclusion

Having now brought to a close the test of divine design in the several books of the New Testament as well as of the Old, I commend the work to the blessing of God on the reader.

It is usual in such treatises to notice objections laid by unbelief against the scriptures. If this were added in any adequate degree to the present volume, it would increase its bulk very considerably. As it already exceeds 600[‡] pages, I think it better to let the positive truth produce its own impression, which difficulties of the kind have no real title to destroy; seeing that the most certain truth, save in matter or in its abstract forms, is necessarily open to such questions. It ought not to be so where God has spoken or caused His word to be communicated in writing. But this is what scepticism disputes or refuses. Legitimate criticism may seek to gather the true text from reliable documents, in time differing more or less through human infirmity or fault. But it rightly supposes an original divine deposit.

[‡] The original edition had a smaller page size [Editor]

No intelligent person would mix this question with God's inspiration: various readings belong to the distinct region of man's responsibility, as scripture does to divine grace. The problem of the true critic is to use all means, external and internal, to recover what was originally written. What is called "higher criticism" is essentially spurious, either denying God as the author or impudently pretending to speak for Him, if they go not so far. Even Christians are in danger of heeding what these enemies of the written word assume, when it is said that it nowhere claims divine authority. Nor is it only inferential evidence that is given throughout the Bible in general, as well as the conclusive proof of the reverence to all then written shewn by our Lord, the Lord of all. It is dogmatic truth, that God's inspiration is claimed for every scripture, not merely for all given before the apostle Paul wrote his last epistle, but for that part which remained to be written. For nothing less is the force of 2 Timothy 3:16: "Every scripture [is] inspired of God and profitable" etc. Had the existing body been meant, the article would have been requisite, as in verse 14 which speaks only of the Old Testament. Its absence was no less correct for accrediting with the same source and character all that God might be pleased to vouchsafe till the canon was complete.

Indeed the apostle had at an earlier date made in substance the same claim in 1 Corinthians 2. Where the Hebrew oracles stopped, the New Testament revealed all that is for God's glory and goodness to communicate (verses 9-12): "Which things also we speak, not in words taught by human wisdom, but in those Spirit-taught, communicating spirituals by spirituals", or, if we supply the gap, "spiritual [things] by spiritual [words]". The words were as positively of the Holy Spirit as the thoughts. Such is the essential property of scripture. Thus all was of the Spirit of God, the revelation, the communication, and also the reception. Rationalism denies God in them all, attributing them to man's spirit, which he may elevate in effect to that of God, being in darkness and walking in darkness, and knowing not whither he goes, because darkness blinded his eyes.

Translation again, like interpretation, as well as editing the text from the varying witnesses, belongs to the responsible use of scripture, and is quite distinct from the fact of its divine inspiration. No doubt the conviction that God inspired every scripture would act powerfully on the spirit of every believer who undertook a work so serious, and is intended to make him feel his dependence on God in the use of all diligence and every means duly to attain the end in view. But inspiration means, as one of those employed in it says, that men spoke from God, moved (or, borne along) by the Holy Spirit. Hence scripture is not of man's wit or will, but of God, as no one more clearly than our Lord ever shows, and so of final and divine authority. Hence too the danger and evil for any one to give, whatever the cause of failure, his own mind and not God's in editing, translating, or interpreting. What God communicated is able to make one wise unto salvation through faith that is in Christ Jesus. "Is it not written?" if truly applied is absolutely conclusive in His judgment Who will judge living and dead. "And the scripture cannot be broken."

How immense too is the privilege! In its later portion it is the revelation of God, not merely from God, but of Himself, and of God speaking to us in a Son, not the First-born merely but the Only-begotten, the revelation of the Father and the Son by the Holy Spirit. O the grace too of His Son deigning to become man, that we might have what is absolute made relative to us in the tender affections of very man, yet of One who was and is God as His Father. Hence the total change for us in looking at things, seen or unseen, according to God, where the greatest are brought down to our hearts, and the least we learn to be near to God's love: nothing too great for us, nothing too little for God, as said another departed from his labours to be with Christ. Christ alone, Christ fully, accounts for both; and scripture is the true treasure-house as well as standard of it all, as the Spirit was sent forth from heaven to make it good in us in every way.

No tradition could avail for such a stupendous task. "But the Comforter (or rather, Advocate), the Holy Spirit, whom the Father will send in my name, he shall teach you all things, and bring to your remembrance all things which I said to you" (John 14:26). Nor is this all. The Spirit would reveal also Christ's glory on high. "But when the Advocate is come, whom I will send to you from the Father, the Spirit of truth which proceedeth from the Father, he shall bear witness concerning me: and ye too bear witness, because ye are with me from the beginning" (John 15:26, 27). More still of the deepest interest appears in John 16:12-15: "I have yet many things to say to you, but ye cannot bear them now. But when he is come, the Spirit of truth, he shall guide you into all the truth; for he shall not speak from himself, but whatsoever he shall hear he shall speak; and he will announce to you things to come. He shall glorify me, for he shall receive of mine and shall announce it to you. All things whatsoever the Father hath are mine: on this account I said that he receiveth of mine and shall announce it to you."

CONCLUSION

The permanent result of His presence and inspiration is, one may say, the New Testament, that inestimable and final gift of God in its kind. But the character of the inspiration in the New Testament becomes the higher and the more intimate in consequence. Every spiritual man must have felt this, in comparing the Psalms, which express the heart of the Old Testament saints, with the New Testament Epistles, which breathe of the indwelling Spirit animating the Christian and the church. But they are alike God's word: there is no difference as to divine authority.

www.ingramcontent.com/pod-product-compliance
Lightning Source LLC
Chambersburg PA
CBHW031958220426
43664CB00005B/59